INDEPENDENT
TELEVISION
IN BRITAIN

Volume 2

Expansion and Change, 1958–68

Other volumes in the same work by the same author

INDEPENDENT
TELEVISION
IN BRITAIN

Volume 2

Expansion and Change, 1958–68

BERNARD SENDALL

First published 1983 by
THE MACMILLAN PRESS LTD
London and Basingstoke
Companies and representatives
throughout the world

ISBN 0 333 30942 1

Printed in Great Britain by
PITMAN PRESS LTD
Bath

To Joseph Weltman
Guide, Philosopher and Friend

CONTENTS

PART III   A NEW BEGINNING: 1962–3

PART IV   YEARS OF ADAPTATION: 1963–8

PART V   END OF AN ERA

PREFACE AND ACKNOWLEDGEMENTS

The previous volume described the establishment of the central mosaic of four companies serving the three main areas dividing the week on a five-day two-day basis. It then went on to relate how the next three areas of greatest population density, Central Scotland, Wales and the West of England and the Central South acquired powerful and prosperous seven-day contractors, working as affiliates to one or other of the original four.

Of the seven companies concerned, ABC Television, Associated-Rediffusion, ATV, Granada, Scottish Television, Southern Television and Television Wales and the West, only two, Granada and STV, survive under the same name today, although strong elements of ABC, A-R and ATV are present in two existing major companies, Thames Television and Central Independent Television. TWW were removed from the scene in 1968 and the Southern Television contract came to an end on 31 December 1981.

We start this second volume with a description of the establishment of eight further regional contractors, one of which, Wales (West and North), collapsed in little more than a year and another, Westward, survived for twenty years, until it failed in the 1980 franchise competition to secure a renewal after 1981. The remaining six are still in operation in their respective areas, the boundaries of which have in some cases been adjusted.

The Pilkington Committee on Broadcasting, which was appointed in 1960, reported in June 1962, and this volume continues with an account and assessment of this report, which was in the main highly critical of Independent Television.[1] The story proceeds with the passing of the new Television Act of 1963 which, whilst rejecting Pilkington's recommendation for 'organic change', modified the system established in 1954, substantially increasing the powers of the controlling authority. The following years saw the contract decisions of 1964, which made no change in the appointment of companies, the period of adaptation to the new Act under the chairmanship of Lord Hill, and the contract decisions of 1967 in which the original mosaic of 1954/5 was abolished and the distribution of power at the centre of the

xi

system was substantially altered. The volume ends with the inception of the new franchises in the second half of 1968, which sets the scene for the story of the seventies to be told in Volume 3.

Following the departure of Sir Kenneth Clark on 31 August 1957, just three years and one month after his appointment began, the Authority had been without a chairman for two months until Sir Ivone Kirkpatrick, former head of the Foreign Office, took up the post on 7 November. Upon Kirkpatrick's departure five years later on 10 November 1962, Sir John Carmichael, who had been the Deputy Chairman, took office as Acting Chairman and served until the arrival of Lord Hill on 1 July 1963. Hill left on 30 June 1967 to become Chairman of the BBC and his place was taken on 1 September by Lord Aylestone, formerly Herbert Bowden, a senior member of the Cabinet in the Labour Government. These comings and goings in the titular leadership mark out various phases in the development of Independent Television. Throughout the period Sir Robert Fraser, whose pioneering work has been described in Volume 1, remained Director General.

During Kirkpatrick's period of office the flood tide of success came rapidly and easily. It was the age of 'People's Television', in which programme popularity was accompanied by great prosperity, especially for the first seven companies. But, as we saw in the last chapter of Volume 1, an adverse climate of opinion about ITV set in during the early sixties culminating in the publication of the Pilkington Report on 5 June 1962. The motto during this period might be said to have been 'Go for Growth' and the consequences were inflationary – in both profits and pride. The popularity of the programme service amongst the rapidly expanding audience and the booming advertising revenue that attended it created a mood of euphoria which ignored, or at any rate minimised, flaws that were becoming evident to some discerning well-wishers as well as to prejudiced antagonists.

Looking back over twenty years we can see an edifice of extremely novel design, hastily planned and hurriedly constructed. That some modifications would be needed could occasion no surprise; and, as we shall see in Part II, the ITA was not oblivious to certain weaknesses. But the prevailing mood was not conducive to serious, collective self-scrutiny. Were relationships all they should be within the ITA, within the bigger companies, between the ITA and these companies and between the companies themselves? At one end of the spectrum were the transitory members of a public authority whose collective wisdom was not infallible. At the other end were directors on the company boards, rather less transitory, but more often than not dabblers in television as one business interest among others. Between them were the varied ranks of professionals for whom television was a career, whether or not their first allegiance was to public authority or private enterprise. If the system was to work they had to seek a broad consensus, bridging the gulf between the two extremes, one of which fell somewhat short of being God and the other somewhat short of being mammon. Independent Television was a master-piece of calculated ambiguity requiring special skills and hard-earned experience if it was to function smoothly and to fulfil its claim to being a genuine public service. Inevitably there were divided loyalties: inevitably some minuses to set against the pluses.

For all his personal reservations Clark had been a remarkably successful catalyst. He had operated *suaviter in modo* and with great panache. His successor, Kirkpatrick – in youth a professional soldier – had just ended a diplomatic career which had brought him to the highest level. During the war he had successfully conducted the European service of the BBC almost as if it were a private army. He was courteous but moody and sometimes decidedly curt. If he had any sense of commitment to ITV as such, as distinct from a fierce liberalism, a marked preference for private enterprise, a non-Reithian approach to broadcasting and a weariness of government in the service of which he had spent the greater part of his life, few could detect it. Seemingly aloof and detached, he held ITV on a loose rein, perhaps more because of a stubborn unwillingness to appease its critics than because of any positive faith in it. A reserved man who did not make many friends, although fortunately Fraser was one of them, Kirkpatrick was not an ideal choice for this particular post. It would in all probability have been better for ITV if Clark had remained for another two years and been succeeded as Chairman by the admirable Carmichael, who, during his acting tenure of the office in 1962/3, acquitted himself extremely well in trying circum-stances.

Carmichael sustained the transition from Kirkpatrick to Hill. A canny Scot, he had valuable financial experience both in government service in the Sudan and subsequently in industry. His talents were well complemented by those of Sir Sydney Caine, Director of the London School of Economics and with varied experience in government, who succeeded Carmichael as Deputy Chairman in 1964. Collectively, the Authority during the Hill period was well-balanced and talented, and it was reinforced in 1966 by Baroness Sharp, formerly, as 'The Dame', one of the most influential civil servants in Whitehall. These were some of the people whose task it was to achieve for the Authority the commanding position in the affairs of Independent Television which the White Paper of 1962 prescribed, and to see through the contract changes of 1967. And of all Lord Hill's attributes perhaps the most valuable, although the least conspicuous, was his capacity for eliciting the views and judgements of others and then distilling them into a viewpoint which he could genuinely call his own.

As for the companies, what was both remarkable and advantageous was, in most cases, their stability at the level of top management; at ATV, Renwick, Collins, Grade and the two Gills, and at ABC Warter, Clark and Thomas. At Granada, the Bernsteins were in their heyday, assisted by such men of resource as Forman. Wills, Herbert (becoming Lord Tangley) and Adorian continued their efficient supervision of A-R, with a good team of professionals headed by McMillan. Amongst the regionals, men of comparable calibre emerged. Anglia were especially strong with the famous 'gang of four', Townshend, Buxton, Scott and Woolf. Grampian moved steadily forward under King, Tennant and Ward Thomas, and so it was even with tiny Channel under large Krichefski and little Killip. ITN continued their almost triumphant progress under the resourceful Cox. The collective talent of ITV in the sixties at all levels was formidable. Small wonder that a number of able people in the BBC sought at one time or another to move across to join it. The interaction between the two organisations was such that British television came to be regarded as the best in the world.

To most of the people who assisted me in relation to the first volume, I turned again for help on this one and it was readily forthcoming. Those on whom I relied especially continued to make themselves available whenever called upon. The gratitude I expressed in the preface to Volume I is that much the greater. Additionally on this occasion I have found myself particularly indebted to Sir John Carmichael and Sir John Spencer Wills, each of whom have treated my enquiries about delicate issues with consideration and forbearance.

My wise helper and counsellor, Joe Weltman (to whom I have ventured to dedicate this volume), would wish me to express his thanks to Dr Richard Hoggart with whom he discussed on my behalf aspects of the Pilkington Report.

I continued to refer, as the notes and references show, to the books by Howard Thomas and Peter Black which I especially mentioned in the previous preface. I have also turned frequently for enlightenment to two autobiographical works, the first being *Behind the Screen*,[2] the broadcasting memoirs of Lord Hill of Luton, and the second *The Greasy Pole*[3] by Reginald Bevins. The first was supplemented by frank and fascinating personal conversation.

To the list of acknowledgements in Volume 1 I gratefully add the following names:

Brian Begg	Robert Lorimer
Kenneth Blyth	Christopher Martin
Robin Gill	Stella Richman
Michael Gillies	Norman Swallow
Ian Haldane	Brian Tesler
Patrick Hawker	Alison Watt
Brumwell Henderson	

I have been most fortunate in retaining for this volume the personal services of the individuals and groups mentioned in the previous preface and I reiterate my warm appreciation.

A selected list of contemporary publications is not included in this second volume, as most works relevant to Independent Television during this period were published somewhat later. There will be a full bibliography at the end of the third and final volume now being written.

B. S.

ABBREVIATIONS

AAC	Advertising Advisory Committee
ABC	ABC Television
ABPC	Associated British Picture Corporation
ABPI	Association of the British Pharmaceutical Industry
ABS	Association of Broadcasting Staff
ACTT	Association of Cinematograph Television and Allied Technicians
AEAC	Adult Education Advisory Committee
AIC	Advertising Inquiry Council
A-R	Associated-Rediffusion
ATV	Associated Television (after 1966, ATV Network)
BBC	British Broadcasting Corporation
BET	British Electric Traction Company
BMA	British Medical Association
BRTA	British Regional Television Association
CAC	Children's Advisory Committee
CCW	Council for Children's Welfare
CRAC	Central Religious Advisory Committee
CWS	Co-operative Wholesale Society
EAC	Educational Advisory Council
EMI	Electrical and Musical Industries
ETU	Electrical Trades Union
ETV	Educational Television (USA)
GAC	General Advisory Council
GEC	General Electrical Company
IBA	Independent Broadcasting Authority
IPA	Institute of Practitioners in Advertising
ISBA	Incorporated Society of British Advertisers
ITA	Independent Television Authority
ITC	Incorporated Television Company (formerly Incorporated Television Programme Company)
ITCA	Independent Television Companies Association

ITN	Independent Television News
ITP	Incorporated Television Programme Company
ITV	Independent Television
LEA	Local Education Authority
LWT	London Weekend Television
NARAL	Net Advertising Revenue After Levy
NATKE	National Association of Theatrical and Kine Employees
NBPI	National Board for Prices and Incomes
NHS	National Health Service
NPC	Network Programme Committee, formerly Network Planning Committee
NTSC	National Television System Committee (of USA)
NVALA	National Viewers' and Listeners' Association
NUT	National Union of Teachers
PAL	Phase Alternation Line
PMG	Postmaster-General
PPC	Programme Policy Committee
PSC	Programme Schedule Committee
QC	Queen's Counsel
RIBA	Royal Institute of British Architects
SCC	Standing Consultative Committee
SECAM	Sequential Couleur A'Memorie
SFTA	Society for Film and Television Arts
SNP	Scottish National Party
STV	Scottish Television
TAC	Television Advisory Committee
TAD	Television Advertisement Duty
TAM	Television Audience Measurement Ltd
TRACK	Television and Radio Committee
TUC	Trades Union Congress
TVR	Television Audience Measurement Rating
TWW	Television Wales and West of England
UHF	Ultra High Frequency
UTV	Ulster Television
VHF	Very High Frequency
VTR	Video Tape Recorder
WACC	World Association for Christian Communication
WEA	Workers' Educational Association
WWN	Wales (West and North) Television
YTV	Yorkshire Television

Part I

THE COMPLETION OF
THE NETWORK: 1958–62

The Structure of Independent Television – 1961/2

ITA regions (14)	Programme companies (15)		Stations (22)	Air date	Population served (thousands)
1. London	Associated-Rediffusion	weekdays	Croydon	22 September 1955	12,910*
	Associated TeleVision	weekends			
2. Midlands	Associated TeleVision	weekdays	Lichfield	17 February 1956	7,450*
	ABC Television	weekends			
3. The North	Granada TV Network	weekdays	{ Winter Hill	3 May 1956	12,452
	ABC Television	weekends	Emley Moor	3 November 1956	
4. Central Scotland	Scottish Television	all week	Black Hill	31 August 1957	3,980
5. South Wales & West of England	Television, Wales & the West	all week	St. Hilary	14 January 1958	3,287
6. Southern England	Southern Television	all week	{ Chillerton Down	30 August 1958	4,269
			Dover	31 January 1960	
7. North East England	Tyne Tees Television	all week	Burnhope	15 January 1959	2,720
8. East Anglia	Anglia Television	all week	Mendlesham	27 October 1959	2,570
9. Northern Ireland	Ulster Television	all week	{ Black Mountain	31 October 1959	1,363
			Strabane	Early 1963	
10. South West England	Westward Television	all week	{ Caradon Hill	29 April 1961	1,601
			Stockland Hill	29 April 1961	
11. Borders	Border Television	all week	{ Caldbeck	1 September 1961	491
			Selkirk	1 December 1961	
12. North East Scotland	Grampian Television	all week	{ Durris	30 September 1961	873*
			Mounteagle	30 September 1961	
13. Channel Islands	Channel Television	all week	Fremont Point	1 September 1962	100*
14. West & North Wales	Wales (West & North) Television	all week	{ Presely	14 September 1962*	1,043*
			Arfon	November 1962*	
			Moel-y-Parc	December 1962*	

* Estimated

Source: ITA Annual Report and Accounts 1961/2 (HMSO)

I

TYNE TEES

By early 1957, with the anxieties of the previous year behind it, the Authority was again actively considering plans for bringing the ITV system to areas beyond those already covered and soon to be covered in London, the Midlands and the North, Scotland, South Wales and the West of England and Southern England. One question examined was the 'rental' that the contractor could be reasonably asked to pay. An annual payment of £95,000 per million population was proposed.

The commitment given to the first four contractors (see Volume 1, Chapter 26) that they would not be required to subsidise through their rentals the cost of later stations was one that could hardly continue if the service was to become nationwide on an equal footing with the BBC. It would be difficult to justify the exclusion of suitable companies anxious to enter the field of television when the only alternative way of achieving the intended national coverage would be a further extension of existing franchise areas. By May, the aim in view had become national coverage by 1960. The standstill in station construction that had been contemplated at a time when the companies' earning capacity was still in doubt, had been counter-manded, and the intended programme of eleven stations extended to fifteen. The development of a genuinely nationwide but decentralised and regionally diverse system could again be contemplated as a realistic option.

The Rank–Associated Newspapers Group had certainly commended itself to Southern England more by its very obvious financial strength than by any regional characteristics, but the next appointment to be made marked a swing of the pendulum back to insistence on the prior importance of a strong regional interest. By early October 1957 a site had been found for the transmitter to serve North Eastern England. It was at Burnhope, in County Durham, some ten miles south west of Newcastle-upon-Tyne.

Applications for the contract were invited on 1 October. The anticipated coverage was about $2\frac{2}{3}$ million, including a small fringe area. The appointed contractor would be expected to establish a studio centre, an outside broadcast unit as well as managerial and sales headquarters in the service area and 15 per cent of programme output would have to be locally produced – all of these by now the more or less standard requirements for the smaller regional contractors. Special emphasis was given to the statutory requirement for independence as to finance and control. The contractor would be 'free to make his own arrangements for purchase and sale of programmes from or to any other company or companies but he must not offer or accept any guarantee of profits or subsidy, nor enter into such arrangements as would restrict competition between programme companies'.[1] The terms of any long-term arrangement for purchase or sale of programme transmission rights would have to be referred to the Authority for approval.

The changed financial climate was reflected in the number of applicants for this new contract. There were seven in addition to the four majors. The new groups included such well-known names as Isaac Wolfson, the Hulton Press, Odhams, Michael Balcon and the *Manchester Guardian*. By 19 November when the interviews took place the field had been narrowed down to three, plus ABC. The three were: the *Guardian* group headed by Laurence Scott in association with John Woolf of Romulus and Remus Films; a group led by Viscount Tenby (Gwilym Lloyd George); a team headed by the local Richmond baronet, industrialist and JP, Sir Richard Pease, and animated by Claude Darling, senior partner in a firm of solicitors with offices in Darlington and Barnard Castle. It had in addition substantial press backing from the *Daily News* company, whose nominees on the Board were Lord Layton and Peter Cadbury; and a show business element was introduced by the brothers George and Alfred Black, members of a long-established North Eastern family firm of theatrical impresarios specialising in variety and revue.

The first and third of these three applicant groups made most impression and it was decided to interview them again on 10 December. The Authority was reluctant to forego what Fraser described as the 'glittering talent'[2] combination offered by the *Guardian* group. In the end it nevertheless came down in favour of the more clearly local Pease group. In reaching this decision it had been impressed less by the *Daily News* and Black connections than by the strong local links and flavour of their programme thinking. Attention was principally focussed on the group's ability to implement their declared programme policies, more particularly as these had been outlined in a supplementary memorandum submitted after the first interview in amplification of their original application.

The aim would be to produce 15 to 20 per cent of output from the company's own local resources. They had little ambition to contribute much in light entertainment, of which the network already offered an adequate supply, but would prefer to concentrate on matters of topical regional interest, children's programmes and informative, even specifically educational output. There was a firm commitment to maximum involvement in regional community life to the extent of establishing a special department to foster local contacts. In connection with their educational plans they announced the recruitment of the former Scottish teacher E. J. R. Eaglesham, by now Professor of Education in the University of Durham who had already put forward ideas for a 'University of the Air' – one of the earliest uses of the phrase.

A formal offer of the North East contract to the Richard Pease group was made in an Authority letter dated 12 December 1957. Negotiations on the terms of the contract turned out to be exceptionally prolonged. Their first choice for a name was 'Three Rivers Television', found attractive by Fraser but thought too obscure by others. The geographically imprecise North Eastern Television was also ruled out. To give the three rivers by name, Tyne, Tees and Wear, was clearly too much of a mouthful. So the choice fell to the shorter, crisper sounding Tyne Tees – thus topographically bracketing the third river.

Not until late June 1958 was the announcement made of the appointment as Managing Director of Anthony Jelly, the thirty-seven-year-old sales director of Scottish Television and a former sales manager with ATV. But in the meantime, Claude Darling and George Black were acting very much as executive directors, urging on the Authority their eagerness to be on the air in time for Christmas.[3] They wanted to start almost immediately their local publicity campaign to stimulate aerial and/or set conversions by viewers in the area. A former furniture warehouse in City Road, Newcastle, was already being prospected as their likely studio centre. It was with the utmost reluctance that they accepted mid January 1959 as the earliest date by which the necessary building and engineering works at the transmitter could be completed. In mid March 1958 it was agreed that the contract reference to opening date would read 'between 10 January and 10 February'.[4]

But the chief difficulty over the Tyne Tees contract, leading to long-drawn-out negotiations, arose from the question of financial control. With each successive franchise award the Authority was learning how complex could be the problems presented by the Act's requirement, as then interpreted, that ITV companies should all be independent of each other as to finance and control. Already the contract offer of 12 December had posed conditions in this sense. Claude Darling and his wife would have to dispose of their holdings in Rediffusion Limited. Peter Cadbury would have to relinquish his Directorship of the Keith Prowse Music Publishing Company which was owned as to 55 per cent of its equity by A-R.

Cadbury's presence on the first Tyne Tees Board was a consequence of his family's connection with the *Daily News* company. He was however already at this stage personally more interested in the prospects for the, as yet, unadvertised ITV contract for the South West. He frankly said so and was told that his own seat on the Tyne Tees Board would have be relinquished should an application for the South West by a group with which he was associated prove successful. In the event, he resigned from the Tyne Tees Board on 20 January 1959.

By the summer of 1958, Tyne Tees was seeking more capital and in August Authority approval was sought for the admission of the Kemsley Newspapers company to a 5 to 10 per cent holding. But Fraser explained that this raised a question of principle and of basic selection procedures, in no way related to any view whatever about the suitability or unsuitability of any new entrant.[5] Programme contracts were offered to groups on the basis that they would not change their composition subsequently[6] and certainly not, as in this case, before the company were on the air. A clause in the draft contract ensured that there could be no share transactions affecting the ownership or influential control of a company without the Authority's prior consent; and that, in particular, shares in the company could not be acquired by individuals or institutions having either direct or indirect significant interests in other ITV companies. But the company was most anxious to be free to issue and market all voting share capital, and eventually, the existing draft contracts were signed and exchanged on a written assurance that some possible easing of the terms of the clause relating to share transactions would be reconsidered at the earliest practicable date.

It was not until the late summer of 1959, when the company had been on the air for more than six months, that the loose ends were tied up with lawyers' red tape. In simple terms the outcome was that the original financial structure of the company, £60,000 voting shares and £30,000 8 per cent Redeemable Loan Stock, would be open to change by an early redemption of the loan stock followed by an issue of further capital in the form of non-voting shares up to a permitted maximum of 60 per cent of the total equity. The Authority made this concession on the firm understanding that the remaining 40 per cent would always consist of voting shares; and that no voting rights would ever become attached to Tyne Tees shares quoted on the Stock Exchange.[7] One year later Lazard Brothers were offering for sale 584,000 non-voting ordinary 2/- (two shillings) shares in Tyne Tees at 25s. 9d. each. The overwhelming public response amounted to more than £4,000,000.[8]

The intervening months had seen the translation of the late 1957 aspirations and good intentions into a bustling regional programme centre with close on half a million viewing homes and an advertising revenue which by the end of the first year would top £2¾ million – with the signal they fed to the Burnhope mast being seen by fishermen on the coast of Denmark. On the by now familiar ('completed in record time') pattern, ten months of feverish preparatory activity had transformed the former warehouse premises in Newcastle's City Road into a compact but technically sophisticated complex of two large production studios plus a small presentation studio for local news reports and interviews. The first TV outside broadcast unit ever to be permanently stationed in the North East had been acquired.

An intensive publicity campaign had been conducted throughout the second half of 1958, both to persuade viewers to adjust their sets (or their aerials) and to recruit local advertisers. By the end of the first week's transmissions the Nielsen Audience Research could report an audience of 37 per cent of all homes in the area, 'by far the highest coverage achieved by an ITV station in its opening week',[9] and, at 306,000 homes, about 50 per cent higher than the company's own forecast. 'We are the eighth child of the ITV family,' said Pease, 'and although we are not as big as some of the other members, we are young and lusty, and we are going to make our voice heard.' He was speaking on the opening night, 15 January 1959. Promptly at 5 p.m. the Duke of Northumberland threw a switch and the studios went live to the strains of the specially composed (or rather collated) 'Three Rivers Fantasy', a medley of traditional North East music, including Bobby Shaftoe, the Water of Tyne, Billy Boy, the Colliers' Rant, and the inevitable Blaydon Races. The evening continued with an episode of *Robin Hood*, *Popeye*, national ITN News followed by local news, distinguished on this occasion by an interview with the former MP for Stockton-on-Tees, Prime Minister Harold Macmillan. 'This is really a very splendid occasion,' he said. He was struck by the energy, enterprise and intelligence of the people of the North East. It was no nondescript no-man's-land between England and Scotland. 'This new service is proof that it is not.'

After the interview came a half hour of *Highway Patrol* followed at 7 p.m. by an hour long special variety programme *The Big Show* featuring Dickie Henderson, Beryl Kaye and Jack Payne, among others. At 8 p.m. came *Double your Money*, then *This Week*, *Wagon Train*, *ITN News*, *Murder Bag*,

I Love Lucy, culminating with a special Epilogue at 11.15 p.m. with the Bishop of Durham and massed local choirs.

This first evening's schedule (to which, in fairness, the occasional productions of a more serious nature in their 15 per cent local output should be added) gives a paradigm of what was to come. As Mary Crozier, the *Guardian* critic, noted in June 1960 Tyne Tees's 'strong line is light entertainment, particularly comedy', a description somewhat at variance with the statement submitted to the Authority at the time of the contract application. She noted in their local output *Sunshine Street*, a half-hour comedy series with music and a satirical slant; *The One O'Clock Show*, four times a week at lunchtime, incorporating 'quick knockabout sketches' before an invited, participating audience of old age pensioners, women's institutes and the like; and *North East Roundabout*, a fifteen-minute magazine on weekday evenings, the Friday edition being devoted to local sport. Two Tyne Tees documentaries had been shown by A-R: one on North Sea trawlers with music and ballads by Ewan MacColl and one on the Darlington Railway. Mary Crozier's final judgement was of 'an energetic, down-to-earth station, very much aware of its regional audience and of what would go down with them. It makes no pretension whatever to meet highbrow tastes . . . it is pragmatic rather than poetical.'[10]

Other observers were less kind. By the time the company reached its second birthday unfavourable comments were appearing in the newspapers, both in the form of special articles and of letters to the Editor. And there was more than a hint of divisions of opinion on programme policy within the company boardroom itself. As early as 30 January 1959, a special correspondent of the *Darlington Northern Echo* was asking 'Is ITV really serious?' and concluding 'after a decent interval when Tyne Tees Television has had time to settle down, I shall investigate the issue of balance. Readers would probably agree that there would not be much balance in a daily programme in which the only items of serious interest were the Epilogue and the news.' A year later the same paper wryly commented: 'The company policy has been . . . to give the public what it wants. This is the natural result of its commercial nature. The bulk of its time has been consequently devoted to American serials, give-away shows, variety and drama.'[11] And in the same week the *Northern Despatch* noted 'after two years . . . a sense of unease'.[12]

This unease was not ill founded. True, the company's ratings were as high as ever. But intelligent and informed observers could hardly overlook the fact that whereas other parts of the ITV system, after acute financial difficulties at the outset, had been responding noticeably to ITA pressures for a return to a more balanced programme offering, here was a regional company which had never known any serious financial worries, apparently persisting with a programme schedule more appropriate to the earlier struggles for survival. 'Taking stock of Tyne Tees is a melancholy task for anyone who cares about the North East and about the quality of what fills our television screens,' said the *Northern Echo* on 12 May 1962, and the article went on to cite programmes like ABC's *Tempo* and other important networked current affairs or documentary programmes that were either not shown at all in the North East or only at infrequent intervals. A Newcastle viewer wrote to the *Guardian* in sarcastic vein:

> While commercial viewers in other parts of the country have been saddled over the past weeks with a series of art talks by Sir Kenneth Clark, we in the Tyne Tees area have not only had the pleasure of seeing *Highway Patrol* instead, but have also enjoyed the privilege of seeing it for the second time . . .[13]

The letter went on to cite other, similar instances. At a time when the Pilkington Committee was about to report, that was a situation the ITA could scarcely view with equanimity. Changes were overdue.

Bob Lorimer, the Authority's Regional Officer, pointed out to George Black, the company's Programme Director, and Bill Lyon Shaw, the Programme Controller, that they were demonstrably 'failing to meet the Authority's requirements in the matter of serious programmes'. Their response to these and other representations led only to some relatively minor schedule changes. A meeting was therefore called at Tyne Tees' London office at which the necessity of achieving a more balanced output was strongly expressed by Frank Copplestone, at that time ITA's Head of Regional Services. 'It would appear,' noted Lorimer in his monthly report for June 1962, 'that the discussions on the inclusion of serious programmes have had a salutory effect which should . . . be reflected in future schedules.'[14]

But these efforts seemed to intensify disputes and tensions within the company over programme policy. Part of the trouble arose no doubt from the dual role of George Black as senior programme executive and founder member of the Board. The Managing Director, Jelly, was himself convinced that it was wrong to have senior executives occupying commanding boardroom positions. In his opinion, the company's regional responsibilities could only be met by a substantial improvement – qualitatively and quantitively – in the company's news and documentary output. These tensions continued until well into 1963, culminating in an uninhibited outburst of indiscretions by Lyon Shaw at the annual television festival at Montreux. He was reported to have said that 'the ITV mentality is to seek money rather than to encourage producers to be creative and adventurous'.[15] He left the service of Tyne Tees soon after.

But in the meantime, sufficiently significant changes had occurred for the Authority to record its pleasure over 'the improvement in the balance of the programme pattern in the Tyne Tees area'.[16] And the *Darlington Northern Echo* declared in January 1963,

> There has been a change for the better. Now Tyne Tees does network *Roving Report, Tempo, What the Papers Say* and the promising new Granada documentary *World in Action*; it put on *Electra* in Greek when other commercial companies turned tail; and its local output shows enterprise and is more often of high quality.[17]

True, went on the writer, it seems that great efforts are still being exerted to prevent a number of serious programmes from being seen by anyone not suffering from insomnia. But 'the fact remains that Tyne Tees is becoming part of the region's life'.

2

ANGLIA

The glittering talent that Fraser had perceived in the unsuccessful *Manchester Guardian*–John Woolf applicant group for the Tyne Tees franchise was not destined to be lost to ITV. The next contract was to be that for the East Anglia area; and applications would be invited as soon as the PMG had approved the preferred transmitter site at Mendlesham, a disused airfield near Stowmarket in East Suffolk. The advertisement appeared on 10 April 1958 with a closing date on 28 May. It attracted applications from four new groups in addition to the existing four major contractors. One of the new groups was headed by the Deputy Lieutenant for the County of Norfolk, the Marquess Townshend of Raynham, and prominent among its members were Laurence Scott of the *Manchester Guardian* and John Woolf of Romulus and Remus Films. Others in the group were Donald Albery of Wyndham Theatres, Glyn Daniel and Aubrey Richards from Cambridge University, Aubrey Buxton, the naturalist and Sir Robert Bignold, President of the Norwich Union. Among the other three new applicants was one described as Viscount Alexander of Hillsborough and Associates, including Anna Neagle and Herbert Wilcox, Woodrow Wyatt, local Cooperative Societies and *Reynolds News*.

The Norwich Union Insurance Society was involved with three of the new applicants. It had been approached by a number of local groups and had decided to offer each of the three most promising ones financial support to the extent of $7\frac{1}{2}$ per cent of the money to be raised up to a maximum of £25,000 without, however, seeking a seat on the Board. The Authority, while emphasising that normally it would not expect to see the appearance of any shareholder in more than one application, raised no objection in this particular case, in recognition of the special standing of Norwich Union in East Anglia.

All four applicants were interviewed on 17 June and it was soon agreed to offer a contract to the group led by Lord Townshend in preference to a group organised round the Norfolk News Company. Determining factors were not only the glittering talents but also the very substantial element of local participation in boardroom and in shareholdings (more than fifty named individuals). Moreover, up to £35,000 out of intended capital of £400,000 (£100,000 in £1 Ordinary Shares and £300,000 8 per cent Loan Stock) was being held in reserve for possible allotment to local newspapers, not yet associated with the group. Declared local programme intentions also impressed. Featured prominently were of course farming topics as well as local music and theatre, women's programmes, sports magazines, local archeology and folklore, and natural history.

The letter to Townshend[1] informing him of the decision contained the proviso that a shareholding of £50,000 (not £35,000) plus one place on the Board should be offered collectively to the Norfolk News Company, the *East Anglian Daily Times* and the *East Midlands Allied Press*. Until the outcome of this approach to the newspapers was known, no public announcement was to be made. The delay was short, and in due course W. O. Copeman, Chairman of the Norfolk News Company and a former Lord Mayor of Norwich, joined the Anglia Board. By August the new contractor's name, Anglia Television, had been approved.

In the meantime, a highly critical article appeared in the *Spectator*,[2] a periodical which had for some time been hostile to ITV, and the ITA especially. The article cited the Anglia decision as a demonstration of the Authority's persistent 'anti-Labour bias in the selection of contractors'. It had accepted 'the traditional approach that anything Tory is non-political and anything connected with Labour is political'. The article could well have been inspired by a member of the unsuccessful group led by the seventy-three-year-old Viscount Alexander. The accusation of an anti-Labour bias was patently false, given the presence of eminent party members such as Dr Eric Fletcher, MP and Sidney Bernstein, to say nothing of the *Daily Mirror* group, among the programme companies. However, the incident was not without its repercussions. Anti-ITV prejudice in some sections of the Labour Party was reinforced by the resentful disappointment of those hopefuls who had looked forward to the creation of an ITV station in which the cooperative movement would have a dominant role. This was to be made very clear in November 1960 when the Parliamentary Committee of the Cooperative Union presented its memorandum of evidence to the Pilkington Committee:

In our opinion the ITA has interpreted its responsibility in awarding contracts in a much too narrow and exclusive manner . . . if our experience is any guide it is totally disinterested [*sic*] in encouraging any form of programme contracts based on local popular and democratic organisations.[3]

That was certainly not how the successful applicant saw the Authority's decision. 'Anglia Television is determined to reflect the life of the area it is going to serve,'[4] said Lord Townshend.

Once again the ITA was to experience the enthusiastic eagerness of a new contractor anxious to get on the air with minimum delay. The Edwardian Agricultural Hall in Norwich had been acquired as headquarters and studio premises; and a bare month after the contract offer the newly appointed Chief Engineer Tom Marshall, who had been in charge of Granada's London studios, was at work planning the transformation of the Hall into a self-contained television production centre. The announcement of 25 June 1958 had looked forward to first transmissions 'during the second half of next year'.[5] But when Townshend, Woolf, Scott and Buxton saw Fraser on 16 September he told them that it would be unwise to count on so early a start. The engineers were dealing with an aerial of novel design, necessary because of the contiguity of the London transmission area. It had been devised to produce an asymmetrical radiation pattern with maximum signal strength towards Norwich, Peterborough, Cambridge and Colchester, towards the Wash and Lincolnshire, with minimum strength in the London direction. It was to be installed on one of the tallest masts so far erected in Europe – some 1000 feet high. Naturally, they wanted to be sure it was working as planned; and this was unlikely to be known before September 1959 at the earliest. 'We must not on any account go into action except with an aerial in every way satisfactory.'[6]

In these exchanges (which were to continue for several months) the young company seemed to betray a certain air of frustration, even perhaps a hint that the Authority might be dragging its feet. 'I do really feel that your letter places rather heavy emphasis on the "delay",'[7] wrote Fraser. With an eye to advance commercial bookings for the pre-Christmas buying spree, the company continued to press for early November or even 29 October. As things turned out they were lucky. They got on the air by 27 October. The earlier start for Mendlesham certainly owed much to the efforts of the ITA engineers and to EMI, the manufacturer of the novel aerial array.

However, it was already apparent that here was a programme company led by four active, managerially-minded directors who were not going to take back seats and leave the driving to senior executive staff. Competent and self-assured on the basis of past achievement, they were as confident in the rightness of their purposes as in their claims to all the support and recognition (and of course the rewards) that such right purposes would justly deserve. They were exemplars of that thrusting but socially responsible entrepreneurial spirit that would eventually make ITV succeed in more than a material sense. This spirit, this belief that doors open only when they are pushed, continued to inform the company's dealings with the Authority throughout the months until air date.

By December 1958 Anglia were negotiating an agreement with A-R that would provide a national network outlet for drama productions, for which the new company seemed to be well qualified by virtue of their connections with the film world through Woolf and the West End theatre through Donald Albery. But although there was, naturally, to be a Post Office link bringing networked ITV programmes to Norwich, at that time no return link was envisaged which would bring Anglia productions to London and hence to the network. It seemed inevitable that the planned six to eight plays a year would have to be produced in London. With some justification the company expressed the hope that these productions would nevertheless be classified as a contribution towards the 15 per cent of 'local origination' to which they would be bound by their contract. But by the end of the month Townshend was writing again expressing the hope that a return link from Norwich would not be long delayed. The Authority was not unsympathetic and placed an order for the line with the Post Office. Donald Stephenson, the former Controller of the BBC's Overseas Services, was by now Anglia's Chief Executive. Asked to substantiate the claim that the line would be needed to feed a significant number of Anglia productions into the network he promptly cited the drama commitment adding, for good measure, a twenty-six episode family serial, a new series on household treasures, a new archeological series exploiting the Cambridge–Glyn Daniel connection, a new science series, a major new agricultural series and a natural history series exploiting the East Anglian landscape and wild life. This was at the end of January. But a bare month after going on the air in the autumn, Stephenson had to report that his company had now come to the conclusion that the link was something they really could not afford at that stage, and asked for the Post Office order to be withdrawn.

What had happened in the meantime? For one thing the assumptions about the immediate programme capabilities of a small ITV company in embryo were much too optimistic. But over and above these evident miscalculations, this return link story had become part of another, bigger one, that of the likely size and eventual geographical spread of Anglia's future audience. Of compelling interest to them was the fact that on 2 September 1958 the Authority approved the construction of a new transmitter near Dover to provide a service for South East England.[8] This decision immediately gave rise to concern about the extent of probable overlap that would exist between the new station and adjacent company service areas. Both London companies were worried, ATV especially because the newly opened Southern transmitter's signal had already encroached into their Midlands weekday franchise area as well as into the approaches to London.[9] The overlap between Dover and the new (and improved) London transmitter, shortly to be built, was expected to be very large indeed, including anything from a half upwards of the population to be served by a South East station. Yet, it had hitherto been the Authority's policy to appoint fresh programme companies having, so far as possible, local roots and interests, as it opened new stations. To do otherwise even in cases where some overlap of coverage areas occurred would mean excluding groups able and willing to set up as new programme contractors, and assigning new areas to existing companies would be favouring the haves at the expense of the have-nots. It was only the size of the anticipated South Eastern overlap that gave the Authority pause.

Enquiries had already been received from possible applicant groups, but, notwithstanding apparently reassuring figures produced for one of them by Nielsen's, the Authority remained dubious about the financial viability of a contractor whose service area would be so far invaded by signals not only from Croydon but also from Southern's Chillerton Down and even Anglia's Mendlesham transmitter. There was some uncertain recognition that Kent and the East Sussex borders, though affected by the south eastward spread of London's dormitory suburbs, did possess a distinctive regional character. But three overlaps, even if the largest – from Croydon – might be mitigated, seemed to make prospects of financial disaster for a new contractor all too real. So the Authority announced its intention to operate the Kent station as a satellite to an existing programme contractor. But which existing company was it to be? That was the second dilemma; and this the Authority took close on six months to resolve. After some hesitation it was agreed to invite all existing contractors to apply.[10] Among the applicants were Southern Television and Anglia. Interviews held on 24 March 1959 included A-R, ATV and Granada as well as Anglia and Southern. The Members had little difficulty in deciding not to give an additional service area to any of the first three companies whose profits were already so high as to attract unfavourable public comment.

Anglia had enlisted some eminent local Kent supporters, who expressed confidence that the people of Kent would welcome a contractor of their character. The company argued that, quite apart from the fact that Dover was much nearer to Mendlesham than to any other regional transmitter, there were certain similarities between the two areas and their inhabitants, such as a long seaboard with both maritime and agricultural activities. Ethnically and geographically the two areas were certainly more alike than, for example, the two parts of the TWW area. Their rivals in Southern, on the other hand, had not recruited any backing from public figures in Kent. They had, instead, committed themselves to a local studio (something Anglia had left open) and to the appointment of additional local staff in order to deal with local advertising and to provide a local news service. Participation of local Kent worthies would be sought if and when they were given the contract.

The Authority decided in favour of Southern. As we saw in Volume 1, Chapter 29, it tended to regard Southern as a virtual 'mini major', one with sufficient independent competitive weight within the ITV system to help counter-balance the power of the network companies. Fraser had come to feel that it was a company with considerable further potential for the enrichment of ITV programming as a whole, backed as it was by the large resources of the Rank organisation. It would be politic, therefore, to give them a more substantial population base. If Kent were given to Anglia 'they would have a distinctly larger service area even than Southern now enjoys, and this would seem to me particularly hard to defend'.[11] Anglia were not yet on the air. They had certainly displayed commendable awareness and understanding of regional responsibilities and the Authority was impressed by this. But they were still untried. Townshend himself had said that they did not expect to become profitable until some two years after their air date, which was still some months away.[12]

The South East decision was felt as a severe setback by Anglia. The ambitious programme plans outlined in Stephenson's letter would certainly have been more appropriate to a larger company, one of the size they would have attained had the additional contract gone their way. The case for a return link from Norwich to London had in fact been supported by describing it as a quite indispensable necessity in the event of Anglia obtaining the contract for South East England.

Inevitably, therefore, Townshend voiced concern over the likely inroads into Anglia's primary area of the Kent transmissions. At the very least, he thought, early consideration should be given to the provision of a satellite transmitter that would carry their signal northwards to more viewers in Lincolnshire. He went with his colleagues to argue their case with Kirkpatrick and Fraser on 12 May; and this meeting was followed up by a letter and memorandum again linking their failure in Kent with demands for compensatory expansion northwards. The overlap with the South East would, they assumed, rob them of 50,000 to 100,000 potential viewers. They argued that the terms on which they had been offered the contract had been altered unilaterally by the Authority. Such an argument was too much for Kirkpatrick. In the course of a letter, explaining the technical inevitability, not to say necessity, of overlaps he said he was:

> obliged to point out that we have never, in the appointment of any programme company, guaranteed or even suggested that its service area would be kept free from overlaps. Instead, the terms of our contracts would not prevent us from appointing and transmitting the programme of a second company in precisely the same area, thus bringing about an overlap of 100 per cent.[13]

He indicated that further argument was futile; even if as many as half of the theoretical 100,000 population overlap were to watch Dover rather than Mendlesham (and this was most unlikely) Anglia's population loss would be no more than 3 per cent.

The episode was not allowed to sour relations, and the after-taste of disappointment may even have been sweetened when it was learned by mid August that early low-power tests from Mendlesham had already revealed good reception well into East Lincolnshire, including Boston. By this time the company were distributing a well-printed glossy monthly bulletin to dealers in their area. And no doubt as a placatory gesture the October issue of this bulletin gave a lot of space to the role and functions of the Authority. It was headlined: 'Full Power Test Signals. Aerial erection roars ahead in all parts of the Region.' The bulletin also reported with pride Anglia's forthcoming contribution to network drama. Although the 'smallest of the ITV companies' they would be providing the 'best of plays, with star casts', to be shown nationally on Tuesday nights in the Play of the Week slot. George More O'Ferrall, 'the man who directed the world's first television play for the BBC in 1936' had been appointed Head of Drama. The first play would be *The Violent Years* starring Laurence Harvey and Hildegard Neff. It would be seen at 9.35 p.m. on opening night, Tuesday 27 October 1959.

'Opening Night' for Anglia began at 4.15 p.m. in the afternoon: it proved, said the *Ipswich Evening Star*, 'a smooth start'. Viewers were first taken on an aerial survey of their area, coming down to earth via the entrance of the Old Norwich Post Office and Agricultural Hall, now renamed Anglia House. Here Lord Townshend introduced Kirkpatrick who, after a few words, proceeded to master control where he threw a symbolic switch – a gesture, commented the newspaper, which lost some of its dramatic impact 'because the station had by then been on the air for some minutes'.[14] The introductory thirty minutes continued with 'trailers' of forthcoming local programmes, including the light entertainment *Midday Show*, featuring a twenty-one-year-old singer–interviewer named Susan Hampshire and Norman Hackforth, mystery voice of the BBC's *Twenty Questions*, now Anglia's Director of Music. Then came three A-R children's programmes up to the 5.55 p.m. ITN news, followed by Local News at 6.08 p.m.; then STV's *This Wonderful World*; a film report specially shot in Germany on the amalgamation of the Norfolk and Suffolk regiments; Granada's *Song Parade*; *Emergency-Ward 10*; a panel game (*Concentration*) and a detective series until the mid evening ITN bulletin at 9.25 p.m. After this came the promised network play up to News Headlines at 11.05 p.m., followed by a repeat of the opening thirty minutes and then, until midnight, the Epilogue. 'A memorable evening that must have ended with a sigh of satisfaction.'[15] Feelings of pride were surely in order. It was unique for a regional company – the smallest so far – to mark its first night by networked drama filling ninety minutes of peak time.

According to Marsland Gander of the *Daily Telegraph*[16] generally excellent reception in the region (and beyond) was achieved. The Anglia pictures from Mendlesham had been received as far south as the London outskirts at Romford, Woodford and Enfield; northwards to Sheringham and Cromer, eastward to Yarmouth and Lowestoft. But these were of course no more than casual, unsystematic 'sightings'. The fact remains, however, that when in mid 1960 an accurate scientific check of Mendlesham coverage was made, the population served turned out to be well over 2 million, whereas the estimated one on which the contract applications had been made was 1.7 million.

The quantity of local productions shown on that first night (more than 50 per cent) was hardly likely to be typical. Anglia's first week, however, did include, as well as the light entertainment *Midday Show* already mentioned, local sports coverage, *Town and Gown* – the first of a regular half-hour discussion series from Cambridge – and, on Sunday, a service from Norwich Cathedral and the first edition of the forty-minute *Farming Diary*.

By the end of their first year one local newspaper felt able to comment: 'In its presentation of local programmes which after all is the real criterion,' Anglia was showing 'increasing self-confidence, poise and polish'. Singled out for special praise were Aubrey Buxton's *Countryman* series ('grown in stature and popularity'), the weekly topical debate *Arena* ('pungent and forthright') and the local talent show, *Glen Mason Show*. The announcement that the news magazine *About Anglia* (presented by Dick Joice, a tenant farmer on the Townshend estate, who also presented the Sunday *Farming Diary*) was to be seen five days a week in future was hailed as good news because it was 'the nearest thing on TV to a local *Panorama*, informative, amusing, and occasionally provocative'.[17] Several of the networked Anglia plays had made national Top Ten ratings and the output was regularly getting an audience share of over 65 per cent, higher than the average of other ITV companies' plays. Financially too, things had gone well. Early losses had been wiped out much sooner than expected. The directors were able to declare an interim dividend of 20 per cent for the period ending October 1960.

But Anglia's early ambitions to make a larger regular contribution to the network were not going to be realised so easily. They soon became aware of the rigidities and drawbacks of the network system. Moreover, it was in keeping with the character of this young company that they should have sought early in their life to influence the structure of inter-company relations. In response to representations from Townshend, Fraser agreed that there were two lacks in the organisation of ITV. One was the absence of any adequate means for the collective consideration and discussion of programme policy by *all* the companies. The other was the absence of any consultation between the regional companies about their own needs, policies and problems. Taken together the six regional companies must now be considered to be a powerful element in Independent Television. 'If the network companies meet separately, as they do in the Network Programme Committee, is there not something to be said for at least occasional meetings between the regional companies?'[18]

Townshend's response was positive. He contacted chairmen of the five other regional companies, inviting them to an informal lunchtime discussion. The meeting took place on 4 February 1960 and was attended by the chairmen of STV, TWW, Tyne Tees and Ulster. John Davis of Southern was represented by another Southern director. Topics discussed included: prospects for 1964 (when current contracts ended); labour relations; programme interchange; joint film purchase; presentation of evidence to Government Committees of Enquiry on behalf of regional companies. It was agreed to meet again at monthly intervals.

This initiative led to the eventual formation of a separate association of regional companies. It might therefore be seen as a welcome and public-spirited first step towards a reduction in the entrenched dominance of the Big Four; and hence even towards greater flexibility in the planning, not to say competitiveness in the supply, of programme output for the network. But that would be over-simplification. There was a fundamental ambivalence in Anglia's position. Given their programme ambitions it was natural that they should react against the rigidities of the networking system of those days. Yet, thanks to their affiliation agreement with A-R, they had become substantial beneficiaries of that system. Thanks to its very rigidities they were assured pre-emptive right to a network showing for eight ninety-minute drama productions each year, sight unseen: and that at a time when television broadcasting hours were still strictly rationed.

The Anglia plays that have since continued over the years to maintain their privileged network place have been by and large popular 'middle-brow' drama; and the company have themselves not been slow to point to their ratings success. Already their first two productions achieved national ratings of 59 and 62, whereas plays from ATV averaged 43+, from A-R 45+ and from Granada 44. Two years later they had provided twenty-six plays, eighteen of which reached the Top Ten. 'We lose money on the deal' John Woolf was quoted as saying 'but we have made Anglia into a name.'[19]

It was with the more demanding 'serious productions' arising in part at least from their Cambridge connections that Anglia's ambitions were less easily fulfilled. Indeed they found themselves in their first weeks showing locally one of the series cited by Stephenson as potential network fare (*Town and Gown* from Cambridge), at the time when the rest of the network (apart from Tyne Tees!) was seeing Sir Kenneth Clark's art lectures. Nationwide showings for the excellent Glyn Daniel-inspired archeological series were long delayed and were occasional rather than regular. Even the increasingly – and deservedly – successful *Survival* programmes did not gain an assured regular network placing as of right. It is, as Maurice Wiggin wrote in September 1961, a 'hard road' to prestige. Of the smaller provincial companies Anglia seemed to him the most ambitious. 'To make money *and* qualify for the status halo is an awfully nerve-racking business.'[20]

The 'nerve racking' strains may have had something to do with the relatively short company careers of some of Anglia's first senior executives. Stephenson resigned at the end of 1959. By the end of 1961 their first Programme Controller was leaving because of 'differences of opinion . . . with the planning committee'[21] and was not replaced. Whatever the 'differences of opinion', one factor must have been the close and increasing involvement – already mentioned – in day-to-day programme matters by the 'gang of four' executive directors, Townshend, Scott, Buxton and Woolf. For many years this small 'management committee' was to exercise most of the functions normally exercised elsewhere by a programme controller. It cannot be said that they made a bad job of it: quite the contrary.

Within two years of its opening night this company had gained a position of exceptional prestige that other small companies could well envy. It was a reputation mainly built on four types of programme: drama, natural history, the local news magazine *About Anglia* and *Farming Diary*; and these reflected in no small measure the personal preoccupations and interests of the members of the four-man 'management committee'.

3

ULSTER

With the advent of Anglia, the ninth ITV company, contractors had been appointed to bring an ITV service to some 90 per cent of the United Kingdom's total population. Of the five areas still to be served the most populous was in the six counties of Northern Ireland. Here there was a potential coverage of some 1,000,000 people, slightly more than that of the proposed station for south-east England. Yet, although doubts about the financial viability of the latter caused it to be eventually designated a 'satellite' station, little hesitation was felt over the desirability of a separate independent programme company for Northern Ireland. Here if anywhere was a population with distinctive regional character; and the possibilities of signal overlap from mainland transmissions were small. More serious perhaps would be encroachment of signals from a future television service in Southern Ireland. By April 1958, proposals for the establishment of a commercial television service in Eire were under active examination by a Commission set up the previous month. The proposals of this Commission, which reported in May 1959, for a self-supporting independent commercial service were later (August 1959) rejected by the Eire Government which opted for a public authority financed partly from licence fees and partly from advertisements. This service did not go on the air until the end of 1961. But any South to North overlaps would most probably be balanced, if not outweighed, by ones in the reverse direction.

From 1956 onwards, there had been enquiries to the Authority from interested parties in Northern Ireland. It was constrained, however, to defer a decision by two factors, both of them as it turned out, short-lived. One was the Government's restriction on capital expenditure which had led the PMG to ask the ITA to postpone entering into any further commitments after the Scottish and Welsh stations. The other was the gloomy financial outlook of early 1956 whose influence had been much in evidence when the Scottish franchise was on offer. Among those enquiring were Commander Oscar Henderson (son of a former Mayor of Belfast whose family owned the *Belfast*

Newsletter), Lt.-Col Cunningham (Managing Director of the *Northern Whig*) and Mr Sayer of the *Belfast Evening Telegraph*. These three highly reputable Belfast papers were Unionist in their politics. No interest was shown at this stage by the leading Nationalist journal, the *Irish News*.

But it was late April 1958 before the ITA was able to set a target date for the opening of its Northern Ireland station at 'late 1959, early 1960'.[1] By late summer of that year plans for a transmitter sited at Black Mountain to the West of Belfast were well advanced and it was decided on 2 September to advertise forthwith.[2] Closing date for receipt of applications was 9 October. Two existing ITV contractors – A-R and Granada – and two new groups applied.

There were probably proportionately fewer television receivers in Northern Ireland than in other ITV regions, but ITV's financial boom by now was well under way. According to the *Belfast Evening Telegraph* there had been originally no fewer than five intending applicant groups 'in rivalry for what on the experience of other regions is one of the money spinners of the age'.[3] The newspaper went on to hint – somewhat cryptically – that the Stormont government would doubtless 'want to have its say' in the appointment because 'the political implications are considerable'. This last remark worried Fraser, deeply conscious as he was of the very great importance in a Northern Ireland context of the Act's requirement of due impartiality.

At their meeting on 14 October, Members heard from Colonel Chichester, their Northern Ireland colleague, that both of the indigenous applicant groups included in his opinion 'competent and highly respected figures from the business and public life of Northern Ireland'.[4] One, headed by the Duke of Abercorn, a son of the first Governor of Northern Ireland, included George Lodge, owner of the Belfast Royal Hippodrome and Grand Opera House, 'an energetic personality with great experience of the entertainment business' as prospective Managing Director; and Captain Orr, the Westminster MP for South Down who had played such an influential part in debates on the 1954 Television Bill. The two newspapers, *The Northern Whig* and the *Belfast Evening Telegraph*, were also associated with this group.

The second group, led by the Earl of Antrim, included Sir Francis Evans, the former British Ambassador to Argentina, Hubert Wilmot, Sir Laurence Olivier, Betty Box, representing Beaconsfield Films and William MacQuitty, a London film producer from a well-known Ulster family, who was to be their first Managing Director. The newspaper interest in this group was represented by the *Newsletter* and the Henderson family. A number of local weekly papers outside Belfast were also represented. They said that 25 per cent of the group's share capital would be reserved for eventual offer, should they be awarded the contract, to the newspapers associated with their rivals.

Both groups showed awareness of special problems particularly as regards relations of Northern Ireland with its Southern neighbour. The Authority would have liked to have as its contractor a combination of elements from both, but discreet local enquiry revealed that the marriage could not be arranged. Interviews therefore took place on 4 November 1958 and the choice fell on the Antrim–Henderson group. Its statement of intent seemed fuller and its membership seemed more widely representative of Northern Ireland as a whole. A formal offer of contract was despatched to Lord Antrim on the following day. The willingness of his group to offer a 25 per cent shareholding to the two other Belfast newspapers was merely noted. Neither that nor any offer of directorship or shares to members of the Abercorn group was made a condition of the appointment. But it was emphasised that any allocation of unissued capital or changes in the membership of the board of directors would require prior Authority approval. The new company adopted the name of Ulster Television Ltd.

The Authority was concerned about the need to ensure adequate Roman Catholic representation both in the boardroom and among the shareholders of Ulster Television, and it had been favourably impressed by Lord Antrim's good intentions in this respect. However, the initial voting share capital of the company was £100,000 of which £25,000 was unissued, £24,000 in the hands of London shareholders, and of the remaining £51,000 in the hands of Northern Ireland shareholders only £3000 was held by Roman Catholics. Antrim felt that the disproportion could be at least partially corrected by the use of some of the still unissued 25 per cent of voting share capital.

It was decided to seek purchasers for 10,000 of the unallotted shares and in May 1959 the company were given approval for the appointment of two new Directors, both Roman Catholics, and the issue of shares to 27 new investors, the effect of which was to increase Roman Catholic holdings in the company to about 16 per cent. The situation was further improved when in August 1959 the Nationalist *Irish News* and two of its directors were allotted between them 1200 £1 voting shares. This newspaper had a circulation of about 40,000, roughly the same as that of the Hendersons' *Newsletter*.

When the newly appointed company began to tackle the nitty gritty of viable operational plans, they were soon aware that their group lacked members with the necessary professional experience and knowledge. No one in the United Kingdom had yet faced the daunting task of running a commercial television station on so small a scale; moreover the percentage of viewers in the Northern Ireland population was almost certainly lower than in any other ITV area so far. The company did not expect to have an initial audience of more than 100,000 homes by its opening night. 'It is clear to us' wrote Antrim, 'that Ulster Television will be a difficult business proposition and, during the first two years, at least, we shall not find it easy to pay our way.'[5] As they became better aware of the complexities and economics of television production they began to harbour doubts about the realism of the plans for local programming outlined in their application.

The prospect of a rental payment of over £100,000 to the Authority was also daunting. Could it be fair, they wondered, to be charged on a population basis, as all other contractors were, when the set-density in their area was so much lower? But here, anxious as the Authority was to nurse this latest fledgling in its flock, it would not be easy to help. Both groups competing for the contract had applied in full knowledge of what the rental would be.

Instead, what the ITA set about trying to do was to increase the size of the service area. The signal from Black Mountain would not reach close on a third of the population in the west of the Province. That was why a channel had been reserved for a second, satellite transmitter at Londonderry. But already more was being heard about the planned television service with advertisements in the Republic. One of its transmitters, so it was rumoured, would cover Western Ulster. Small wonder that the ITA engineers were asked to step up the priority of site finding in the area. With the best will in the world, however, this was going to take time. All that could be promised was: 'when there is anything we can say about Londonderry, we will let you know, but a station there before 1961 doesn't look a possibility'.[6] In the event it was to take much longer.

In his reply to Antrim about UTV's programme problems, Fraser was not unsympathetic: 'I am sure you will find that the Authority appreciates the special nature of your situation'. But he had also to point out that 'during the interview . . . you left the Authority with the impression that you would feel able to undertake a good deal more than now seems to be suggested'. Because the company obviously needed avuncular advice as well as paternal reproof he went on to say:

One modest studio and a staff of less than one hundred represent the furthest stage to which you should prudently go at the begin-ning . . . much will . . . depend upon the imagination and ingenuity shown in giving your transmissions a local colour without too great an outlay . . . Ulster Television will in fact be pioneering in this respect, and may perhaps serve as a model for other relatively small companies.[7]

What UTV needed more than anything else at this delicate stage was an infusion of television professionals. To lay foundations of success in what was bound to be in the first instance a shoestring operation they needed more than enthusiasm and energy combined with a fund of experience in business, theatre, film production and newspapers. They got what they needed through an affiliation agreement with ABC Television. This extended to obtaining Authority agreement to an arrangement whereby ABC would sell air time for UTV on a commission basis for a limited number of years until they were strong enough to have a fully staffed organisation of their own in London. But ever mindful of the need to keep companies independent of each other as to finance and control, in appearance as well as in fact, Fraser had to add:

We cannot promise to continue this approval indefinitely . . . It is important that . . . Ulster Television's separate identity should be continuously emphasised by the issue of separate rate cards, separate promotion material . . . as well as by the appointment of a London sales manager. On no account should any printed material or circular lose their separate identity.[8]

The UTV Board seemed to be taking too gloomy a view of the company's financial prospects. They were clearly preoccupied by the heavy initial outlays that would be repaid only gradually over a slow and uncertain future. Yet a TAM survey in March 1959 should have encouraged them. It showed that of the 127,000 TV homes in the Province 103,000 already had multi-channel receivers – a higher proportion (81 per cent) than in any previous ITV region; and these homes contained, on average, more than four people each, again a higher figure than elsewhere. But the directors of UTV remained acutely money conscious. In their minds they faced painful inner conflicts. Their application had promised an hour a day of local programmes. The enthusiastic urge to create a truly regional station reflecting the distinctive character and culture of their area (and which had so commended their application to the Authority) had to come to terms with the prudent, deep-rooted instincts of people temperamentally inclined to preparatory anticipation of a rainy day. Until that conflict was resolved Antrim was unable to give any substantial details of his programme plans.

Progress on the Black Mountain transmitter had been good and opening night for the new station was fixed at 31 October 1959. So when the second week of June arrived without any firm programme plans from UTV, Fraser become seriously concerned. With barely four months to go, Ulster Television were, he said, 'in a miserable plight . . . worried about their income . . . nervous and puzzled about what can be done'.[9] He had seen a memorandum (dated 19 May) from Ulster's Managing Director, William MacQuitty, to his Board, and found it 'diffuse and depressing'. The long list of programme 'possibilities' in this document bore little relation to the production resources of a single studio station with no recording equipment and no outside broadcast facility. A meeting followed at Princes Gate which Antrim, MacQuitty and R. B. Henderson (General Manager) attended on behalf of the company. Fraser insisted that it was high time a qualified person was appointed to take responsibility for UTV's own programmes, even though for the time being the company's total production effort should be concentrated on a single magazine type programme to be put out at the same time each day.

A discussion followed immediately in which the Authority's Regional Officer, W. H. Wilson, and Ron Rowson, ABC's Programme Controller, participated, and a three-phase plan for UTV's own programme activity was worked out. A 'tentative' schedule embodying Phase 1 was sent to the ITA by Rowson on 18 June.[10] Local production would be limited, on each of the five weekdays, to the twenty-minute news magazine immediately following the ITN bulletins at 6.10 p.m. One or two 'serious programmes' shown on the network would be replaced by popular film series. Most likely to give the Authority pause was the absence of a local news bulletin. Perhaps the need would be met by topical items in the news magazine. In Phase 2 when the station had become established, there would be more 'balance' and a 'slight increase' in local origination. This latter, it was hoped, would include one item in MacQuitty's May memorandum, namely a series of late night lectures by dons of Queen's University, Belfast, tentatively entitled *Midnight Oil*, giving a diploma or some recognition for viewers who followed the courses. Phase 3 would have maximum possible local origination and a much more balanced programme schedule. The route by which this draft arrived (i.e. from an ABC not from a UTV source) naturally caused concern at Princes Gate; and Fraser, when he saw a press reference to UTV's dependence on ABC, immediately wrote to Howard Thomas, expressing concern.[11]

Preparation of their first programme schedule was not the only task in which UTV was getting help from ABC. The latter's Chief Engineer, Howard Steele, was supervising the design of their studio in Havelock House, the reconstructed clothing warehouse which was to be their Belfast HQ. S. E. Reynolds, a senior producer with ABC, was to be appointed UTV's first programme controller, but he went into hospital for a serious operation almost immediately.

However, the young company were beginning to emerge from their early confusions, and to show signs of being able to look after themselves. They made plans to publish their own weekly programme magazine with the title *TV Post*. It was noticeable that in this atmosphere of growing self-confidence and clearing of minds, an increasingly important role was being played by UTV's General Manager, thirty-year-old R. B. ('Brum') Henderson. In July Hubert Wilmot resigned from the position of Production Manager, and it was Henderson who conducted further programme discussions with the ITA, establishing an excellent working relationship with Wilson, the Northern Ireland Officer. He quickly acknowledged the wisdom of giving public evidence of forward programme thinking if local opinion was not to be too disillusioned. After all, when they were awarded the contract, MacQuitty had proclaimed 'Ulster TV is for Ulstermen. Our interests are rooted in Ulster, our programmes are for its people.'[12] That was in March. But on 24 October 1959, the *Belfast Telegraph* was telling its readers that one week later, when the company went on the air, 'the initials UTV . . . will suddenly assume an important new significance . . . as the symbol of an Ulster company's own assessment of Ulster prestige, intelligence and culture'; and that this 'symbol' would be represented initially by one local product, *Roundabout*, a twenty-minute weekday news magazine. True, the paper was able to add 'I am assured that even before Christmas we can look for an increase'. As Henderson saw it *Roundabout* which they were determined, he said, to make into a successful and worthwhile Ulster programme, could also be in part a testing ground for programme ideas that could be more fully developed later into additional local programmes as soon as finances would permit. ITA officers for their part sought firmer commitment not only to a phased increase in local output, but also to rather more serious 'balancing' material from network sources in the UTV schedule. But the Members were also very conscious of the experimental nature of their newest station and were not prepared to push too hard. As Wilson himself put it, 'I do not think we can expect a lot in the formative months', adding cautiously, 'How many formative months there are going to be I would not like to say!'.[13]

Still the Hallowe'en first night which opened with a strong Northern Irish flavour turned out by all contemporary accounts to be an encouraging, hitch-free success. There were, it is true, a few complaints of poor reception from viewers in the Dublin area! At the preceding celebratory luncheon,

Lord Brookeborough, the Northern Ireland Prime Minister, welcomed the advent of ITV as 'a vote of confidence in the stability of the Northern Ireland government'.[14]

The inaugural transmission itself was less political. It was introduced by Sir Laurence Olivier, in his capacity as a director of the company and was deemed locally to be 'smooth, efficient and entertaining'.[15] The Governor, Lord Wakehurst, pronounced a ceremonial speech of welcome and a Hallowe'en party, compèred by Sir Laurence, was held in the studio. Six Belfast schoolboys, invited in from nearby streets, joined in the revelry, to which Beatrice Lillie, a shareholder and daughter of a well known Ulsterman, contributed some characteristic 'poetic brevities'.[16] Richard Hayward, Ulster folklorist and singer, gave in words and music a quick introduction to the character, culture and products of each of the six counties in turn. And then after swift glimpses at other ITV studios, rehearsing future programme treats in store, the station joined the network and the latest episode of *Robin Hood*. At the evening's close, Sir Laurence returned to speak the Epilogue.

The next day, in place of the network's fortnightly Sunday afternoon *Bookman* programme, a film shot by the Governor was shown. Under the title *Rich and Rare* it featured in thirty sequences a series of traditional Ulster country crafts and activities from fishing and farming to turf-cutting, scything, bagpipes, the Lough Neagh ferry and the May Fair at Ballyclare. But from then on programming was to be mainly, in the words of Marsland Gander, 'a one-way traffic in the usual Anglo-American pattern . . . from across the water'.[17] Apart from station announcements and some commercials, only the weekday *Roundabout* was both for and of the region. One month later Fraser wrote 'What they are now doing is not permanently defensible . . . It isn't so much a question of what Ulster is doing now but of proposing to them a . . . time-table of improvements.'[18] Thanks largely to the understanding between Wilson and Henderson, a timetable was established and the improvements came. By January 1960 local origination had risen to four hours a week, and there is no doubt that even within that limited compass an impression was being made. In that month the Dublin Senate were debating the Bill for the introduction of television in Eire and one speaker in urging cooperation with neighbouring broadcasting authorities referred to the programmes shown in Northern Ireland as 'extraordinarily effective in their Irish local flavour'.[19] 'UTV', said the TV critic of the *Belfast Telegraph*, 'needs more people, more equipment, more space and clearly a bigger programme budget . . . The management remains a little too preoccupied about paying the rent' but 'for all its shortcomings –

and I have never belittled them – [UTV] is striding forward.' In comparison with the local BBC he thought they were 'making the greater impact'. That they were able to do so despite their restricted programme formats 'is quite extraordinary'.[20] *Roundabout* was regularly getting ratings in the 70s and 80s.

In announcing his January increase, Henderson also told Wilson that they were formulating plans for the following autumn. By that time they would have built up two adequate production teams. He was as good as his word. That autumn schedule, when it came, showed just over six hours a week of local programmes – precisely the amount he had promised the company would achieve by the end of their first year.

The early money worries had by now shown themselves to have been unnecessary. Already in June 1960, when Antrim presented the company's first Annual Report, he announced a trading profit of £50,903 after a full twelve months' expenditure had been set against only six months' income. By 1962 their profits for the year had topped £250,000. Only a few days after Antrim's statement, Henderson spoke of the impending purchase of an Ampex video tape recorder, which would significantly increase the productivity of the single studio. It came as no surprise when in September he succeeded to the post of Managing Director. That same month, when the Authority Members met for the first time in Belfast, Fraser was describing the UTV news magazine *Roundabout* as a 'remarkable programme' whose 'unique success' had led to its being copied in other ITV regions, including Scotland, Wales and the North East.[21]

And when UTV's first birthday came along, *Roundabout*, which to mark the occasion was allowed to run for fifty minutes (including another pictorial record of Ulster life called *Richer and Rarer*, from that distinguished amateur film maker, the Governor) was singled out by Mary Crozier of the *Guardian* on a visit to Belfast as chief among the surprising number of programmes making up 'a more varied output than I expected from so small a station'.[22] This varied output included an afternoon series for very young children, a women's programme, a children's quiz, a 'lonely hearts' type discussion series on personal problems called *Share the Load*, a regular Friday evening sports commentary as well as the early *Roundabout*. All were getting exceptionally high ratings. In that first year the number of ITV viewing households had risen from 97,000 to 165,000; and *TV Post*, the weekly programme guide, had a circulation of 100,000.[23]

Another local birthday comment in the Belfast *Northern Whig* confessed to enjoyment of UTV's 'handsome concession to oomph and publicity, its liberal ration of middle brow entertainment and its occasional excursions into the byways of culture'. That fairly describes the company's screen image.

Excursions into culture were indeed occasional and from time to time the relatively low proportion of serious 'balance' was a bone of contention with the ITA. But, apart from those items they took from the network, the company's own serious contributions were nearly always enterprising. An outstanding example was the realisation in 1962 of the *Midnight Oil* project, first mooted by MacQuitty in 1959. From 2 July 1962 on every weekday evening between 10.40 and 11.15 p.m., over a period of two months, seven groups of six broadcasts – forty two in all – were given by Professors and other members of the teaching staff of Queen's University in Belfast. The topics were medicine, law, literature, music, physics, history and economics. Audiences were better than expected. Although the description 'first University of the Air' was an excusable exaggeration, such enterprise from a diminutive regional company certainly merited Kirkpatrick's comment: 'a very remarkable effort'. The Authority was sufficiently impressed seriously to contemplate making Northern Ireland the area in which to experiment with the future possibilities of an educational channel.

A year later in July and August 1963, UTV renewed this initiative with another late evening series called *The Inquiring Mind*, giving popular introductions to microbiology, architecture, aviation, music, the visual arts and Ulster's contribution to United States history. By this time, however – since December 1962 – extra broadcasting hours were being allowed by the Post Office for approved Adult Education programmes – a fact that makes the earlier *Midnight Oil* series seem that much more enterprising.

In November 1962, shortly after the success of *Midnight Oil* the company put into service improved studio facilities more commensurate with their programme commitments. With an additional studio twice the size of the one with which they had so far made do, and with appropriate additional technical installations, a fuller local news service became possible and *Roundabout* was replaced by *Newsview*, a Monday to Friday programme intended to combine a news bulletin with topical magazine and comment; and there would be regular local news bulletins in mid afternoon as well. Further reinforcement for this developing service came early in 1963 when with the opening of the Strabane transmitter at least another 180,000 people in Londonderry and to the West were brought within range of UTV programmes.

At the time, it might have been difficult to foresee the quite exceptional contribution this development of an efficient local news and current affairs service of high professional integrity would make to the uniquely important, if unenviable, role that Ulster Television would be called upon to play before the end of the decade. The merest inkling of things to come had been given by one careful sentence of the company's Pilkington evidence: 'The area also has its own set of sharp and often bitter political divisions and tensions'.[24] Long before these sleeping dogs of violence were once again unleashed UTV had been established firmly in the region's mind not only as a purveyor of 'oomph and publicity' but also as a trusted and respected medium of public information whose management and staff would be able to face their coming ordeal with confidence, skill and courage.

4

WESTWARD

The ITV station to serve Devon and Cornwall was, said the *Daily Express*, 'the last big plum in the present commercial TV set-up'.[1] So it was not surprising that Fraser would tell the Authority in September 1958[2] that he believed there would be strong applicants for the South West franchise. He had already (Chapter 1) had notice of Peter Cadbury's interest; news of other eager aspirants had also reached him. Technical surveys had confirmed that two transmitters would be needed and, given the nature of the region, the search for suitable sites would certainly have to take into account objections from local amenity preservation groups. Air date would therefore, he said, be probably late 1960 at the earliest.

Almost a year elapsed before the Television Advisory Committee recommended to the PMG approval for the two transmitters, one at Stockland Hill, between Honiton and Axminster in Devon; and one at Caradon Hill, 5 miles north of Liskeard. The signals radiated from these two masts would reach an estimated 'rental population' of between 1 and $1\frac{1}{2}$ million, comfortably above the minimum figure which the Authority at that time thought necessary to support a viable company. A related question concerned the service for the Channel Islands. If and when such a service came about, consideration would have to be given to its relationship to the contractor for the South West.

Applications for the South West contract were invited on 14 October 1959. The detailed particulars sent to would-be applicants contained a paragraph explaining that 'the Authority had intended to invite applications from persons interested in the provision of programmes in the Channel Islands at same time' but that unresolved problems had prevented this. In anticipation of their resolution, the Authority would want to discuss with the company awarded the South West contract the nature of their relations with the Islands, whether or not the service there was provided by themselves or by an independent Channel Island company.

Twelve applications were received from new groups. A full application also came from Southern Television and undocumented formal ones from A-R and TWW. The last named company had already raised with the Authority the possibility of cooperation – including shared studio facilities in Bristol – with the successful applicant for coverage of the more northerly parts of the new ITV region.

The twelve interviews gave the Members an unusually long day on 8 December. But only five of the competing groups were thought to be serious contenders, by virtue of the distinction of their members, their degree of regional commitment and the attractiveness of their programme plans. Out of these the choice fell on the group brought together by the energetic Peter Cadbury.

The Authority were unanimous in their conclusion that in all three relevant respects this group outshone all the rest.[3] Not only did it have support from the Lords Lieutenant and County Council Chairmen of all four counties, of the current Chairman of the TUC and of many other local trade unionists, among them Lord Netherton (formerly Sir James Turner of the National Farmers Union), of local representatives of the Red Cross, the WVS, the Townswomen's Guilds, the Mothers' Union, the British Legion, the Council of Social Service and the St. John Ambulance Brigade, of Cornishmen A. L. Rowse and Exeter University Vice Chancellor J. W. Cook, of Daphne du Maurier, Henry Sherek, Ted Willis and Ronald Smart of Billy Smart's Circus, but also out of 208 named individual shareholders 194 were residents in the area, accounting together for 12,000 of the proposed issue of 20,000 voting shares. It was further intended that residents from the area should always be in a majority on the Board of Directors. But, above all, the Authority could not fail to be convinced by the evident care and professional know-how with which, in a ten-page Appendix to their application, the Cadbury group had set out their detailed programme intentions under nine separate headings: farming, the arts, women's programmes, children's programmes, sports magazine, light entertainment, news and news magazine, religion, and miscellaneous programmes on such varied topics as tin mining, local cheeses, sea fishing, local careers for school leavers, mead, oysters and Axminster carpets.

It was proposed that Peter Cadbury would, in addition to being company chairman, share the duties of Managing Director with Frank Hoare CBE, a man with considerable management experience in the film industry. Baynham Honri, a former member of the BBC's Engineering Research Department, with experience with Stoll theatres and Ealing Studios, was to be the company's technical director. So the Cadbury group were offered the contract, subject to agreement on the rental which would be fixed initially at £150,000. This agreement was readily obtained plus an assurance of cooperation with any separate company that might eventually be appointed to operate in the Channel Islands. The new contractor took the imprecise geographical name of Westward TV.

Almost immediately afterwards, on New Year's Day, Cadbury wrote asking for an air date intimating that the company could be ready by November. He got a disappointing reply. The Post Office had encountered difficulties in providing the necessary links and it was not at that stage possible to promise an earlier date than August 1961 – this notwithstanding the fact that the two ITA transmitters could, if necessary, be operational at least six months earlier. But as Cadbury himself confessed, patience was 'left out of my character'.[4] He and his colleagues had, as they put it, set their hearts on an opening date in mid-March 1961. In spite of the financial risk therefore they decided to proceed with the recruitment of staff (including the enrolment of theatrical impresario Emile Littler as Programme Controller), and with the construction of their purpose-built studio centre in Plymouth on the assumption that the Post Office could be persuaded into completing the link between Plymouth studios and the rest of the network by the earlier date.

Westward had affiliated with ABC and the management of that company had convinced them of the advantages of a March opening as against a late spring or summer one. Cadbury got Authority engineers to bring pressure to bear on their GPO opposite numbers and himself unmercifully badgered the PMG and Assistant PMG. He campaigned so vigorously and vociferously that he succeeded in getting a tentative half-promise of a possible 1 March start. It was a shortlived success. Having taken the step of issuing a rate card and an invitation to advertisers to make provisional bookings with Westward TV, from 1 March 1961 onwards, Cadbury was not a little mortified to learn in August 1960 that the Post Office no longer found it possible to meet a March opening date but that, subject to unforeseen circumstances, the links to the South West could be expected to be available for a programming opening date at the end of April.

Though disappointed, Cadbury remained unabashed. He saw in this setback a case for getting from the Authority some remission of rental. As he put it to Fraser, to go on the air on 29 April would be to start operations at the worst time in the year for advertising revenue; and that even though they had expected to operate at a loss in their early months, the company (and its shareholders) would be £80,000 worse off with that starting date than they would be if they delayed their start until 1 September.

The Authority felt it had no option, unless it was to have two stations lying idle for over six months, but to agree that there should be some waiver,[5] and the outcome was a rent-free period of four months for Westward from the planned end of April opening date until the end of August 1961. This would have to be repaid before the end of the contract period in 1964, but no interest would be charged on this deferred payment.[6] Cadbury, who had really brought the dilemma on himself by his premature announcement of a March air date, expressed gratitude for this help but, never a man for half measures, he could not restrain himself from also expressing regret that the fee had not been waived completely.

But the air date drama was even now not over. The devastating floods in the South West that autumn made the Post Office once again doubt their ability to complete the link even by the end of April. And the work on the Stockland Hill transmitter came to a standstill for fourteen days when the rains turned the site into a sea of mud. This return to uncertainty did not deter the born optimist from continuing his plans to send out during the first months of 1961 a travelling exhibition that over thirty-six days would visit twenty-three centres in the region in order to give to advertisers and the population generally a foretaste of impending delights. The exhibition was housed in railway coaches drawn by the specially hired fifty-seven-year-old steam locomotive, City of Truro, said to be the first locomotive to reach 100 m.p.h.

This time he was vindicated. By herculean efforts Post Office and ITA engineers succeeded in overcoming their difficulties, and Westward Television were able to start broadcasting to an estimated population of at least 1,363,000 as promised on 29 April 1961. Initial audience was estimated at around 650,000, using well over 200,000 multi-channel receivers. The company were reported as having already booked £250,000 of advertising up to September.[7]

In the run-up period to that event Cadbury and his senior executives had been continuously active in the region, addressing meetings, giving press interviews, generally seeking to influence public opinion. Something well over £30,000 was spent on press advertising, dealer promotion, posters, direct mail and the exhibition train, and during the six months before air date, so local dealers reported, 22,000 new sets were sold. But would-be viewers whose expectations had been perhaps raised over-high by news-paper statements about 'the West Country . . . on the brink of an adventurous development'[8] had to be prepared for the relatively modest offering of local programmes that was now planned. At the same time, they had to be encouraged to go on believing that the new television service in the South West was just what they had been waiting for. No easy task even for a man with the drive and publicity appetite of Cadbury. Thus, he was quoted in one paper, referring to the very many letters of suggestions he had received, as saying 'for every letter the company received asking for local programmes another two said: "Don't give us that rubbish, we want to see *Gun Law* and the 'London Palladium' ".'[9] Repeatedly in interviews and public speeches he reverted to this theme that most correspondents were asking for the programmes that the rest of Britain had been getting via the network. At the same time, Littler, while making known that there would be at the start 'no more than 2 to 3 hours of local programming a week' (including a ten-minute daily local news and a 'new type' of light entertainment show at midday), was also saying, naïvely, that having the choice of the transmissions of the Big Four, Westward would be able to pick and choose; and 'we will be a little more discerning than some in the past'.[10] The region would have its own programme magazine called *Look Westward* and the output of local programmes would be substantially increased, perhaps even doubled, by September. Further claims to membership of the company of angels were made in the revelation that there would be two hours of school broadcasting (from the network) every weekday afternoon, that a committee of local educational advisers had already been formed and that an equivalent religious committee was being appointed in anticipation of a home-produced religious programme in May.

One aspect of this intensive publicity campaign during the first three months of 1961 brought into prominence a dormant problem which was to prove a continuing source of irritation and concern. This was the question of the overlap between the service area of TWW served by the St. Hilary transmitter and that of Westward served by the Devon transmitter at Stockland Hill. Back in October 1959 TWW had been told that there would probably be an overlap of over 100,000 population between St. Hilary and the Stockland Hill transmitter, at that time still under construction; and in April 1960 it had to be added that the overlap population looked like being more like 190,000.[11] Lord Derby expressed concern, but on receipt of an explanatory letter he accepted the position as inevitable.

But this was not the way of a man who had once registered protest by tethering an elephant to a Mayfair parking meter. When Cadbury became aware of the extent of the overlap in Somerset and North Devon and saw on a coverage map issued to advertisers by TWW that it actually included the Stockland Hill transmitter itself and extended virtually to the Channel coast between Exmouth and Weymouth, he gave voice in no uncertain fashion. It was 'unrestricted piracy'[12] he said. This was of course wild talk, based in any case on a badly printed map which TWW promptly withdrew.

But the fact of the overlap was real, nor could the Authority initially see anything in principle wrong with an area in which two of its contractors were competing for audience. Was not competition between programme providers the very principle on which ITV had been founded? But that of course was not what had so far happened. Most of the programmes in all regions were the same and the system, as it developed, had created a chain of local monopolies in the sale of television advertising. Overlaps were resented as an invasion of these monopolies. Competition between rival programme offerings, when it existed, was one thing; but competition in aggressive salesmanship was quite another matter. Cadbury could hardly relish TWW sales drives in Weymouth or Exeter. When he riposted by declaring to the Press and in other public places that TWW was a Welsh company without any real claim to viewers South of the Bristol Channel, tempers began to flare. And things were not improved when he set out to woo viewers in Bristol, well outside Westward's contract service area. There was talk by TWW of legal action and the ITA had perforce to intervene to impose a measure of self restraint. These were early skirmishes in what was to prove a recurrent frontier war, albeit punctuated by lengthening periods of calm and cooperative good sense. The Authority was to remain over the years uneasily aware that at any time ill-considered words or over-zealous sales initiative could give matter for more newspaper stories of domestic squabbling within ITV.

Yet when air date, 29 April 1961, arrived Westward went on the air very quietly. Perhaps knowledge that they were starting simultaneously with the introduction of the new tax on TV advertising played its part. There was no ceremonial or birthday revelry. It was a Saturday and transmissions began simply with the networked Saturday afternoon sports programme, *Let's Go*. This was followed by the usual network fare. Nothing was seen of the prestigious new £175,000 Plymouth studio centre at Derry's Cross with its £150,000 worth of gleaming new equipment until late that night, at 11 p.m., when the first local production carrying the Golden Hind symbol was shown. Called *Hello from Westward*, it introduced regional viewers to officers and staff of their new television station in their working environment. 'A scrappy affair, with forced continuity and plenty of meaningless statements' said the *Western Morning News*, which then went on to concede that 'it conveyed well enough the spirit of enthusiasm among the new production team'.[13] This was followed by the Epilogue given by the Bishop of Exeter, introduced by Cadbury himself. Then closedown.

For the time being the rest of Westward's local programming was to consist of local news, Littler's promised lunch-time light entertainment, *Look in for Lunch* and a quiz show, *Ordinary People*, presented with a participating audience from Plymouth's Athenaeum Theatre next door.

By September ambition began to flower and a substantial increase in local production took place. So far, as the *Plymouth Independent* put it, Cadbury's wish 'that the station should be strongly identified as a West Country station' had remained 'wishful thinking' with 'the superbly equipped television centre in the heart of Plymouth . . . barely ticking over'.[14] Now there were to be local discussion programmes, a twice-weekly local magazine, *Westward Diary*, a local sports programme and a monthly programme on local arts. 'The Westward train is perhaps overdue' said the same newspaper, 'but it is getting up steam.' Alas, the locomotive was soon to run out of steam.

The Equity strike which affected the whole of ITV throughout that autumn and winter was bound to be most damaging to a small regional company just starting up. But that was only an aggravating factor in a worsening situation. Although the company ended their first year's trading with a net profit of just under £100,000, this left them when set against the previous, non-trading year's debit balance, with a deficit of £66,654 to be carried forward; and with a commitment to a further £20,000 capital outlay on their studio centre (which had in fact already run away with more than half a million). Virtually everything was proving more costly than planned and revenue, affected both by the strike and by the Television Advertisement Duty, was flagging. 'The Golden Hind has struck a squall'[15] said the *Daily Express*. By September 1962, the debit balance had reached £173,000 and Cadbury told his shareholders that not only would no dividend be paid for the past year but that their company looked like losing between £50,000 and £100,000 in the year ahead. Some of them must have ruefully compared this statement with the information that TWW had declared a dividend of 110 per cent for year 1961. In competition for audience with the BBC, Westward were consistently getting lower audience shares than nearly all other ITV companies, achieving little more than 50 per cent. In many weeks five or six BBC programmes featured in the regional TAM Top Ten.

With only a couple more years of their contract still to run, something drastic had to be done, and that quickly. The Westward Board, notwithstanding its many local people, insisted that current ambitious plans for local production should be severely pruned, something Cadbury felt reluctant to do. While himself campaigning vigorously in newspaper articles, speeches to MPs and others against the 'iniquitous' Television Advertisement Duty that threatened, he claimed, the very survival of small

ITV regional companies, he once again turned to the Authority for help, in particular to the ever-patient Fraser. There were long personal letters and many very long telephone conversations. Fraser told him plainly that he was shocked by what he had heard about the company's finances but that the unrealistic campaign he was conducting for the abolition of TAD and/or the extension of the Westward franchise area to include Bristol and Bath would not help his cause. Cadbury argued a case for reduction in Authority rental and permission once again to reduce the amount of local programming from the contractual six to seven hours (i.e. 15 per cent) to at most four.

The ITA remained unresponsive to Cadbury's appeals. It did not accept that he and his colleagues were totally without blame for the company's misfortunes, innocent victims of their own good intentions. It had other sources of information. It knew that there was serious discontent among Westward's Plymouth staff over the way the company was being managed, largely at a distance, from their Chairman's office in London. It knew from its Regional Officer that this discontent was shared by local members of Westward's Board who had also been kept in relative ignorance of the way things were going by the small inner group of executive directors round Cadbury himself. 'Westward has had a lot of bad luck', Fraser reported 'but it has also had a lot of bad management. The internal quarrels . . . are a byword in the business and it is still rather erratically conducted with too much part-time absentee direction.'[16] One belated concession to staff and local feelings had been made by the appointment of a Plymouth-based joint managing director in the person of Bill Cheevers, the company's Chief Engineer.

By comparison with the operational cost of comparable regional companies, there can be no doubt that Westward's expenditure on both fixed assets and operations were on an extravagant scale. Any concessions made to them would have been rightly seen by other companies as rewards for inefficiency, over-staffing and poor management. The company had to be told to put their own house in order; that there could be no reduction in the local origination requirement of six hours a week; and that the economies they had in mind did not seem to be anything like enough. As for Cadbury's claim that Westward's actual viewing population was at least one third less than the 1,400,000 for which they were paying a rental, he was told that the possibility of a rental concession would not be considered before completion of a TAM audience survey which Westward intended to commission. In the meantime, proposed economies in expenditure of £100,000 in 1963/4 were nothing like enough. A more reasonable amount would be £200,000.

The ruthless economies that Westward were thus compelled to make inevitably demanded a cutback in staff; and this, equally inevitably, led to difficulties with the trade unions. The ACTT threatened strike action. The union's Westward shop, faced with a proposal for eighteen redundancies (a cut of 25 per cent in the company's technical staff) remained unimpressed by the recent liquidation of the press and public relations department and were not in the least mollified by the news that the company's twenty-two directors had waived their fees for the year, thus saving a little more than £6000. The bad relations between management and local staff offered a poor basis for negotiation. The Authority, having already considered what steps they might have to take in the event of Westward going out of business, were now faced with the possibly more delicate task of ensuring mainten- ance of the service while the company's studio centre was temporarily out of action. But when the dispute began to look likely to escalate into a nationwide ITV stoppage the central labour relations office of the ITCA intervened and a peace formula was found. Westward agreed to keep on four of the eighteen and the network companies undertook to find jobs for the other fourteen. 'This is the first time I know [of],' said George Elvin, General Secretary of the ACTT, 'that any industry as a whole has accepted responsibility for anybody losing his job in a single firm in that industry. It is a great step in the right direction.'[17]

But the outlook for Westward was still not good. Relations between Cadbury and his local directors remained strained. They felt diminishing confidence in him and his management methods; they disliked the rarity of his appearances in Plymouth and they resented the way so much was being done from the London office without their knowledge or concurrence. Cadbury for his part was still apparently not convinced that the rational response to the crisis was to cut his coat according to his cloth. The whole mosaic of the ITV regions must be redrawn, he told *The Sunday Times*. Without more and better programmes from outside, without a slice of Southern TV territory and a bigger share of the TWW audience the company was doomed,[18] he said.

More realistically important for Westward's future, however, would be further reductions in outgoings. Local programme output had been maintained at just over six hours a week: but with budgets pared to the bone. The ambitious local arts programme, the much appreciated farming, gardening and religious programmes had disappeared. In what was left, much simpler more economical formats were being used, some of the lost time being made up from the short items from outside sources such as road or weather reports. Although these changes had been reluctantly accepted by the ITA, sacrifice of quality to maintain quantity could not be allowed to go too far.

However, in April the promised TAM survey of viewer behaviour became available, and seemed to bear out some of Cadbury's complaints, though not his claim that it justified a rental reduction of 40 per cent. Consequently, the Authority did now decide to grant an abatement of 20 per cent which would apply retrospectively to air date on 29 April 1961.[19] The effect over the total period of the Westward contract would be a saving of close on £108,000. In consequence of this concession, gratefully received and without quibble, Cadbury was able to negotiate for – and obtain – a reduction in the charges paid to the network companies for the use of their programmes.

When one took into account the impending abolition of TAD announced by the PMG in February 1963 and the likelihood that the new levy, much disputed though it was, would bear less onerously on small regional companies, it began to look as if the Golden Hind would weather the storm and was in sight of smoother waters ahead. A further step towards a rationalisation was taken with the resignation in August 1963 of several members of the company board, some of them London-based like Frank Hoare (a member of the original applicant group), some local, like Daphne du Maurier and Michael Chapman, managing director of Torquay's Imperial Hotel, who said, 'we felt the very large board was not able to be as effective as it could be if smaller'.[20] By this time too in autumn 1963, advertising income was beginning to rise once more. With an increase over three months of nearly 15 per cent, prospects seemed to be improving that before the end of the contract period Westward shareholders would at last receive a dividend; even perhaps that their company's outstanding debts would be paid off.

5

CHANNEL

In the summer of 1959 when the Authority was considering plans for the West Country, reference was also made to recent approaches by an 'apparently influential and able' group from the Channel Islands.[1] This group had declared their interest in the possibility of setting up a local ITV company that would provide a service for the islands, including even programmes made in their own studios. The idea of a company able to survive with an audience of at best 25,000 viewing homes and a total population of around 100,000 had hitherto not been contemplated. The BBC service to the islands treated them as part of the audience for their West Region television output from Plymouth. But the Authority concluded that it would be unwise to proceed on the assumption that the Channel Islands would be a pure satellite when it was known that a group existed willing to originate programmes there.

Two preliminary steps were, however, necessary. Orders in Council would be needed authorising extension of the provisions of the 1954 Act to the islands; and the technical problems of getting a usable signal to them had to be solved. Not least among the latter was the proximity of the French coast and the risk of interference with French TV transmissions; and it was not until the following January 1960 that means were devised of allaying French apprehensions.

There being no reason to expect a refusal of the necessary Orders in Council, it was agreed to invite applications as soon as possible. A start to transmissions in the second half of 1961 was anticipated. In view of the very small scale of the operation the annual rental to be asked would be £11,000 although the costs to the ITA would probably be four to five times that amount.[2] Cadbury had of course promised full cooperation with any eventual contractor for the islands, but it seemed only sensible to make the decision before the Westward contract itself had been finalised.

By closing date, 8 March 1960, two applications had been received. Interviews were fixed for 22 March. In the intervening fortnight enquiries were made about the relative standing locally of the two groups of islanders involved. The contract particulars issued to applicants differed in important respects from previous ones. The Authority was not able to offer anything more than a qualified commitment to a planned starting date for the service or to a specified location for the transmitter. The likelihood was that there would be a single transmitter on Jersey, covering all the islands save Alderney from some time towards the end of 1961 or shortly thereafter, but ITA engineers had yet to establish that an acceptable service could be given for a reasonably high proportion of the time.

All programmes not produced locally would have to be those network programmes being currently transmitted in the South West area. These transmissions would be picked up 'off air' in Alderney, the northernmost island, and relayed for retransmission from the Jersey mast. Since, however, signal strength from the mainland would vary, there might be times when the Channel Islands contractor would have to provide additional local output to stop unavoidable gaps in planned network supply. Moreover, because the local service would have to be on a Channel 9 frequency, as were the transmissions received from the mainland in Alderney, interference with the latter could be avoided only by drastically reducing signal strength from Jersey in the northerly direction so that Alderney itself would not be able to receive Jersey programmes.

Applicants were also told they would be expected to put forward persuasive evidence that an ITV company serving the islands would be able to pay its way. A population in the service area of some 100,000 would after all be smaller than that served by any other television station in Europe.

One of the two rival applicant groups was led by Jersey schoolmaster Jurat G. Malet de Cartaret. Its intended Chairman–Managing Director would be Frank Darvall CBE, former First Secretary at the British Embassy in Washington and, until 1957, Director General of the English Speaking Union. All the intended directors were Channel Island residents, including six from Jersey, two from Guernsey, the President of the Alderney States and the Dame of Sark. There would be initially 181 shareholders, ninety-six from Jersey, seventy-eight from Guernsey, one from Alderney and six from Sark; and only three of them were not islanders. No individual would have more than 8 per cent of issued capital.

The second group had as Chairman Senator George Troy, a leading Jersey citizen, governing director of the largest firm of stevedoring contractors in the islands. Working closely with him was Senator Wilfred Krichefski, owner of a large Jersey clothing store and President of the Jersey Tourism Committee. Also associated were the respective Managing Directors of the local newspapers of Guernsey and Jersey, Gervase Le Gros

Peek of the Guernsey *Star* and *Evening Press* and Arthur Harrison of the Jersey *Evening Post* and *Weekly Post*. Two non-resident directors were Harold Fielding the well-known London theatrical impresario, and Sir Reginald Biddle, retired manager of Southampton Docks. Both had strong connections with the islands, especially the latter who was born and educated in Jersey. All the proposed share capital of £110,000 would be subscribed from within the islands; £82,500 by the ten directors and the remaining 110,000 five shilling ordinary shares by 184 widely representative islanders, 108 from the Jersey Bailiwick and 76 from that of Guernsey which includes the islands of Alderney and Sark.

Members of this second group had, it transpired, been trying to start commercial sound broadcasting since 1952 and commercial television since 1953. Extracts from their relevant correspondence with the PMG were attached to their application.[3] They also emphasised their links with the local press, which they considered absolutely vital because of the economies they would permit in local news coverage. Their rivals on the other hand stressed their independence from the press: a competing television service would avoid the dangers of media monopoly. Both groups expressed confidence in their ultimate financial success, quoting advice and figures from existing ITV companies, advertising agencies and the TAM organisation. Both assumed a set count by air date of 20–25,000. The de Cartaret group anticipated first-year advertising revenue of £110,000 plus £5000 profit from a local programme magazine against expenditure of £99,000. The Troy group estimated advertising income at £126,854 and outgoings at £101,000. This more optimistic forecast was justified by reference to the 'vast concourse of holiday-makers who, each year, more than sextuple the total population of the Channel Islands'.

De Cartaret planned a main studio with two vidicon cameras, an announcer's booth and two telecine channels on Jersey and, possibly also, a relay point on Guernsey into which occasional local items could be fed via one fixed vidicon. Troy foresaw initially nothing more ambitious than telecine facilities with a small announcement and presentation studio: he believed that by means of 16mm film cameras and quick processing there could be infused into the network programme enough material of both Jersey and Guernsey origin to stimulate regional interest and to justify their independent status.

The interviews confirmed what had already been learned from local enquiries: that either group would clearly provide a responsibly conducted service. However, on balance the Troy group seemed to have more business competence and it was decided to offer them the contract. Both groups had in the Authority's judgement seriously underestimated the eventual costs to them of network programmes. Although both gave assurances that they could still cope with such charges at least twice as high as their estimates, the Members appear to have found the Troy response to this criticism more persuasive. Because of the constitutional niceties attendant on the extension of a British Act of Parliament to the legislatively independent Channel Islands, Troy was asked to keep the decision confidential to himself and his fellow directors. But this was not to be. The story broke in the local newspapers that weekend, much to Troy's embarrassment, because the press members of his consortium were precisely the ones he had not been able to reach.

It seems to have become almost a rule that the smaller the company the more numerous and complex the difficulties over getting them on the air. However that may be, the period between contract decision on 22 March 1960 and air date for the Channel Islands company on 1 September 1962 was certainly more prolonged and more fraught with problems and frustrations than most. The need for Orders in Council was the least of their worries, and these were in due course obtained.

The site for the transmitter in Jersey too was not easily found or acquired. In January 1961 negotiations began for purchase of what appeared to be a suitable site at Fremont Point.[4] But it was the end of April before there was any certainty it would be acquired, and even that was not the end of the story. The mast to be used was one intended to be replaced at Lichfield in order to improve the reception in the Midlands region, and because it could not be dismantled until the new one was satisfactorily operational it would not be available for transport to Jersey until October. Subsequent erection on site and fitting of an aerial and feeders would take, subject to weather, until well into 1962 before test transmissions could begin. And even then, transmission of actual programmes could not start until the Post Office link from Alderney to Jersey was established. Even if the site for the Alderney mast was to be fixed without difficulty – which proved to be far from the case – delivery of the equipment for the link thence to St. Helier would take several months and was unlikely to be working before June 1962. So Fraser, in a letter to the restless Troy on 5 May 1961,[5] had to say in reaction to continuing company pressure that any idea of an air date of 1 January was quite out of the question and that it would be wise to take for planning purposes an air date of Saturday, 1 September 1962.

In the meantime, the company, which was now registered officially under the name of 'Channel Television',[6] entered into negotiations with ABC for an affiliation agreement. Three ABC staff members were to be seconded. One of these was Ken Killip, at that time Technical Manager of the Mobile Division of ABC, who was made General Manager of Channel. Immediately on appointment Killip began energetically to put the new company on to a workmanlike basis. He was hardly in office before trouble with Alderney broke out.

As reported in the *Guernsey Evening Press* of Friday 4 August, at a meeting on the previous day 'The States of Alderney rejected by 5 votes to 3 a proposal to grant a 99 years' lease to the GPO in respect of an $8\frac{1}{2}$ acre plot on Les Rodiers above the Battery Quarry for the purpose of erecting a 100 foot mast for relaying ITV programmes from the United Kingdom to Jersey and Guernsey'. As the States' members left the court, the newspaper reported, there was spontaneous applause from the crowd gathered outside. 'I am no Bolshie,' one member was quoted as saying, 'but I have not heard a single soul speak in favour of this TV mast. The people do not want it.' Not surprisingly perhaps since, as another member had reminded them, the mast would not provide programmes for Alderney. Strong public feeling had obviously been roused. Troy was reported in the same newspaper on the following day as saying that the Post Office, the ITA and the company had all entered into commitments for the supply of equipment amounting to hundreds of thousands of pounds. He found it inconceivable that the Alderney decision should frustrate plans to give the people of Jersey and Guernsey what the people in the United Kingdom now had – an alternative television programme. 'Channel TV will go on the air in 1962. I cannot believe otherwise.'[7]

Ultimately – and of course, inevitably – Alderney was persuaded not to be dog in the manger. A letter of 13 September from Krichefski said: 'You will be as glad as we are to know that when the States of Alderney met yesterday they reversed their previous decision'.[8] The PMG was to be granted a ninety-nine-year lease and the right to immediate entry on to the proposed site in order to start installation work.

The story of mast trouble was not quite ended. Local preservationists started to get worried about the ITA's own mast at Fremont Point. Belatedly the National Trust took a hand and a petition was presented to the Jersey States, which voted to uphold it. But the move came too late, for a valid decision had already been taken by the Island Development Committee to allow the mast, and work had begun. Preparations for the station opening, now firmly fixed at 1 September 1962, moved on apace. On his return from a brief visit to Jersey, Pragnell of the ITA reported: 'Killip . . . has revolutionised things. The studio is going up very quickly and there is a purposeful air about . . .'[9]

One of the matters that concerned Killip – and indeed continued to do so throughout the contract period – was the quality of the picture picked up from the mainland that the company would be able to offer its viewers. There could be no absolute guarantee that reception at Alderney would be consistently of sufficient standard; and stand-by arrangements had to be made. The ITA's original intention was to ask the Post Office to take the signal from the Stockland Hill transmitter some eighty miles away on the mainland, relying on the other transmitter in that region at Caradon Hill as a first line stand-by. But Killip thought a better stand-by might be the Chillerton Down transmitter on the Isle of Wight which served the Southern Television area. The problem was that Southern's programme schedule differed from that of Westward, not necessarily taking the same network programmes nor showing those it did at the same times. A separate agreement with Southern would also have to be negotiated, to say nothing of the changes in the Authority's arrangements with the Post Office over the Alderney relay. On the other hand, Killip saw in the change not only a possibly more reliable stand-by but also an alternative access to the network, giving him, potentially at least, a greater flexibility of choice when compiling his own schedule. He was successful in persuading the Authority.[10] Negotiations with Southern were duly concluded a month after opening the service.

Channel Television's first draft schedule showed that right from the start the company would be providing three hours a week of local origination. It also showed clearly the disadvantage of dependence on another company's scheduling decisions in the use of networked material. Channel Television's viewers would not, for example, be able to see *Tempo*, the Sunday arts programme from Channel TV's 'parent' company, ABC, because it was not scheduled by Westward. Equally, on Monday evenings, Granada's *All Our Yesterdays* was not available; although here a local purchase of similar content, *Time to Remember*, was to be substituted for the record programme shown at that time by Westward. There was also to be a regular five minute late night news bulletin in French.

So this smallest ITV company went on the air as planned at 5.00 p.m. on Saturday, 1 September 1962, in the presence of most Members of the Authority, who the next day journeyed to Herm in glorious weather for an al fresco lunch. Out of a total staff – including their London sales team – of fifty, only three of those involved in the opening night programmes had any previous experience of television broadcasting. Yet all went well. After the National Anthem accompanying stills of The Queen's recent visit to the islands, the Lieutenant Governor of Jersey, ceremonially declared the station open, in the presence of Carmichael, the Bailiffs of Jersey and Guernsey and Fraser. And at 5.10 p.m. Channel Island viewers joined the network for the delights of *Robin Hood*. After the ITN five minute bulletin at 5.40 p.m. came, at 5.45, *Serenade*, a local programme of 'early evening music' and at 6.05 p.m. local news and weather. Following the first-night pattern of other regional companies, there came at 11 p.m. – after a customary Saturday evening network menu of variety and thrillers – *Meet Channel*, a look around the station, including interviews with local people about their first impressions of this new factor in their daily lives. The next day, Sunday, brought the first of a local weekly series for farmers at 12.45 p.m. and at 3.05 Channel's film cameras presented coverage of Guernsey's annual *Battle of Flowers*. A local religious programme at 6.15 p.m. followed the ITN bulletin at 6.05 p.m. It took the form of a discussion of televised religion by the members of Channel TV's own Religious Advisory Committee.

Apart from the regular local news and weather reports and the nightly French news at or around 11.15 p.m., there were two thirty-minute broadcasts of the local news magazine, *Studio Wednesday* and *Studio Friday*, shown not, as in other regions, after the early evening news but at 10.45 p.m. on these two nights. Despite their limited resources the company transmitted the network's weekday afternoon broadcasts to schools as soon as the new term started on 17 September.

An independent local programme magazine, *Channel Viewer* was published. It was destined to make a very welcome contribution, through sale of advertising space, to the company's annual income – over £11,000 in its first year.

There were, however, a bare 25,000 Channel 9 homes in the islands on opening night. True they were, on average, homes better off than those in other ITV regions: 52 per cent in the A, B and C classes – as against the 40 per cent average elsewhere. But the company was going to have a tough struggle. Initial viewing figures were not encouraging and before the end of the first month Killip was making urgent requests for measures to improve the quality of local reception. On 3 October, Senator Troy, who had been ailing for some time, died. He had realised his ambition to create an independent Channel Islands television station and to see it on to the air. He did not live to see it achieve success. That was left to Krichefski, who took over as company chairman at a time of growing anxiety. By the end of the year 1962, audience figures were still disappointing. In December the weekday peak time share was 38 per cent (as against the BBC's 62) rising to 41 per cent on Sundays. The company had precious little time in which to make good. Hardly a year would pass before they would have to decide whether or not to apply for a new contract. Courage and determination would be needed if they were to win through. Both were displayed. Early in 1963 things did begin to look up. The ITA Regional Officer reported in February that there had been a remarkable change in the last two months, and this was partly due to improved reception conditions but mostly to Killip's leadership. TAM was already showing that local programmes were increasingly successful. The farming programme *Island Farmer* had been outstandingly so. A feature of the local viewing figures was the relatively low popularity at that time of network favourites like *Coronation Street* and *Emergency-Ward Ten*. In this respect the resident population apparently differed in their tastes from the hordes of summer visitors who, in so far as they continued to view in their hotels and boarding houses – and very many did – persisted in the viewing habits they brought with them from the barbarous North.

But the main contribution to the young company's public acceptance was being made by its local news service, both in the daily local bulletins and in the twice-weekly news magazines. This was undoubtedly helped by the fact that on Jersey, for example, the single edition of the local *Evening Post* appeared daily at 4.30 p.m. and there was no equivalent morning paper. Those who had protested earlier over the threat of news monopoly were no doubt surprised at the degree of fiercely competitive rivalry that developed between the local press and the journalists of the television company. The latter were providing a directly competitive alternative service, 'in no way just an illustrated version of the local paper', wrote Geoffrey Cox to Fraser after a visit to the Channel Islands some time later. 'The job they are doing, in the news field,' he said, 'struck me as a particularly good example of the value of a local ITV station.'[11] 'Of all the regional companies,' said the *Daily Telegraph*'s Peter Knight in June 1963, 'Channel TV is the most local in its outlook. . . . It may be TV in miniature but it has a character of its own.'[12]

By their first birthday Channel's audience share had risen to 60 per cent and more than 80 per cent of all local multi-channel viewers looked at their programmes at some time in the week. True, they would still be trading at a loss when their contract expired and their bank overdraft would be large. Their total income in their first nine months' operation was £82,900 against an expenditure in the same period of £169,595, a total which excluded earlier capital expenditure on premises of another £23,000. At the end of 1963 it looked as if their accumulated trading loss would be well over £70,000 by the end of their second year. Although expectations of a steady rise in advertising income seemed well founded it could never be very large. If survival was to be ensured, stringent remedies would be needed both in the form of lower payments for use of network programmes and a substantial reduction in the rental payable to the Authority. Both were to be readily forthcoming. By the end of its first contract period the company was still, like any other sturdy and promising youngster, largely dependent on parental support. And this youngster's eventual emergence into vigorous, in-dependent adulthood would continue to owe much to freely given – and justly merited – family backing.

6

BORDER

The new year 1960 found the Authority considering the 'progress we have made towards nationwide coverage for our first service'.[1] Ten transmitters had so far been constructed, covering between them some 80 to 90 per cent of the population of the United Kingdom. With the appointment of Westward eleven programme contractors had been appointed. Future programme companies, if any, would have service areas with populations well below one million. Inevitably the question arose whether a population much below that level could ensure an advertising income sufficient to support an independent, as distinct from a satellite, programme operation.

Fraser did not think the Authority could properly refuse suitably qualified groups access to ITV if they were prepared to accept the financial risks. He conceded, however, that in practice such companies might well be in need of some form of subsidy, at least in their early stages. This was a noticeably different line of thought from that followed when a contract for South East England was under consideration. At a less explicit level – and as the ITV system generally became more prosperous – factors other than potential advertising revenue were figuring larger in the minds of those at Princes Gate.

It had in any case always been assumed that independent programme companies would be sought for North East Scotland and the Borders. The latter area, however, would include viewers both north and south of the Border. Although there would have to be two transmitters, one near Carlisle and the other at Selkirk, the former would serve a viewing population of which 30 per cent would be in Scotland and 70 per cent in England. The relative percentages for the latter would be 15 per cent in England and 85 per cent in Scotland. But the actual numbers of Scots within range of the Carlisle transmitter would be greater than those within range of Selkirk. The question arose whether Scottish public opinion would accept the attachment of Selkirk to a Carlisle based company rather than its allotment as a satellite station, to Scottish Television. But STV were an extremely prosperous company. Whereas the estimated 90,000 rental population of Selkirk would be a tiny addition to the millions already served by STV, that number could make a very important difference to the survival chances of a Carlisle based company. The views of the ITA Scottish Committee were sought, and they were unanimous that Selkirk should be linked with Carlisle, provided the company appointed were genuinely representative of all parts of the Borders.[2]

Two of the major companies had other ideas. ABC and Granada put to the Authority a detailed submission arguing for an extension of their common Northern franchise to include the Carlisle service area.[3] Nevertheless the Authority, whilst remaining uncertain whether the Border region could support an independent station, decided to invite applications in order to give potential candidates an opportunity to make a case for the award of a contract.[4] An advertisement duly appeared giving Wednesday 6 April as closing date. The notes issued to applicant groups included this statement:

> . . . the combined Border area is small and likely to be only marginally profitable . . . The Authority will therefore need to be fully convinced both as to the financial stability of applicant groups and as to their ability to provide programmes of high quality, including a certain number of programmes produced in the Borders, before it offers a contract. Applicants are, in effect, being invited to make out a case for the grant of a contract.[5]

Two applicants were interviewed on 3 May 1960. The first of these called themselves Solway TV, and was made up by the amalgamation of two earlier groups of which one was mainly Scottish, the other mainly English. Although it appeared from the proposed financial structure that control of the company would be with a small inner group of directors, £50,000 of B (non-voting) shares and £100,000 of 7 per cent loan stock would be offered to the public, represented in the first place by a long list appended to the application of so-called sponsors from all walks of local life ranging from farmers and Masters of Foxhounds to doctors, dentists, lawyers, headmasters, clergymen and trade unionists.

Border Television, the second group, was headed by the Managing Director of Cumberland Newspapers Ltd, John L. Burgess OBE, who was also Chairman of Reuters, Deputy Lieutenant for the County of Cumberland and President of the World Federation of Cumberland and Westmorland Societies. Associated with him were Sir Michael Balcon, the film producer, the Earl of Lonsdale, Sir John S. Muirhead, Chairman and Managing Director of the Scottish newspaper and magazine publishers, George Outram and Co, Sir Hector Hetherington on behalf of Glasgow University of which he was Principal and Vice Chancellor and Norman Leyland, the College Bursar on behalf of Brasenose College, Oxford.

John Burgess had shown active interest in the possibility of a commercial television service in the area since 1954; and had indeed approached the PMG at that time. He emphasised in the interview his belief in the independent-minded character of the region which would resist any suggestion that it should become a satellite area to a larger outside company rather than be served by its own local programme contractor. His study of the financial prospects had persuaded him that such an independent operation was possible. Wide local participation in shareholdings would be sought, for which purpose $14\frac{1}{2}$ per cent of ordinary non-voting share capital would be held in reserve. A list was included in the application of some 100 people from the counties and towns on both sides of the Border who had given signed undertakings to take up those shares. Robin D. Gill, a young former Unilever executive with family ties in the area, was to be Managing Director. In spite of the participation of Glasgow University and an Oxford College, the group had no immediate plans for educational programming, but thought that, having regard to the need for financial realism, a more useful contribution might be made in Adult Education rather than in schools broadcasting. Initially local programming would have to be on a modest scale, within the limitations of a small two-camera studio with telecine. Some suitable programmes could be supplied from Tyne Tees or STV local output.

The Authority found it very difficult to choose between the two applicant groups, but, after taking the views of the staff, came down in favour of the Burgess group. A condition of the offer was to be the appointment of at least one further Scotsman from the area to the small executive group of directors with which it was intended to run the company's day-to-day affairs. The letter to Burgess making the formal contract offer went further.[6] Two other named directors should join the company executive board: Lord Dalrymple, a landowner whose family owned the local newspaper in Wigtownshire and J. I. M. Smail, Chairman of the Tweeddale Press, owners of the *Berwick Advertiser*. The Authority also reserved the right to require a higher output of local productions than was envisaged in the Burgess group application. The rentals were to be £37,000 for the Carlisle station and £10,000 for the Selkirk one. The conditions were accepted.

In the more detailed negotiations with the Authority that followed,

familiar problems arose over differences between company opening intentions and anticipated dates for the completion of transmitters. The problems
were complicated because the area was to be served by two transmitters and
there was little hope of their being completed simultaneously. The Carlisle
transmitter to be sited at Caldbeck (birthplace of John Peel) was not likely
to be ready before May 1961, later than the promised 'early 1961' because of
the difficulties of working on a 1000 foot mast during winter weather on a
bleak exposed northern site. The company disliked the idea of opening at
the beginning of the worst period of the year for advertising: it would mean
starting with a period of four months when their outgoings would greatly
exceed their income. They were able to persuade the Authority to forego the
four months rental and agree to an opening date of 1 September.[7]

The Selkirk transmitter was to be of a relatively untried design: an
unmanned repeater picking up Caldbeck's signal and retransmitting it on
another frequency. Consequently the manufacturers (Marconi) were
reluctant to commit themselves to a firm early delivery date, merely hoping
to get the job done and transmissions started by the end of 1961. In order to
be as helpful as possible to the young company the Authority later decided to
go further. To the evident delight of Gill who had pressed for as small an
interval as possible between the two dates, it was decided to erect a
temporary 200 foot mast at Selkirk whilst work continued on the permanent
one.[8] Notwithstanding the reduced coverage secured by this temporary
arrangement, the Authority was thus able to ensure some reception of
Border programmes in both parts of the region before Christmas 1961.

Gill was also anxious to have recognised coverage in the Isle of Man, as it
was very likely that good pictures from Caldbeck would be picked up,
especially in the north of the island, in and around Ramsey. But the
Authority, ever sensitive to the political niceties of programme incursions
into adjacent territories not subject to Westminster legislation, was
unwilling to have such relatively small coverage shown on published maps.
It had followed a similar policy in connection with the availability of UTV
programmes in the Irish Republic (and indeed also on the western coast of
the Isle of Man) although it does seem to have turned a blind eye to a TAM
coverage map for Granada which showed Winter Hill viewers in eastern
parts of Man. With Border a compromise was reached whereby the
company would be able to mention on its rate card the existence of an Isle of
Man audience (without showing it on a map) and the Authority would not
charge any rental for the 4000 odd predicted rental population in Ramsey.

In the meantime work had been started on a purpose-built studio centre
at Harraby, a new housing and industrial estate two miles south of Carlisle

centre. Sales offices were set up in Carlisle and London. A station symbol was chosen which would suggest in abstract design the two distinct parts of the Border region brought together by the electronic medium. Staff was recruited, and it was estimated that a total of about 100 would eventually be employed. Patrick Campbell, a former BBC North Region drama producer, was appointed Presentation Controller and Maurice Lindsay, a well-known writer and broadcaster from BBC Scotland, was named Programme Controller. Negotiations were started with Granada for an affiliation agreement giving access to network programmes and an ambitious local publicity campaign was launched.

There was to be a Border edition of *TV Times*. An article by Gill in the *Cumberland Evening News*[9] promised Border viewers the pick of ITV programmes whose titles would already be well-known to them. Border would balance these programmes with those originated in their own studios. These would bring local news and regular features covering topics of particular interest to people in the area, beginning modestly but increasing in amount later.

Shortly before opening, the publicity campaign was extended to the Isle of Man. 'Get Ready to Switch to Border TV' said a full page advertisement in the island's newspaper in the last week of July 1961. 'Border TV is Coming'.[10]

A company decision at the time made, no doubt, for reasons of economy, but which the *Television Mail* called 'startling',[11] was not to subscribe to TAM. They intended to rely instead on seven-day aided-recall research and the provision to advertisers of audience composition analyses. But useful marketing information was not lacking. It was pointed out that, notwithstanding its predominantly rural character with few populous centres of industry, the Border region was in per capita terms the wealthiest regional market in the United Kingdom, apart from the big urban areas of London, Midlands and the North. Consumer spending per retail outlet was higher in the region than any other area, save only London, South East England and Scotland. But, said *TV Mail* in the same issue, 'The entry of Border Television into the independent system marks . . . the realisation of truly local television'.[12] For a company with so small a service area, they were producing even in their first week, remarked the paper, more than might have been expected.

The ceremony of going on air on 1 September was brief and businesslike. Promptly at 5.45 p.m. John Burgess appeared, made an opening statement and introduced his Managing Director. Gill in his turn then presented other members of staff to the viewers. Then came the normal ITN early evening bulletin to be followed at 6.05 p.m. by the very first local Border news and weather; and five minutes later the first broadcast of Border's own twenty-minute topical news magazine, *Focus*, introduced by Maurice Lindsay. It was 10.30 p.m. before the next local production appeared, *Borderline*, first of a monthly series of celebrity interviews. On this occasion Lindsay interviewed George Macleod of the Iona Community. Before close down at midnight came the Epilogue spoken by the Bishop of Carlisle.

During the first week, and for several months to come, local output remained at about 2½ hours. Transmission began each weekday at 12.55 p.m. with farm prices. On Mondays, Wednesdays and Fridays at 1 p.m. the STV light entertainment *One O'Clock Gang* was shown; on Tuesdays and Thursdays at the same time, the *One O'Clock Show* from Tyne Tees. Apart from the regular local news bulletins and the three times a week *Focus* magazine, there was a four-headed discussion *What say They* dealing largely with local issues and *Time out of Doors* covering local sport and other outdoor activities, introduced by staff interviewer Derek Batey, former ventriloquist and sound broadcaster. There were no school broadcasts. Very few schools in the area seemed to have television receivers, but a circular letter to schools and LEAs had been sent enquiring whether they would welcome a schools service. It was to be some years before Border felt able to afford participation in the ITV service to schools. Full participation in religious output was also delayed. The first-night Epilogue with the Bishop of Carlisle remained for long an isolated exception. Instead, brief Sunday evening readings from philosophical and devotional texts were used.

However, by the end of their first year of operation, the company had increased their audience from 64,000 homes to over 110,000, equal to more than two thirds of all private households in the region. Moreover, in doing so they had achieved a profit on the year of more than £10,000. They were, it is true, also carrying a deficit of £28,000 from their previous thirteen month run-up period without any revenue. But in the following year up to April 1963 with pre-tax profits at £27,424 the debit balance was completely wiped out.

If one overlooks the failure of the prestigious educational figures on their board to influence them to any participation in ITV's educational programming, it can be truthfully said that Border amply fulfilled the expectations raised in 1961 by their successful application. They had again demonstrated the practicality of the Authority's pursuit of regional diversity, provided the appointed companies combined genuine feeling for local interests with sound business judgement. Their local origination figure of barely 5 per cent at air date had grown to well over 10 per cent of total output. Local news bulletins with stories from both sides of the border and the Isle of Man were regularly achieving ratings of 40 and above. An audience share *vis-à-vis* the BBC consistently between 55 and 60 per cent was sustained not merely by the wide appeal network fare, but also by the devotion of local viewers to the regular topical magazine, the sports and farming items and the more light-hearted series of popular music and inter-town talent competitions. The professional quality of the monthly celebrity interviews by Maurice Lindsay and the occasional one-off documentary feature had earned them the respect of their colleagues from both ITV and BBC. Several of their occasional productions had been shown in other ITV regions. Notable among these were religious programmes, for while showing persistent reluctance to follow the fashion of regular nightly epilogues – as a relatively inexpensive and trouble-free method of clocking up local origination – Border had demonstrated originality and skill in devising special miscellany programmes of words and music to mark the main religious festivals.

The placing of eight Border productions in their local Top Ten in May 1963 can only have served to reinforce the attitude of the company's management towards the rigidities of the networking system as it was. Robin Gill and his chairman John Burgess were among the more outspoken critics of this system at the time of Pilkington.

In the company's first annual report Burgess said: 'We believe we have proved that a station such as Border is of value to the community and can be commercially independent and profitable, although the margin of profit is far less than the larger stations'.[13] Outside observers agreed. When the *Daily Telegraph*'s Marsland Gander visited Carlisle in July 1962 he wrote:

No Pilkington member . . . came near Border TV. If he had strayed so far he might have concluded that a hundred honest men and women who believe in TV were devoted to trying to give what they can day after day.[14]

7

GRAMPIAN

When Roy Thomson was awarded his contract the predicted coverage of the Authority's Central Scotland transmitter at Black Hill included a number of viewers in the lands towards the Tay and Dundee. But in practice it was found after the station had become operational that reception in these parts was poor. The changes necessary to correct the performance of the transmitter were expected to improve reception in that direction, but even so they did not seem likely to give anything better than fringe area reception of STV. Predicted coverage was a purely theoretical figure based on drawing board calculations, and it implied no contractual commitment. When, however, it was rumoured in early 1960 that the possibility of a new transmitter near Perth was being examined in order to ensure the best possible reception for Dundee and Tay area viewers, James Coltart wrote to the ITA to lay claim to it as an STV satellite, to which he said they had at least a moral right.[1]

But the ITA had long since harboured ideas for the extension of the ITV system to Aberdeen and the North East. For that, two transmitters would be needed and sites for these were being investigated. The more southerly and higher-powered one near Aberdeen would predictably overlap into the Tay area. When faced with the question whether to add the 300,000–500,000 Tayside population to STV's $3\frac{1}{2}$ million or to the 700,000–800,000 predicted for the North East Scotland contractor, there would be little doubt which was the right course to take.[2] STV could hardly claim they were getting less than they bargained for, since a recent TAM map had credited them with a coverage from Black Hill of over 4 million against the ITA's rental base of $3\frac{1}{2}$ million. For the time being, however, the decision whether or not to proceed with a Perth transmitter was deferred until such time as it was established how far southward and how clearly the Aberdeen signal would eventually penetrate. The more urgent immediate task was the appointment of a programme company for North East Scotland. The chosen transmitter sites were at Mongour (Durris), fifteen miles south west of Aberdeen and at

Roskill (Mounteagle) on Black Isle, north of Inverness. It was decided to start their construction that autumn 1960 and, by working through the winter months, be ready for programme transmissions some time in autumn 1961.

So early in May 1960 applications were invited for the contract under which a rental of £73,000 p.a. would be payable in return for a predicted coverage from the two transmitters of some 870,000 people (including 182,000 in fringe areas). Closing date was 28 June. Because they were anxious to get the matter settled before the summer break, ITA Members agreed to interview applicants as early as 5 July. It was known that at least seven new groups would apply. The contrast with the situation in Central Scotland could not have been more marked, and the groups included a wide range of prominent people who had rejected Roy Thomson's overtures four years earlier.

At the end of a full, tiring day of interviews, the Members were left with a short list of three groups and these, they felt, they would have to see a second time. The first of the three groups were Caledonian TV, led by Thomas Johnston, Chancellor of Aberdeen University and a former Secretary of State for Scotland, which included John Grierson, Alex Gibson of the Scottish National Orchestra, the two novelists Neil Gunn and Neil Paterson, representatives of local farm and fishery interests and a very long list of ordinary local folk as would-be shareholders. Their proposed Managing Director was J. J. Hardy, the then General Manager of STV and James Buchan, ex-BBC, was to be Programme Controller. They stated confidently that they could start with 10 per cent of local production rising within two years to 15 per cent.

Secondly there was North Caledonian, led by Donald Cameron of Lochiel, including Eric Linklater, George Elrick, R. N. Bruce Lockhart, and the Duke of Fife. Of the 350 other named interested people 326 were residents in the area and represented a complete cross-section of local life. Their Programme Controller was to be Tom Singleton who had been successively an Executive Producer and Deputy Controller of Programmes with ABC and had been one of those who advised UTV in the difficult run-up period.

Finally, there was North of Scotland TV, a group formed round a nucleus of directors of the largest chain of independent cinemas in Scotland, the thirty-year-old Caledonian Associated Cinemas Ltd. But it was emphasised that these men were participating in the group as individuals. Chief among them were their Chairman, Sir Alexander King, a self-made seventy-two-year-old Glaswegian who had started in the world of entertainment at the age of fourteen selling theatre programmes at Glasgow's Princes Theatre, and a man Roy Thomson would dearly have liked to associate with; Captain Iain Tennant, owner of the 8000 acre Innes estate near Elgin; and Provost Wotherspoon of Inverness, Managing Director of Caledonian Cinemas. Other associates included Lord Forbes, Scotland's premier baron and Deeside landowner; the Hon. Angus Ogilvy; the Dowager Viscountess Colville, Chief Commissioner of the Scottish Girl Guides; E. O'Donnell, a director of London Film Productions, formerly with ABPC; and Dr Honeyman, one-time Member of the ITA. In their first application the group had said little about their local programme intentions, apart from promising as many as possible, including two daily local news bulletins and a local magazine programme. Before their second interview they submitted a further document outlining programme plans in more detail, even giving a specimen week's schedule, evening local news, sport, weather, epilogues, local chat shows, native Scots music and a weekly series for small children. Captain Tennant admitted that there was an apparent paucity of backers from the immediate Aberdeen area in their group but pointed out that competing groups had to some extent pre-empted them by roping in several hundreds of the people most likely to be interested. If appointed they would be ready to offer shares to these people. Over a third of the proposed share capital had been reserved for this very purpose. Close cooperation with the local press and with Scottish Television was also intended.

The Authority ended its second interviews with the feeling that any one of the shortlisted groups would be a suitable contractor. It needed a majority vote finally to decide in favour of the King–Tennant group, and even that only on conditions.[3] These were first that Thomas Johnston, Neil Paterson and Cameron of Lochiel should all be invited to become directors, and (if they accepted) be each of them offered the opportunity of subscribing for 1000 voting and 2000 non-voting shares. These shares were to be taken from the proposed holdings of King, Tennant and Wotherspoon, with the result that no single director of the company would hold more than 1000 voting shares. Secondly, proposals for larger institutional holdings should be dropped and individuals from the region, from the Aberdeen area in particular, be invited to take up these non-voting shares instead, sympathetic consideration being given to the numerous private persons associated with the Johnston and Cameron applications. Thirdly, the cinema chain's 5 per cent holding in ABPC (ABC TV's parent company) should be disposed of.

All these conditions were accepted. Tom Johnston and Neil Paterson accepted directorships, but Cameron declined. Both Cameron and

Johnston supplied the King group with their lists of small local subscribers. In the consequent reorganisation of the company's finances, the number of shareholders was increased from 225 to nearly 700, but the majority of voting shares, and therefore control, remained with the Board.

At the interview with the King group the Authority had sought and received assurances that Tennant would be able to find time for the affairs of the company, in spite of the demands of his 8000 acre estate. Immediately after appointment he and his colleague O'Donnell swiftly set to work establishing the new company on a working basis. They started planning for an air date of 1 October 1961; and by mid-September they had taken over the old tram depot at Queen's Cross, Aberdeen, for their studios. But although workmen were soon busy pulling up old tramlines at Queen's Cross, it was by no means certain – especially in a part of Britain where weather conditions could be severe – that technical engineering problems might not cause unforeseen delays. The ITA engineers were confident they could have both the Durris (Aberdeen) and the Mounteagle (Inverness) transmitters ready by autumn 1961 (with perhaps a week or two interval between them), and the Post Office were also hopeful that they could complete the extension of a vision link from Glasgow northwards to Aberdeen by that time. It was, however, very doubtful whether they could carry the extension further as far as Mounteagle before the following year. Faced with the likelihood that this small company might therefore be operating in only one part of their area for more than a year, the Authority decided to provide a temporary link between the two transmitters out of its own resources. But this was not to be the end of the new company's engineering problems, as we shall see.

In January 1961 the company's management adopted the name Grampian Television and shortly afterwards Gwyn Ward Thomas was appointed sales controller and Alex Mair company secretary. As with several other companies during their formative period, Grampian were advised and guided by ABC Television, the network company to which they became affiliated. Senior members of their staff visited Belfast to see how the Ulster company was managed and operated. Howard Steele, the ABC engineer who helped design the UTV studio, played a similar role for Grampian. One of the incidental matters broached when he, in company with Tennant and O'Donnell, went to Princes Gate to discuss the technical problems of opening date, stirred echoes of the earlier exchanges with STV about the Tayside overlap. Grampian spokesmen were understandably concerned to know whether the changes being made to the Black Hill aerial would materially affect, in STV's favour, their potential share of the audience in this area. Early research had established that about one third of TV receivers in the total Grampian area were located there. ITA engineers tried to reassure them that the likely changes would not be significant; and told them about the possibility of a satellite transmitter near Perth whose attribution had been left for the time being undecided.[4]

The association with UTV was made quite fortuitously even closer because Bill Wilson, the ITA Northern Ireland Officer, became temporarily acting Scottish Officer as well. In March 1961, Wilson was in consultation with David Brown, Grampian's newly appointed General Manager, about the amount of local programming the Authority would be expecting during the company's first year. Drawing on his Ulster experience Wilson advised what came to be known as the 2:4:6 pattern of local origination:[5] that is to say that there should be no more than two hours local production during the first six months, increasing to four for the second and amounting by the beginning of the next year to at least six hours. For the initial weekly two-hour offering he strongly recommended a well balanced weekday magazine similar to UTV's *Roundabout* which had done so much to establish the Belfast company's identity in Northern Ireland as a genuinely regional television service. This advice was accepted.[6]

By the end of May Tennant was in a hopeful frame of mind. David Brown had had to resign as General Manager for personal reasons and his place had been taken for the time being by Edward O'Donnell, one of the executive directors. Jim Buchan, an experienced BBC producer, who had been a member of the unsuccessful Caledonian TV applicant group, had been appointed production controller. The sales department in London under Ward Thomas was doing well. Building work on the studio centre was up to schedule and an opening date of 30 September 1961 seemed a reasonable possibility. A series of local meetings with dealers and aerial manufacturers was planned to begin on 1 July. A station symbol had been chosen in the form of a 'Saint Andrew's Cross which evolves itself on the screen into a picture of the Grampians, with suitable music attached'.[7] O'Donnell had listened to 600 traditional Scottish tunes and had finally settled for a five-second recording incorporating Scotland the Brave as melody line and the Psalm tune Crimond as counterpoint.

It came as a veritable bombshell to learn a month later that, in addition to their worries over viewing of STV in the Tayside overlap area, and the makeshift nature of the link between their two transmitters, Grampian's access to network programmes was in serious jeopardy. In late June, the Post Office disclosed that, because they had been let down by an equipment supplier, they would be unable to complete the promised link between

Glasgow and Aberdeen before February 1962. To make matters even worse, the proposed second link from Carlisle to Glasgow that would give independent access to programmes from the south was going to be delayed several months. Apparently oblivious of the paramount importance to an ITV company that it should be, and appear to be, patently distinctive and independent in its programming, the best the Post Office engineers were prepared to offer at this stage was a temporary link that would retransmit the STV signal from Black Hill.

Consequently the only network programmes Grampian could broadcast would be those being shown at the same time by STV; and, much more serious, there was obviously going to be a large disparity between the amount of local production screened by Grampian and that shown by STV (now some ten hours a week). This would mean that whenever they were not putting out their own local programmes, Grampian would be transmitting not their own choice of network fare but several hours of STV's local productions. To say Grampian's management were dismayed by this news is to put it mildly. They were to be reduced to the role of a mere satellite, their ambition to establish the new company's distinctive identity in the minds of the region's viewers set at naught. Any hope of competing with STV for viewers in the Dundee–Tayside overlap area would have to be abandoned. Their publicity campaign in the area had already begun. Planned, and in some cases booked for the weeks ahead, were meetings with local press men and with television set dealers. There was to be a luncheon meeting with Scottish MPs for the area. A six page supplement giving information about the company, their programme plans and their starting date had been prepared for the local press.[8] As a first reaction all recruitment of staff was stopped and a formal protest was made to the Authority, including a hint at possible claims for financial compensation, even though it was known and admitted that the fault lay elsewhere. The possibility of not producing any local programmes at all was also contemplated.

ITA staff were indignant at the belated and apparently light-hearted admission by Post Office engineers of their failure to honour a commitment on which the Authority had relied in its dealings with its latest programme contractor. Intense personal pressure was brought to bear on the Post Office at all levels both from the Authority and the company. Lord Forbes, on behalf of the company, made approaches to the PMG and had a not wholly satisfactory interview with the GPO Director of Telecommunications. However, impressed by the evident concern expressed to him, the latter agreed to offer something better. He would provide two temporary channels (main and reserve) from Glasgow to Aberdeen which would operate full time from early September. These would be fed, not from off air reception of Black Hill but from the Glasgow switching centre, the point at which network material from outside was received before being passed on to STV studios. This would mean that Grampian would at least have independent access to the network during those periods when STV did not need it because they were transmitting locally-originated material. There would, however, still be another three or four months after air date before the second Carlisle–Glasgow line would be available to give Grampian completely independent access to network programmes.[9]

It was a solution well short of the ideal, but it was the best that could be done. The company were thus able to resume their build-up and preparations for a 30 September opening date. The *Aberdeen Evening Express* of 29 September 1961 was moved to expatiate on the technical miracles achieved over the past months in the transformation of the old tramshed into an ultra-modern showpiece HQ and studio centre with two studios, to say nothing of 'the ornamental goldfish pond with miniature fountains in the forecourt'. As for programme expectations, the press had been told that commercial television seen in the North East of Scotland would be less dependent on 'alien and mid-Atlantic mediocrity'.[10] There would be more opportunity for native speech, native song and traditions and more employment for local artists. In the first local edition of the *TV Times* King referred to the 900,000 inhabitants of the area as the Grampian family. True, local production would not exceed about three hours a week to begin with. But this would expand to at least twice that amount soon; and £10,000 had been set aside for research into original programme ideas.

All that happened by way of ceremonial on the Saturday afternoon opening at 2.45 p.m. on 30 September was a brief word of welcome to viewers from Kirkpatrick who then threw the symbolic switch. One minute later they were at Catterick races with the rest of the ITV family. After the wrestling which followed came STV's *Scotsport*, the news, ABC's *Thank Your Lucky Stars* and *Gun Law*. Then at 7.00 p.m. the Grampian Chairman appeared in *Greetings from Grampian*, inviting viewers in the region to see over the new studios with him and to see excerpts from some programmes still to come. The movie that followed at 7.30 p.m. was obviously chosen with local viewers in mind: *The Eye Opener Man and Robert Burns*. Apart from the local weather report, the next local origination was the Service of Dedication conducted from the studio by the Lord Provost of Aberdeen.

During the following week the pattern for the next three months became apparent: on the five weekdays the news magazine *News and Views* was shown for thirty minutes from 6.15 p.m., with the exception of Thursdays, when it was reduced to fifteen minutes from 6.05 p.m. in order to make room for *ITN's Roving Report*. Brief local news bulletins were shown for two and five minutes respectively at 12.40 and 1.22 p.m. on weekdays. Lunchtime was dominated on four days of the week by ATV's light music entertainment *Lunch Box*. ('I am an Aberdonian at heart,' wrote Noele Gordon, in that week's *TV Times*.) And there was a second *Scotsport* from STV on Wednesdays at 10.35 p.m.

One week after the station opening Edward O'Donnell was able to hand over the task of chief executive to Ward Thomas, who was offered a seat on the Board and would take up residence in Aberdeen. He was very shortly plunged into a looming crisis in the company's affairs. It was a situation which King in a letter to Kirkpatrick described as 'disastrous' and 'calamitous'.[11] The audience being reached was very much smaller than had been anticipated when the company's rate card had been issued to advertisers. This had assumed an audience of some 135,000 homes increasing to 160,000 by January 1962. The TAM report for Opening Night had shown that less than 100,000 were in fact Grampian viewers. A later survey carried out in mid-November 1961 had shown little improvement. As a result the company were compelled to reduce their advertising charges substantially in order to be able to offer an acceptable cost per thousand; and this in its turn meant a drastic revision of revenue estimates, leading to the expectation of a loss of £20,000 in the first year of operation and a level of profits in subsequent years that would seem to rule out any dividend payment before 1964, when the contract would end. Stringent programme economies had to be imposed.

The main factor contributing to this situation was the company's failure to attract many viewers in the Dundee–Tayside overlap area. According to TAM estimates, 20 per cent of all homes in the Grampian service area equipped to receive ITV were in Dundee. Most of these had hitherto been viewing STV programmes and, although some must have been getting rather poor reception, by the end of 1961 they had shown little inclination to change over to Grampian. And now recent improvements in the Black Hill transmitter had led to better reception for these STV devotees. The mid-November survey showed that only 5500 out of 40,500 multi-channel homes in Dundee itself were viewing Grampian. It looked as if STV had a considerable and, in the absence of other factors, permanent advantage. King, Tennant, O'Donnell and Ward Thomas went to Brompton Road on 19 December to seek Authority help. Their first suggestion, to reduce the power of the Black Hill signal in the Dundee area, was rejected out of hand. Their second, provision of a satellite of Durris in the area, was also turned down. Their third suggestion, reduction in rental, was one the Authority could consider.

Members appreciated that Grampian had 'some reason to be in an extremely nervous state about their financial prospects'.[12] Quite apart from the overlap problem, they had come on air at an unfortunate time. All companies had been hit by a general fall in advertising revenue to which the recent imposition of the 10 per cent TAD had probably contributed, to say nothing of the prolonged Equity strike. And the smaller companies were hit the hardest. It was agreed to allow deferment for six months of 20 per cent of the £77,000 Grampian rental. At the end of the six months the position would be reviewed. It was after all early days to decide that the company would never be able to increase its share of audience in an overlap area considerably more extensive than the city of Dundee alone, where STV seemed so firmly entrenched. In the opinion of the Scottish Member, Professor Talbot Rice,[13] confirmed by Carmichael, there was at that time little in Grampian's local output to tempt viewers away from STV (or indeed the BBC). To this judgement, which they shared, the Authority's Scottish Committee added the comment that Grampian had very much over-estimated the speed with which they would be accepted by a population notoriously conservative in its habits.

But King and his colleagues pressed for more: a permanent reduction – not a deferment – of rental and that by 30 per cent, not 20; and, they argued, the reduction should run from air date and not from 1 January 1962.[14] Confronted by this further request on 30 January the Authority so far relented as to concede an outright reduction from 30 September 1961 but it stood by its figure of 20 per cent, adding moreover that the concession should be reviewed at the end of the company's first year of operation. This revised offer was gratefully accepted.[15] With the help of Fraser, Grampian also started successful negotiations for a reduction in their payments for network programmes. In due course, having confirmed that no significant change had since occurred, the Authority agreed to extend the rental abatement – subject to a 7 per cent cost of living increase – until 31 March 1963, the end of its own financial year.

Not only was Grampian's potential audience much smaller than could have been expected but they had launched their service into a region where influential elements of public opinion were antipathetic to the very idea of commercial television. In connection with the station opening, the Lord Provost of Aberdeen had actually said that he was uncertain how far it was proper to 'dedicate' a commercial enterprise of that kind. During their early months the company's audience share, at 49 per cent, was the lowest of any

ITV company so far. (Compare Tyne Tees with 74 per cent or even Ulster with 54 per cent.) Whatever the failings of their own productions the dour, reticent character of their local public played its part. By late 1962 their viewing homes had increased to 142,000, very little more than they had expected to start with; their average viewer correspondence amounted to six letters a week and if they sought to include 'vox pop' interviews in their news magazine only one person in ten would respond. It took much persuasive effort to succeed, as they did, in selling all the advertising time they had forecast; but the income was far less because of the very substantial rate reductions they had felt constrained to make. At the end of February 1962, after five months' operation, their deficit on profit and loss account was just over £46,000 to which had to be added some £50,000 spent in preliminary expenses in the formation of the company. For the year ending February 1963 income had risen to £592,000 against revenue expenditure of £545,000 and capital expenditure of nearly £26,000.

And yet in spite of all difficulties, much was achieved. By June 1962 Tennant felt able to claim that the company already stood for something valued in the life of North East Scotland and this view was shared by the Authority's Scottish Officer, John Lindsay, notwithstanding a period of hostile newspaper reports carrying stories of difficulties with staff. By November of that year, shortly after his promotion to Managing Director, Ward Thomas could proudly point out that three of Grampian's local programmes had just appeared in the local Top Ten. They were *Pick o' the North*, a local talent show; *A' the Airts*, a Scottish knowledge quiz programme and *Calum's Ceilidh*, featuring Calum Kennedy, a Gaelic singer. These programmes, which were regularly attracting large audiences, reflected the extension of the company's local origination from the limited formulae of news magazine and sports reports into the fields of local popular music and light entertainment. Not that their local news and current affairs were by now any less appreciated. In the first week of January 1963 six Grampian productions appeared in the regional Top Ten and of these *Sportscope* was at number three position with a 61 rating and *Grampian Week* at number seven with a rating of 56. This last was attracting consistently higher ratings than any other serious factual programme on British television – ITV or BBC. By the end of their first contract period Grampian had advanced from having the smallest audience share to fourth position in the league table.

Local newspapers, which for a time had been sharply hostile, speaking slightingly of 'TV Service on a Shoestring' and exploiting any story (such as an occasional staff difficulty) that might be made discreditable to the company, had by the end of 1962 become almost unanimously favourable.

Necessarily so. They had perforce to acknowledge that after a shaky start Grampian were living up to their early promises and had become very much a part of the region's life. The picture was, as John Lindsay pointed out, one of a small well-organised company with a strong sense of public service, economically run but at no time over-profitable, striving above all to achieve through its own programmes a true sense of identity with its audience, even though that audience's highest words of praise remained limited to a laconic 'nae bad'.

Such were the beginnings of a company which first secured its contract by a knife-edge decision and subsequently never had a challenger to face.

8

WWN

Obviously the Authority was approaching the limits of the practical in its quest for decentralised regional diversity. A fortnight after Channel Television went on the air, on 14 September 1962, another company started operations with certainly as great, if not greater, claim to distinctive independence. Its story was to be very different.

When in January 1960 thought was being given to the completion of the national system, particular attention was paid to the technical problems of providing a service for the as yet uncovered regions of North and Western Wales. The rightness of establishing national companies outside England was surely even more patent in the case of Wales with its live spoken language and cultural tradition. Yet Nature had made the job much more difficult.

The concentration of population on the southernmost part of Welsh territory had made almost inevitable the placing of a transmitter in that area and the consequent creation of a company with responsibilities to viewers on both sides of the Bristol Channel. It would of course have been possible to construct satellite transmitters in other parts of Wales in order to make TWW more fully a national Welsh programme company. But, quite apart from its substantial West Country audience, there was the added complication that, whereas the company's Welsh audience had only a minority of Welsh speakers, those parts of the country as yet uncovered by ITV transmissions were predominantly Welsh-speaking. Thus, although the Authority did not rule out the possibility of extending TWW's service area northwards and westwards, the Members preferred first to see whether any additional wholly Welsh group could be found able and willing to form a company to do the job. Of the willingness they could have had few doubts. The Welsh Member, J. Alban Davies, had kept his colleagues informed of the state of opinion in the Principality. As television viewing came to occupy ever more of the waking hours of the British people, so there grew also among influential minorities in Wales the belief that this all-pervasive medium could be the sovereign means for preservation and possible renascence of Welsh language and culture. Such groups were increasingly vocal in their insistence that any further extension of television broadcasting in Wales should be entrusted to a Welsh company, totally owned and controlled by Welshmen and committed to their cause. It should have as first priority the transmission in peak hours of a significant amount of Welsh language and Welsh interest programmes. But would such a company have a sufficiently large audience to guarantee financial survival?

The territory occupied by this additional population presented peculiar topographical difficulties for the engineers. The plan they devised was for two medium power transmitters, one in Pembrokeshire and one on the Lleyn peninsula. The former would direct sufficient power northwards to enable the latter transmitter to receive and re-broadcast the signal. By July 1960 further work on this plan made possible cautious predictions of the approximate likely coverage of the two transmitters. The estimate was that a total population of over 700,000 might be reached. But about 400,000 of these would be in areas of 'fringe reception', some of them already adequately served by TWW output from the St. Hilary transmitter. On these figures it seemed reasonable at least to consider inviting applications for the franchise. But, as in the case of Border and Channel Television, the Authority would expect applicants to make the case for their chances of financial survival. The knowledge that some Welsh television enthusiasts were thinking in terms of a non-profit making, but self-supporting, company was in itself encouraging.

There would almost certainly be a long delay before the Post Office would be able to provide a link to the proposed Pembroke transmitter from the anticipated site of the new Welsh company's studios in the capital city, Cardiff. In the meantime, given the manifest eagerness of pressure groups in Wales, it was agreed to make public the Authority's good intentions as soon as possible. Fraser was visiting the National Eisteddfod in Cardiff and was duly reported as having declared on 4 August 1960 that the ITA proposed to create a new independent television service area in West and North West Wales, and in the autumn would be seeking to appoint a programme company for the area. He hoped to be able to begin the service in 1962 or at the latest in 1963. This announcement was warmly welcomed in Wales. The TWW Board decided they would consider applying themselves for the additional contract; but even if they were not successful they would be ready, they said, to offer support to any other Welsh company eventually apointed.[1]

At this time there emerged the possibility of further extending the proposed Welsh service by the inclusion in the technical plan of a third transmitter to carry the signal into the area north of the Snowdon massif, and into Flint and Denbighshire. On 29 September there was a meeting between the PMG (Reginald Bevins), the Minister for Welsh Affairs (Henry Brooke) and representatives of a Committee set up by Welsh local authorities and voluntary bodies to press the claims for a national Welsh service. According to a letter received from Dr Haydn Williams, Director of Education for Flintshire and a leading member of the Committee, Bevins showed himself 'very helpful and seemed to want to do something immediately to meet the demands which have recently arisen in Wales'.[2] The Welsh spokesmen were led to believe that there would be 'no insuperable difficulty' in allowing a Flintshire transmitter to meet the needs of North East Wales. The snag from the ITA's point of view was that a Flint station would have a very large overlap indeed with the Granada and ABC transmissions received in North Wales from the Winter Hill transmitter. The estimated primary and secondary coverage in Wales would total 286,000 people of which 255,000 were also in the corresponding coverage area of Winter Hill. A large number of these were Welsh speakers, and Granada were already providing for them in off peak hours. However, there could be no doubt that it would be in the interests of Welsh viewers if this addition could be made to the service area of a Welsh company based in Wales.[3] Any audience loss suffered by Granada or ABC would be a tiny part of the huge total population of the Northern region.

Another worry was cost. First estimates suggested that the annual running cost of the three transmitters would be about £200,000, while only a fraction of that could be taken in rental. The Authority would therefore be subsidising the service at an annual rate of about £150,000. It believed, however, that, as it had a duty under the Act to extend its service to as much of the country as was reasonably practicable, there was nothing against its subsidising stations whose rentals did not meet their costs.[4]

Knowing the strength of feeling in Wales, Members were anxious to issue some preliminary advertisement inviting interested parties to get in touch on a provisional, non-committal basis if only to gain some idea of the likely field. But it was to be well on into 1961, and only after continuing pressure from Welsh interests on Ministers, that any further positive step could be taken. The Pilkington Committee was by now at work, and, in spite of the earlier encouraging noises from Bevins, the Post Office officials were apparently less eager to settle a go-ahead for something so clearly related to the future of British broadcasting. They argued that the Flint/Denbigh transmitter could hardly be described as a further extension of the existing service since nearly 90 per cent of the population in its proposed service area were already getting more or less adequate programme reception from Winter Hill. That part of the ITA's plan therefore fell more logically into a consideration of future broadcasting policy (in this case for Wales) rather than into a continuing fulfilment of an existing statutory duty.

But the Authority did feel committed. In default of a firm decision from the Government its advertisement appeared on 7 April, couched in terms which left the question of the third transmitter open and referring merely to stations to be erected in West and North Wales. Closing date for applications was 19 May. The simultaneous press notices,[5] however, mentioned specifically the three stations for which Post Office approval had been sought, on the Prescelly Hills in Pembrokeshire, on the Lleyn Peninsula and 'one to cover the Flint/Denbigh area'. The total population lying within the overall coverage of the three transmitters would be about one million. But that would include large 'fringe-areas'. The primary and secondary service areas would perhaps have 640,000 of which some 360,000 would be people outside the coverage areas of any existing ITA transmission. 'We must take it absolutely for granted,' wrote Fraser, 'that we must appoint an independent company for West Wales if there is any prospect that a group of people will appear who are ready to accept the responsibility.'

Because any company appointed would be expected to make a genuinely distinctive contribution, it almost went without saying that there would be a contractual requirement that the company should broadcast a number of programmes in the Welsh language during the evening viewing hours. These would include both locally produced Welsh programmes and re-transmissions of some of those already being provided – in off-peak hours – from TWW and Granada studios. Rental for the three-station plan would be of the order of £72,000; for the two-station plan proportionately less. Interviews with applicant groups would be on 30 May 1961 in Cardiff.

A bare four days before those interviews the Director-General at the Post Office, Sir Ronald German, came to Princes Gate in order to discuss the Flint/Denbigh proposal. His message was that it would be most unlikely to get his Minister's approval unless the company appointed provided 'a distinctively Welsh service'[6] different from that coming from Winter Hill and containing as much as 50 per cent of locally originated material, two-thirds of it in peak hours. For the Post Office so to prescribe the balance of programme content was unprecedented and certainly incompatible with the spirit if not the letter of the Act. The conditions were also breathtakingly unrealistic in relation to the likely earnings of the proposed new Welsh company; and German was told so. The hope was expressed that the Minister would share the views of responsible Welshmen that a distinctively Welsh service could be provided with a lesser origination. It was agreed that all four applicant groups would be told of the PMG's expectations and asked to state how far they thought they would be able to go towards meeting them.

The four groups were Television Wales Norwest, led by Lord Tenby (Gwilym Lloyd-George); the Wales Television Association (Teledu Cymru) led by Dr Haydn Williams and Colonel Traherne, the Lord Lieutenant of Glamorgan; Cambrian (North and West Wales) Television with the Marquess of Bute as President; and Cambrian Television, led by Lord Ogmore. All four applications carried the conventional array of distinguished names from the area, representing the arts, the professions, business and places of learning, and peers, journalists and landowners. In their interviews all four groups were warned of the continuing uncertainty about the dates at which the planned transmitters would be operational and, more especially, about the limited prospects of an early approval for the Flint/Denbigh transmitter. They were questioned closely on their likely capital resources and the factual basis of their predictions of income and costs. The financial risks of the enterprise were emphasised, risks which would be that much greater if only two, rather than three, transmitters were eventually available.[7] All declared themselves willing to accept a contract on such a reduced basis but added, with varying degrees of prudence, that their own productions would have to be, initially at least, on a modest scale.

The Authority quickly concluded that the choice lay between Lord Tenby's group and that of Dr Williams, with a preference, on balance, for the latter. These two were therefore called back for further discussion. The Members were very anxious that the contractor appointed should be fully aware of the uniquely difficult task of gaining and holding a sufficiently large audience in a service area having such large overlaps with the territory of other contractors who would often be offering mass appeal network fare in competition with offerings of Welsh language and culture.[8] A final decision was not made until three days later,[9] after a special meeting between the Williams group and Authority senior staff, when firm confirmation was obtained of the group's acceptance of suggestions about their capital structure and their Board of Directors. Their equity capital should be increased to £350,000 (of which 10 per cent would be voting stock): they should also make clearer to all would-be investors their declared intention that increasing programme expenditure would always have first claim and any dividend distribution only second claim on any profits earned. In addition it was suggested that a member of Lord Tenby's consortium, Eric

Thomas, the chairman of Woodalls, a leading Welsh newspaper publishing company, should be invited to join the Board.

The offer of the contract was made public on Wednesday 7 June and, although lingering resentments from their defeated rivals would soon make themselves evident, there seems to have been general satisfaction among Welsh nationalists that the choice had fallen on a group including such respected figures as Haydn Williams, Llewellyn Heycock and Gwynfor Evans, the President of Plaid Cymru.

Fraser wrote to the Post Office telling them that the stated conditions of approval of the Flint/Denbigh transmitter, that nearly half of its output should be originated by the new Welsh company, exceeded all that was normal and possible. It amounted to an apparent expectation of some thirty hours a week. He demonstrated the 'total abnormality' of that figure by comparison with the weekly production efforts of wealthy established companies like A-R ($12\frac{1}{2}$ hours); STV ($9\frac{1}{2}$ hours); Anglia ($7\frac{1}{2}$ hours). The most that could be reasonably expected of the company would be a couple of hours a week at the outset rising, given a three-station operation, to an hour a day by the end of their first year. To this could be added approximately three hours of Welsh from TWW and Granada. German's reply said that the PMG could not agree to anything less than ten hours of Welsh language and Welsh interest programmes, all in good evening viewing hours. These requirements would have to be included in the contract.

Though a considerable climb down, the terms were still onerous, but Williams and his colleagues felt they had no option but to accept, although the company would now have to originate much more than they would be wise to undertake. Foreseeing inevitable financial difficulties, Fraser secured approval for a substantial reduction in the rental charged during the first year of the Flint/Denbigh transmitter.[10] He followed up this initiative on behalf of the young company with an approach to Granada, their intended 'parent' company, suggesting that the charges for network programmes could also be correspondingly reduced. This was readily conceded.

Thus, whereas the rest of ITV would be subsidising the new Welsh company to the tune of about £150,000 a year, Bevins and his officials had, by their unreasonable demands, done all they could to put the infant company's chances of survival in jeopardy. The production they demanded would require a scale of staffing, studio space and equipment that certainly neither Ulster nor Border would have been able to support in their first year. It could of course be said (and was) that Haydn Williams and his colleagues were a bunch of over-enthusiastic amateurs and that only their total lack of the necessary hard-headed professionalism could explain their acceptance of impossible conditions. Evidence for this view could be found maybe in the early resignations of those two of their original directors, Sir Miles Thomas and David Vaughan of Barclays Bank, who might have sustained a stronger element of financial realism.[11]

The further history of this company is one of a mounting series of setbacks and disappointments. If any blame for the damaging consequences of those events – most of which were well outside their control – could be laid to their door, it could only be in terms of lack of prudent foresight and an impetuous excess of zeal to which might be added those occasional failures of tact and public relations sense common to men who are convinced of the rightness of their cause. True, when Fraser saw Williams and Traherne at the end of June to talk about programmes, he began to feel forebodings. 'We must at once constitute a Welsh Nursing Party and keep it in being until baby is safely with us.'[12] The outcome was the preparation by ITA staff of a suggested draft schedule of Welsh output amounting to over ten hours a week, of which about $4\frac{1}{2}$ hours would come from the new company, the rest from TWW or Granada.

In the first week of September, the company announced their acquisition of a two-acre site for their studio centre on the outskirts of Cardiff, conveniently close to the Pontcanna studios of TWW, with whom, said the announcement, some programmes would be shared.[13] Shortly afterwards Nathan Hughes, who had been an engineer with A-R and later with TWW, helping to design their studios, was appointed General Manager. A private company, Wales Television Limited, was formally registered. The very necessary negotiations for coexistence and cooperation with the other Welsh company now had to begin. It must be said that if these negotiations turned out – as they did – to be long, difficult and at times even acrimonious, the blame was not always TWW's, even though it did occasionally require Fraser's skills in diplomatic cajolery to persuade them to forebearing tolerance. Chief among bones of contention was the title chosen by the younger company. Its implied claim to be the national Welsh company, covering and serving the whole country, was rightly resented. The bickering went on for many months. Even after the Authority had ruled that the company should be called Wales (West and North) Television Ltd and the use of the national name always so qualified, there were periodic revivals of the argument.[14] It covered such trivia as the actual placing of the qualifying words on letter headings or on the sign outside the studio centre; the use and placing of the symbolic red dragon; the exclusive use of the words Teledu Cymru; the title heading of a new programme weekly originally called

Wales TV Weekly to be published by a company calling itself 'Wales Television Publications Ltd'. And agreements once reached were not always honoured either by Williams or the company staff. Switchboard operators, for example, consistently identified themselves to callers as 'Wales Television Ltd'.

These disagreements began to get in the way of a satisfactory workable arrangement for the supply of Welsh language and Welsh interest programmes from TWW. That an agreement was finally reached, in which TWW showed themselves more generous than their strict commercial interests would seem to dictate, owed as much to the mediating efforts of ITA staff and to TWW's own sensitivity to Welsh public opinion as it did to the tactics of Williams and his colleagues. The latter were happy to receive TWW's Welsh language programmes virtually free but were very reluctant to commit themselves in advance to purchase any of the English language Welsh interest ones. Matters were further complicated by Granada's disconcerting decision to cease production and transmission of Welsh language programmes from September 1962, which meant that WWN's ten hours minimum commitment would have to be made up by additional programmes from either their own resources or from TWW's.

For their part TWW continued to show a generous regard for the still dubious financial resources of WWN, in contrast to the bleak rigidity of the Post Office. Could not a regular children's programme in Welsh between 5 and 6.00 p.m. count towards the ten hours, asked WWN, even though this would not be in the contractual 'good evening viewing hours'?[15] The ITA thought it could. Not so the Post Office whose official wrote: 'The condition laid down by the Postmaster-General (a minimum of ten hours a week of "Welsh programmes all in good evening viewing hours") still holds . . . We are quite sure that . . . Ministers did not have in mind the period between 5.00 and 6.00 p.m. We know of nothing to make us think that Ministers would be willing to vary the condition in this way.'[16] Nor, evidently, were Ministers going to be asked!

This frosty response may have been influenced by the furore caused some months earlier by some incautious remarks by Haydn Williams in which he had suggested that the Welsh language and Welsh interest programmes were likely to be screened between 6.00 and 7.00 p.m. and 10.00 and 11.00 p.m. – leaving the 7.00 to 10.00 p.m. period for more widely popular network programmes. 'Wales TV will not have Welsh in peak hours' headlined the *Western Mail* on 26 November 1961. A spokesman for one of the unsuccessful applicant groups was quoted as saying: 'They have had to compromise their ideology for commercial viability'.[17] Before long Haydn

Williams was defending himself on the BBC against the accusations in a pamphlet titled *Teledu Mamon* that his company would be sacrificing Welsh language and culture on the altars of mammon. These reports had aroused excusable doubts at the Post Office whether the company would be honouring its programme commitment, and the Authority had had to remind Williams that complete exclusion of any Welsh programmes from the hours of 7.00 to 10.00 p.m. would be politically indefensible.

On 24 April 1962, the company's first Rate Card was issued claiming an estimated potential viewership of 247,000 homes and an air date of 14 September. This date was later confirmed by the ITA. The Pembrokeshire transmitter (Presely) would certainly be ready by then. Unhappily completion of the Lleyn one (Arfon) was likely to be delayed by appalling weather. In the event this transmitter was not operational until 9 November.

The long intervals between the opening dates of the three ITA transmitters were bound to add to the difficulties of the company's management. A postponement of their air date might have been more prudent, but their programme plans were by now far advanced. It was their intention to open with five weekly half-hours plus a Sunday religious programme. They had engaged a staff of seventy-five, soon to be raised to more than a hundred. Their deal with TWW for use of the latter's programmes had been concluded in May, offering them three hours of Welsh language in return for repeat fees plus incidental expenses and two hours of Welsh interest at a cost related to population coverage. Later TWW agreed that for the time being their Welsh language programmes would be available cost free. At the end of August John Baxter, their Managing Director, wrote confirming promises of all possible help in operational and other matters.[18]

So the last ITV company to be appointed under the round of contracts which began in 1954 took the air at 6.00 p.m. on Friday 14 September 1962. About 700,000 out of the 1,070,000 people who would be able to receive the new service were reckoned by the ITA to be able to receive signals already from stations in other areas. How many of them could be persuaded to switch to WWN depended in part on the content of the programmes and in part on the relative strength of the signals. Those who observed that the challenge lay in the bare eighteen months in which the company had to prove itself before the ITV contracts ran out were missing the point. The question was whether they would be able to survive even that long. Out of that majority of their potential viewers now offered a choice between ITV channels, the ones WWN must aim to attract would have to be both Welsh speakers and also able and willing in most cases to spend the money on changing their aerials.

To the professional eye the first week's local programmes were not unpromising. Opening night started with a special production of the national anthem, *Land of My Fathers*, devised and produced by Ernest Byrne, the company's Executive Producer. In the words of the programme magazine, it gave the song 'a new dimension by giving it a visionary [sic!] background'. The pictures included Llewelyn's monument, Cathays Park, Harlech Castle, Swansea University and City Hall, Cardiff, Llyn Gwynant, the sea off Lavernock, Pembrokeshire and the Black Book of Carmarthen. This was followed by *Croeso* (Welcome), a series of extracts from forthcoming local programmes. Then came at 6.06 p.m. the news and weather in Welsh and the first issue of *Heno* (Tonight) the local magazine programme, a miscellany of serious and light topical items, a short sports item and *Impact*, a two-headed discussion in English, news and weather in English, and a brief musical item *Moment for Melody* until 7.00 p.m. when the networked quiz *Take Your Pick* was shown.

During the course of his viewing of the first week the Authority's Welsh Officer in Cardiff, Lyn Evans, was led to wonder whether the 'company may well have overstretched their resources in trying to do five hours per week at the start'. By the end of the week however he concluded: 'if the company can maintain this output and reasonable standards they won't be doing too badly'. Maintain it they did. On 28 January 1963 Moel-y-Parc (Flint/Denbigh) started programme transmissions and both the Post Office and the Authority were duly informed of the extent to which the ten hour commitment (which now became operative) was being fulfilled. In the average week, 10 hours 51 minutes of Welsh and Welsh interest programmes were being transmitted, made up of 5 hours 11 minutes in the Welsh language from TWW and 5 hours 40 minutes of WWN's own local origination in both languages. More than ten hours of this total fell between 6 and 11 p.m. It really was a very creditable achievement. The reported ratings for the company's own productions ranged from 27 to 42 with many in the mid thirties, a level which seemed encouraging.

Alas, while such progress was being achieved on the programme front, the financial outlook was getting ever more gloomy. The set count was disappointingly low and income was far behind expenditure. Initial capital expenditure had been £330,000 and by the end of 1962 estimated revenue had been £55,000 against expenditure of about £119,000. The Authority felt obliged to grant a moratorium on rental payments[19] and Fraser persuaded Baxter of TWW to take a sympathetic attitude over payments overdue to them. Before long Pragnell was asking the ITA lawyers what other possibilities existed under the Act for the Authority to give financial assistance to a company in difficulty. There could be circumstances, and, he said, he feared this situation may have been reached with the Welsh company, in which mere abatement of rental would not suffice and some form of subsidy might be needed if the company was to stay solvent. The lawyers saw no way in which that could be done. But one cannot help reflecting what might have been possible had it been feasible for the Authority to draw on that vanished fund of £750,000 for which the Act had provided (see Volume 1).

The cruel economic reality was that WWN was totally failing to attract anything like the hoped-for advertising revenue. With the addition of Moel-y-Parc transmissions their set count appeared to be about 106,000. On that basis they were earning about £2.25 per home per year as against the national average for ITV companies of about £5.00. So there should have been considerable room for expansion. But some of the available audience figures, by concealing the amount of 'split viewing' in the very large areas of overlap, totally misrepresented the true position. Only some 40 per cent of the area's total viewership were exclusively WWN homes. The advertiser was not being offered access to a share of a 100,000 plus market but to that of a 40,000 plus one.

An added complication in the split viewing situation came from the relatively numerous small wired-relay companies originally formed to overcome the problems of reception in the difficult terrain of South Wales especially. There were at least a score of these with subscriber totals ranging from 20–25 homes to several thousand. Only about half of them carried any WWN programmes and one company in the Port Talbot–Neath area with over 15,000 subscribers was actually providing Westward programmes, claiming it saw no demand for those of WWN.

In March 1963 the Authority decided to drop all hope of payment of its deferred rentals.[20] It had just learned that the company's expected deficit over the next twelve months was £100,000 bringing the accumulated deficit on profit and loss to £290,000. 'Members might well ask themselves whether there is any prospect of the ultimate survival of this company'[21] wrote Fraser. But he still continued to hope against hope. He did not see the crisis as one of imprudent expenditure on staff, equipment or programmes: it was essentially one of income. Once the full effects of the addition of Moel-y-Parc to the company's programme outlets were felt things could still change. By May it was clear this had not happened. Average monthly income seemed likely to be £20,000 instead of a predicted £30,000, and expenditure was running at an annual rate of £470,000. The Members concluded that there was 'on the figures available no possibility of Wales (West and North) being able to continue in being'.[22] But it would be disastrous if an ITV company were to go into enforced liquidation. The only possibility, they decided, would be to bring about a merger with TWW and to grant the latter the franchise for the WWN area but without any guarantee of the post-1964 contract. The Authority should, they said, take on the role of marriage broker in order to ensure terms that would inflict the least possible hardship on WWN shareholders.

Even so, the struggle for independent survival continued. Concessions were made all round. The network companies claimed no payment for programmes supplied, as did TWW. The Authority rental was reduced to a peppercorn token £100 p.a. The Board of WWN, meeting at Shrewsbury, on 17 May decided they could not do otherwise than cease all programme production and reduce the size of their staff. This would mean making 80 redundant (out of 140). Haydn Williams resigned and Eric Thomas was appointed Managing Director. He and Emrys Roberts kept in close, almost daily, touch with Fraser in the continuous efforts to stave off the inevitable. 'I no longer quite despair of the company's independent future,' wrote Fraser.[23] He had already written to the Post Office asking for release from the ten hours commitment. There was a meeting of Alban Davies and Carmichael with Keith Joseph, Minister of Housing and Local Government, Lord Brecon, the Minister for Welsh Affairs and the PMG in which it was made clear that the Government 'wished everything to be done to enable WWN to continue until the expiry of its contract'[24] and at which it was therefore agreed that the PMG would release the Authority from the ten hour commitment.[25]

But now WWN's bank became restive over their overdraft. In the circumstances it was clearly neither wise nor responsible to seek further risk capital. So reluctantly but as an act of considered judgement Thomas, Roberts and Fraser, all three, agreed that the merger with TWW was the only possible and honourable solution.

The terms that emerged from the consequent negotiations were not ungenerous. WWN would continue as programme contractor as a subsidiary of TWW until expiry of their contract. Shareholders of WWN were offered five half-crown non-voting TWW shares for every six one pound WWN shares held by them. The current market value of TWW's 2/6d shares was 17/-. So the WWN shareholders would get a £4.25 investment in a profitable company for every £6 they had invested in one that was virtually bankrupt; and, with the yield on TWW shares at 13.4 per cent they could even look forward to a dividend that would give them 9.5 per cent return on their capital. These terms were sent out on 23 September 1963. As Fraser commented to the recently appointed new ITA Chairman, Lord Hill, if the necessary 90 per cent acceptances were not received 'a trainload of psychiatrists should be dispatched to Cardiff and points West and North'.[26] No such mass migration of psychiatrists took place.

The formal takeover took place in January 1964. By that time TWW knew they had been awarded the post-1964 contract for the two franchise areas now combined into one. As Fraser had said in his note to Hill 'They can hardly be expected to buy WWN one day and be dismissed from television the next'. To Nathan Hughes, the General Manager of WWN he wrote: 'The end of WWN as an independent company is a sad event for us all but . . . it became inevitable'.[27] At a time when, as other pages of this volume show, there was much else of first importance in the affairs of ITV to claim his attention, he had given much time, effort and care to a cause in which he clearly saw, among other things, both realisation and ultimate justification of the very principles of the Authority's regional policy. The words of Gwynfor Evans to him deserve to be recorded: 'In the midst of the bitter disappointment . . . the selfless and generous sympathy and help you have given from the start stands out as the finest thing in our experience of independent television. You could not have done more.'[28]

Part II

GRAND REMONSTRANCE: 1962

9

'DISQUIET' AND 'DISSATISFACTION'

Although, in their emphasis on the future, the terms of reference for the Pilkington Committee differed from those given the Beveridge Committee, its members were in no doubt that before they could make defensible recommendations about the future they would need to scrutinise the broadcast services as they were at that time and had been operating in the immediate past.

A paragraph in the introduction to the Report reminded us that on 1 March 1961 the Lord Chancellor in the House of Lords had confirmed that the Committee were 'entirely free' to recommend how the existing services – as well as any hypothetical new ones – 'should be constituted and organised in future',[1] including for example (as they saw it) the possibility that ITV should be financed otherwise than by advertising. If they were to be in a position to contemplate such a far-reaching proposal going to the very root of existing legislation, they would obviously need to examine the whole apparatus of contemporary broadcasting services in order to determine how far these, in their make-up and operation, could be related to failings or inadequacies in programme output which called for correction. But more than this, the Committee decided – rightly or wrongly – that they would have no sound basis for judgement of a broadcasting service's shortcomings (or of the organisation which may or may not have caused them) until they had succeeded in formulating to their own satisfaction a definition of the purposes of broadcasting as a social institution.

The members of the Committee took themselves and their task very seriously. They had, after all, been reminded by Lord De La Warr himself that in discussing television they were dealing with a 'force' of 'almost equal importance to the future of mankind as . . . nuclear power'.[2] The late 1950s and early 1960s were not only a time when conspiracy ('pressure group') theories and 'dismay' at exorbitant ITV profits were rife; they were also the years in which the now flourishing academic industry of media sociology was being born. In particular the cult figure of Marshall McLuhan was beginning to emerge, with his guru-like utterances.

This is not to say that the chairman and members saw themselves as media gurus. It was rather that, collectively, they displayed a general puritanical spirit. More than one of the statements that appear in their report, and to which they put their names, seem to betray an air of almost arrogant moral superiority which as individuals they would no doubt be most eager to disown.

Chapter 3 of the Pilkington Report which discussed specifically 'The Purposes of Broadcasting' was in some respects disarming. It was (as has been since admitted) written later, after the main body of the report and its recommendations were already in draft.[3] It opened, for instance, with the admission – agreeing in this with both the BBC Chairman, Sir Arthur fforde, and the ITA's Director General – that 'good broadcasting is something experienced rather than defined'. It disclaimed having any preconceived principles by which to judge the quality of the services provided.[4] It was necessary therefore to approach the matter empirically, judging the respective achievements of the two television services by the reported experiences and reactions of their viewers. In practice this seems to have involved basing judgement on the evidence of those organisations and individuals who told the Committee they had something to complain about. Not, it should be noted, on any attempts to understand the motives and satisfactions of the many millions of television viewers who in those areas where they had a choice were at that time choosing to watch ITV. Presumably the Committee considered such an investigation beyond their means or outside their terms of reference.

From the evidence presented to them the Pilkington Committee drew the conclusion that all was not well with the British television services and it saw this expressed in terms of public opinion under the two general headings of 'disquiet' and 'dissatisfaction'. In both respects it concluded that the major offender was Independent Television. 'Disquiet' was the word used to describe concern over the failure to appreciate the medium's supposed ability powerfully to influence moral values and attitudes and the apparent consequent proclivity towards the brutal, sordid and unedifying; under 'dissatisfaction' the Report subsumed general complaints over the limited range, variety and quality of the material chosen for programme treatment; and the 'unsuitable' times at which minority interest programmes were shown.

The second of these related in particular to what the Television Act had called 'proper balance'. Evidence on the subject reached the Committee from a wide variety of sources and the concept of balance was interpreted in an almost equally wide variety of ways. The first most obvious interpretation was a requirement to include programmes of local, or regional, interest. This category differed from other so-called 'balance programmes' in that they could be presumed to appeal to a majority rather than a minority of the viewers of the particular station from which they were broadcast. Otherwise they would not be doing their job. At the same time, they helped to illustrate the fact that not only were members of majorities also members of minority interest groups – as the several memoranda to Pilkington and indeed the Report itself insisted – but that the converse was also true, a fact that some of the critics often seemed to be disposed conveniently to ignore. There could be no member of a minority group who did not regularly find himself in a variety of contexts a member of the majority. Even regular and dedicated viewers of programmes of specialised regional interest were reluctant to sacrifice for their sake access to those networked programmes in which they shared an interest with the majority of their fellow citizens in other regions.

Certainly the size of that majority share of the output had to be carefully judged. Chief among those giving evidence calling for more regional television were of course, as they have always been, the Welsh and Scottish Nationalists. But the former, on whose behalf no fewer than eleven different groups presented memoranda to the Committee, were principally concerned to have a separate Welsh language broadcasting service for Wales rather than merely 'such facilities as would be appropriate to a region of England'.[5] Yet at the same time oral evidence from the Welsh Member of the Authority (J. Alban Davies) emphasised a reluctance to relinquish what they were already getting. They wanted a national channel as well. The half dozen Scottish groups were in the main more modest in their claims. With the exception of the Scottish National Party (who wanted a full blown Scottish Broadcasting Corporation) they urged a better and larger place in the output for programmes of genuine Scottish interest and origin. Indeed little of the written evidence from Scotland expressed satisfaction with the locally produced output of Scottish Television at that time. Provocatively differing from most other critics of ITV, the SNP even went so far as to say: 'If anything we approve of the amount of material from the United States. It at least gives our people a viewpoint other than that of London.'[6]

The Pilkington Report provided printed evidence of dissatisfaction with the regional programme output of ITV from three sources other than Welsh and Scottish Nationalists: first from the Radio and Television Safeguards

Committee of the unions concerned with broadcasting, which recommended reconstituting and strengthening the representative character of the Regional Councils and Committees of the broadcasting organisations, *without* any specific reference to ITV; secondly from the 'Liberal Party Committee' which, after tabulating percentage local viewing from eight of the twelve ITV regions, said 'Liberals would like substantially more';[7] and thirdly from the Parliamentary Committee of the Cooperative Union which recommended that ITV programme contracts should be awarded to 'popular and democratic organisations with strong roots in local life',[8] but which made no comment at all on existing regional output.

On the other hand all the programme companies giving evidence to the Committee had supplied information on their respective services of local news and other studio series of local interest as well as their local outside broadcasts. The Authority also recalled[9] that whereas in 1954/5 (i.e. eight years after the postwar resumption of the BBC television service) the Corporation had produced 254 hours of television in all its regions, in 1960 the five-year old ITV was already producing at the rate of 3750 hours a year outside London, and the BBC in that year – whether or not under the stimulus of competition – some 1220. It pointed out that every programme company was contractually bound to produce a prescribed number of hours in its own studios. There was to be no 'riding the network'; because in addition to meeting the 'local tastes and interests' requirement, equally important so the Authority believed, was the establishment of centres for local creative endeavour via the new medium in the eleven provincial cities[10] where ITV regional companies had set up their studios. This factor was also an important consideration for the three major companies based outside London, as the Granada evidence, in particular, emphasised.

The ITA also listed some of the locally produced and locally viewed programmes from Anglia, Scottish Television, Southern Television, TWW, Tyne Tees and Ulster. (An additional memorandum had dealt in further detail with the question of the national television service for Wales.) On that evidence these regional companies were producing on a regular weekly basis amounts of regional programming varying, according to their respective size and resources, between five and eleven hours a week. True, when one looked more closely at the detail of this output, some of the programmes – in some cases up to one half perhaps – did not seem to be specially regional in their appeal. But the Authority's memorandum also recorded that in the Midlands the contractors, ABC and ATV, mainly and necessarily occupied in the provision of nationally networked programmes, were between them offering at least five hours a week exclusively for Midlands audiences. A proportion of these local news bulletins and news magazines, local gardening, local farming, local sport, interviews with local personalities and local talent spotting and variety programmes was not of outstanding intellectual or artistic quality. One could perhaps look critically, even sceptically, at the reasons given for placing most of these programmes at 'off peak' times. There could be some justification too for saying certain regional companies should, in circumstances of ever-growing prosperity,[11] have done more for their respective audiences and that this was especially true for the companies appointed to serve the Scottish and Welsh nations. But there is little to support the curiously dismissive attitude adopted by the Pilkington Report towards the regional programmes of Independent Television generally. Still less is it easy to follow the logic of the comment: 'One might have thought . . . that the emphasis would have been much more on regional than on national broadcasting'[12] – if by that the Committee meant that they had actually expected each regional station to devote more hours of its output to local rather than national, networked programmes. In fact, over the system as a whole at the end of the year 1961/2 some 360 separate programmes were being produced each week. Of these 230 were local programmes.

10

PROGRAMME BALANCE

It should be expected of a 'balanced' programme service, as the Report pointed out, that it finds space for a reasonable number of programmes dealing with a variety of different and divergent minority interests, by no means all of them so-called 'high brow'. At the end of Chapter 9 of the Report there are listed some two dozen broad but specialised topics that had been mentioned in communications to the Committee from more than fifty individuals and organisations complaining that their particular interests were getting inadequate coverage on television, and in some cases none at all. The Report did point out that 'within the number of programmes possible, it would not, of course be possible to fulfil all requirements . . . and the claims made for their subject by some of the organisations listed cannot merit much attention'.[1] It went on, however, to recommend that both BBC and ITV should consider how much more they might do to meet such special needs.

One aspect of 'balance' had always been given special importance. In keeping with the moralistic tone adopted by so many vocal public commentators on the mass media, the assumption was consistently made that entertainment needed to be 'balanced' by a suitable proportion of improving material. And such material was identified with programmes of an 'informative and cultural' nature.[2] Over the years the epithet 'serious' was used to apply to those programmes on whose presence in the output 'proper balance' was deemed to depend. This identification was not just a feature of the thinking of the high-minded critics. It was embodied on the initiative of the ITA in the thinking and related programme discussions between it and the companies. Nevertheless, it was in respect of the supply of such 'serious' material that, according to most of the evidence given to Pilkington, and in the apparent judgement of the Committee itself, ITV was most signally failing to provide proper balance.

This failure was seen to apply both to the total quantities of such programmes shown and to the proportions of them screened in peak viewing hours. The Report quoted to this effect evidence from the TUC (sections of the audience with special interests were being ignored); the Radio and Television Safeguards Committee (a failure to serve 'any but the mass audience'); the Society for Education in Film and Television ('a very low proportion of topical, documentary and educational items').[3] Emphasis was laid on the fact that the Safeguards Committee represented a wide range of organisations professionally involved in broadcasting. But no mention was made of the evidence from the Society of Film and Television Arts, also professionals, which, while agreeing that it was 'questionable whether it (ITV) produces the balanced programmes the Television Act requires' also made the point that 'commercial television has clearly been much better than its strongest opponents forecast'.[4] Also unquoted were the comment from the Unitarians that a good episode of *Emergency-Ward Ten* was more worth having than a poor *Panorama*;[5] and a similar one in general terms from the Church of England that statistics showing the amounts of serious programmes were less important than the quality of the programmes, whether serious or light entertainment.[6] On timing, complaints were cited from the National Union of Teachers and the TUC that ITV serious programmes were mainly shown off peak. The Association of Education Committees were quoted as saying that ITV seriously underestimated the public when it put on 'nearly all' its 'better programmes' late at night.[7]

In a reference to the Authority's claim that 'the broad pattern of programmes' was 'reasonably satisfactory in its balance'[8] the Committee said that 'those who have written to us as viewers' believe the contrary.[9] But the list of the names of those individuals and organisations whose memoranda to the Committee on this topic were printed in the second volume of the Report's Appendix appeared to contain few who could be said to be truly writing as typical 'viewers' rather than as spokesmen for certain predictably committed groups or as individuals with specialised interests to defend or propagate. They included, in addition to the religious bodies and nationalist organisations already mentioned, and those listed at the end of Chapter 9 of the Report (e.g. the RIBA, Scottish Ornithologists, English Folk Dance and Song Society, the Amateur Rowing Association, the Automobile Association, the National Anti-Vaccination League etc., etc.) educational bodies such as the Workers' Education Association or the Educational Institute of Scotland, the Northern Ireland College of Education; also the Co-operative Union, the Council for Children's Welfare, Townswomen's Guilds, Women's Institutes, ISBA, the Federation of British Industry and a group of Conservative MPs. Additionally there was a miscellaneous collection of individuals, including Christopher Mayhew MP, Professor

Hilde Himmelweit, Denis Howell MP and Sir Kenneth Clark.

In the nature of things those responding to an open invitation to submit evidence to a Committee of Enquiry will be self-selected and seldom if ever representative of the public at large. In such circumstances it was surely unduly presumptuous of the Pilkington Committee apparently to claim to be offering an objective picture of viewer opinion. For such a claim more scientifically based research would have been necessary; and although they showed themselves ready enough to criticise the broadcasters for their inadequate exploitation of the right kinds of research, they do not seem to have made much use of research evidence in reaching condemnatory judgements. This is not to imply that a broadcasting authority, like any other important social institution, should seek to base and justify its conduct of affairs solely on the findings of social research to the exclusion of considerations of public policy or even of philosophical value judgements. But it is both dishonest and inimical to development of sound workable policies to confuse the two complementary sources of judgement and decision.

And yet, after one has duly discounted the unrepresentative nature of its evidence and the selective use made of this evidence, there was validity and justice in some at least of the criticisms that the Pilkington Committee made of the programme services of ITV. This is not to say that there were not already programmes of outstanding merit in drama, documentary, current affairs and light entertainment (to say nothing of the news and the excellent schools service) but there were not enough of them sustained over the weeks and months or, possibly, transmitted in peak viewing hours to make the necessary impact.

As has been told in Volume 1, there had been a 'retreat from balance' before the looming menace of financial collapse in early 1956, and this had been, however reluctantly, condoned by the Authority. It had meant multiplication, in the main viewing hours, of relatively cheap programmes of wide mass appeal, such as quiz programmes, party games or audience participation shows, as well as a heavy reliance on crime and Western telefilms imported from the United States. Although, as we also saw, there had been since 1957 steady, firm and persistent – and by no means unsuccessful – pressure from the Authority on the companies to re-establish the claims of balance, there was still sufficient of the lightweight things in the output to support the verdict of predominant triviality and even, perhaps, to lend an air of plausibility to Kenneth Clark's pessimism about public taste ('you cannot go low enough') and his fears of a 'Gadarene descent'[10] if the amount of television in Britain were to be increased. And when, as had become increasingly apparent, the turning of the commercial tide had been swollen to a great and increasing tidal wave of profit, the relatively slow return to balance lent some credibility even to the sour comment to the Committee of another former Authority Member, Dr T. J. Honeyman, when he said 'it was frequently stated . . . "we don't want speculators". As it turned out and with mighty few exceptions, that is precisely what we got.'[11]

With two former Authority Members, one of them its distinguished first Chairman, decrying ITV's achievement, it was hardly surprising that the Pilkington Committee was not over-impressed by the Authority's own less hyperbolic exposition of its policies.[12] When for example the Report records what it seems to interpret as conflicting explanations respectively from the Authority and programme companies for the off-peak transmission of serious minority programmes, it was the Authority's version which was deemed unsatisfactory. The Authority was quoted as saying that serious programmes tend to get substantially larger audiences at off-peak times than they do when scheduled in peak: that their placing at such times was therefore considered policy. 'The Authority supported this argument' says the Report, 'by tables showing that Independent Television's programmes shown outside peak hours achieved higher ratings than did BBC programmes shown during peak hours.'[13] For whatever reasons, this piece of written factual evidence from the Authority was not chosen for reproduction in the printed selection of Memoranda submitted to the Committee. It showed for instance that *Panorama* at 8 p.m. was getting a rating of 20, while Granada's *What the Papers Say* at 10.35 p.m. was getting 27; that Kenneth Clark's *Lectures on Art* from ATV were getting at 10.30 p.m. more than three times the rating enjoyed by the BBC's *Monitor* at 10 p.m.. Nowhere in this ITA memorandum was it actually stated that off-peak placings were 'considered policy'. It just gave the facts, including the timing of *This Week* at 8 p.m. with an average rating of 42.

'The evidence of many of the companies' the Report continued, 'suggests another reason . . . that it was commercially inevitable.' Admittedly there followed a qualification: 'By saying that some of the companies recognise these consequences of commercial considerations we imply neither that all did, nor that they saw no other reason. But this explanation was put to us by some companies, and was widely believed to be true.' It does not seem to have been realised that the two explanations were by no means incompatible. Indeed A-R were quoted in support of both explanations: 'Associated-Rediffusion in their written evidence agreed with the Authority; they said that the majority need inevitably had preference in peak hours, then added to our surprise, "it should not be assumed, however, that the most convenient and popular times for viewing on the part of minorities are the same as those for the majorities" '.[14] Why this should be surprising was not explained.

On one more detailed aspect of programme balance, namely the question of the acceptable proportion of foreign (i.e. substantially us) programmes, the Committee showed itself less dogmatic. This could well be because BBC and ITV policies were very similar. A number of organisations representing performers, film makers, writers and musicians made submissions recommending that there should be a statutory quota limit on the amount of foreign material screened. The Report registered sympathy with the objectives of these organisations but concluded that such a measure would not be desirable; controls should remain flexible. It was noted that ITV were showing on average no more than about eight hours per week, amounting to around 12 per cent of total output. On that basis the Committee declared itself satisfied that the requirement of the Television Act relating to 'proper proportion of British material' was being met.

After the passage of time the real truth of the matter can perhaps be seen more clearly. When Pilkington was attempting to assess the programme achievement of ITV, five highly remunerative years had passed since the recession of 1956. As was seen in Volume 1 the proportion of serious programmes was, even before Pilkington reported, virtually as high as it has ever been, before or since; but their impact on the intelligentsia – all light rather than heavy viewers – had been minimal. It seems obvious now that, on grounds of expediency if none other, more of the revenue should have been lavished on programmes and less taken as profit. Or, put another way, some of the immense revenue potential should have been sacrificed in order to present in peak time programmes more conspicuously in harmony with the public service tradition in broadcasting. Through a combination of parsimony and stubborn devotion to the concept of people's television, ITV missed an opportunity to acquire easy merit in the eyes of the Committee. In the long run, as we shall see, the system gained strength from the experience, painful as this proved to be.

TELEVISION VIOLENCE AND THE YOUNG

The Committee was less happy about the content as distinct from the quantity of the imported material. For this was one of the factors which it felt had contributed to public 'disquiet'. Whereas 'dissatisfaction' about ITV was attached by the Committee to the companies' alleged failure to anticipate (and provide for) a wider range of potential interest and enjoyment in their audience, 'disquiet' was attached to the more debatable hypothesis of the television medium's power to influence the minds and behaviour of its viewers. For many of those giving evidence, the objection to the screening of film series from the United States was not simply that they were non-British, but that they seemed to be predominantly either Westerns or crime series. They portrayed acts and scenes of violence; and a lot of this violence was being shown in early evening hours when many children were still viewing. Not all the evidence to the Committee expressed the same level of concern about this problem. The BMA, for example, expressed the belief that the effect on children of TV violence was probably not as great as had been feared; and the NUT also thought some of the fears had been exaggerated, repeating the by-now hackneyed argument that violence portrayed in costume (or in otherwise conventionalised form) was relatively harmless. Yet then, as now, and quite irrespective of the Committee's deliberations, the issue of televised violence and especially its effects on the young, was very much a matter of continuing live public concern.

There had been the 1958 Himmelweit Report (*Television and the Child*) followed by the report of the joint BBC–ITV O'Conor Committee. Although much of the public worry related to the output of both broadcasting services, the Committee was in no doubt that ITV was the more blameworthy. In reaching this conclusion, it cited the evidence of the self-appointed Council for Children's Welfare (CCW), whose memorandum had included an analysis of programmes shown between 6 p.m. and 9 p.m. on both services.

This showed that 'in a week typical of most in the year 1960 the BBC's programme between 6 p.m. and 9 p.m. devoted rather less than one hour to Westerns and rather more than an hour and a half to crime programmes' whereas 'the independent television programme devoted two hours to Westerns and three to crime programmes'. The Pilkington chapter giving an appraisal of the BBC service goes on to note 'Some Westerns are shown in the BBC's programme between 5 p.m. and 6 p.m. but this is children's hour and the Westerns shown during it are usually of the conventional, stylised kind. Provided that there are not too many of these, and that they are counter-balanced by other programmes, these are regarded by the public, the sociologists, and the producers as harmless.'[1]

In the equivalent chapter for ITV no reference at all was made to the possibly greater acceptability of 'stylised' or 'conventional' violence. Both chapters referred to the recommendations of the O'Conor Committee; but it was apparently not considered relevant to record that the preamble to the report was a joint BBC–ITV statement rejecting the proposal for additional machinery in the form of a new permanent joint advisory body; and stating that in the opinion of *both* broadcasting bodies it would be wrong to allow the needs of children to determine the nature of all programmes shown between 6 p.m. and 9 p.m. in 'family viewing' time. Also ignored was the fact that the Authority, before subscribing to the joint statement, had consulted its Children's Advisory Committee, a body whose advice it was statutorily obliged to carry out. Instead the BBC were quoted as saying that they had accepted the O'Conor proposal 'that the period between 6 and 9 each evening be recognised as family viewing time'; and an internal note of guidance to producers of which the BBC issued a summary to the Press in March 1960, was referred to approvingly as a 'code of practice . . . showing active concern to prevent the objectionable portrayal of violence'.[2] It was noted that by contrast the Authority, after discussion in the SCC, had agreed with the companies that programmes before 6 p.m. should be suitable for children, those between 6 p.m. and 7 p.m. 'not unsuitable', and that subsequent programmes should be graded so that 'tough adult programmes' did not appear until after the main news, at 9.25 p.m. The Committee showed itself unimpressed by what it was told about an SCC discussion of the BBC's code,[3] which had concluded with the decision that

the practice of Independent Television could not best be regulated by a written code and that the problems could best be tackled by the directorate and management of the programme companies giving their personal attention to seeing that their producers and other staff concerned with the production and previewing of programmes were aware of company policy[4] and realised that anything of which they were doubtful should be referred for further attention.

The Authority's participation in this decision was described as a 'surrender of authority'.

The Committee did not 'find it easy to understand what the objections to a code are',[5] despite, or regardless of, the considered opinion that had been expressed by the O'Conor Committee:

The experience of the Hayes Code for films in the United States has, however, not always been a happy one and the Committee believes that a written code has certain positive disadvantages. While a code can save time, it can also serve as a scapegoat on to which a producer can pass off his responsibilities. It is only too easy to argue that, because a particular theme is not specifically banned in the code, there is no harm in exploiting it. A code may, therefore, become a shield for irresponsibility and it may become an excuse for the mediocre programme or the programme which plays safe.[6]

The scc decision and the discussion which preceded it faithfully reflected those comments. The Pilkington Committee had every right to disagree with them and give its reasons for doing so; but simply to ignore them and consequently to describe the subsequent decision to leave regulation of practice uncodified as a surrender of authority was scarcely fair or responsible. It might be thought that the least that should have been done would have been to invite Miss O'Conor to elucidate her committee's point of view.

THE IMPACT OF TELEVISION
ON SOCIETY

There seems to have been in the Pilkington Committee a certain predisposition to attribute to the Authority a cavalier disregard of its public responsibilities amounting to positive dereliction of statutory duty. The members had not liked Kirkpatrick's remark to them in his oral evidence that it was an over-simplification to say that television 'would be a main factor in shaping the values and moral attitudes of our society in the next decades',[1] a judgement which they held to be in conflict with the main weight of evidence from other sources, and, so it seems, with their own views. This remark had been bluntly supported in the same oral session by the ITA's Roman Catholic religious adviser, Monsignor G. A. Tomlinson, who considered the statement that television was going to have a profound influence on moral values to be a very exaggerated one. He thought it would be truer to say that it could modify.[2] Nor, in the context of the violence problem did they like the Authority Chairman's statement that television was more likely to reflect life than influence it and that anything reflecting life must reflect violence.[3] The Report also noted – with implied disapproval – two statements, one in a speech by Fraser that 'the test was not . . . whether a play or story contained violence; it was rather its values – the moral values implicit in its presentation. Particular classes of programme must not be dismissed *en bloc*; each programme must be examined on its merits and one must ask if there was humanity in it';[4] and one from Kirkpatrick in oral evidence 'that the portrayal of violence was objectionable if it was out of balance, or placed in a wrong context: it might be objectionable to show to children what was proper to show to adults'.[5]

Neither of these two statements gives much support to a charge of irresponsibility. They would seem to bespeak a greater degree of considered open-mindedness than the Committee itself possessed. How else do we explain its total failure to make any reference to the announcement made in

Parliament by the Home Secretary on 29 March 1962 that the Authority had undertaken – on the initiative of its Chairman – to bear the cost of an enquiry into the effects of television on young people? This offer, which eventually amounted to a total of £250,000 over a period of five years, had been made the previous November in the course of a national conference on crime prevention. In making it Sir Ivone had said: 'I believe we cannot draw conclusions in relation to the damage which television does without much closer examination. But what interests us more is the manner in which we can exercise a positively beneficent influence on our society and about this we know very little.'[6]

Ironically enough, Richard Hoggart, who as we have seen was one of the more influential members of the Pilkington Committee, felt able to write in 1968 in an article for the International Encyclopaedia of the Social Sciences as follows:

> Although television is important and pervasive in its effects on attitudes and behaviour, it is probably not as important as is commonly thought. There are not at present a great many reliable studies on the effects of television, nor are their results definitive . . . television probably cannot change taste radically or upset deep-seated assumptions, but where it follows the grain of personal or social predispositions, it can reinforce them.[7]

It might well have been more politic for the Authority to have at once publicly declared itself committed to the 'family viewing' concept with a watershed at 9 p.m. as the BBC had done. But the factual programme evidence on which the Committee based its case against ITV can scarcely be seen as persuasive. As has been noted, the Report quoted from a memorandum submitted by the CCW which gave tabulated figures comparing BBC and ITV output between 6 and 9 p.m. during one week in 1960. The figures given were:

	Westerns	Crime
ITV	2 hrs 00 mins	3 hrs 30 mins
BBC	50 mins	1 hr 25 mins

However, when the actual programmes that hide behind such figures are named, one sees the unreliability of such simple quantitative analysis. Included in the ITV Westerns, for example, was *Flicka*, a thirty-minute story of a romantic kind about a boy and his horse. And the ITV crime total included two

half-hour transmissions of *Biggles*, a children's adventure story, thirty
minutes of *Knight Errant*, a largely non-violent story about a hero who goes to
the rescue of people in distress, a thirty-minute Douglas Fairbanks romance
with a mild detection interest and the courtroom series *Boyd Q. C.* If those
five programmes were left out, the comparison between the two services in
terms of actual titles for the week in question would be:

ITV Western:	*Cimarron City, Whiplash, Riverboat*
BBC Western:	*Tenderfoot*
ITV Crime:	*Dangerman, Police Surgeon*
BBC Crime:	*RCMP, Portrait of a Murderer, Here Lies Miss Sabry*

These titles would give ITV $1\frac{1}{2}$ hours of Westerns against the BBC's 50
minutes; and ITV's crime 1 hour against the BBC's 1 hour 25 minutes. An ITA
paper dated 29 June 1962[8] following publication of the Pilkington Report
gave an analysis of the output for the two weeks immediately preceding that
date, using the same method of classification adopted by the CCW two years
previously. It showed:

ITV Westerns total:	3 hrs 50
BBC Westerns total:	3 hrs 30
ITV Crime total:	5 hrs 50
BBC Crime total:	6 hrs 55[9]

Such figures might perhaps give credence to the general sense of 'disquiet'
which Pilkington had detected, but they do not support the assertion that
ITV was the main, or only, culprit.

However, the Committee concluded its consideration of the problem of
violence by making just such an assertion and laying the blame at the
Authority's door. 'The Authority cannot, by relying on policies towards
violence of the individual companies, properly discharge its responsibilities.'
It therefore recommended that the Authority should issue if not a Code at
least a clear statement of policy; and that in particular it should also
establish a Family Viewing Time concept whereby all programmes shown
before 9 p.m. would be 'not unsuitable' for children.[10]

Other television programmes apart from those portraying violence were
held to have potentially harmful social (and moral) effects. These included
quizzes, programmes which 'ridiculed or humiliated ordinary people'[11] and
some drama. And here again the Committee was inclined to go along with

its informants in seeing the independent companies as the main culprits. It was not just that programme balance was unsatisfactory, because there were too many 'party games' in the output. The implied moral content of these programmes was felt to be bad. The Committee therefore recommended that quiz programmes with studio participants should have prizes of lower value than the existing £1000 maximum; and that the skill or knowledge required to win should be more closely related to the value of the rewards. This was a view largely shared by the Authority itself. As early as February 1957 the companies had been persuaded to start to reduce the excessive number of programmes with prizes so that by the end of that year Fraser was saying 'we have pulled ourselves together in the matter of cheaply won prizes'.[12] By 5 June 1962, when the Pilkington Report was published, quizzes and panel games occupied on average no more than 2 hours a week on ITV, compared with 75 to 80 minutes on the BBC.[13]

On the more difficult topic of television drama, the Committee was less prepared to draw conclusions. Much of the critical evidence it received lumped together for moral condemnation the triviality of ITV's light entertainment and an alleged preoccupation with 'sordid domestic subjects'[14] in much television drama. The Committee evidently did not accept this assimilation of the two sources of disquiet. Since the dramatist might be presumed to have higher aspirations than those of a mere entertainer, since his aim might be to explore and illuminate the human condition, the members felt it right to concede to him greater freedom to choose his subject matter from those aspects of human experience that moved him most deeply. At the same time, as the Authority and the companies had found, this could well lead at any one time or with any one important group of writers, to concentration on a relatively limited range of topics, and those not always the most attractive or optimistic. Kirkpatrick was quoted in the Report as saying that there had been an undue predominance of 'kitchen sink'[15] plays on ITV; but that as a result of representations made to the companies at the SCC the number of such plays had fallen.

Although it does not seem to have led them to any firm conclusion on which to base a recommendation in their Report, the Pilkington members felt that there was something wrong about the Authority's censorship function in relation to serious drama. They quoted with apparent approval from a submission by Granada which emphasised the separation of Authority staff from the creative activity of production. After looking at the papers relating to one case in which the Authority had made cuts which proved unacceptable to the author,[16] they emphasised the extreme difficulty facing a body which must, though playing no part in the creation of the programmes, exercise a statutory responsibility for censorship – and try to do so, 'without damage to the moral and artistic integrity of a work'.[17]

Having convinced themselves that the ITA lacked a proper sense of social responsibility because it did not appear to share the belief that television would have effects on society comparable with those of nuclear energy, they did not apparently know how to formulate clearly their disapproval of an Authority which chose to show concern (even perhaps *moral* responsibility) over the possible hurt that a specific programme, however meritorious artistically, might inflict not on the Human Race or Society but on individual viewers and fellow citizens. Part of their difficulty arose from the fact that the viewers at home knew when they were being shocked or offended by bad language or unseemly behaviour and were likely to protest. On the other hand, they perversely liked the quiz shows without realising (as their betters seemed to do) that their moral fibre was being destroyed by them.

The Report applauded the BBC's approach to the dilemma of serious but potentially disturbing drama, which was to continue to show such plays but to intersperse them over the year with a sprinkling of more anodyne, less serious-minded productions. The oral evidence demonstrated that the Authority and the companies were in agreement with this approach and it was self-evident from the programmes as published in the journals that such interspersing was taking place. But ITV was accorded no credit similar to that given to the BBC.

13

ADVERTISING

The Pilkington Committee's comments on ITV advertising also clearly reflected its belief in, and consequent anxiety about, the supposedly unique power of the medium to influence and mould the minds and actions of viewers. It emphasised that the ITA's statutory responsibility to maintain so far as possible a high general standard of programmes applied equally to the advertisements. At the same time it had to acknowledge that, because of the mandatory force given by the Act to the recommendations of the Authority's statutory Advertising Advisory Committee, the standards applied in the control of the advertisements had not been established solely by the Authority itself. The Committee did not like this division of responsibility and thought it should end. Further, while welcoming the assurances given by both Authority and programme companies that (although advertising was the dominant source of ITV revenue) it had none the less to be treated as secondary to the main purpose of providing a good public television service,[1] the Committee was less happy with the arrangement which allotted to the companies and their joint 'copy committee' the practical tasks of advance scrutiny and approval of the advertisements offered for transmission, leaving only 'difficult' cases for consideration by the ITA and/or its advisers. It would indicate a greater sense of public responsibility if the ITA's advertising control staff played a more central role. The Authority as the legally appointed controlling body of the ITA service should take full responsibility: should appoint its advisory committees not under statutory compulsion but out of that very sense of responsibility, and should make its own judgements as to the responsible use to be made of their advice.

In any case, it was suggested, that advice would be more to the point if the Advisory Committee had more members representing consumer interests and the number of representatives from the advertising world were correspondingly reduced. The fact that, because of earlier Authority action, three of the six advertising representatives on the original fourteen-member

Committee had been reduced to the status of non-voting 'observers' did not impress. Housewives and mothers 'to whom much advertising is addressed'[2] should also be on the Advisory Committee as well as representatives of special interests such as the British Medical Association.

The Committee was aware that the AAC included a member from the BMA (as well as nominees from the British Dental Association, the Ministry of Health and the Pharmaceutical Society). But it could hardly fail to be struck by the BMA's own evidence, which had been sternly critical of the advertising for proprietory medicines. The Association had said that not only did such advertisements create exaggerated fears of illness and lead to undesirable self medication but they also included misleading and sometimes false claims. Ideally all commercials for drugs, medical treatments and preparations should, they said, be prohibited, and if that were not to be, then no such advertisement should appear before it had been approved by a special panel of doctors. This evidence, when published, raised eyebrows at the ITA, since it seemed to imply either that the BMA had not been kept properly informed by their distinguished representative (Dr Guy Dain) on the Committee or that they were not willing to accept shared responsibility for the decisions of a committee on which he was their nominee.

Moreover, the publication of the BMA evidence had been followed by criticism of all television advertising for medical products by Lord Taylor in a House of Lords debate on 1 March 1961 and by a Commons question on the same subject from George Darling on 17 May 1961. After the Lords debate, the Committee had asked the ITA for its comments on Lord Taylor's strictures. The Authority replied in a lengthy memorandum dated July 1961 describing the procedures for the checking and control of all advertisements for medical products. The memorandum went on to say that immediately after Lord Taylor's speech in the Lords, the Authority had asked the companies urgently to review all medical advertising and their acceptance procedures. Steps had been taken to tighten these up; in future *all* scripts for medical products and treatments would be referred automatically to an appropriate consultant who would have freedom himself to take a second opinion. The AAC had welcomed these steps and Dr Dain had declared himself impressed with the action taken. An abbreviated version of this memorandum was published in Appendix E to the Report. Yet, although the Report itself contained a reference to the BMA criticisms, it made no mention at all of the Authority's response to them.

The 'Principles for Television Advertising' devised nearly three months before the first ITV transmission were accepted as binding on the ITA and the companies. They were intended primarily to achieve exclusion of misleading advertisements of all kinds (not merely medical ones). However, in the light of the evidence it had received, the Pilkington Committee declared itself unconvinced that the principles were not being subtly evaded and that no misrepresentation was taking place. In this it relied not so much on bodies like the Cooperative Union which spoke of 'measures close to direct deceit'[3] as mainly on the evidence of the 'Advertising Inquiry Council'. This body had been orginally set up at the instigation of Mayhew, Francis Noel-Baker and other members of the anti-ITV lobby, but by 1962 it had recruited some Conservative Party members and had appointed Lord Fisher of Lambeth (the former Archbishop) as its chairman. 'The Advertising Inquiry Council told us in oral evidence,' said the Report, 'that it was their impression that 5 to 8 per cent of all advertisements on television were false or misleading and that they were moved to investigate some ten to twelve new cases each week.'[4] One might perhaps detect a note of mild scepticism in the Report's comment: 'There are of course no statistics showing how many advertisements do in fact infringe the Principles'. Some scepticism about the Inquiry Council's 5 to 8 per cent, or the validity of the ten to twelve weekly complaints seems justified since, with the exception of two advertisements which had been withdrawn three years earlier, there had been no specific mention either to the Authority or to anyone else of any of the other advertisements concerned.

Nevertheless, the Pilkington Committee concluded that the belief of the Authority and companies that the ban on false or misleading claims was being very well observed was too sanguine. Unless the most exacting standards were observed, the Principles would come to be of little value. The most difficult cases were when claims were not expressly made but were there for the viewers to infer. The Authority should not rely on several statements of principle, leaving to the companies' copy committee their practical implementation. Case law was of overriding importance and should be formulated by the Authority itself. 'We recommend therefore that the Authority should assume effective control of the work of the Copy Committee.'[5]

The impression conveyed in this as in some other cases is that the Committee was saying – not in so many words, of course – 'This may or may not be an accurate description of the facts, but it is clearly what responsible individuals or organisations say they believe to be the case'. It was probably inevitable, given the method it had adopted for collecting its evidence, that it should have relied so much on hearsay, out-of-date information and imperfect memories, and sometimes indeed on proffered judgements and opinions designed more with the aim of supporting the public image of the witness than of clarifying the facts. Such a method of work certainly left the Committee considerable freedom to interpret and use the evidence in the light of its own philosophy. But it was not always likely to do fair justice to all the activities of a relatively new public institution which was still discovering problems and dilemmas inherent in its public task and exploring ways, not always unsuccessfully, of overcoming them. It is therefore worth noting that when it came to report on the Authority's control over the amount, frequency and incidence of television advertising the Committee was disposed to give credit where it was due in spite of some of the critical evidence that it received.

As we saw in Volume 1, the Authority had settled for a ration of six minutes of advertising an hour but had decided that this figure could be averaged over a day's broadcasting. Averaging, as some critics were not slow to point out, could lead to the transmission of much more than six minutes in peak hours where the charges to advertisers were high. In reply the ITA pointed out that the need to exclude advertisements from some programmes and the fact that some programmes offered better opportunities than others for 'natural breaks' made averaging unavoidable. The Committee found this reasonable. It also noted with approval that after the first two years (1955–7) (and as the demand for advertising time had grown) the maximum allowed by the Authority in any one 'clock hour' had been progressively reduced from eight minutes in 1958/9 to seven-and-a-half minutes in September 1960 and by the end of that year to seven minutes.

The practical interpretation of the term 'natural break' (as the appropriate place in a programme for the showing of advertisements) had come in for criticism, which was repeated in some of the evidence submitted to the Committee. But here again the Report duly recorded that the Authority had already reacted to such criticism and had tightened up its controls. The Committee agreed that to forbid the use of the 'natural break' could well increase the number of short programmes ('which would be bad') but added that the definition of a 'natural break' should be kept under constant review 'subject to the overriding needs of good broadcasting'.[6]

On two further advertising issues, one general and the other concrete and specific, the Committee declared itself in flat opposition to ITV principles and practice.

The general issue arose from what might be described as a conflict of philosophies. As we have seen, the Committee, in its essay on the Purposes of Broadcasting, had declared that 'television does not, and cannot, merely reflect the moral standards of society. It must affect them, either by changing or by reinforcing them.'[7] It therefore concluded that many advertisements, by projecting what it regarded as a false picture of the world and undesirable models of behaviour, were bound to have a socially undesirable effect. Quoting in support the evidence it had received from educational bodies like the NUT and the WEA, it deplored the ready acceptance in the TV commercials of 'discreditable' human impulses like acquisitiveness, snobbery, uncritical conformity, 'keeping up with the Joneses'; and those portrayals of happy homes where the happiness, it seemed to be implied, depended on the possession of the products advertised. The Report registered the Committee's disappointment that neither the Authority nor the company representatives, when challenged orally on this matter, accepted the validity of the criticism. Fraser 'rejected absolutely the view that the image of a way of life portrayed by television advertisements was regrettable'.[8] Company spokesmen 'could see nothing wrong in an advertisement which, for example, showed family affection or a happy home so as the better to sell a product'.[9] The Committee for its part concluded that advertisements which appeal to what it described as 'human weakness' 'could well in the long run have a deplorable individual and social effect'.[10] It consequently recommended a revision of the Authority's Advertising Principles so as to prevent the acceptance of such advertisements. But it then went on, with becoming and overdue modesty, to 'recognise the difficulty of drawing up a watertight code to prescribe advertisements of a kind which can never be precisely defined'.[11]

In the specific case of the Advertising Magazines the Committee was on more solid ground. These broadcasts figured in the ITV output by virtue of several references in the Parliamentary debates on the Television Bill (as well as in the 1953 White Paper) to 'shoppers' guides'. The Authority had decided to allow programme companies to transmit one of these per day; and (more important as the demand for advertising air time began to grow) not to count them against either of the six minutes hourly average or the seven-minutes maximum in any one hour. But there was from the start a virtually insoluble dilemma implicit in the whole concept. The Television Act had stated unequivocally that advertisements should be clearly distinguishable from programmes. To justify their designation as a distinct and special category, the goods or services advertised in the 'magazines' had to be related in some way, e.g. by being all of one kind, related to one area of use, or obtainable only in one store, and this interrelationship was to be made clear by the linking presentation. In several cases presentation was done by well-known television performers whose familiar, recognisable voices and personalities served to give the item an additional cohesion and conviction (occasionally in a near fictional or even semi-documentary setting). According to the Authority's earliest formulation of the rules, the linking material itself did not need to 'look like advertising' and could legitimately serve the purpose of *'more effectively commending the product(s) to the audience'*; at the same time it should not be such that it *'could only be reasonably said to serve the purpose of attracting a larger audience'*.

In order to make the distinction between advertising magazines and normal programmes more complete, it was initially insisted that the linking material as well as the naming and descriptions of the products should be paid for by the advertisers. This requirement, which was subsequently relaxed, gave formal expression to the distinction between advertisement and programme but did little to remove the appearance of sponsorship. On the contrary. There can be little doubt that, however carefully they were labelled, the more successful advertising magazines were seen (even enjoyed) as *programmes* by at least some viewers. The Authority's own evidence to the Committee had actually described advertising magazines as 'a form of advertising which could be so intrinsically interesting as to attract an audience in its own right'.[12]

Considering the kind of tightrope act the companies were expected to perform[13] it is hardly surprising that over the years there had been repeated public criticisms of advertising magazines and repeated attempts by the Authority and its officers to redefine the position in both practically workable and legally defensible terms.[14] During the first three years of ITV several hundred advertising magazines were screened. But the underlying dilemma persisted. The more plausible and 'intrinsically interesting' the linking theme of an advertising magazine was, the more readily it would resemble a programme and incur, however unjustifiably, the charge of programme sponsorship. The less plausible the theme and the less effective the linking, the more the magazine would seem to be no more than a bunch of unrelated spot advertisements which should rightly be counted against the daily allowance for such.

By the end of 1961, in fact, companies were already finding it increasingly difficult to produce 'themed' magazine programmes.[15] They did, however, continue to regard the magazines as an important element in their advertising, and insisted on their continuing popularity with viewers. They were, therefore, most reluctant in their acceptance of the Authority's decision taken at that time to allow no more than three per week because, in the Authority's words, 'it has not been possible for the companies to develop this form of advertising along the distinctive lines envisaged by Parliament and by the Authority when it allowed for magazines in addition to the spot advertising quota'.[16] It was probably true that, as the Report said, by the time the Committee started work many advertising magazines were merely strings of advertisements – in some cases only distinguishable from spot advertisements because the same voice and same person appeared throughout.

Among those giving evidence to the Committee on this subject was the Authority's first Chairman. He said they were, in effect, sponsored television and 'he strongly recommended that they should be forbidden in any new Act'.[17] The Committee itself concluded that even if the magazines were within the letter of the Act, they offended against its spirit. It therefore recommended their prohibition, uncompensated by any increase in the time allowed for 'spot' advertising, and the recommendation was subsequently implemented by a formal direction from the PMG. They had survived as hostages to fortune for too long.

14

MORE CHANNELS AND
LONGER HOURS?

As has been seen the Committee's chosen method was to solicit facts and opinions from spokesmen for the broadcasting bodies and from whatever individuals or organised groups responded to an open invitation to give 'evidence', and then compare what it had thus learned with the definition its members had collectively reached of the 'purposes of broadcasting'. Theoretically at least, any desirable changes or further developments in the broadcasting services should follow self-evidently from such a comparison. The flaw in this approach was that evidence submitted by groups and organisations (usually established for purposes not related to broadcasting) did not necessarily reflect accurately the attitudes and expectations of the general public as consumers of broadcasting. The Committee might, of course, have enlisted the aid of social scientists as Barbara Wootton was to suggest later in a letter to *The Times*[1] – to provide it with apparently verifiable objective data on which to base judgements and recommendations. This it chose not to do.

Some half dozen of the companies, as well as the ITA, gave their views of the future. The ITA memorandum of November 1960 on the subject was in tune with the motives that had led to the creation of Independent Television in 1954: that is to say those very classical liberal impulses that had brought an end to monopoly required that any future extension of broadcasting should lead to more diversity and more competition between mutually independent providers.[2] As we saw in the previous volume, when it created the national pattern of ITV transmitters and programme contractors, the Authority felt it to be an unwelcome (and, it hoped, temporary) impediment that the frequencies at its disposal prohibited it from bringing about any more than the limited degree of competition in the supply of programmes that could arise from the weekday–weekend split between companies serving the three central areas from London, Birmingham and

Manchester. Its long-term expectation had been to have more than one competing programme provider in the main transmission areas, and its preferred solution to the problem of the 'scandalously' high profits of the ITV companies was more competition. More companies competing for advertising revenue would inevitably mean lower profits. Such had been its response to the criticisms of the Public Accounts Committee. To Pilkington it emphasised that 'the principles of independence and separation'[3] were more important than the form any additional services might take. A first step should be the creation of a third service (for which the VHF frequencies were now available) on the decentralised pattern of the existing ITV service, for which the programmes would come from new independent competing providers. However, the evident need for uniformity of standards in such matters as 'good taste', 'due impartiality', 'offence to public feeling', permitted amounts of imported foreign material, as well as the probable need 'within limits' for some degree of coordination to ensure wider programme choice did point towards a common supervisory body, which could well be the ITA itself.

As for future technical possibilities the Authority had first argued that a change from the 405-line to the 625-line picture and the introduction of colour should be delayed to 'some point within the next ten years'. But in a later memorandum of July 1961, it expressed a radically different view. Since it had become evident that the UHF Bands IV and V would have room for four and not three services (as had previously been believed), it would be better, the Authority now thought, to plan for a change-over to a 625-line colour service as soon as possible. Three of the four services should be general interest ones (BBC plus two on the ITV competitive, self-supporting pattern). The fourth should be a specialised educational service, directed and controlled not by an existing broadcasting organisation but by educational bodies, financed in part at least by public funds and so constituted as to be, like the educational system itself, plural and decentralised. It should, however, not be used as a pretext for reducing the proportion of serious 'cultural' material on the three general services. Particular attention was drawn to the use being made of ETV in the United States. Although there were important fundamental differences between the educational systems of the two countries, the ITA suggested that the American example demonstrated that a service exploring the great potential of the audio-visual medium could make an important contribution to British education at all levels, both locally and nationally: and would be more in the national interest than a fourth general service. What the memorandum did not go out of its way to explain was that adoption of such a plan would successfully block BBC aspirations to expand with a complementary second service of their own.

The BBC reacted sharply and critically.[4] The ITA proposals were, they said, based on misconceptions and 'open to serious disadvantages', not least because they gave no room for the second BBC service which the Corporation wished to 'provide in order properly to fulfil its obligations under its Charter and, in particular, to meet the needs of educational broadcasting as they develop'. Indeed such development could well ultimately justify, they went on, a third national BBC service. The commercial, self-supporting third service proposed by the Authority would not lead to greater diversity and range of viewer choice. This was clearly illustrated by the results of competition between commercial networks in the United States: 'monotony and limited range of programmes'. On the other hand, the allocation to the BBC of a second network would make possible 'planned alternative programmes', giving viewers a genuine choice such as was not possible in the competitive situation then existing and which would be even less possible, were there to be an additional competing commercial service. The ITA's reference to North American ETV was misleading. These American educational programmes were inadequately financed, viewed by minute audiences and of very poor quality. In the view of all competent educationalists, educational broadcasting in Britain should remain part of the general services (as foreseen by the Charter) and not segregated as the ITA proposal would imply.

The Pilkington Committee was to find no difficulty in concluding that the BBC had had the better of the argument. Thus was born the doctrine of 'complementarity', against which the later Annan Committee's plan for an Open Broadcasting service under a new Authority was to founder.

Faced with proposals for a third television service the Government might well have considered that a possible (if by no means wholly satisfactory) compromise could be an extension of the permitted hours of broadcasting on the existing channels. The Pilkington Committee acknowledged this possibility when it recorded the view that the PMG should retain powers to prescribe broadcasting hours, because it remained a government responsibility to decide what proportion of national resources should be devoted to broadcasting. But the Committee also recorded a marked difference of opinion between broadcasters and those claiming to speak for listeners and viewers on the question of an increase in permitted hours. Few of the latter advocated increase; many doubted its desirability. The BBC had told the Committee they wanted hours of television to be extended step by step in a carefully planned fashion over the years 'to give priority to particular needs and opportunities as they arose, and to ensure against any falling away of standards'.[5] They looked forward to an increase over the period 1964–70 from about sixty hours on one BBC service to a total of about a hundred hours on two. They did not think it was necessary to maintain exact parity of total hours between themselves and ITV, but they were opposed to any 'wide disparity' which could operate to their disadvantage. So their approach was markedly more cautious than that of the ITA and the companies, which was one of outright opposition to restrictive limitations on the freedom of the media of public communication.

As long ago as June 1958 the Authority, in agreement with the companies, had asked the PMG to authorise an increase in the basic daily allowance from eight hours to eleven. More recently in February 1960 a modest request had been made for an extra half hour per day plus the addition to those programme categories (school broadcasts, religious programmes, live outside broadcasts, and broadcasts in the Welsh language) for which extra broadcasting hours were already permitted,[6] of adult education programmes, repeats of school broadcasts outside school hours, Parliamentary reports and recorded outside broadcasts. The BBC had agreed to the request for an extra half hour per day but did not favour the proposed additions to the exempted categories, on the grounds that they should properly be regarded as part of a balanced general service, not as extras. No doubt a more weighty factor was the assumption that more hours for the Corporation meant more expense; whereas more hours for the ITV companies meant more potential advertising revenue.

However, the PMG had explained that the Government was unwilling to approve any change in the hours rules in advance of the report of the Pilkington Committee. It was abundantly clear that for the time being no useful purpose would be served by pursuing the matter further with the Government.[7] ITV was thus reduced to waiting on the Pilkington response to the case for greater freedom put to it by the ITA, ABC, ATV and Granada. The ITA had said that it could see 'no reason in the public interest why it should not extend the hours of transmission ultimately to the hours of the present sound service';[8] it did not think limitation to some eight hours a day (as against seventeen to eighteen hours for sound radio) could be justified merely on the grounds that the BBC 'might not . . . be able to increase its hours correspondingly'. The aim of television, after all, was not that one service should win an advantage over another, but to provide the public with programmes which they may or may not view according to their free choice. The memorandum went on to draw attention to those sections of the population who could be served by additional hours of day time television:

housewives, shift-workers, the retired and those on holiday. The same point was made in more sweeping terms by ATV in their claim to be allowed 'to broadcast programmes at any hour throughout the day when there is evidence to show that an interested audience is available'.[9] ABC were more specific, advocating extra hours in the earlier part of the day to be used for morning news bulletins, specialised programmes and above all adult education. Granada's case rested on the opportunity they would have to serve minority interests (unavoidably crowded out by the majority looking for entertainment in peak evening hours); and the wider training ground thus afforded for burgeoning talents among writers, performers and production teams.

In the event, the conclusions of the Committee proved to be against anything more than a 'moderate' increase.[10] In its view, the provision of additional complementary services would better serve the viewing public and the 'purposes of broadcasting'[11] than would any substantial increase over the eight to nine hours daily on the existing services (which could 'hardly be regarded as scarcity').[12] Moreover, in the interests of competition in good broadcasting between the two systems they recommended that 'there should not be a marked disparity between the number of hours for which each of the two competing systems is allowed to broadcast'.[13] The Report gave no support to the proposed increase in the 'exempted categories' with the exception of adult education programmes, provided they could be closely enough defined as genuinely instructional broadcasts, that is rather than generally informative (or educative) ones.

Suggestions from the companies about the future were limited to proposals for the third (VHF) channel, as were those from virtually all the other bodies, educational, professional, religious and commercial which also gave evidence on this topic. There is no indication of any attempt on the part of the companies to agree a collective view with one another, let alone with the ITA. Diversity was the order of the day.

Two of the companies and the National Broadcasting Development Committee (the successor to the Popular Television Association) supported the idea of a second commercial service competing in each area for audience and advertising. Significantly the two companies were ATV and TWW, which respectively included in their managements those early pioneers of commercial television, Collins and Chapman–Walker. A Liberal Party memorandum took the same view. It was also the preferred solution of the IPA, as well as a group of Independent Conservatives and the Association of British Chambers of Commerce who were anxious to break the monopoly in the sale of television advertising. Southern Television (and the Rank

Organisation) thought that existing transmitter areas would need to be redrawn so as to achieve seven-day companies of approximately equal size; otherwise the introduction of a second commercial competitor could prove disastrous for smaller regional companies. Ulster Television were not certain they would remain viable if faced with a commercial competitor.

ABC Television agreed that the Third Channel should be a commercial one financed by advertising, but they emphasised the heavy losses it would have to carry before it became viable and they urged the Committee not to recommend a further channel unless they were convinced it was necessary. A-R too had doubts about the need for another channel. If it were to be established they said, it should be designed to create an additional and hence wider range of programme choices for significant minorities than was so far possible. The programmes should come, they proposed, from both the BBC and the ITV companies, the latter recovering their costs from advertising also designed for particularly minority tastes and interests.

Anglia agreed that the third service should be made up of programmes from both the BBC and ITV; but they believed it should be a minority, cultural channel not financed by advertising and controlled by an independent non-profit organisation. Joint BBC–ITV programming was suggested in several submissions including those from the Church of England and the Congregationalists, and it was a feature of the much more radical and ingenious proposal from the ISBA. The Society held that a separate channel serving minorities was undesirable because it would tend to segregate minority interests and thus lead to impoverishment of the other services. They suggested instead *three* commercial channels. The three transmitters in each region would each carry equal amounts of programming (in terms of hours) from the BBC and two commercial companies. There would be a supervising and coordinating authority to ensure fair shares of peak time. It would be open to the BBC to carry advertisements if they wished; if not there would still be no need to increase the licence fee because the Corporation would not be producing more hours even though its programmes were appearing on three competing channels. Such an arrangement, said the Society's memorandum, would offer the viewer genuine balanced services. This was clearly preferable to competition between an all-BBC and two wholly commercial channels, since these would inevitably be competing for the majority audience most, if not all, of the time. Granada declared their opposition to a segregated 'cultural channel'[14] but thought the universities should have access to a channel of their own in order better to serve their wide and growing social responsibilities. The company did not doubt that such a University Channel could count on programme offerings from the BBC and other ITV companies, as well as Granada: but they could see no valid reason why it should not carry advertising.

Most of the suggestions about the future dealt, as can be seen, with the relatively simple questions of the need, nature, allocation and financing of a third service for which it was assumed the necessary frequencies were already available. The consensus view was that a further service was needed, although in the case of one or two of the religious bodies – as in the case of one or two of the ITV companies – this agreement was qualified and reluctant. Most wanted the extra programmes to offer something different. Yet whilst this clearly seemed to mean more variety of choice, more for minorities, more education, and, in some cases, of a higher cultural level there was little enthusiasm for a specialised channel. Few went so far as the County Councils Association in rejecting the idea of an additional balanced service in favour of one addressed to the 'peaks of our common culture'.[15] The Society for Film and Television Arts said that, 'Culture need not be the watchword, but intelligence should'.[16] Even the Royal Society, which of course wanted more specialised science programmes, did not favour putting them all on the new channel. Rather should the extra air time thus gained be used to achieve a higher proportion of science in the schedules of all three services. Opinions were divided on the question whether greater variety would come from planned complementarity or from more competition, although it was only a few who supported the latter. It was noteworthy that the television professionals like the SFTA, the screenwriters, ACTT and Equity (*and* Christopher Mayhew) while being in varying degrees critical of the ITA service, did not favour giving the new channel to the BBC. ('Not bold enough', 'too big already', 'too bureaucratic' and 'Establishment'.) But the ITA had even fewer friends. Even the group of Independent Conservatives saw the two competitive commercial channels it recommended as operating under a strengthened, re-organised Authority because 'in our view the ITA have not used their powers under the Television Act of 1954 as effectively as they should'.[17] Sir Kenneth Clark 'told us that the introduction in 1964 of a third service financed from advertising would be the worst of all things to do'.[18]

However, Sir Harry and his colleagues had too strong a belief in the power of the broadcast media and their potential influence for cultural, social and moral good to accept the status quo. Whereas the Authority had looked forward to the establishment of four separate television services, the Committee was prepared to contemplate no fewer than six. Four of these would be on 625 lines in the UHF bands.[19] The other two would come later when, after an interval of some years in which output was duplicated to allow for gradual obsolescence of 405-line receivers in viewers' homes, the channels carrying the two 405-line VHF services became vacant. But for the time being they were concerned to make recommendations about the third and fourth services. The former should be given to the BBC; the latter, ultimately, *and only after far-reaching structural and operational changes*, to the ITA.

It seemed evident to the members of the Pilkington Committee that given the dissatisfaction they had recorded with the range and variety of the existing television services, the most pressing future need was the creation of another general channel. Both British broadcasting tradition and the Committee's own understanding of 'purposes of broadcasting' implied a comprehensive service. The subject matter of broadcasting was in principle all-embracing; and each of the two public corporations was to treat all of it. But if the two additional services were to be in the UHF Bands IV and V, there would still be the available frequencies for another service in VHF Band III. The Committee did not think it sensible to use them for a national service which would also have to be duplicated over the transitional period in UHF. Instead, it concluded, on grounds of practicality and fair dealing, that the unallotted frequencies in Band III should be used to allow the BBC to establish a separate service for Wales under the supervision of the BBC's National Broadcasting Council for Wales. If that were done there would be no need to readjust the structure of ITV in order to provide another exclusively Welsh service on the commercial channel. The aspirations of the other two national regions should be satisfactorily met by the local adjustment of the two national services to permit the inclusion of more material of specifically Scottish or Northern Irish interest. The same should be done for the English Regions. The Committee omitted to note how much provision for the three 'national' areas had already been made through the deliberately re-gionalised structure of Independent Television. Even if it was less than might ideally be wished for, it was significantly more than anything the BBC had so far shown itself prepared to do.

Subject to that limited degree of local flexibility, the recommendation was for additional national services of a non-specialised comprehensive nature; and this should mean the continued inclusion of educational broadcasts for schools and adult learners. The ITA proposal for an educational channel was rejected. The development of such a service would, in the opinion of the Committee, 'strike at the concept of education (in both the specific and general senses we have described) as a purpose of all services of broadcasting'.[20] The importance and scale of ETV in the United States and the relevance of American experience to British conditions had been exaggerated.

Such an additional comprehensive service would best serve the 'purposes of broadcasting', the BBC had said, if it were planned to be complementary to an existing service in such a way that the audience would have a wider range of choice through the regular offer of simultaneous alternatives. The Committee dismissed the Authority's contrary proposition that diversity was more likely to appear as the result of competition between independent providers rather than from coordinated planning of two services by the same people. The Authority had said that, thanks to competition, there was already enough diversity of choice to satisfy the ordinary, non-specialist viewer. All that was needed was the contribution of more independently creative approaches to the same wide range of material.

The Report declared that the ITA's claim was in total conflict with the weight of evidence the Committee had received to the effect that the range was not nearly wide enough. 'This was a major criticism and probably the view most generally held.' It was 'the widely held view that an effect of competition had been to narrow the range of the BBC's programming'.[21] The BBC themselves always strenuously contested this verdict.

However, the Pilkington Committee was probably right in its criticism of the Authority's generalised use of the concept of competition to cover a variety of discrete things – competition in the world of ideas, competition for a major share of the audience and competition in the sale of advertising time. An extension of this last form of competition would be a practical measure for reducing the excessive profits of those enjoying a monopoly of television advertising time; but the ITA conflated these different connotations of the word competition in order to argue that there was a causal connection between competitive broadcasting and increased programme diversity. Such an increase had certainly occurred since the coming of Independent Television in spite of the contrary evidence on which Pilkington relied, and it is not certain that it would have done so had the BBC been left with their monopoly. However, this was attributable not only to the arrival of competition itself, but to the structure for Independent Television which, within the framework of the Act, had been devised. In other countries and in different circumstances, the existence of competitive services had led to quite different results.

Convinced by their perception of the Authority's faulty reasoning on the one hand, and the misleadingly inaccurate evidence they had chosen to accept on the other, the Pilkington Committee decided to recommend an early start for an additional 625-line UHF service planned and produced by the BBC to extend and complement the national service already provided by BBC 1. It rejected the various ideas for an additional broadcasting authority or for joint programming between the Corporation and ITV, agreeing with the BBC's contention that proper complementarity could be achieved only by a single planning and producing body. At the same time, however, the Committee, notwithstanding its ill-concealed dislike of advertising, was, as we have seen, prepared to recommend the allocation in due course of a second UHF channel to the ITA, provided the Authority was enabled to play a much more dominant role in the processes whereby programmes reach the screen. To achieve this Independent Television would need to be 're-constituted and reorganised'. All possibility of evolutionary change was rejected. 'We can find nothing in the present circumstances of independent television to suggest that its failings are those of an organisation needing only time to correct them . . . They are not curable by adding to the existing specific controls.' Further progress along the course set in the previous seven years was not enough. 'Organic changes . . . are necessary.'[22]

15

'ORGANIC CHANGE'

The Pilkington Committee had been disposed to accept the accusations levelled against the Authority by several of those giving evidence that it had failed to live up to its public responsibilities and was not in effective control of the ITV service. All too often, it was said, the Authority had appeared in the subordinate and undignified role of a public relations spokesman defending, even extolling, what were seen as the misdeeds of its programme contractors. The Committee was not persuaded that the Authority exercised the necessary degree of responsible control over what appeared on the screen, either in the form of programmes or advertisements. From the evidence received and from the responses of ITA spokesmen to its questions, there was no escaping the conclusion that the Authority did not fully accept its own understanding of the purposes of broadcasting; and that to the extent that it did, it was either unable or unwilling to exercise the control over the programme contractors necessary in order to bring about a more adequate realisation of those purposes. The range of programme experience available to British viewers had been impoverished rather than enriched since the coming of ITV: too much material of doubtful social, moral or aesthetic value was being transmitted both in programmes and in advertisements, some of it even definitely harmful.

Moreover the plural, decentralised organisation that the Authority had created for Independent Television had not brought about a service displaying the hoped for variety and diversity of character and attitude. On the contrary, on the Authority's own admission, the networking structure that had grown up had not brought about a free trade among programme contractors in buying and selling programmes leading to the adequate competition in programme supply required by the Act. Nor could it be contended that the system of affiliations established between the major and the minor companies was wholly in keeping with the requirement for competition between a number of companies independent of each other as to finance and control. The Committee conceded that even in a decentralised plural system some form of networking was unavoidable, because no one programme contractor was likely to have the resources to provide a full service and because it was essential that the best productions should be available to all, irrespective of where they were produced. But the networking system being operated under the Authority did not in practice provide the requisite ITA control. Networking was manipulated by the Big Four under a minimum of constraint.

It was recognised that in one important respect the Authority had already gone beyond the insufficient regulatory powers given to it by the Act. In a proviso to Section 6(1) of the Act, the Authority's powers to demand advance information about programmes, and to forbid the broadcasting of any material it considered unsuitable, had been made conditional on the Authority 'apprehending' a breach of the Act. Such anticipation of a 'sin of commission' was, as the Report put it, 'seldom possible'.[1] So in the course of actual workaday practice there had been established between the companies and the Authority's staff a regular flow of advance programme information, as a matter of routine. In its evidence the Authority had asked that any new (or amending) legislation should give this practice unconditional statutory force. But since such a change would merely regularise existing practice, the Committee thought it of small importance. Existing practice was after all producing the service of which they so clearly disapproved.

In the view of the Committee the failings of the ITV service were an unavoidable consequence of the way in which it was organised. No real improvement would be possible until the relationship between Authority and companies had been radically changed. Since the Authority's role was a largely negative, regulatory one, the creative production and planning functions being left to the companies, it followed that everything depended on the Authority's initial assessment and appointment of its contractors. It had to choose applicants who, in its judgement, would be prepared and able to provide good programmes while seeking to earn by the sale of advertising time sufficient money to pay not merely the costs of those programmes but also reasonable dividends to their shareholders. They would, however, be expected to be above all prepared if need be to subordinate their natural commercial propensity to maximise profits to the claims of good broadcasting. Risks of the abandonment of good intentions would be less real if the sanctions that the Authority could impose on offenders were stronger: the power to impose fines of £500, £1000 or £1500 for successive confirmed breaches of the Act was utterly derisory. The ultimate sanction in the power to terminate a contract was also of little practical significance because it was unlikely ever to be used. A suggestion made by the Authority that there should be shorter-term contracts might be a help, but only if the possibility of non-renewal were seen to be a genuine one. To all intents therefore 'the appointment of a programme contractor is virtually irrevocable; and once appointed a contractor cannot be effectively disciplined'.[2]

Whereas the Director General had said that he and his colleagues had no difficulty in securing through persuasive advice the compliance of a programme company with the decisions of the Authority, the Committee pointed to the evidence of a widespread public feeling that the Authority was not in effective control. It was a mistake for it to regard the companies as its partners in pursuit of a common purpose. As guardian of the public interest the Authority should have the role of master employing the companies as its agents. But this could not be brought about within the existing structure, merely by increasing or strengthening the Authority's regulatory powers. As long as companies were expected to realise the 'purposes of broadcasting', whilst at the same time ensuring their success as commercial enterprises, there would be conflicting aims to reconcile.

The Committee's reasoning did not stop at that. In broadcasting at any rate, the notion that commercial success would in the long run depend on the provision of a good service to the consumer was only partially true. More often than not, the primary functions of a broadcasting service would, when choices had to be made, be subordinate to the protection or maximisation of profits. Even to place the overall programme planning function in the hands of the Authority would not be enough so long as the programme contractors were the sellers of advertising time. Real and effective power, commensurate with its public responsibilities, would belong to the Authority only if it were also the advertising salesman. Independent Television should therefore be reconstituted so that the Authority would plan the overall pattern and content of the programme schedules; and would sell advertising time and have total responsibility for the nature and content of the advertisements it accepted for transmission. Programme companies would produce for the Authority, against suitable payment, the programme items to be included in the schedule planned by the Authority; and any surpluses earned by the system thus reconstituted would accrue to the Authority, which would pay them to the Exchequer.

Such fundamental 'organic' changes would ensure the elimination of all the major and minor failings of which ITV stood charged. A programme company's success would henceforward depend on its ability to produce 'good programmes', that is programmes consonant with the Authority's dedication to the purposes of broadcasting. In the existing arrangements, only the Authority and the producers employed by the companies were interested in good programmes while the company administrative staffs had the continuing problem of reconciling the aspirations of their creative people with the commercial success of their companies. ITA administrators would have to face no such division of interests because they would have no commercial motivation. They would nevertheless continue to secure all the revenue the system needed because the Authority would be, like the companies, a monopoly seller of advertising. But the problem of excessive company profits arising from their monopoly would no longer arise.

The Committee believed that even under its proposed new order, advertising revenue would continue to grow; and that this would happen even if the ITV audience were reduced by the advent of a second BBC service. It would eventually be sufficient to support a second ITV service. And a second ITV service organised in this new way would no longer pose the threat to survival of the smaller regional companies, fears of which had been voiced in the evidence of Ulster Television and Anglia, for example. What the Committee regarded as the Authority's very reasonable wish to have the right to fuller information about the programme companies' costs would also no longer be a problem. It would, moreover, also find itself with the funds necessary to conduct the technical and audience research which it should have done and had so far failed to do. Finally, the nature and composition of the companies would be no longer of such crucial importance once the Authority – company relationship had been changed.

It is difficult to understand why a Committee which had attributed such importance to the initial appointment of the companies should decide that the nature and composition of those companies would be no longer of such crucial importance once the Authority–company relationship had been changed. The companies would after all still be making the programmes and making them (under Pilkington's more detailed proposals) with the *contractual guarantee of a minimum take* of their products by the Authority. It might well be asked whether some guarantee against having to choose between unsatisfactory programmes and blank screens was not of fairly crucial importance to a broadcasting authority.

16

NEWSPAPER INTERESTS

The issue of press participation in the television companies was seen by the Pilkington Committee as a subsidiary matter. A reader of the Report might even have taken away the impression that the Committee dealt with it primarily because the issue was raised by the Government. A letter of February 1961 from the PMG to the Committee had posed for its consideration the question 'whether control over newspapers and television stations should be vested in the same hands'.

The decade of the 1950s had witnessed an increasing concentration of newspaper ownership into ever fewer hands. In 1960 Associated Newspapers purchased the *News Chronicle*. By 1961 the three main newspaper empires (Beaverbrook Newspapers, Associated Newspapers and the *Daily Mirror* Group) controlled 65 per cent of total newspaper circulation in Britain. Shortly after the merger in 1961 of Odhams (publishers of the *Daily Herald*) into the *Mirror* Group, the Government set up a Royal Commission on the Press under Lord Shawcross with terms of reference which, *inter alia*, invited examination of the revenue derived from television as one of the factors tending to 'diminish diversity of ownership and control'.

If the Committee held that large press holdings in television companies were of secondary importance, the Authority (and not a few of its critics) certainly did not. Its memorandum to Pilkington dated April 1961 explicitly recognised the concern that must inevitably be felt 'lest the means of communication should fall into fewer hands than would be consistent with the needs and nature of a free society'.[1] Indeed, as we have seen, the informing principle of its creation of the decentralised, plural ITV system had been a similar concern to ensure as much 'diversity, variety and independence' as limited broadcasting frequencies could allow in a means of communication at least as important as the press. Equally, and for similar reasons, the Authority had striven to ensure, as its memorandum also pointed out, that, so far as possible and other things being equal, the programme companies it appointed had a 'diversified and multiple ownership' rather than a 'single or concentrated one'. The problem with which the Authority was faced in this context was both novel and socially important, and it was one the Committee might have analysed more searchingly in its published report.

An essential distinguishing feature of the infant independent system was the requirement to have programme providers who would be commercial entrepreneurs operating for profit. Quite apart from its obvious relevance as the only other commercially based mass medium of public information, the fact that the press had long faced the problems of reconciling substantial dependence on advertising revenue with a commitment to public service made it in the eyes of the Authority a natural participant with 'a great and constructive part to play in the development of independent television'.[2] Any ban on press participation must, it told Pilkington, 'impede initiative, confine talent, restrict the growth of the energetic and artificially separate two means of communication between which some mutual influence is beneficial'.[3]

In the event, as we saw in Volume i, because of a variety of circumstances, the successful applicant groups did not include all the press representation the Authority might have desired. In its written evidence the Authority pointed out that of the Big Four only ATV had any press shareholders, and that it was mainly in the regional companies that such holdings were substantial. The chief contribution of these television companies to ITV output and a valuable innovation in British broadcasting was in their local news and current affairs programmes, in respect of which associations with newspapers had been helpful. Moreover, in the context of anxiety over newspaper mortality, participation in a profitable television enterprise could well be, for local papers especially, a helpful assurance of survival. There were in all some seventy-five newspapers involved in the nine regional companies, of which only four were national press companies. Scottish Television was predominantly press controlled with 80 per cent of the voting shares held by Roy Thomson, who also controlled Thomson Newspapers which had all the non-voting shares. The *News of the World* had 21 per cent voting and 12 per cent non-voting shares in TWW. In Southern Television 38 per cent of the voting shares were held by Associated Newspapers Ltd, and in Anglia the *Manchester Guardian and Evenings News Ltd* held 21 per cent of both voting and non-voting shares.

During oral questioning, Kirkpatrick readily admitted that he and his colleagues would have preferred less national, and more regional, press participation in the regional companies; but he pointed out that at the time when the contracts for TWW, Southern and, especially, STV were awarded, the commercial prospects for an ITV company had not seemed so rosy and the Authority could only choose from the limited number of groups who applied. It agreed that in the case of STV any renewal of the contract would probably be dependent on a more diverse and more local ownership; for, of course, at the time the contract was awarded it was *The Scotsman Publications* which had exercised control, and the expansion into Thomson Newspapers had not yet taken place.

The key policy question that arose, however, both from concentration of newspaper ownership in fewer hands and the ownership or control of television companies by newspapers was the threat they could represent to the number, variety and independence of the means of communication, of facts and opinions. When Kirkpatrick was asked whether he thought there was a threat to democracy by participation of newspapers in television companies he asserted bluntly that there was not. Both the general requirement of due impartiality and the specific ban on expression of their own opinions on matters of political or industrial controversy by company managements or officers was, in his view, a sufficient safeguard.

Various aspects of this possible 'threat to democracy' were discussed at length in oral exchanges. Not only was the risk examined of newspaper interests exerting influence to jeopardise the due impartiality of a television company in which they had a shareholding, but the questioning even went so far as to consider the contrary case of Authority insistence on the statutory restraints constituting a threat to traditional press freedoms. In its Report the Committee recorded that it had found no evidence that participating newspapers had been in any way inhibited or biased in their handling of broadcasting matters. It was not however persuaded that, even though there may have been advantages at the outset in helping some companies to develop programmes of news and comment, press participation in the ownership of programme companies was now as helpful an influence as the Authority had suggested. While it agreed with the Authority that the impartiality requirements of the Act made the threat to democracy most unlikely to materialise, 'it would be unwise to dismiss it too lightly'.[4] As a precaution therefore, some limits should be set on press participation. The Committee did not think it necessary to recommend an absolute ban but felt that a suitable formula should be devised whereby in no independent television company was the press interest allowed to be dominant, by which it meant holding more than half the voting shares. Thus the Scottish Television contract should not be renewed unless the press interest was sufficiently reduced.

Before concluding its observations on press participation the Committee could not resist making yet one more slighting reference to what it believed to be the Authority's feebleness.

> The problem of the participation of the press in the programme companies is important precisely because the present constitution and organisation of independent television vests the reality of power . . . in the companies while the regulatory arm – the Authority – can exercise little effective control.[5]

Of course, the Committee was confident that if their proposal for 'organic change' were implemented, the problem arising from press participation as well as all the other problems, perils and failings of the ITV system would virtually disappear.

MISCELLANEOUS PILKINGTONIANA

Scattered through the pages of Pilkington, and sometimes overshadowed by what the Committee regarded as major issues, were varied observations and recommendations bearing on subjects which have received attention in this history. A selection of these are described in this chapter.

(i) ADVISORY COMMITTEES

The Committee recommended that the Authority should appoint its own Central Advisory Committee for religion instead of making use of the BBC's CRAC; and it recorded its surprise that the Authority had not appointed a General Advisory Council, more especially as the Authority did not apparently conduct any proper surveys of public opinion of its services. Such a Council should be made a statutory obligation. Naturally, given the 'negative and regulatory' role of the Authority, the informed opinion which a GAC might be expected to provide would have little influence so long as the network programmes continued to be the responsibility of 'a small group of men from the large programme companies'.[1] But the organic change previously recommended would alter all that. The Committees for Scotland and Northern Ireland should not be made obligatory, but 'we would expect that the Authority should continue to see the need for them and would set up a similar Committee for Wales'.[2]

Pilkington shared the Authority's own dislike, expressed in its evidence, of the requirement under Section 8(2) of the Act making compliance with the advice of the three statutory committees (Children's, Religious and Advertising) virtually binding. This was a derogation of responsibility 'wrong in principle and contradictory in terms'. The law should be changed; it was wrong to 'diminish the responsibility of the answerable public corporation'.[3]

In recommending that the ITA should appoint its own separate body of religious advisers, the Committee undoubtedly had in mind reservations expressed to it by the BBC. And here, as in so many other matters, it found BBC arguments persuasive. Irrespective of the undoubted convenience to the churches, a single joint advisory body for both services was wrong in principle, it concluded. 'It must detract from the authority and responsibility of each of the broadcasting authorities.'[4] Joint consultation of both broadcasters with the same religious advisers had been originally the BBC's own suggestion and Church leaders had agreed. It was common ground that there should be no competition in religious broadcasting; but by the time of their evidence to Pilkington, the Corporation were voicing doubts about the attendance of Authority representatives at CRAC meetings. It had, they claimed, inhibited the sort of open discussion of their programme plans in the friendly collaborative atmosphere that they had previously known.

The Report noted that all designedly religious broadcasting in the United Kingdom had, for understandable reasons, been virtually limited to the Christian religion and, within that, to those so-called 'mainstream' denominations represented on CRAC: i.e. the Church of England, the Church of Scotland, the Methodists, Roman Catholics, Baptists, Congregationalists and Presbyterians. It was acknowledged that the 'general tenor' of the evidence received about religious broadcasting from spokesmen for the general public was complimentary and that 'the religious programmes put on by some of the programme companies of independent television were particularly commended'.[5] Nevertheless, the Report conceded the justice of the claims for greater recognition by many of the minority religious groups. If the membership of CRAC was widened, said the Committee, so as to include some lay members 'chosen for their personal qualities rather than on a denominational basis',[6] this would make it easier to advise the broadcasters on the claims of the lesser religious groups. Moreover, 'religious broadcasting need not be restricted to Christian religious broadcasting'.[7] However, while going on to consider the claims of the Humanists and others 'who believe that morality is independent of revealed religion',[8] the Report concluded that in a nominally Christian country the spokesmen for the Christian tradition *should* have a special claim on the time allocated to religious broadcasting. But it also emphasised that the non-religious bodies should be allotted a fair share of time in controversial broadcasting in the general output.

A further recommendation about advisory committees was that the Authority should appoint its own separate committee to advise on schools broadcasting, and not continue to rely on the Children's Advisory Committee. This was necessary, said Pilkington, because in this field the broadcasters are acting 'largely as agents for the educationalists',[9] whereas programmes for children should be wholly the responsibility of the broadcaster. If the recommendation to place the Authority 'fully and effectively in control'[10] were implemented there should be no further need for such a committee.

(ii) DURATION OF THE ACT

The Report recommended that in view of the 'far reaching [technical] developments'[11] expected in the next decade, the duration of a new Television Act (and, incidentally, the renewed BBC Charter) should be for more than ten years in order to give the broadcasting authorities time to adjust to the changes. The Authority had recommended a duration of fifteen years; the BBC had suggested renewal of the Charter for twelve years. Pilkington concluded that twelve years would be the right period.

(iii) POWERS OF GOVERNMENT

There was the question of the PMG's reserve powers of direction. Under the Television Act (Section 9 (2)) and the BBC's Licence and Agreement (Clause 15 (4)), the PMG had the right to serve a notice on the broadcasting authorities requiring them to refrain from broadcasting any matter or class of matter specified in the notice. In the BBC licence it was expressly stated that the Corporation had the right at its discretion to make known that it had received such a governmental direction. The Committee recommended that a new Act should explicitly give the Authority the same right. Regarding the Fourteen Day Rule (Volume 1) it was pointed out that the 'experimental' suspension of the rule had already lasted for five years, and that there had been no dire consequences. It was therefore urged that the PMG should turn the interim suspension into a final and formal act of revocation. The reasons given were ones which corresponded closely with the arguments put forward five years earlier by Independent Television.

As for the requirement of Section 3(2) of the Television Act (embodied also in a direction by the PMG to the BBC) which forbade both the Authority and its programme contractors from broadcasting their own opinions on matters of current public policy or industrial controversy, Pilkington recommended that the restriction should continue. It was, the Report said, necessary because manifest impartiality was the best guarantee and justification for the broadcasters' independence from political control.

(iv) MINISTERIAL AND PARTY BROADCASTS

The Committee also took note of the established arrangements for the more committed political broadcasts in the form of the so-called 'ministerials', the election broadcasts and annual series of party political broadcasts by the main parties. It had received criticisms of these arrangements both from the Welsh and Scottish Nationalists and from minority parties like the Communists, the Independent Labour Party and Commonwealth. As a result there emerged in the Report a firm recommendation that separate party political broadcasts for Scotland and Wales should be allowed and that these should be additional to the broadcasts for the whole United Kingdom.

On the question of access for smaller political parties, there was insistence that both the BBC and the ITA must see to it that minor parties are given a fair opportunity to take part in normal controversial broadcasting. Whether this policy should be extended to involve some revision of the system of party political broadcasting 'must remain a matter to be settled empirically'.[12] No encouragement was given to ITV's long-standing desire to break away from the traditional form of party political broadcasting as established between the BBC and the leading political parties (see Volume 1). Given the Committee's conviction that 'the BBC should remain in future, as it is now, the main instrument for broadcasting in the United Kingdom',[13] the subordinate role thus assigned to the ITA was only to be expected.

(v) THE OPTION AGREEMENT

This was the arrangement reached in 1954/5 between the Authority and the first four contractors to the effect that, in the event of the opening of a second station in any of the three areas (London, Midlands and the North), the company currently holding a franchise for part of the week in any one of those areas would be given first refusal of a seven-day contract for the area. While expressing an understanding of the motives that led the Authority to enter into such an agreement, the Committee thought it a bad mistake.

We can understand that the Authority would have sympathised with the point of view expressed by the first four contractors. But it is altogether another question whether the Authority should have committed itself as completely as it did, and we find it difficult to understand why, as an important body concerned with the public advantage, they should have given the option.[14]

As a formal contract between the Authority and the four comapanies, the agreement would come to an end on 29 July 1964. It should not be renewed. 'It is, after that date, destitute not only of all legal, but also of all moral, force.'[15] This was something of a bravura performance by Pilkington, but it showed little understanding of the ITA's early problems in getting Independent Television off the ground.

18

A SUITABLE CASE FOR TREATMENT?

The Report of the Committee on Broadcasting, 1960 (Pilkington) was formally presented to the Postmaster-General (Reginald Bevins) on 5 June 1962. Whether the members of the Committee had any confidence that the Government would accept their recommendations for the re-fashioning of the ITV system it is difficult to say. They can hardly have been reassured by the debate on broadcasting policy which had taken place on 1 March 1961 in the House of Lords on the occasion of the publication of the Annual Reports for 1959/60 by the two broadcasting authorities. Speakers included Lords Boothby, Beveridge, Shackleton, Taylor, Alexander of Hillsborough, Longford and the Bishop of Manchester, all of them repeating the familiar criticisms of ITV. Lord Kilmuir (by now Lord Chancellor) was at pains to emphasise that the Government would not want anything said in the course of the debate that would influence or prejudge the findings of the Pilkington Committee. But he also went on to say 'Although this process will be of immense value, it does not relieve either Parliament or the Government of the ultimate responsibility of making up their own minds'.[1] Whether, as was quite possible having regard to the avalanche of adverse comment about ITV which was reaching the Committee and being published, the Government judged that a hint to Pilkington not to get carried away was timely is hard to say. But this would certainly explain why, in winding up for the Government, Lord St. Oswald declared:

> I think Independent Television as a concept and as a system has justified itself. I believe it was needed when it came and that its results are a dynamic, highly efficient and highly responsible industry.

Here Lord Alexander interpolated, 'That is the view of the Government'. To which St. Oswald replied, 'My Lords it was right, in the view of the Government, to set up Independent Television and we are very pleased at having done so'.[2] However, by this time the Committee already had the bit between its teeth and more than a tug on the reins would have been needed to deter it.

After the Report was published the speed with which the first White Paper followed – within a couple of weeks – must have given cause for further discouragement among the advocates of radical change. The impression is given of a Government anxious to make known before the Parliamentary recess (during which the Report's findings and recommend-ations would be widely discussed) what its own reactions were likely to be. In his own account of the events Bevins claims that, soon after the appointment of the Pilkington Committee, he realised that it might be difficult to get a new Bill through Parliament before a general election if he waited for Pilkington to report. At his suggestion the Prime Minister therefore appointed a Committee of Ministers to consider 'the main issues in advance'. This Committee had already reached 'provisional conclusions' by the time the Report was received. 'We made a quick re-appraisal . . . in the light of the Report and reported the results to the Cabinet. Most of our views secured general acceptance . . .'[3]

The members of Pilkington can hardly have felt gratified by the direct and dismissive statements in the White Paper:

> So fundamental a change in the structure of independent television requires the most thorough examination, and the Government wishes to be satisfied that any new structure would remedy the defect it was designed to overcome and would not throw up equally serious difficulties of its own or deprive the system of those features for which it can fairly claim credit.[4]

At all events the terms had been set for a new round of vociferous, doctrinaire debates to put beside those of the early fifties. In their course most of the by now threadbare arguments were to be heard again. But the important difference was that this time the disputants were no longer arguing about a bogey man. Some of them, at least, knew what they were talking about. And, as the politicians were not slow to realise, so did the general public.

Part III

A NEW BEGINNING: 1962–3

19

FIRST REACTIONS

Although the Pilkington Report is dated 5 June 1962, it was not publicly available until Wednesday 27 June, advance copies having been received (subject to the customary publication embargo) by lobby correspondents and the Authority on 25 June.

The *Daily Express* had the first leak. As early as 7 June it published a report by Martin Jackson headlined 'Pilkington Report gives a shock to ITV', which accurately foretold several of the Committee's findings though not the proposals for organic change. The ITV system as a whole found itself faced by a decidedly less hostile press after publication of the Report than it had been getting ever since the company profits had started to boom. In the judgement of not a few observers the Pilkington Committee had too readily cast themselves in the role of champions of the BBC and in that role had overplayed their hand. By the time the Authority met in Belfast on 3 July, the Members had more than enough to feed and stimulate their reflections.

Seldom can the press, both popular and serious, daily and periodical, have occupied so many column inches with coverage of the findings of an official Committee of Enquiry. Members learned from more than one source that the Pilkington Report was a 'bombshell' which had caused a sharp fall in the Stock Exchange quotations of ITV shares. They may also have read that Lady Pilkington's housekeeper had threatened to resign if *Coronation Street* were stopped because of the Report; or that Sidney Bernstein had exclaimed 'To hell with it!' before he'd read it. From the *Daily Mirror*,[1] a Member would have learned that it was the public that was being told to 'Go to hell!' by what its rival paper, the *Daily Sketch*, called 'The Piffington Report'; and from the *Daily Telegraph* that 'this amazing document' was saturated by 'a haughty conviction that whatever is popular must be bad'. The *Daily Express* (and *Evening Standard*) continued to plough their lonely, bitter furrow ('in its condemnation, the report merely voices opinions long held by the people'). But if any Members read the *Daily Worker*, they would have been informed that 'many people will find it impossible to accept the almost uncritical praise of the BBC'. From the *Daily Mail* they would have got the verdict: 'An extraordinary mixture of sense and nonsense, impartiality and prejudice . . . its diagnoses are often good but its main remedy is fantastic'; a remedy, explained *The Economist*,[2] that would turn the Authority into 'another sort of BBC . . . on ticket of leave . . . tarred as little as possible by the wicked commercial sources of its revenues'.

But encouragement to less emotional reflection may have come from the stately, mandarin prose of *The Times*: 'Since this is at variance with the conferment of popular applause as expressed in the way most people use their switches, it requires some justification'. With admirable detachment *The Scotsman* had added: 'The committee's attitude is academic and austere . . . whether these virtues are the best equipment for passing judgement on TV programmes is extremely doubtful'; whereas Roy Thomson, the newspaper's proprietor (and, of course, Chairman and owner of Scottish Television) had, somewhat less moderately, given voice – from distant Toronto – to feelings of 'amazement and disgust'.

Other ITV company spokesmen had been scarcely less hasty and emphatic in their reactions. They were all of them behind Peter Black who in the *Daily Mail* on 28 June said: 'I don't think Pilkington has given the companies enough credit for what they've done . . . commercial TV considerably broadened and vitalised the range and style of programming. News and presentation, drama, current affairs and children's TV are obvious examples . . .'; but they expressed themselves in less moderate terms. 'Outrageous . . . this sorry document.' 'Utterly contrary to the whole tradition of free enterprise.' So said Renwick of ATV. 'The best place for this report is the waste paper basket,' said the flamboyant Peter Cadbury of Westward who, according to *The Times* and the *Telegraph*,[3] then went on to plan a garden party on the following Saturday at which Sir Harry would be burned in effigy together with copies of the Report. 'A disquieting document with disturbing social implications,' said TWW's Chairman, the Earl of Derby. But most of the companies followed the Authority example and withheld comment until the Report had been properly digested.

A reaction to this welter of criticism came in 1963 from Richard Hoggart (who had been, as has been seen, a highly influential member of the Committee) in an essay entitled 'Difficulties of Democratic Debate: the Reception of the Pilkington Report on Broadcasting'.[4] He recalled, *inter alia*, that the Report had argued that broadcasters have to recognise that they are in 'a constant and sensitive relation to the moral condition of society'. The word 'moral', he said, 'affronted respected organs of opinion like a Gideon Bible found at his hotel bedside by a roving atheist'. This essay might well be thought to have given a clearer indication of what those who wrote the Report were trying to impart than the document itself. In his concluding remarks he says:

> The Report sought to extend intellectual and imaginative freedom, to give more room for variety and dissent. Its view of society was based on the idea of change and possibility, on the view that there are within the huge majorities lots of overlapping minorities, on thinking not only about what we are but of what we might become if we were given more varied chances.

Today, after twenty-six years of the duopoly, any speaker using Hoggart's words could well expect to receive a warm round of applause.

There were also in the first press reports some intimations of the reactions of the politicians and the likely attitude of the Government. There can hardly have been doubts about the generally favourable response of many rank and file members of the Parliamentary Labour Party; nor, for that matter, of the TUC's George Woodcock (the TUC's own Pilkington evidence had described ITV output as excessively 'shoddy'[5]). But leading Labour politicians, including Hugh Gaitskell himself, were reported to be cautiously non-committal about the Report's recommendations for fundamental change in the structure of ITV. As for the Government's supporters some newspapers – following no doubt the journalists' natural penchant for drama – claimed to see signs of a possible revival of the division of opinion of the early fifties, with only fifty to sixty back-benchers, so it was said, prepared to come wholeheartedly to the defence of commercial television. 'Some Tory MPs are saying that they are delighted with the Report and hope it will be fully implemented' recorded *The Scotsman* (thereby demonstrating its editorial independence from its proprietor). But *The Times* probably got nearer the truth: 'Inside the Cabinet and on the back benches many who would not flinch from the actual recommendations, considered on their own, deeply resent the moral judgments not only of commercial television, but of the capitalist principle, in which they consider them to have been framed'. *The Daily Telegraph*'s political correspondent, H. B. Boyne, wrote of the commercial TV lobby 'leaping to the aid of the programme companies like tigers defending their young'. But Ministers were, he suggested, still uncertain how widespread this anti-Pilkington feeling was. The composition of the Conservative Party in the Commons had changed a good deal since the passage of the Act. It could not be assumed that all members returned in the 1955 and 1959 elections thought the 1954 Act produced a permanently ideal framework for the future of British television.

On the evening of 27 June Reg Bevins, the PMG, had attended a seventy-five-minute meeting of Tory back-benchers called to discuss the report. His opening comment that Pilkington had painted the BBC 'whiter than white' had apparently been greeted with applause. What he was able to tell the Cabinet on 28 June about the balance of party sentiment reassured Ministers that their own feelings were widely shared. It seemed reasonable to deduce, as did the *Guardian*'s political correspondent, Francis Boyd, that, given the initial expectation of a revival of earlier Parliamentary battles with the Opposition 'the Government will approach the future of broadcasting with caution but with the object of rescuing more of commercial television than the Pilkington Committee proposes'. On the morning of 29 June, Ian Macleod confirmed in Parliament that a White Paper would appear on the following Wednesday, 4 July.

Such then was the background to the Authority's meeting in Belfast on 3 July.

20

MORE MATURE REFLECTIONS

At the Authority's meeting Kirkpatrick reported that he had tried unsuccessfully to see the Home Secretary, who was Chairman of the Cabinet's Home Affairs Committee and as such concerned with any Government action on the Pilkington Report. He had therefore written to Mr Butler and passed on the contents of his letter in an interview with the PMG, in which he had also expressed his anger at the tone of the Report. In his letter of 2 July to Butler he had said:

> I completely repudiate the Pilkington Committee's statements of alleged fact. In particular I repudiate the statement that the ITA falls far behind the BBC in showing serious programmes in good evening hours . . . The Pilkington Report is loaded with prejudice and abounds in misrepresentations and distortion. . . . The Authority has been publicly attacked. In deference to the request of the Postmaster-General it has hitherto remained silent . . . it cannot be expected to do so much longer . . . [1]

He had even hinted that if the White Paper adopted a similar attitude towards Independent Television, the Members of the Authority might well 'feel compelled to take drastic action' (presumably resign *en masse*).

But the PMG had reassured him about the 'objectivity' of the forthcoming White Paper. Accordingly, it was agreed to make only a brief general statement to the expectant press. This was duly done by Kirkpatrick at the luncheon which followed the meeting and at which a number of Northern Ireland dignitaries were present. He said that the Authority wished however to repudiate the attitude towards television which had been attributed to it. That was not in accordance with the evidence which the Authority gave, and the account of the character and balance of independent television programmes was incorrect and misleading.

To reinforce the latter point, the Authority decided to issue for public distribution a booklet of 'Facts and Figures' (based on papers prepared by

the staff) intended to disprove the accuracy of Pilkington's description of
ITV programme output. One table showed that the only significant discrepancies between ITV and BBC output were in 'entertainment films' (ITV 20
per cent, BBC 8 per cent), and in sport (BBC 22 per cent, ITV 15 per cent).
Others showed that in an average week of June 1962, the BBC was putting
out in the London area 22 hours 47 minutes of 'serious material' against 19
hours 24 minutes from ITV; and that in evening hours the respective
percentages of 'serious material' were:

6–8 p.m.:	ITV 34 per cent	BBC 52 per cent
8–10 p.m.:	ITV 20 per cent	BBC 20 per cent
10–closedown:	ITV 38 per cent	BBC 38 per cent

However, the ITV serious programmes were usually reaching outstandingly
larger audiences than the BBC ones (in some cases twice as many).

Kirkpatrick obviously felt strongly about the apparent interpretation in
paragraphs 156–60 of the Report of his views on the social influence of
television. In a letter to *The Times* on 12 July he rejected the Pilkington
assumption that the Authority took the irresponsible attitude that television
had negligible influence. But 'the belief that television by itself will "mould"
society is a dangerous illusion'. It is as dangerous to overestimate as to
underestimate the influence of the medium, he concluded. 'A realistic
appraisal is not equivalent to an abdication of responsibility.'

When the White Paper[2] itself appeared it was relatively short, comprising
some 5000 words, and was 'largely concerned with those changes that could
be made without too much controversy'.[3] It accepted that both BBC Charter
and a new Television Act should run for twelve years from 30 July 1964. The
traditional independence of the broadcasters from day-to-day government
supervision was reaffirmed but the reserve powers of the PMG as responsible
Minister were to remain unchanged.

Agreeing with Pilkington about the educational possibilities of television,
the White Paper said that additional hours would be authorised for bona
fide adult education. Education should continue to have a place in the
general services and not on a specialised educational channel. In order to
make available a wider choice of programmes, including more educational
and informative ones, the BBC would be authorised to start a second service
and that would be on 625 lines in UHF starting in London by mid-1964 and
spreading nationwide as quickly as possible. It accepted that all new TV
services should be similarly on 625 lines UHF and that the existing two
services should also be changed over to this standard 'in due course'. But

these two would need to be carried on 405 VHF in Bands I and III as well as in the higher frequencies until existing receivers could reasonably be expected to have become obsolete. The BBC would be encouraged to introduce colour 'on a modest scale' into its BBC 2 transmissions; as would ITV as and when a second service for the latter was authorised. On advertising, Pilkington's conclusion in favour of the existing average of six minutes per hour with a seven-minute maximum was accepted, but so also was the recommendation that advertising magazines should be abolished. Subliminal advertising would be explicitly banned in future legislation and there would be discussions with the ITA on a possible change in the permitted length of the interval between advertising breaks; on the vetting of medical advertisements; on advertisements shown during children's programmes and on the nature of the possible social undesirability of the appeal made by some commercials. And then (Bevins' 'objectivity') there was praise for the achievements of Independent Television:

> A novel partnership between public and private enterprise, producing between them lively and certainly popular television . . . it has undeniably contributed something of value and by bringing competition into the world of television exercised an enlivening effect on television in general.[4]

Consequently the Pilkington proposals for 'organic change' were, as we saw in the previous chapter, treated with cautious doubt. Full account would be taken of the views which would be expressed in public debate and the Government would be submitting a statement of its own proposals later. These would also cover such matters as the second ITA service (for which 'there will be scope')[5] as well as the nature of the ITV companies and their relationship with the press. Informed newspaper comment suggested that the Government had also recognised the need to do something about the companies' excessive profits, the dominance of the network by the Big Four, and the powers of the Authority to influence the balance and quality of programmes.

On the day that the White Paper appeared with its praise for ITV's contribution to British television, some unnamed ITV company executives were being reported in the *Daily Express* and the *Daily Mail* as putting the blame on the Authority for the Report's 'devastating attack on ITV'. The *Mail* said that 'ITV company executives feel they were let down by the way the Authority put its case to the committee'. And there were also suggestions that a new and 'more efficient' Authority was needed. This was in contrast to the behaviour of company representatives at the first post-Pilkington meeting of the scc on 12 July, at which Fraser told them of the wide distribution to be given to the 'Facts and Figures' booklet. Brownrigg said the ITA was to be congratulated on producing so cogent an account of the programme output of Independent Television.[6] Satisfaction was also expressed over the White Paper's reference to extra time for adult education. ABC and ATV made known their plans for three regular twenty-minute programmes on Sundays at noon. However, Fraser warned the companies that the current negative reactions to the Report might well be shortlived, and he expressed the view that not enough had been done to bring out the fact that ITV was substantially more than a purely entertainment service. To his suggestion that companies should look after their relations with those persons in the community likely to influence political decisions, companies were quick to respond with claims of good and developing local public relations.

Fraser had himself just given a practical demonstration of the way to put over the ITV case to those able to influence political decisions. He had been invited to address a meeting of trade union MPs at the House of Commons. In the event, it appears, a number of other interested Labour Party back-benchers also attended. It had been reliably reported that at a recent meeting of the Parliamentary Labour Party, the zealous Mayhew and his friends had been within an ace of getting a resolution carried committing it to support for the Pilkington proposals for 'organic change'. Gaitskell and some of his colleagues in the Shadow Cabinet were doubtful about the electoral advantage that would be gained from such a commitment; and a vote on the resolution had been deferred on the grounds that too few members were present at the meeting. The encounter on 10 July was therefore bound to be a difficult one for Fraser. Newspaper accounts suggest that he scored something of a personal triumph. He had also distributed the 'Facts and Figures' booklet and had answered questions from MPs and the Parliamentary press at the end of the meeting. According to the *Daily Mail*'s correspondent, it 'ended in a storm of applause'.[7]

In detailed comments sent to the PMG, the Authority, whilst adhering strictly to its own stand on all the major issues, expressed agreement with Pilkington on some subordinate matters and conceded ground wherever it could decently do so without compromising its own principles. But it did not accept that any increase in hours should be moderate: on the contrary it reiterated its strongly held view that there should be a substantial extension in order to be able better to serve special interest minorities and those many others who were not able to view in the evening hours. Nor could the

Authority accept the Pilkington argument against any 'marked disparity' between the hours of broadcasting permitted to the two competing television services. The case, such as it was, had even less force now that the Government had decided in favour of BBC 2.

The idea of 'family viewing time' was, said the comments, in accordance with long-standing existing policy and a fresh public statement to that effect would be made after consultation with the Children's Advisory Committee. It was emphasised that, notwithstanding the absence of a formal 'Code on Violence', Pilkington was quite wrong in its assumption that the Authority left exercise of control to the discretion of the companies: on the contrary there were constant regular exchanges between Authority and company programme staff both about the content of programmes and their appropriate placing in the schedules. However, consideration would be given to the advisability of making a formal declaration of the Authority's policies.

The Authority accepted that the value of prizes offered in quiz and games programmes should bear some relationship to the skills required, and recommended that future legislation should give it the power to control this. An ITA obligation to conduct audience research was also accepted and an undertaking given that ways of extending it would be explored. But the Committee's failure to acknowledge the Authority's initiative in providing £250,000 for research into the effects of television on young people came in for some sharp comment.

Turning to the control of advertising, satisfaction was expressed that both Pilkington and the White Paper accepted that the permitted amounts and their distribution were matters best left to the ITA and not be a subject for legislation: but it was also claimed that the difficulty in defining 'natural breaks' was not as great as both the Report and the White Paper seemed to assume. Years of practice had led to a 'fairly narrow and common sense' definition and to a reduction of the area of difficulty to a relatively small number of cases.

The paper accepted that some interpretative amplifications of the rules about advertising content could be useful; asserted that the Report's recommendation on false or misleading claims went no further than current Authority practice; and took leave to doubt the validity of the assumption of socially harmful effects. Though not accepting all the strictures on advertising magazines, the Authority noted the Government's decision to abolish them and recorded its discussion with the companies on the timetable for their withdrawal.

Comment was brief on the White Paper acceptance of the recommendation that the next television service should be BBC 2. The Authority saw no reason to alter its view about future television services as described in evidence to the Committee. But faced with a Government decision it felt it right to draw Ministers' attention to the possible financial consequences of a second BBC service both for ITV and for the Exchequer. This brief comment was developed at length in a Financial Appendix to the paper, which aimed to show the effects on ITV income of a reduced audience share arising from additional competition, and to indicate the extra ITA and programme company expenditures arising from the proposed concomitant technical changes. The assumed outcome would be less Television Advertising Duty (to say nothing of other taxes on company earnings) and consequent loss to the Exchequer.[8] There was a marked flavour of special pleading in this argument from a body which had previously favoured more competition as the preferred method of reducing excessive company profits.

As regards the Pilkington proposals for major changes in constitution and organisation, the paper commented that the image of an allegedly unsatisfactory and disquieting ITV programme output which was cited by the Committee as the justification for its proposals reflected a false and misleading account of the character and balance of the service. It expressed satisfaction that the Government saw 'practical difficulties' in a plan which the Authority for its part regarded as totally unworkable. But there was readiness to discuss what practical steps could be taken to improve the ITV system.

Although the Government had followed Pilkington in rejecting the idea of a specialised education channel, the Authority continued to maintain that the proposal was one worthy of further study. It went on to express satisfaction at the decision to authorise additional hours for adult education; and recorded its intention to develop the informal contacts already established with a view to appointing an Adult Education Advisory Committee.

These are but a selection from the voluminous comments which Bevins and his officials were invited to digest. Less formal notes sent to Butler and Hailsham were more concise. They referred to Pilkington's misrepresentation of the Authority's approach to its responsibilities and to the social role of broadcasting; to the contrast between Pilkington's description of the absence of an ITV code on violence as 'surrender of authority' and the O'Conor Committee's contrary conclusion on this subject; to the inaccurate statistics of western and crime programmes produced by the Council for Children's Welfare; to the inadequate treatment in the Report of the Authority's views on the problems of networking; to the total failure on the part of the Committee to appreciate the regional achievement of ITV. With regard to the 'denigrating and misleading' treatment of the Authority's and the companies' part in patronage of the Arts, it was pointed out that at the end of 1961 the companies' disbursements to the Arts totalled about £1,000,000. Finally the notes contrasted the Authority's own submission on the likely effects of more competition on company profits with the 'distorted' version of the argument printed in the Report.

LORDS AND COMMONS HAVE THEIR SAY

At five minutes to three on 18 July, Viscount Hailsham rose from his seat in the House of Lords to move 'That this House approves the Memorandum on the Report of the Committee on Broadcasting 1960', in other words the White Paper. The speech contained little to recall the vituperative onslaught he had delivered in 1954. True, he declared himself unrepentant; but added: 'obviously one has learned, and I hope forgotten, something in the last seven or eight years'. He suggested that 'the time has come to move away from the possibly somewhat superficial and academic generalising about paternalism, commercialism, monopoly and free enterprise which have dominated this subject so long, and to move towards a return to an agreed broadcasting policy based upon technical necessity and practical politics'. That set the tone. In the two-day debate that followed,[1] and which on its first day went on till well after 11 p.m., some three dozen Peers made speeches. Little was said that was original. Said Lord Longford: 'A bell ought to be rung if anybody made a new point in this debate . . . I don't think many bells will be rung during my oration'. But it was a good-natured debate much more in keeping with the traditional mores of the Upper Chamber than the near hysterical outbursts of moral indignation noted by Lord Salisbury in 1953.

A close approach to partisan acerbity came at Lord Astor's revelation of a 'quiet subterranean' investigation into the political allegiances of BBC programme staff, carried out at the end of the war, he said, by a representative of the Conservative Party. It had revealed that many of them were socialists, he claimed; and that was why he and his fellow Conservatives had then determined to put an end to an established broadcasting monopoly whose programmes betrayed such a 'strong pink tendency'. One or two Labour peers objected strongly to the implication they read into his remarks that producers' political opinions should be taken into account when they were appointed.

For the rest, their Lordships exchanged reminiscences about their own viewing and broadcasting experiences, Lord Morrison in particular revealing his addiction to Maigret, Perry Mason and the BBC's [*sic*!] *No Hiding Place*. There was general agreement that both BBC and ITV had excellent serious programmes and that in many respects there was little to choose between them. *Panorama* and *This Week* came in for special praise; and if from the Labour side it was claimed that the BBC showed rather more such serious programmes in peak, Government supporters (relying no doubt on the ITA's 'Facts and Figures') were quick to point out that *This Week* reached twice as many viewers as *Panorama*. It was not always clear whether speakers realised they were debating the White Paper and not the Report. The Bishop of Chichester (speaking for His Grace of Canterbury, as well as for himself) thought Pilkington had done very much less than justice to ITV's contribution to religious broadcasting. 'Done with more freshness, independence and originality by ITV than by the perhaps rather more stilted approach of the BBC.'

Lord Beveridge told the House that he had changed his mind about the recommendation of his Report on Broadcasting that the BBC monopoly should be maintained. Lord Shackleton, long time opponent of commercial television, agreed with the Earl of Derby that insufficient credit had been given for ITV's regional achievement and added that it would be regrettable if a reorganisation of ITV were to lead to the demise of any of the regional companies. More than one Peer expressed his belief in the fundamental common sense of the average British viewer and his consequent ability to protect himself – and his children – from the allegedly corrupting influences of 'sordid' drama, fictional violence and even 'misleading' advertisements. Those were in varying degrees the views of the Bishop of Leicester ('the Kingdom of England is not the Republic of Plato'); Lord St. Oswald, winding up at the end of the first day (quoting Chesterton: 'All this talk is based on that complete forgetting of what a child is like which has been the firm foundation of so many educational schemes'); and Lord Francis Williams, himself a regular and successful performer on both channels.

The last named criticised the Report for being 'out of touch with the geography of real life'. He confessed that he felt a certain shiver running down his spine as he read the Report. He had been at the BBC's studios at Lime Grove on the night it appeared and was interested to find that the 'more creative producers and younger people' there were not rejoicing, but on the contrary displaying an air of despondency and gloom because Pilkington appeared to have fastened on the Corporation the 'image of smug goodness, of being the perfect establishment organisation which does only what the right people think', just what, under the leadership of Hugh Greene, they were hoping to get away from.

There was all-round approval of the White Paper's technical proposals about 625 lines; and, on balance, general agreement with the award of an extra channel to the BBC, although one or two (like for example Lords Swinton and Bessborough) still thought ITV should have at least a part in the third channel, and several hoped its access to the fourth channel would not be long delayed.

Most speakers took the view that the White Paper was right in its cautious approach to the more fundamental Pilkington proposals for the reorganis-ation of ITV. Even though it was widely admitted that there were faults to be corrected, such as the dominance of the Big Four, the rigidity of the networking arrangements, the excessive profits and inadequate programme balance in peak, Lord Shepherd was able to say on behalf of the Opposition that the ITA 'is here and we must live with it'. What faults there were could probably be more sensibly corrected by giving the Authority stronger and more explicit powers rather than by adopting proposals for 'organic change' of doubtful practicality. All in all the occasion scarcely merited the *Evening Standard*'s description of 'a great debate raging'.[2] Its predominantly non-controversial character was underlined by the new Lord Chancellor, Lord Dilhorne, formerly the Attorney General, Manningham-Buller, in a maiden speech of which the central thesis was the compatibility of genuine public service with profitable private enterprise.

Although Hailsham's speech (to say nothing of the White Paper itself) had shown that the Government already had strong doubts about the practicality of the Pilkington proposals for fundamental reorganisation of ITV, the Authority thought it prudent, in the days preceding the ensuing debate in the Commons, to supply Ministers with its own reasons for believing that they would be wrong in principle and unworkable in practice. A further paper argued in careful detail that a system 'based on an unreal divorce between responsibility and execution, between the planning of programmes and their preparation'[3] could not produce a good television service; and that the resultant centralisation of programme planning would tend to stultify, if not eliminate, the pluralistic diversity that had been one of the acknowledged achievements of ITV.

The Commons debate[4] on 31 July 1962 was conducted in much the same atmosphere as the earlier one in the Lords. In his opening speech Bevins said he felt there was more 'convergence of views' in the House than there had been some years ago and in his winding up for the Opposition, W. R. Williams felt able to say 'we have left behind the old battle' about commercial television; it was 'not a debate in the normal sense' but an exchange of ideas. To which the Assistant PMG (Miss Mervyn Pike),[5] replying for the Government, added 'the debate has been concerned mainly with realism and it is in this spirit that our arguments and discussions will go on in future'. Bevins reaffirmed the Government's conviction that the creation of ITV had on balance been a good thing for British broadcasting. Conscientious and hardworking as the Pilkington Committee had been, their praise of the BBC and their criticism of ITV had been overdone. But, he reminded members, it had always been intended to check on the success of the competing service when renewal of the statute was imminent. The Government were now taking the 'promised second look' in order to decide how the system should be shaped in the future. Certainly there were failings in the commercial system which needed corrective action: the dominance of the four major networking companies should be reduced; profits were excessive; above all, ways had to be found of giving the Authority a more positive role in the supervision and control of advertising as also of the content, standards and balance of the programmes. 'I should not myself shrink from a limited element of paternalism'. Such an admission made it that much easier for that stout defender of the monopoly, Gordon Walker, to say in his reply on behalf of the Opposition that 'competition has done some good'. Duty done, he could not forbear from going on to say that, in his view, standards in general had been depressed by competition. 'None the less, ITV is here now . . . for good or ill, it is part of our national life.'

Such a prudent awareness on the part of the Labour leadership of the possible electoral repercussions of too hostile an attitude towards ITV was not to the liking of Mayhew who, not surprisingly – as several of the newspapers observed – had recently resigned his position as Party spokesman on broadcasting. In the debate he was as vehement as ever in his condemnation of Independent Television and in his support for the 'organic change' which had, of course, been a feature of his personal evidence to Pilkington. Ness Edwards, another Labour veteran of the earlier campaign, was un-characteristically restrained: 'Today we are having only a skirmish before the great battle which is yet to come'. But there was further food for thought in his warning to the Government not to exploit 'divisions on this side of the House' in order to avoid the pressures for reform.

Hard words for both Kirkpatrick and Fraser came from speakers as diverse as Sir Harmar Nicholls, Woodrow Wyatt and Captain Orr. The first of these, a bluest of the blue Conservative if ever there was one, agreed that the ITA should be strengthened and, noting Kirkpatrick's imminent departure added: 'Let us ensure that someone is put into it (the Chairmanship) who really can ensure that Parliament's intentions are carried out'. For Wyatt much of the trouble with ITV could have been avoided if only the Members of the Authority had been 'more vigorous men'; or if those in office had shown more inclination to use the powers they had. Captain Orr saw legitimate cause for pride in the achievements of British TV, whether BBC or ITV, when compared with the services in other countries. Nevertheless it seemed to him essential for the Government to find a 'man of stature' as the new ITA Chairman – 'someone who has been engaged in the business and knows something about it, and about industry generally, and who knows how to act as a member of a board of directors and can control his managing director'. The Directors General of both BBC and ITA were in his opinion altogether too powerful. They should be made more amenable to the wishes of their respective governing bodies. The debate ended without a division.

TENSION AT
ST. MARTIN'S-LE-GRAND

Bevins had received the congratulations of the Prime Minister for his work in producing the first White Paper, and he was determined not to let grass grow under his feet. Consequently, whilst Parliament was debating during the summer of 1962, the 'too-powerful' Director General of the ITA and his senior colleagues found themselves involved in continuing discussions with the civil servants at the Post Office. Spontaneous reactions to Pilkington by press and Parliament had on the whole been reassuring; and the fact is that the fight in which the ITA eventually found itself engaged was not with the forces of public disapproval but with a tough, ambitious Minister of the Crown aided and abetted by a top official of unusual acumen and tenacity.

Relations at first were harmonious enough. There were meetings to discuss the control of advertising, programme standards and networking and the dominance of the Big Four, the position of the press, a possible code on violence, future television services for Scotland and Wales. The expressed intention behind all these discussion meetings, which continued throughout the autumn, was to reach agreed formulations on the various issues of policy involved in the future pattern of the Authority's control machinery. These would be used as the bases for statements by the PMG in the House or in the forthcoming White Paper. They were also expected to offer helpful pointers for Parliamentary Counsel when the time came to prepare a draft of the new Bill. A great deal of time (and paper) was devoted in particular to the content and nature of advertisements, the Authority's executive responsibility *vis-à-vis* the ITCA Copy Committee, the composition and status of the Advertising Advisory Committee. Whereas these exchanges on the question of advertising generally led to specific commitments by the Authority (albeit emphasising that these were little more than a tightening up of existing practice), those on the less tangible issues of programme and scheduling control were characterised by a marked preference on the Authority's part for discretionary powers rather than for too specific a series of requirements embodied in the Act.

As far as the paper record goes these negotiations with the Post Office seem to have been conducted in an outwardly frank and formally courteous fashion. Yet there began to emerge some signs of growing tension, not to say resentment, in the relations of the Authority and its staff with their Minister and his officers. Perhaps this was an aftermath of some of the harsher criticisms of the Authority voiced in the Commons debate and left without correction from the Government Front Bench. It could also be a reflection of the fact that Bevins had made no bones about his conviction that there were still some things very wrong with ITV and that he was the man tough enough to resist all pressures towards compromise in his determination to put them right.

At the Authority meeting of 11 September Fraser, when reporting progress of the talks with Post Office officials, was asked whether it might not be desirable for the PMG himself to discuss 'the salient questions'[1] directly with the Members. He agreed, suggesting three broad topics: first the system for the inter-company trade in programmes; secondly the Authority's powers to influence programme balance and content; thirdly the basis on which new rentals should be calculated. At the meeting of the SCC which took place on the following day the companies were also told about the same three broad issues affecting the future which were to be discussed with the Post Office. They were asked in particular to supply factual data for discussion of the rentals. These included estimates of expenditure and gross revenue for 1961/2 and 1962/3, the latter before and after the incidence of Television Advertising Duty, together with forecasts of anticipated audience shares once BBC 2 was fully operational and of the likely effects on advertising revenue. The company managers at this meeting expressed themselves reasonably confident of their ability to cope with increased BBC competition – at least in peak hours – even though in the words of Val Parnell, the Corporation had become a 'highly professional competitor'.[2]

It was the rental issue which was destined to become in the months ahead by far the most troublesome. This was not so much because of the practical complexities of the problem: on the contrary. Intervention of third party control in the creative areas of programme planning and judgement was obviously a much more tricky matter. But, as was to be made increasingly clear, Bevins had made up his mind that it was here – in dealing with the 'scandal' of ITV's excessive profits – that he would reveal himself a politician of vigour and decisive action. In his references to programme content during the debate he had readily conceded the principle of 'de gustibus'; but it was obviously much easier to commit oneself to a judgement commending itself to the general public on what was an excessive profit. As a politician and member for a working-class constituency, Bevins was as alive as was the Labour Shadow Cabinet to the possible electoral repercussions of television legislation. Votes might or might not be lost by paternalistic interference with the people's favoured entertainment. Few, if any, would be lost by the imposition of restraints on over-prosperous entrepreneurs. The PMG committed himself to the view that the rentals should be made up of two parts, a fixed amount to cover the Authority's costs and a variable amount which would be a tax on profits. By 2 October Members were voicing concern that the PMG appeared to have taken no steps to consult with the Authority either about the July White Paper or about 'the important matters with which the Government proposed to deal in the second White Paper'.[3] It was decided to inform the PMG of these feelings and to ask for an early meeting. The forthcoming change in the chairmanship did not, in the Authority's view, lessen the need for the Minister to consult with it.

In the event Kirkpatrick himself had two meetings with Bevins on 23 October, a day when the Authority was also meeting. The first of these two encounters took place in the early morning and lasted three hours. The second was later that day, after the Chairman had reported to his fellow Members and secured their views.

Preparations had been made in a preliminary discussion on 11 October between the Deputy Chairman, Sir John Carmichael,[4] and the Director General of the Post Office, Sir Ronald German.[5] This was followed by a letter from German to Fraser enclosing a note defining the 'much more prominent and powerful position'[6] the Authority was expected to have under the new Act. It would 'correspond to their position as the answerable public body . . . go hand in hand with a diminution in the power of the Big Four . . . and a correspondingly enhanced public prestige for the Authority'. Such phraseology seemed to carry the implication that the Authority had not previously conducted itself as 'the answerable public body'. As for the implication that the ITA's position and public prestige were related in inverse proportion to the power of the Big Four, Fraser did not see that as a correct representation of the position and he found it offensive.

Kirkpatrick's meeting with Bevins on 23 October was his last as Chairman. His report on his discussions with the Minister covered: networking and the arrangements for programme supply; the control of programmes; the pattern of the contracts; the second ITV service; the control of advertising; and the problem of company profits. On some of these broad general agreement had been reached, as for example on the Authority's proposals for closer involvement in advertising control, or for 'free trade' in programme supply. But on other issues shared views on objectives would, it appeared, need to be complemented by further discussions about the appropriate means of achieving them. By far the trickiest of these would be the practical steps required to limit company profits. The Minister was clearly determined not only to reduce the earnings of ITV companies to defensible levels, but also to achieve a reduction in the power both of the four major companies *vis-à-vis* the regional companies and of all the companies *vis-à-vis* the Authority as custodian of the public interest. And he wished to be seen to be doing these things. The Chairman had made efforts to persuade the Minister that some of the measures contemplated could be self-defeating if taken too far. Bevins had apparently accepted the argument that a small nucleus of relatively large (and wealthy) multi-competent programme contractors was essential if a reliable supply of high quality programmes for the national service was to be available. He had recognised moreover that this meant that the strength of such companies was a consequence of the size and population of the areas they had been contracted to serve; and that it would therefore be unwise to contemplate changes in those areas.

Two days later, on 25 October, Fraser was able to send to German a summary of the Authority's views. On the supply of programmes for networking, it proposed that it should be empowered to require the four majors to make their programmes available without strings to the regionals; and that the price paid by the latter for the programmes they took should be proportionate to their ability to pay at an hourly rate fixed with the agreement of the Authority. Such 'price fixing' would apply only to programmes supplied by majors to regionals: not to deals between the regionals themselves.

The Authority was reluctant to assume the power (which the Minister apparently thought it should have) to tell companies what programmes they should include in their output. Such an arrangement would be contrary to the whole spirit of ITV, a system in which the component companies were on principle expected to display the main virtues of competitive private enterprise, independent initiative and responsibility. It would indeed be more in keeping with the paternalistic attitudes of Pilkington and that Committee's recommendations for 'organic change'. What the Members did feel they should be given under new legislation was the power of scrutiny and approval of all company programme schedules in advance, and a reserve power to demand further detailed information about the content of any particular programme, without the existing proviso that such a demand could be made only if a breach of the law was apprehended. In practice, as it had told Pilkington, the Authority was already exercising such powers. It merely wanted the *de facto* to be made *de jure*. It declared its readiness to set up a Programme Committee under its chairmanship on which all companies, large and small, would be represented, to keep the whole programme provision under regular review.

On advertising control, the Authority explained that it was already proceeding, in association with its statutory Advertising Advisory Committee, towards a general revision and extension of the existing Principles for Television Advertising, in order to make them, by means of interpretation and illustrative example, more patently related to particular cases. In addition, there would be a move towards a more direct participation of Authority staff in decisions on the application of the revised Principles, even though the day-to-day acceptance of advertisements would continue to be in the hands of the programme companies' Copy Committee.

On the programme contracts, the Authority again spelled out its case for the existing pattern of service areas with four major companies, dividing the week so that no one was too powerful but none too small, but with a strong and distinctive regional element. It emphasised the desirability of maintaining as much of the regional structure as circumstances allowed. The continued survival of smaller companies providing a highly valued regional service would depend firstly on their access to an assured supply of programmes of national interest from the major companies; and secondly on the impact of increased competition from two BBC services, as well as the possible effects of a still hypothetical second ITV service.

The Authority remained cautious about the much-publicised issue of company profits. It reminded the Minister that it had always accepted that some means of reducing them must be found. It would therefore prepare for consideration a formula for calculating additional payments by the companies, over and above the rentals which were paid to the Authority for its own use to cover its operational needs. The additional payments (or levy) would be on a sliding scale, falling most heavily on the companies with the largest profits. Equally non-committal were its comments on alternative methods of assessment, collection and transmission to the Exchequer. But on one thing it was forthright. Once a statutory levy on ITV company profits was imposed, the existing Television Advertising Duty should disappear. The accumulation of taxation on gross income (which did not reflect profitability), on profits before normal taxation, and normal income taxes would be unjust. If a competitive service were initiated, it would also be impracticable because of the anticipated fall in profitability.

Doubts about future profit levels in the presence of competition made the Authority unwilling to commit itself at this stage to a second ITA channel. It preferred not to have its hands tied, despite its continuing belief in the principle of competitive television.

On suggestions for coordination of programme output between the BBC and ITA in certain fields, the Authority was less than enthusiastic. The intention of Parliament as embodied in the 1954 Act had been, it recalled, that there should be competition between the two. Indeed, it was precisely because of the competitive initiative of ITV companies that the BBC had felt compelled to move as far as they had in the supposedly non-competitive fields of education, religious and Welsh language television. Nevertheless, in the interests of a common audience wishing to use both, the two services were already in the habit of meeting to arrange avoidance of clashes in timing. In ordinary sports coverage and in children's programmes competition was both defensible and beneficial. But the Authority did deplore the BBC's unco-operative attitude towards proposals for an alternation agreement to avoid wasteful duplication of coverage of big national sporting events as well as Royal and State occasions.

The Authority was forthright in its opposition to the idea of an ITV Code on Violence: it declared itself 'satisfied with its present arrangements for the control of violence in its programmes' and doubtful that a Code would make them more effective in any way. More valuable than written codes was the development of a climate of responsible opinion among producers. In fact, it was claimed, the recent record of ITV without a published code seemed to be better than that of the BBC. The internal statement of the Authority's general policy towards 'family viewing' was relied upon by those members of its staff who acted as programme 'censors', calling for (and getting) advance information and even previews of all programmes about which they harboured any doubts.[7]

These carefully compiled summaries had a cool reception at the upper level of the Post Office. Further symptoms of tension seemed to be emerging. According to German what the Minister was really hoping to get was a fresh appraisal by the Authority of the working arrangements, with the ITA in control and seen to be in control of programme planning and networking.[8] He was critical of the proposals for future control of programme standards: what he found unsatisfactory was that apparently 'virtually no change' in the Authority's current practice was being contemplated, even though changes in the 1954 Act were being asked for. He felt the Authority would be expected to participate 'in the detailed planning of programme schedules right from the start', even seeming to imply at one point that the decision to make any individual programmes should be made dependent on Authority consent. He pointed out that the Minister had agreed, at the Authority's wish, to regard its power to nominate programmes for the network as a reserve one. He was sure the PMG would be sorry if the Authority felt unable in its turn to move its own position in any important respect from what it had been when it gave evidence to the Pilkington Committee.

Writing on 16 November, and reflecting the Members' irritation as well as his own, Fraser stoutly denied that the Authority had not advanced beyond its Pilkington evidence. That had said that no further powers were needed in relation to the selection, planning and preparation of programmes, but merely the removal of the 'apprehending a breach' restriction on the supply of advance information. What was now being proposed – consultation about, scrutiny and advance approval of individual company programme schedules, plus a statutory committee to consider network schedules, chaired by the Authority – went far beyond that. He then added, in what was clearly intended as a rebuke to German, that the Authority was disturbed at the possibility that Ministers might have the impression that its present proposals were of scant significance, and that, in so far as this impression might be current in Ministerial circles, it was important that it should be removed.

It was not a happy situation and the Members had some reason to feel 'in disgrace with fortune'. There had been a hostile and, as they thought, unfair Report, some harsh words at Westminster and clear indications of a hawkish Minister. The companies were anxious and restless. Now it seemed they had to deal with an over-zealous top civil servant.

As for the question of the proposed formula for a levy on company profits, this was a matter which the Authority took very seriously indeed, bearing as it did upon the future livelihood of the whole ITV system. They saw it as something needing discussion with the Minister himself, and it figured prominently on the agenda of a meeting with Bevins on Wednesday 14 November. (By this time, Kirkpatrick having departed, the Authority spokesmen at these discussions were Carmichael, now Acting Chairman, and Sir Sydney Caine,[9] assisted by Fraser.) At this meeting, Bevins appeared to be impressed by the arguments in favour of substituting a graduated levy on company profits for the TAD.

Consequently, on 29 November Carmichael wrote to him personally spelling out in a step-by-step logical argument why the Authority believed that TAD should be abolished and a graduated levy substituted, as the most reasonable and defensible way of dealing with excessive profits without damaging the regional services of Independent Television. After a further meeting, Carmichael was able to report to the Authority on 4 December that 'discussions with the Post Office had gone well'.[10] He had come away with the impression that the officials were now in favour of the abolition of TAD and its replacement by a graduated impost on profits. Indeed Bevins had agreed that there would be no need to include details of the proposed charge on company profits in the White Paper. That could be settled subsequently at official level. In the meantime he had even seemed prepared to entertain the proposition that the serious impact of TAD on the smaller regional companies might justify some appropriate adjustments in that duty in the 1963 Budget. However, whether the Treasury would be persuaded to go along with him in his thinking on the major and minor issues was still to be discovered.

Throughout these discussions the Authority had repeatedly affirmed its distaste for the role of tax collector. It would have much preferred the graduated, profit-related payments to be collected directly by the Inland Revenue, in the form of a royalty payable to government by the commercial exploiters of a scarce national asset (the allotted radio frequencies) in much the same way as an international oil or mining company might pay a national government for a fixed-term concession to exploit the mineral resources on that government's national territory. Ever since the first Public Accounts Committee's enquiry into ITV profits, it had consistently regarded the 'rental' payments it took from the companies as designed exclusively to cover the costs of its own necessary statutory activities as the publicly accountable supervisor and controller of the programme services and as the provider of the technical transmission facilities, that is to say the physical means of access to the allotted frequencies. To the last the Members were prepared to accept only with great reluctance the inclusion of tax collection among the statutory duties laid on them by the Act.

During the three to four months of discussion between the first and second White Papers of 1962 one senses the distinctive presences of three interacting, more or less personalised, roles: those of the Authority, the senior Post Office civil servants and the Minister. With the departure of Kirkpatrick and the absence of an immediate successor, the main burden of focussing, interpreting and putting forward persuasively the views of the Authority fell, as so often before, on Fraser. Although he had stalwart backing from Carmichael, the personal contribution which he made during this period in particular to the future basis of ITV's growth and success was unique. The attitude he embodied and conveyed was of an Authority convinced that it had been unfairly treated and misrepresented by the Pilkington Committee; that it had brought into being and established high in popular esteem a public television service of a completely novel kind which had certainly some inadequacies and obstinate perversities but which had been progressively improved under gentle but persistent moral pressure, reinforced at times by public praise for progress as much as for achievement; but a system which had in any case been responsible, spontaneously and without external prompting, for significant innovations, artistically and socially, in British broadcasting; and which with no more than a few changes in organisation and inner power balance could become not merely a good television service of which no government need feel ashamed, but a service of excellence.

On the other hand, there was a PMG who was determined, as the chapters of his memoirs[11] covering this period confirm, to make his personal mark as a man of firm decision and clear views of the public interest;[12] embarrassed by the black and white dogmatism of Pilkington, but no less embarrassed by the equally exaggerated public reactions to that Committee's report; persuaded of the rightness of a competitive commercial broadcasting service but equally conscious of the political bonuses to be earned by the taming of over-mighty subjects and the mulcting of the over-swollen money bags. He may even at times have entertained the thought that, given the near bipartisan attitudes at times apparent in the July Commons debate, he could, by displaying the right firmness on well-chosen issues, ensure a less turbulent and time-wasting passage for the Bill than had been afforded the earlier measure, and in so doing earn for himself some credit in the Cabinet. But if he did, he would have found little in the speeches at that autumn's Labour Party and TUC Conferences to encourage the belief that Labour back-benchers would readily adopt the cautious approach of their leaders in the Shadow Cabinet. In fact the Labour Party Conference at Brighton on 2 October had passed a resolution unanimously supporting the Pilkington proposals.

The role of the Post Office civil servants between these two parties was obviously a delicate one. Naturally, with a piece of legislation on their hands, the Director General of the Post Office himself was closely involved, even though broadcasting was only one of his responsibilities; and both he and his colleagues would have had perforce to reflect on paper at least the attitudes of their Minister towards ITV. German was nothing if not zealous in doing just that.

When new legislation is in train to regulate the activities of an existing service, the traditional independence of broadcasting is inevitably at risk. Bevins' eagerness to show where the ultimate power lay might to some extent have been satisfied by the decision to abolish advertising magazines

made known in the July White Paper. Obviously 'interference' from on high
in the conduct of advertising could hardly be stigmatised as an attempt by
government to control the freedom of information. But the task of the
patient negotiators cannot have been made much easier when, after all the
sound and fury unleashed by the Pilkington Report, the ITV companies
came on the air with their autumn schedules not markedly changed in their
general pattern and balance from the previous quarter – still including even
advertising magazines, for example. 'The companies were showing utter
contempt for the Government's intentions and for public opinion'[13] quoted
Reynolds News from a statement by the Cambridge don, Peter Laslett, who
was chairman of the Viewers' and Listeners' Association. 'Quiz shows
return as ITV defies Pilkington'[14] headlined the *Daily Express*. The companies' defence could have been of course that changes in so far as they were
genuinely necessary could only be made as and when existing programme
contracts ran out. But, challenged, they continued to display a proclivity to
question the need for drastic change.

In all the circumstances it must surely be held remarkable that the second
White Paper when it appeared on Tuesday 18 December, conformed so
closely in its treatment of all main issues with what the ITA spokesmen had
proposed.

23

THE WHITE PAPER AND BILL: DECEMBER 1962

This 'further memorandum on the Report of the Committee on Broadcasting, 1960',[1] while not discounting the evidence of disquiet with certain aspects of ITV, rejected the Report's recommendations for radical change. What faults there were could be remedied by less drastic measures. The achievement of the existing system was such as to justify its continuance. But a decision on a second ITV service would be left in abeyance for the time being: the possibility that it would eventually be authorised was not ruled out, even though there was as yet no evidence of public demand for it and its financial prospects could be doubtful.

The section on networking recapitulated the Authority's own description and justification of a system built up around the three main areas of population, served by four large contractors and a number of smaller regional contractors. However, though indispensable, the four large companies should not be allowed to dominate the system: the rigidities of the networking arrangements would have to be removed, and to do this the ITA would be given increased powers and responsibilities, so as to assume 'a commanding position in the affairs of independent television'.[2]

The Authority would chair a scheduling committee representing all companies, and it would supervise the financial arrangements for buying and selling of programmes on their merits. The final responsibility for 'the shape, content, balance and quality of the service as a whole'[3] would rest with it; and it would be given a reserve power to nominate programmes for inclusion in the network schedules should the proper discharge of that responsibility make that necessary. It would be obliged to ensure that sufficient time was allotted to the news services of ITN and that adequate finance would be provided to enable them to carry out their functions, 'which include the provision of other types of information programmes'.[4] The companies would continue to be responsible for programme production and sale of advertising time. Their contracts would come up for renewal after three years and could be terminated if performance had been unsatisfactory. The Government was not prepared to place specific statutory restrictions on the participation of press interests in the programme companies, but it was proposed to give the Authority the right and duty to suspend or cancel a contract 'should newspaper holdings give rise to abuse'.[5] The PMG himself would be given a similar reserve power, subject to 'suitable Parliamentary safeguards'.[6]

The White Paper accepted the Authority's view that profits could well decline after 1964, once there was two-channel competition from the BBC. Nevertheless, 'they are still likely to be substantial, at any rate in the larger areas while there is only one commercial programme'. The forthcoming Bill would therefore have a specific provision requiring the Authority to collect adequate rentals, which would include 'a substantial payment calculated by reference to the profits of the companies before tax'.[7] (The present rentals, said Bevins in his press conference, were 'derisory'.[8]) Contrary to its own wishes, the substantial additional payment was to be collected by the Authority and then remitted to the Exchequer.

The Authority would not in future be required by statute to comply with the advice of its advisory committees; but it would be under an obligation to set up committees which were clearly necessary, i.e. committees to advise on programmes for schools, on religion and on advertising. It would be left to the Authority to decide whether or not to establish a General Advisory Council. There would no longer be any obligation to have a Children's Advisory Committee, for it would in any case be part of the Authority's general duty to consider the nature of programmes for children, as well as to consider the effect of the other programmes on children when large numbers may be expected to be viewing.

Taking a leaf from the Pilkington book, the White Paper said that the Government was seriously concerned about the dangers of excessive violence and excessive triviality in programmes, and discussions had taken place with both the BBC and the ITA. It did not think that prescription of detailed programme standards by legislation could be effective, but written codes of standards and practices did serve a useful purpose in focussing attention on problem areas requiring care and the broadcasting authorities would be expected to make effective use of them.

The Authority would be expected to take on more formal and direct control of executive decisions on advertisements; and it would be given additional statutory powers to regulate distribution, presentation, tone and style of advertisements, between programmes and in natural breaks within them. As the Authority had undertaken, there was to be increased consumer representation on the Advertising Advisory Committee which had already been asked to review and amplify its Principles for Television Advertising, special attention and care being given to commercials addressed to, or presented by, children. Lastly, it was recorded that the PMG had already issued a direction that advertising magazines should not be screened after 31 March 1963.

In response to the Government's readiness to grant extra broadcasting hours for adult education, the BBC and the ITA had consulted with educational bodies and had jointly put forward an acceptable formula defining the nature of such programmes. The PMG had expressed the hope that the two services would cooperate as fully as possible in this field of programming.

On coordination of output in general the White Paper accepted the ITA's contention that this would lead to a measure of joint planning which, even if it were feasible, would undermine the benefits of competition, but the two services had been told to cooperate as far as possible in education, religion and Welsh or Gaelic language programmes, areas where competition was inappropriate.

Most of the terms of this second White Paper had been generally anticipated. The *Financial Times* commented that the Government's proposals were 'with one exception much as expected',[9] the exception being postponement of a decision on ITV 2; but the newspaper still seemed to harbour doubts about the Authority's ability or willingness to assume a dominating role *vis-à-vis* the companies. On the proposed levy, judgement was perforce suspended until more was made known of the details. On the whole criticism was muted. As the *Yorkshire Post* said, 'although the unfortunate Pilkington Report gave birth to both White Papers, neither of them looks much like mother'.[10]

A foretaste of the subsequent Parliamentary haggle seems to have been given to Bevins almost immediately by the Government's own back-benchers, according to a report in *The Times* on a private meeting of the Conservative Party's broadcasting committee. Members were apparently sharply critical of the three-year contract proposal, believing that no new companies would enter the field on such limited security of tenure. Some back-benchers had complained that the Government seemed determined to reintroduce restrictive provisions which had been removed from the original Act as a result of back-bench pressure. Other speakers seem to have asked for more definite action on newspaper holdings in ITV companies. On the decision not to authorise a second commercial channel in the near future, the Minister appears to have been forced on to the defensive. His claim that the programme contractors did not want a second channel and his doubt about its probable financial viability were, said the report, both challenged. 'Competition with the existing commercial network was desirable and possible.'[11]

Of the spokesmen for ITV companies, only Renwick of ATV was reported as expressing sharply critical views of the Government's intentions. ATV had always been the company which were most unequivocally in favour of the extra competition that a second commercial service would provide. Despite its doubts about the viability of two ITV services competing with each other and also with two BBC services, the Authority too would have preferred a more forthcoming attitude, which would not exclude the possibility of ITV 2 starting at or about the same time as BBC 2, i.e. before the latter had succeeded in getting hold of additional audience at ITV's expense. Moreover, as long as the ITV 2 question remained undecided, an area of uncertainty was introduced into the ITA's engineering plans in respect of the proposed change-over to 625-lines UHF and the associated introduction of colour. In any case, the new contracts for the period after 1964 for which the Authority would be inviting applications would need to take into account any possibility that a second ITV service might be authorised within the period covered by such contracts.

The second White Paper was evidently intended as 'background reading' rather than as a discussion document, for it was swiftly followed on 20 December by the new Television Bill. Its preamble and opening clauses highlighted the main points in the Paper. The television service to be provided was for the first time described in similar terms to those used for the BBC: 'a public service for disseminating information, education and entertainment.'[12] It went on to be even more specific. The programmes would have to be of high general standard, properly balanced in subject matter and – this with obvious implications for the expected future role of the Authority in networking decisions – it would be an Authority duty 'to secure a wide showing for programmes of merit'.[13]

Stronger requirements figured in the subsequent provisions placing on the Authority the duty to draw up a code giving rules not only in respect of the screening of violence but also governing 'standards and practices'[14] for all programmes, especially when large numbers of children and young persons may be expected to be watching. It would be an obligation of the Authority to secure compliance with the code. All company programme schedules would have to be drawn up in consultation with the Authority and submitted to the Authority for approval in advance. No programme could be transmitted if not included in an approved schedule and the Authority would have in reserve the statutory power to give an unqualified direction to a company governing the inclusion or exclusion of any programme item or class of item.

Clause 4 of the Bill proposed that all programme contracts between companies and Authority would have to include provisions making clear its reserve power to ensure that a programme from one company would be shown by one or more other companies at the Authority's discretion; and that the financial arrangements for the supply of such a programme as well as those for any other bought-in programme from whatever source would have to be approved by the Authority. This provision for mandatory Authority approval of all programme prices went well beyond anything previously discussed. The most the Authority had ever contemplated was the use of discretionary rather than mandatory powers of approval, save only in the case of the supply of programmes from the four major companies to the others. The Authority would continue to have powers to produce or obtain programmes from outside sources, should that prove necessary in order to ensure 'programme balance' or in an interval which might occur in any area between the ending of one contract and the start of the next; but the famous provision for an annual grant of £750,000 would disappear.

The duty to draw up the Advertising Code was to be taken from the Advisory Committee and given to the Authority itself, although the Committee would remain a statutory one with the task of keeping under review and making recommendations to the Authority on desirable changes in the Code. But the Committee's advice would no longer be mandatory and it would be the Authority's obligation to secure compliance with the rules in the Code. It would have additional discretionary powers to impose any other specific requirement as to advertising it considered appropriate in particular circumstances and to make changes in the Code where it deemed that necessary.

Further discretionary powers were also spelled out, whereby the Authority could regulate by direction the timing, amounts and distribution and placing of the advertisements: and in these matters the PMG would also have permissive powers to impose his own rules after consultation with the Authority. Among other things, the rules would place a ban on advertising magazines, on 'subliminal advertising' and on 'excessively noisy or strident'[15] sound in advertising: these in addition to the existing bans on political and religious advertising. It would also be a duty of the Authority to have a medical advisory panel appointed after consultation with the PMG as to the professional organisations to be represented; and there would be an obligation to consult with this panel about the rules in the Code and to seek its advice before transmission of any commercial for medical, surgical or toilet products and treatments.

Clause 7 placed beyond doubt that Bevins intended to be tough about company profits. It dealt with the expected two-part rentals and in particular with the levy on profits which the Authority would have to collect for the Exchequer in addition to the payments received to meet its own expenses. The formulas for working out the levy would be settled by the PMG after consulting with the Treasury and the Authority, and the latter would have to include them in its contracts with the companies. These were to be 'framed by reference, among other things, to the annual profits of the programme contractors'[16] and steps would be taken to forestall evasion by taking into account also, where necessary, the profits of subsidiary or associated companies of the programme contractors. The profit figures to be used would be the gross figures before tax. In apparent response to an earlier Authority contention about the probable unfairness of a flat uniform rate, it was added that the formulas might be different from one company to another, and it could be left to the Authority to decide how the agreed formulas were to be applied in particular cases. If necessary the PMG would have power to direct the Authority to get the necessary financial information from the companies; and failure on their part to provide the information or the giving of false information would be made criminal offences.

There was a clause specifically dealing with the news. To the requirement of the 1954 Act of 'due accuracy and impartiality' was added one that 'a sufficient amount of time'[17] should be given to news, an addition which seems odd given the more general requirement of programme balance already in the Act. The White Paper commitment to the maintenance of ITN was to be honoured in the contracts ('at least one body . . . effectively equipped and adequately financed'[18]) and it was to be a supplier of other appropriate programmes besides the news. Provisions were included making it obligatory for future contracts to have legal safeguards against any changes in the control or ownership of companies which would have made them less acceptable as contractors in the first place. The Authority was also to have the option of including in the contracts even wider prohibitions against any changes in ownership or control; against the possession by any director or officer of one company of shares or profitable interests in another, either directly or indirectly via another holding company. Also to be covered in the contracts was the supply to the Authority of detailed information about programmes in advance, irrespective of any apprehension of a breach; and information about all other matters financial or technical which it, the Authority, might need in order efficiently to carry out its statutory duties. Its unused (and unusable) power to impose fines for breaches of contract was to be done away with, leaving merely the power to terminate after three breaches. If and when the Authority had responsibility for a second service, the two services should so far as possible be provided by different companies; but, nevertheless, they should be planned so that the same kinds of programme were not on the air at the same time.[19]

The Pilkington observation about the lack of qualitative audience research was reflected in a clause of the Bill requiring the Authority to bring the programmes and other activities 'under constant and effective review' and in particular to ascertain 'the state of public opinion about the programmes'.[20]

A modification of the 'due impartiality' requirement in the handling of controversial current affairs would be introduced putting beyond legal question the Authority's power to allow 'balance' or impartiality to be achieved over a series of broadcasts and not necessarily within single programmes.

Such were the main proposals of a piece of amending legislation that was being introduced in fulfilment of the Government commitment given in 1953 and 1954 that the scheme for Independent Television was an experimental one, which might well need to be modified in the light of experience. Two months were to pass before it came to be debated in Parliament. In the intervening weeks the Government would have ample opportunity to gather reactions from press, programme companies and the Authority.

The press reaction was singularly lacking in the stridency of its earlier response to Pilkington. Attention was concentrated on three issues: the attack on company profits; the failure to award the ITA a second channel; and the tightening of Authority controls. To the *Financial Times* the Bill seemed to go 'a good deal further'[21] than the White Paper in the powers which would be given to the Authority. 'The hostile attitude of the Pilkington Report has been retained but its positive suggestions ignored'[22] said the *Sunday Telegraph*, and then went on to echo the by now familiar argument that a second ITA service would at once be both the logical next step against broadcasting monopoly and the simplest way of reducing company profits. Most took for granted that the as yet unformulated profits tax would be tough, but the *Financial Times* reminded its readers that television profits were probably past their peak. On programme control, apart from the inevitable clichés about the dead hand of bureaucracy interfering in 'creative' work and some natural doubts about the practical value of codes, the general consensus was that much would depend on the willingness of the Authority to use its extensive new powers. The Bill 'will make it possible to improve the quality of the service'[23] said the *Observer*. 'It certainly amounts to something more than the benevolent supervision of the network,'[24] added the *Financial Times*.

Reactions amongst the ITV companies to the White Paper and the Bill were mixed and, in general, there was a marked reluctance to nail their colours to the mast. Robert Renwick of ATV hardly exaggerated in his statement in his company's annual report for 1963 when he said that within Independent Television there were nearly as many points of view as there are companies and that it was only in respect of certain limited objectives that there was any measure of agreement at all. The Granada Group report for 1963, whilst indicating Bernstein's dislike of what was by then the new Television Act, because of its seemingly restrictive nature, had nothing to say about its financial provisions. Likewise Wills, in his review at A-R's Annual General Meeting in September 1963, confined himself to a factual description of the eventual terms of the levy and to an assessment of its likely impact, *inter alia*, on the company's future prospects.

In marked contrast to the others, however, ATV had been unable to contain themselves. Renwick found the 'discriminatory' profits-based tax utterly repugnant and he said so in no uncertain terms to his shareholders, to the press, to Members of Parliament, and to the PMG himself. 'It is now proposed,' said an ATV brief to potential supporters at Westminster, 'that a member of the Government should decide the amount and the manner in which the companies' profits should be taken from them and that this money shall not be spent in any way on the furtherance of television but shall be paid direct into the Exchequer.' The provisions 'invite the Postmaster-General to behave in the most arbitrary fashion, ranging far beyond the consideration of operations directly deriving from the business of acting as a programme contractor'.[25]

Later, when – as we shall see – this 'levy' became a tax on turnover, Renwick's indignation knew no bounds. In his 1963 report he came near to admitting that his efforts, and those of colleagues like Norman Collins, to bring about a change in Government policy were not only unsuccessful but in all probability counterproductive. If it had been possible at the time the Bill was published for the major companies collectively to have declared their acceptance, however reluctantly, of a levy based on profits, the subsequent decision to change it to one on gross advertising revenue might perhaps have been avoided. In the event it was only when the much more restrictive 'turnover tax' came to be adopted by the Government that the Big Four began to speak with one voice in a memorandum sent to MPs. But by this time it was April 1963; the Cabinet had been persuaded that a profits-based levy would not work and the Bill had already reached the Committee stage. In the meantime, the ITA and the Government had been locked in discussion for more than three months.

After the Authority's meeting on 10 January 1963 the Members were joined at lunch by the PMG who was thus able to hear their comments on his Bill at first hand. These were subsequently summarised and sent to him.[26] They hoped it could be assumed that such broad definitions as 'high general standards in all respects' and the interpretation of expressions like 'programme of merit' would be left to the Authority's judgement and realisation 'so far as possible'. They expressed doubt about the proposed comprehensive code 'governing standards and practice for all programmes' which could in its application 'stifle creative programming' and by its very generality might pre-empt necessary particular acts of judgement. It would be going unnecessarily far to require Authority approval for the financial and other arrangements governing *all* programme transactions. A more practical approach would be to give the Authority discretionary power to intervene where it thought fit. The Members looked forward to getting as soon as possible more information about the financial provisions: about the future of the TAD, about the formula determining the amounts of the 'additional payments'. They welcomed Bevins' assurance that they would be invited to participate in discussions with the Post Office and Treasury on these matters.

A second part of this note marked a significant step in the Authority's recoil from its initial cautious hesitations over the financial prospects of a second commercial service. 'To avoid any doubt the Authority wishes to put on record its willingness to introduce as soon as possible a second programme in those areas where it can be demonstrated that two self-supporting services can be sustained.'

In the ensuing weeks the familiar exchanges between Post Office and ITA senior officials continued on details of the published Bill. This activity did not go unnoticed. 'At talks between the Post Office and the Independent Television Authority, the ITA have, in effect, said: "If you want our co-operation, give us a second channel",'[27] wrote Clifford Davis in the *Daily Mirror*. This interpretation reflected the fact that, by some back-bench Tory MPs, and amongst the companies by ATV, this deferment of ITV 2 was seen as symptomatic of a Government attitude less favourable to commercial television than good Conservatives were entitled to expect. Bevins had to defend his Bill before more than one private meeting of Party members. It was felt that the hitherto effective challenge to the old monopoly would inevitably be weakened once ITV with still only one channel was facing the BBC with two. Moreover, the powers which the Bill proposed for the Government and the Authority over the companies' activities were regarded as a denial of free enterprise. Apart from the excessive 'grandmotherly' controls, particular concern was naturally directed towards the powers to be given to the Minister 'to impose a levy of any size on any or all of the companies'.[28] Reporting the general expectation that Bevins would be making a more explicit statement on this subject, *The Times* noted that he had already been trying to allay uneasiness, and the 'fear in some Conservative quarters that in this way ITV will in effect be milked to provide a subvention for the development of its rival, the BBC'.[29]

The clarification of the already notorious Clause 7 was in the meantime being handled in a manner which proved not just more explicit but also disconcerting for ITV. On 31 January the staff had informed an Authority meeting that no reply had been received to the letter sent after the PMG's visit; and that, in particular, no further information had been received on the progress of discussions between the Post Office and the Treasury about Clause 7. Members were reminded of Bevins' undertaking that they would be invited to participate in those discussions at an appropriate stage. Almost immediately thereafter Fraser was informed by German that the Government had changed its mind: the 'additional payments' to be exacted from the companies would be levied not on profits before tax, but on gross advertising revenue. They would be calculated on a sliding scale, after allowing for all companies a 'free slice', not subject to levy. It was scant comfort that German was able to assure Fraser that in the 1964 Budget the Television Advertising Duty would be abolished. The Authority had always taken it for granted that TAD would end once a more equitable impost on ITV company earnings had been introduced. But the change in the basis of the additional payments appeared to be a virtual *fait accompli*, for the new 'formula', it was learned, was to be submitted for Cabinet approval on 7 February.

Carmichael at once told Bevins that, while welcoming the proposed abolition of TAD, he was sure the Members would find the switch to a levy on income rather than profits objectionable in principle. It would also make the eventual introduction of a second service, which the Government apparently intended, much more difficult. The Authority were now, he said, persuaded that it would be feasible to introduce a second service in the three central areas – London, Midlands and the North. It would prefer to do this sooner rather than later for two good reasons. First in order to secure its share of the UHF frequencies and secondly because the commercial television system would be placed at a clear competitive disadvantage if a second ITV service in UHF had to be introduced after BBC 2 had had time to establish itself with the audience.

But by this time Bevins was evidently too far committed to be able to offer any concessions either on the second service proposal or on the additional payments. On the latter and more immediate issue, he recalled the many critical comments made publicly of Clause 7 by press, other politicians and some of the companies. It is a safe supposition that by early February the Treasury had told the Post Office that they found no merit in a levy on ITV company profits. It would offer too many loopholes which it would be difficult to close. For the Treasury, and now – in spite of the wording of his Bill – for Bevins himself, the most rational way of establishing realistic rentals would be a levy assessed on the true value of the public concessions granted to the companies, that is to say on the basis of the gross income which exploitation of those concessions brought in.

When the Authority next met on 21 February, Carmichael was able to report that he had by then received an invitation from Bevins to submit draft changes to Clause 7 which would enable the Authority to make appropriate representations to the PMG at any time that the current levy formula was operating unfairly in individual cases. He had already agreed that changes in the levy formula would be necessary in areas where a second commercial service would eventually be launched. The scale of the levy in any event would, it was proposed, be subject to Parliament's approval each year. As we shall see in Chapter 24, the battles around Clause 7 came to dominate the course of the second Television Bill's passage through Parliament.

Bevins seems to have recognised that his behaviour may have appeared high handed and he went out of his way to make one or two conciliatory gestures. He undertook to consider amendments to any parts of the Bill which the Authority regarded as putting ITV at a disadvantage *vis-à-vis* the BBC. He also agreed that the Authority's reservations about the all-embracing application of the proposed programme Code were well founded. These were, however, matters on which Members of Parliament would soon be claiming their say. The uneasy interlude between publication of the White Paper and Bill and the process of legislation was over at last.

24

PASSAGE OF THE SECOND
TELEVISION BILL: 1963

The Second Reading debate in the Commons[1] might well have further encouraged Bevins to believe that he would have a relatively easy, bipartisan passage for his Bill. Apart from his announcement of his intention to introduce an amendment to Clause 7, changing the basis for assessment of the 'additional payments', it was an unmemorable occasion. The change from a levy on profits to one on gross advertising income apparently came as a surprise. Neither Fred Willey, leading for the Labour opposition, nor Jeremy Thorpe for the Liberals, seem to have been properly briefed and had to be corrected on their factual assumptions.

For the most part Opposition speakers took the line that it was no good trying to turn the clock back. Independent Television was obviously here to stay. Generally speaking they thought the Bill was on the right lines, even if it did not always go far enough in its efforts to correct the shortcomings of ITV. But they looked forward to the Committee stage when they would seek to put that right.

There were the familiar arguments for and against a second ITV service; on the desirability of codes on programme and advertising standards; on press holdings; on the impracticability of three-year contracts; on the control and amount of advertising; and on networking. What venom there was from the Opposition benches was directed mainly against the Authority as scapegoat. It had been feeble and irresponsible in its exercise of controls over programmes and advertisements. It was even suggested that the new Bill would not have been necessary had the Authority not failed to make full use of the powers it already had under the 1954 Act. 'The House has been let down by these people,' said W. R. Williams, winding up for the Labour opposition. The effectiveness of the improvements proposed by the Bill would be doubtful, they thought, if the Authority did not begin to assert itself more forcefully. The new Chairman would have to be a remarkable man 'capable of telling the Authority, and the programme contractors what they must do'. So, said Williams, 'we mean to give the ITA another chance'.

Several members were at pains to demonstrate their broadmindedness by expressing a liking for the BBC's currently successful satire show *That Was The Week That Was*, including especially its satirical comments on politicians. Notwithstanding the need for a stronger hand at the ITA, they felt it would be wrong to prevent the independent companies from being equally free to poke fun at the Establishment. Iain Macleod, winding up for the Government, also drew attention to the liberalising tendency of the clause which allowed due impartiality and political 'balance' to be achieved over a series rather than within a single broadcast. Since the end of the monopoly both the BBC and ITV had achieved much worthy of praise. We want the best of both worlds, he said; and this was what the Bill aimed to get. He was confident it would work, especially if there was a 'strong man' in charge of the Authority. It seemed a very far cry indeed from the libertarian outlook of the One Nation Group some ten years earlier.

The Bill was read a second time without a division, with all the appearance of a preliminary formality. The real business of forging an effective new statutory instrument would be done upstairs in Committee. As more than one Opposition member was to imply when that stage was reached, they regarded the document before them as a draft which it was their intention substantially to rewrite. Small wonder then that the weeks ahead were to witness extensive lobbying from interested parties on all sides. Letters, pamphlets, memoranda, luncheon invitations and requests for interviews poured in to the forty members of the Standing Committee B from at least as many sources as those which had previously stated their case in evidence to Pilkington. Spokesmen for actors, writers, musicians, technicians, advertisers and others all sought to enlighten and influence the MPs; this of course in addition to the ITV companies, individually and collectively, and the ongoing, uninterrupted activity of the Authority with the Minister and his officials. A lengthy memorandum of detailed clause by clause comments was, for example, sent to the PMG on behalf of the ten regional companies, which felt entitled to see in the Bill an intention to further, in part at least, their common interests *vis-à-vis* the Big Four. They were also clearly concerned that improved flexibility in networking arrangements might – because of the greater powers of direction by the Authority that these entailed – lead to additional financial commitments, administrative complications and restraints on their responsible exercise of desirable planning freedoms.

With a Bill likely to influence, however tangentially, the daily lives of most of the population (but which left important issues still inviting amendment) there was bound to be press attention focussed on the responsible Minister. *The Greasy Pole*, Bevins' own account of his political experiences (which was serialised in the *Sunday Express*), leaves the reader in no doubt that for him this period was among the most memorable in his whole political career. He remembers it as a time when he was the object of almost continuous pressure, not least from his own party back-benchers and fellow Ministers. 'I could hardly turn in the Palace of Westminster without being badgered.'[2] Small wonder that he committed what he himself describes as an 'indiscretion'. Under the mistaken impression that the conversation was 'off the record' he talked too freely to a journalist from the *Daily Express*. On 5 March, two days before the first sitting of the Standing Committee, an account of that interview appeared under the headline 'The Postmaster-General Confesses'. True, the Minister later claimed that words had been 'put into his mouth' and the verbatim quotation 'until now the Government has failed in its duty to the taxpayer as far as ITV is concerned' bore a family likeness to similar phrases used from time to time in *Daily Express* leaders. But his reported references to 'pressure groups' in the Tory party, to 'the 1945-55 boys who have somehow or other become entangled with ITV' can scarcely have done much for his popularity in the party. Still less will back-benchers have appreciated his apparent assimilation of both the Conservative Party Broadcasting Committee and the 1922 Committee with these 'two channel boys' who wanted a second channel, and eventually more profit for ITV. 'I have not said some of these things publicly before because if I did I should have half the Tory Party round my neck.' He did. The day after the article appeared, he attended a meeting of the 1922 Committee. He claims in *The Greasy Pole* that the meeting was satisfied with his justification of many of the statements attributed to him. Others, including Sir Harmar Nicholls and several of the newspapers, claim that he apologised.

Bevins asserts that the incident merely served to stiffen his resolve to go his own way, and he identifies this with the proposals for additional payments based on advertising revenue. But the interview did also deal with his intention to appoint a strong man 'on the same wavelength as myself' to be the new ITA Chairman and with his low opinion of the programmes he had seen: 'A lot of what I see is awful'. These remarks too were to be recalled in the Standing Committee discussions. The reaction of the ITA to this 'indiscretion' was that it was, as Caine put it, 'more damaging to the Conservative Party than to the Authority'. 'What was more regrettable,' he thought, 'was the total absence of any convincing defence of the Authority by the Postmaster-General on the floor of the House.'[13]

The situation presented an uneasy dilemma for Bevins. Parliament was being asked to approve a Bill whose main purpose could readily be interpreted as a specific prescription from central Government on the way a national broadcasting service was to be run. It was not simply a question of the excessive profits of a group of commercial enterprises. If Bevins' *Express* interview was anything to go by, the Opposition said, he did not particularly like much of the ITV programme output either and wanted stricter, more effective controls to provide the kind of programmes he felt able to defend. Since the Authority was to be the public instrument of those controls, should its performance not be subjected to more regular scrutiny by the legislators? Why not require its annual report to be debated in Parliament? After all, they claimed, it was the failure of the Authority to do the job properly that had made this Bill necessary. These were arguments the man introducing the Bill must have found difficult to square with a political commitment to the principles of competitive free enterprise, freedom of opinion and non-interference with information media – those very principles indeed which had justified the successful attack on monopoly and the creation of ITV ten years previously.

However, the ensuing dialogue between Government and Opposition took on a markedly different character from that of the 1953/4 debate. Relatively far fewer of the debates were pushed to the point of division. There was this time little sign of the fundamental conflict of principle: whether or not commercial broadcasting should exist at all in Britain. After all, not even Pilkington, not even Mayhew, had argued for the abolition of ITV. So perhaps, notwithstanding the criticisms, the first eight years of this young television service had pragmatically proved something. The realities with which all politicians must reckon were no longer what once they were.

Yet it would be wrong not to take into account as well the political situation in early 1963. Even before the Profumo scandal which was soon to break, Macmillan's administration was losing authority and popular esteem. The Labour opposition on the other hand, notwithstanding the untimely death of Hugh Gaitskell in January, were on a wave of growing optimism, confidently anticipating a return to power at a general election which did not seem likely to be much more than twelve months away. Under the pragmatic leadership of Harold Wilson they were not going to fritter away their appeal to floating voters by a display of doctrinaire attitudes towards a popular television service. A spirit of unity prevailed. In Tory ranks, on the other hand, there were increasing signs of disarray.

Rejection of Britain's EEC candidature, the Vassal spy case, rising un-employment in the North, dissensions about defence policy, the Beeching plan, and a series of by-election defeats had all contributed. And there was more to come.

Against such a background, Bevins' hopes of ensuring an easy passage for his Bill seemed to be in the adoption of as much of a bi-partisan approach as possible. His apparent concessions to Pilkingtonian attitudes provoked largely ineffective protest from Tory members; the group of anti-monopoly crusaders in the party were no longer the vigorous fighting force that once they had been. Nor were they very well represented by their spokesmen on the Standing Committee. The Minister's feelings could well have been somewhat mixed when on 28 March he heard a Labour member say that the Opposition would be delighted to support him if he proceeded on the lines they believed he intended. To which Fred Willey added, for good measure, that they would not oppose him if he found himself being opposed on the benches behind him.

There was almost total agreement that the ITV contractors should be subjected to stricter controls. What differences emerged concerned means rather than ends. Bevins could of course count on general support from the Labour members for measures to reduce the companies' profits. What tussles he had over these took place not only, as we shall see, within his own party but also to a large extent outside the forum of Parliament. Indeed when the controversial Clause 7 in its final amended form came to be debated on the floor of the House the battle had already been fought and lost and it was approved with little more than token resistance. But the absence of overall opposition to the Bill did not mean that important issues of broad-casting policy were not given a full and proper airing. Quite the contrary.

Several Labour speakers were especially concerned about the difficulty of exercising Parliamentary control over the activities of the ITA, and indeed of the BBC as well. This was, as one Welsh member pointed out, only a special aspect of the more general constitutional problem created by the existence of a whole range of virtually autonomous statutory public bodies apparently answerable to no one but themselves. In the present case, the problem was all the more grave, they felt, because it related not to a body like the Coal Board or British Rail but to one supposedly in charge of a medium that touched the minds and hearts of men, to say nothing of the young and innocent. If, as they believed, Pilkington was right in saying that the Authority had failed in its public duty, then it was not good enough to set up such a body and leave it free to run its own affairs unchecked for another twelve years. There should be at least a full debate on the ITA's annual report in each year on the same scale as on a Defence White Paper. To deny the elected representatives of the people the right to judge the fulfilment of a public trust by a body they had themselves established was 'intolerable to democrats'.[4] The Opposition's present willingness to accept television with advertising, said Donald Chapman, rested on the assumption that it would in future be better controlled by an Authority less remote and more vigorous than the one they had known.

Their persistent doubts were strengthened by an article by Kirkpatrick which appeared in *The Times* on 21 March. The recently retired ITA Chairman not only strongly criticised the intended levy on advertising revenue and the proposed new programme controls, he also concluded: 'In this whole business the Postmaster-General is thrashing about like a stranded porpoise on the beach . . . It is high time that political responsibility for broadcasting was transferred to a Cabinet Minister equipped to grasp the complicated issues.' Such an attitude, if it was shared by existing Authority Members, to say nothing of its senior staff, hardly augured well for conscientious fulfilment, in an atmosphere of mutual trust, of the wishes of Parliament as expressed in the new Bill.

Some comfort was given to the harassed Authority when Bevins said that he did not think some of the members' criticisms had been wholly fair 'to the ITA staff . . . and to some of the many worthy people who work for it and who are dedicated to television and who are trying, often in the face of considerable difficulties, to make the best of their jobs'.[5] Eventually a measure of more or less reluctant agreement was reached that there was no practical alternative to choosing the best available people, and letting them get on with it; and that it would not be easy to get such people for the Authority if they were not allowed some latitude for the exercise of responsible independent judgement. The Minister was pressed to name the man he wanted for the vacant post of ITA chairman. He had, after all, said in his *Daily Express* interview that he had in mind a man 'with the necessary drive'. But at this stage Bevins was not able to oblige. Rumours were already current that Kirkpatrick's successor was to be Dr Charles (soon to be Lord) Hill. But the standing in the country of the Conservative Party had at that time caused the Prime Minister to put off for the time being the risk of another by-election defeat in the marginal constituency of Luton for which Hill was the sitting member.

When finally the official announcement was made in July by way of a written answer to a Parliamentary question, it came inevitably under fire in the Upper House. This amounted to something more than the customary partisan gibes at 'jobs for the boys'.[6] There appeared to be a significant break with tradition in the appointment of a well known, controversial party politician to head the controlling body of one of the two national broadcasting services, especially when that politician had himself been PMG in ITA's early days. As will be seen in Part IV the expected consequences of the Hill appointment did not come about.

If the Authority was to enjoy such a degree of independent responsibility in its future exercise of a dominant role in the affairs of ITV, Labour members were concerned that the law should spell out as unequivocally as possible what in detail the responsibilities of that role should be. Yet when applied to questions of programme control such intentions encountered dilemmas. The decisions that had to be made were essentially value judgements, qualitative and subjective, and this fact was also reflected in the ambivalence of Parliamentary attitudes. Thus when Bevins, after further exchange with the Authority, moved an amendment to the sweeping generality of the Bill's requirement for a Code of programme 'standards and practices', he appeared to make it at once more specific and more indeterminately general. It would apply specifically to the showing of violence, particularly when children and young people might be viewing; but also to such other matters as the Authority itself might decide, and the purpose of the Code was re-defined as 'giving guidance' instead of 'governing standards and practices'.[7] The amendment was approved but the Minister seemed himself half inclined to accept the ITA's arguments against the use of programme codes. But he concluded pragmatically that, given known public disquiet, it would offer some reassurance if there existed a formal document, at least, signalling the fact that here was an area of special concern and responsibility for the Authority. At the same time, he resisted a Labour proposal that the Code should be drawn up in consultation with himself and subject to his approval. So a programme code in its amended form remained a requirement of the Bill in spite of a last minute, intelligent and witty attempt to remove it by Lord Conesford in the Upper Chamber.[8]

With such limited Ministerial control and no direct supervision or control by Parliament – by what John Reith once called in a similar context 'the Mother of Abominations' – how then was the ITV service to be kept accountable to public opinion and sensitive to public feeling? This has been (and will doubtless always be) a vexed question for public broadcasting services, given that public opinion, public sensitivities and public interest are not invariably identical. The Bill was apparently intended to make the ITA's relationship to independent outside advisers more rather than less discretionary than in the past, and this left the Opposition uneasy. Willey proposed a General Advisory Council appointed by the Minister, reporting to him annually and he in turn laying the Report before Parliament. Governments had been slow to recognise, he said, the need for adequate consumer representation *vis-à-vis* the public service corporations.[9]

Some members thought there should be a body analogous to the Press Council for all broadcasting, to deal with all public complaints about both BBC and ITV programmes. Published codes were not enough. It was their observance which mattered. Bevins thought that a Consumer Council for ITV would not be able to do anything the Authority could not already do. Personally, he favoured the idea of a GAC and he felt the Authority would no doubt appoint one,[10] but he was averse to anything implying regular Ministerial intervention into the activities of ITV. He was of course echoing Pilkington's rejection of the idea of a Broadcast Consumers' Council. 'The task envisaged for it is part of what the Governors and Members are themselves appointed to undertake.'[11] The Opposition had to rest content with the new requirement that the Authority should in future engage in audience research rather than rely on ratings statistics compiled in the interests of advertisers.

The Authority's future control of advertising content, quantity and distribution were debated at much greater length. All Labour spokesmen were persuaded that this was an area where the public was in even greater need of protection. This applied not just to the possible influence on programmes of the advertisements but above all to their content. Yet in the outcome much the same general attitude as had been displayed towards controls over programme standards and practice came to be adopted (*mutatis mutandis*) towards such questions as the Advertising Code, the degree of consultation with the Advertising Advisory Committee, the degree of consultation with the Minister and his powers of direct intervention. Roughly speaking the final position reached was on the following lines. It was better not to have too many rules, too narrowly drawn, once Minister and Authority have reached agreement on what may not be advertised; and provided, for the rest, proper advice was taken. The Authority should have adequate powers of enforcement but latitude within which to apply responsible judgement in the exercise of those powers. After Bevins had explained what would be the Authority's executive role in advertising control under the new provisions, doubts and hesitations seem to have been allayed and the relevant clauses of the Bill were approved virtually unchanged.

Yet the Opposition continued to hanker after more precise rules. Even Moses, it was said, found there was a need for the Ten Commandments, however much he preached about good conduct. It would be wrong to leave an impression that violence was the only matter for concern. There was blasphemy, obscenity, emotionally disturbing and other offensive material, all too often displayed on television. But eventually Fred Willey parted company from some of his colleagues, saying that what was 'vitally important' was not the formulation of rules, but 'the character of the Authority, its sense of public duty and the steps it takes to discharge that duty'.[12] He went even further, urging that the Code should be drawn up in consultation with the programme companies, to which the Minister replied that such consultations would surely take place in any event without the need for a statutory obligation.

If there were to be rulers, all members were anxious that there should be parity of treatment between BBC and ITV programme-makers. And so inevitably back into the debate came *That Was The Week That Was*. 'This programme has offended me occasionally, and I do not think it would have been worth while if it had not' (Willey); 'when I was lampooned on this programme the members of my family . . . laughed their heads off, and so did I' (Bevins).[13] There was general regret that because of the prohibition in Section 3 of the 1954 Act against offensive representation of living persons, ITV had been prevented from transmitting similar programmes. 'So long as the BBC is allowed to do it, what is wrong in allowing ITA to do it?'[14] asked Ness Edwards; and Bevins had all-party support for his declared intention of introducing an amendment that would remove the discriminatory prohibition.

On such and similar lines the discussions proceeded throughout all the twenty sittings of the Commons Standing Committee, the four debates in the Commons and the four in the Lords, with a noteworthy absence of displays of doctrinaire passion. The overall trend that emerges from study of the debates is a desire to produce a workmanlike Bill, to define more clearly the duties and powers of the Authority, particularly in those areas where experience had revealed possibilities of abuse. The objective was a defensible compromise between that degree of control deemed desirable to defend the public interest on the one hand, and on the other the practical demands of commercial viability and creative freedom in the supply of a wide range of education, information and entertainment. Virtually all amendments that were accepted were framed in this way. Though a few were defeated and many withdrawn (usually because it had been made clear that their intentions were implicit in existing provisions), it was more than once emphasised that this time round at least both companies and Authority would be expected to take guidance from what had been actually said in the debates in order to interpret and carry out more adequately the intentions behind the bare text of the law.

Although the proposed new powers included some the Authority had itself asked for and which it was already exercising *de facto* if not *de jure*, others went further than it would have wished. It continued to be unhappy with the proposed power to command inclusion of particular programmes in a schedule, especially those so termed 'programmes of merit'. It felt that the duty to satisfy itself that a schedule was as a whole up to standard in content, quality and balance should suffice. But while stressing that it should be seen very much as a reserve power of last resort, the Minister insisted that it must be there. He rejected as otiose the suggestion from Tory back-benchers Wakefield and Harmar Nicholls that the Authority should be required to give reasons for refusing to approve a schedule.

At one stage there was an amendment moved by W. R. Williams which looked suspiciously like a revival of the ill-fated £750,000 (see Volume 1). 'The Authority should have the power to produce some programmes if it thinks there is a need to do so.'[15] Willey mentioned that some producers would welcome the sort of support an Authority empowered to produce could give to research and new developments in programme production. This amendment was pressed to a division which was lost by 179 to 133 votes. The same proposal was given a second and slightly longer run in the Lords on 18 July. 'I know many excellent television producers and writers who have ideas for new experiments in television,' said Francis Williams '. . . who it is important should be encouraged.'[16] On a division it was again decisively rejected. And in the Act as it finally emerged, the section of the 1954 Act under which the PMG was able to make grants to the Authority was formally annulled.

However, late in the proceedings in the Lords an interesting new power for the Authority to take part in the provision of programmes was inserted. Moved by Lord Eccles, himself a former Minister of Education, what consequently came to be known as the 'Eccles Amendment' made it possible for the Authority, with the consent of the Minister, to arrange with outside educational bodies for the provision of 'educational broadcasting services of an experimental nature'[17] which would be additional to those already provided by the programme contractors in their approved schedules. Lord Eccles was full of praise for these. They were an ample demonstration of the educational potential of the television medium. He recalled the Authority's submission to Pilkington proposing the creation of a national ETV service to be controlled by neither BBC nor ITA but by a consortium of educational organisations. Until such a scheme became practicable the new clause would make it possible for appropriate limited experiments to be conducted. The background to this proposal was threefold: the existence of an unused VHF broadcasting frequency in Northern Ireland; the interest expressed by the governing body of Queen's University in Belfast for this possible extension of their extra-mural teaching; and the ready cooperation of Ulster Television, already enthusiastic would-be pioneers, notwithstanding relatively limited resources, for televised adult education.

Eccles was able to add that the Authority would itself be prepared to finance such an experiment for a period of up to three years, should the Minister agree to the use of the vacant channel. The Eccles Amendment did not of course come as a total surprise. Mention had already been made at Commons Report stage by Fred Willey for the Opposition of UTV's enterprising *Midnight Oil* venture and the interest shown by educationalists in the Province.[18] He also drew attention to plans already being made for a further experiment, this time a series of early morning lectures by Cambridge dons under the title *Dawn University* to be provided in cooperation between Anglia Television and the Cambridge Television Committee. But at this stage such experiments had received rather a cool reception from the Post Office.

On 30 July the Commons readily gave their blessing to this Lords amendment. Although the powers given by it were never in the event to be used and the Queen's University project fizzled out, it can without exaggeration be counted, together with *Midnight Oil* and *Dawn University*, as one of the sources of Harold Wilson's initiative about a University of the Air, leading to what has since become a notable British educational achievement, the Open University.

The additional Authority power to require a company to include a named programme in its schedule was justified as a necessary instrument for breaking the rigidities of the network and ensuring programme balance. But it was also seen by the PMG as a means of improving the position of the small regional companies, giving them a possible prospect of networking for some of their local productions. But encouragement to the regionals was also seen by many members as desirable on financial grounds. Although it was only the three or four smallest companies which were less than handsomely prosperous, the Big Four were acknowledged to be inordinately so: and this was attributable in part at least to their domination of the network through the affiliation agreements. These, in their present form, would have to go. But in addition the Minister and both sides of the House agreed that the fiscal measures designed to reduce excessive company profits would need to be so framed as to protect the regionals. Members were at that time inevitably impressed by the difficulties (and impending collapse) of the ill-fated Wales (West and North) company. For a Welsh member (and former PMG) like Ness Edwards, this was an outstanding example of the regional principle, the very epitome of a company with local roots formed to serve a clearly defined distinctive regional interest.[19]

The miscalculations that had led to the creation of WWN were taken by Edwards and other Welsh members as a cue for strong criticisms of the Authority's whole approach to the designation of contract areas. It was absurd, they urged, to have two Welsh companies, one of which needed a slice of the West Country to have a viable population base and the other of which was unable to survive because of the smallness of its audience. There should be a single exclusively Welsh ITV company; and the Bristol area attached to South West England. If Ulster could have its own ITV service, why not Wales?[20]

The familiar note of linguistic nationalism was sounded by the veteran James Griffiths, asserting that television with its great social influence 'can help to preserve the Welsh language or it can kill it'.[21] He looked forward to an all-Welsh ITV company, with obligations towards the language and culture of Wales, acting in cooperation with the BBC. Bevins, in his response, underlined the Government's expectation that ITV and BBC would cooperate in areas of programming where competition was inappropriate such as education, religion and, naturally also, Welsh language programmes. Nevertheless, it remained the Government's view that designation and allocation of ITV franchise areas was strictly a matter for the Authority. It was, he knew, looking again at the problem of transmission frequencies as it affected the situation in Wales. But over and above the technical, topographical facts of life which placed a limit on what could be done, were the commercial realities faced by a service financed not by licence but by advertising.[22]

The Welsh lobby were not satisfied with Bevins' reply. One Labour opponent of the amendment annulling the Government's power to make grants to the Authority suggested that such grants ought to be maintained for the purpose of subsidising Welsh language programmes should these prove to be uneconomic.[23] This was the very claim that TWW had made in 1956/7 when the ITA lost its battle to secure the promised £750,000. The issue was raised again and forced to a division in the Lords and defeated by the narrow margin of 42 to 38.

The question of how much and what kind of imported material should be permitted was of course another of the perennial broadcasting issues debated more than once during the passage of the Bill. The motives of the Parliamentary Opposition were partly the customary anxiety over a flood of cheap American rubbish, partly concern at the high rate of unemployment in the British film industry. But they were not all of one mind on the desirability of fixed quotas. To demand a minimum proportion of all film material shown to be of British origin could, it was recognised, as easily lead to a flood of cheap British rubbish. It was even recognised that by no means all US material was poor. Fred Willey liked an idea put to Pilkington by Granada that a means should be found for selecting such worthwhile meritorious programmes (perhaps a panel from unions, Authority and companies?) so that they could be shown irrespective of any existing quota agreement.

What was needed was not so much more restrictive measures (which could provoke retaliation) as the development of a lively and efficient British 'telefilm' industry, exploiting the wealth of home grown talent that the growth of British television had revealed and capable of successful competition in world markets. And attention was drawn to the achievements of one of ATV's associated companies, ITC, which under Lew Grade's direction had achieved an export revenue of four million dollars.

In both Houses there were fulsome all-party tributes to ITN. Viscount Swinton did not think anything could be better than the presentation of the ITN news broadcasts.[24] They were, thought Willey, a most successful contribution to the development of British television with a beneficent influence on both the BBC and ITV as a whole. ITN had done a 'grand job' said Ness Edwards.[25] Such remarks have a somewhat ironic ring when one recalls the anxieties expressed by Labour in the 1953/4 debates over the baneful and disastrous influence that base commercial motives would have on the integrity of the news service.

Lingering vestiges of such anxieties were perhaps behind the suggestion that the Authority should have more say in the appointment of the Editor and Chief Executive of the news company. But it was not pressed. Readily agreed, probably no doubt on the basis of safety in numbers, was a Government amendment requiring that all the programme contractors – rather than just the early 'founder members' – should have the right to financial participation in the news company organisation. The Authority had suggested to Bevins – without success – that it should not be made responsible for ensuring that ITN is 'suitably equipped and financed'.[26]

The Bill's other provision that the news company should be financed and equipped to supply other factual programmes apart from news gave an opportunity for discussion of one persistent unresolved problem of broadcasting policy, namely, whether or not there should be a clear organisational division between the providers of news bulletins and those of current affairs programmes. But it was not pursued in any depth, which was just as well for the waters here were much too deep for Parliamentarians to dabble in. Whatever the theoretical policy arguments, the emergence of numerous regional ITV 'news magazines' had in simple practical terms already added a significant new aspect to the question.

Members did, however, revert, and at some length, to the latent threat to democracy (as they saw it) in the apparent concentration of power and control over the media of public communication represented by the substantial financial participation of the press in some ITV companies – STV and Southern TV in particular. Morrison and Willey wanted total exclusion of the press; and Roy Mason drew attention to the current campaign by the interested press against the financial provisions of the Bill. But not all their colleagues agreed. Chapman wondered (with some reason) whether profitable participation in a regional ITV company had not been a means of keeping more than one local newspaper alive. The matter was finally left, much as Pilkington and the Bill had proposed, for the PMG and Authority in consultation to decide whether in any particular case drastic action (e.g. contract termination) needed to be taken. As a placatory gesture to the Opposition Bevins did, however, change the grounds for such action from 'abuse' to 'leading to results which are contrary to the public interest'.[27] But in so doing he shrewdly recalled that without the Roy Thomson group there would have been no Scottish company at all, a development scarcely 'in the public interest'.

As we have seen, the Conservative back-bench supporters of ITV did not play a very prominent part in most of the early debates. Their position was not an easy one. They were no longer the defenders of the very principle of a commercially-financed competitive television service. The Opposition had now conceded that. The victory had been won: the service was successful, all too successful for some people. They were faced instead with a Minister of their own party (with Socialist antecedents) who was determined on change and who could if necessary count on Labour support for much of what he proposed. In the circumstances, all the Tory members could do was try to ensure that the new measures did not go too far; did not, that is, weaken too drastically the independence and vitality of the ITV companies and their competitive strength *vis-à-vis* the BBC. Their overriding objection to the Pilkington Report lay in its apparent conclusion that the BBC was virtually all white and ITV if not all black, a pretty dirty shade of grey. They did not therefore greet with much enthusiasm the Government's decision to grant a second channel to the BBC whilst putting off ITV 2 into an ill-defined future. Nor did the knowledge that the BBC was being thus rewarded in order to provide an alternative complementary service particularly recommend the decision to advocates of anti-monopolistic and competitive broadcasting services. More competition was, as they saw it, the one most effective device for raising programme standards as well as for removing the undesirable new monopoly in the sale of advertising time.[28] And, amongst the programme companies, only ATV stood truly four-square behind them.

It was perhaps predictable that a man like John Rodgers with a commitment to advertising as a necessary public service should have argued the virtues of competition when he introduced an amendment at report stage to oblige the PMG to licence ITV 2 'not later than 1 October 1965 . . . to present competition to the present television tycoons'.[29] There had in fact been an ISBA paper deploring the television advertising monopoly. As long ago as the very day of the Bill's Second Reading, Selwyn Lloyd himself, the 'Father of ITV', had in a *Daily Telegraph* article expressed his satisfaction at the way in which the success of ITV had vindicated the anti-monopolistic argument of his Beveridge minority report. But at the same time, he had regretted the monopolistic tendencies which had developed within commercial television and he urged the immediate grant of a second ITV channel to counter these tendencies. He returned to this position when he spoke in the debate on the Rodgers amendment.

> The present position where there is only one provider of advertising time . . . is not what I had in mind . . . [it is] a situation which should be changed as quickly as possible . . . I want as many channels as possible as quickly as possible . . . One of the great dangers about this medium which I have always felt . . . [is] that a single channel or a single programme can have too much power.[30]

The Opposition too favoured the second ITV service but differed about the wisdom of any commitment to a particular date. Willey even went so far as to suggest that the timing might be left to the Authority, in the light of circumstances and taking account of the effects of the new levy on company finances. Bevins also subscribed to the principles enunciated by Selwyn Lloyd. 'In broadcasting no Government has any right artificially to deprive the public of services for which the technical frequencies are available.' He then went on to declare, 'It is the Government's intention to authorise the introduction of a second independent television programme as soon as the Government are satisfied that conditions are such that it can be made a success'; they 'would therefore hope to issue a licence for ITA 2 during 1965 unless, and this is unlikely, it seems that the financial or other obstacles are insurmountable at that stage'. Given the decision to introduce new channels on UHF, he thought it better, however, to wait until there was a sufficiently large UHF audience to generate the advertising revenue needed for a new independent and genuinely competitive service. An immediate start for ITA 2 was not a financially viable proposition. That, he believed, was why all ITV companies save one were opposed to an early start for the second service. It would be foolish to risk repetition of the near financial disaster of 1955/6. The new service would in any case probably cost more than it brought in for some time. Even 1965 could be too soon for actual transmission; but he would hope to make a firm decision in the course of the year. Pressed by Selwyn Lloyd whether that meant issue of a Post Office licence for the new service to 'come on the air in 1966', he replied: 'That is perfectly correct'.[31]

This statement was, according to the *Financial Times* 'mainly well-received'. For Robert Renwick of ATV it was 'a return to sound principles . . . healthy competition'; and the IPA said, 'now at last we have the first real promise'.[32] On the other hand, the postponement until 1965 and the PMG's qualifying remarks that the go-ahead would depend on the likelihood of adequate advertising revenue was, said the paper, welcomed by Sir Edwin Herbert, vice-Chairman of A-R who, on this occasion, was speaking also on behalf of ABC and Granada as well. One of the main factors influencing the financial prospects of commercial television would, of course, be the impact of the Government's proposed new levy on advertising revenue. And with the controversies surrounding that proposal Herbert had been, as we shall see in the next chapter, closely involved.

It was not only in this respect that Renwick and Collins could feel that all their strenuous lobbying had born fruit. Back in Standing Committee B during May Bevins had conceded, with full support from the Opposition, that the permissible length of the new company contracts could be extended from three to six years. This was precisely half the loaf that ATV had been seeking, but it was in all the circumstances as large as they could reasonably expect. However, the compliance of the Opposition stemmed more from the representations by the unions than from those of the managements.

As will be seen in the next chapter, it was in relation to Clause 7 that Renwick and Collins encountered their most serious rebuff.

25

THE LEVY

In early scc meetings of 1963 programme companies were already pressing for a statement of the Authority's likely interpretation of its role under the new Bill as regards control over programmes and advertising. Fraser told them that he expected the eventual outcome in those fields 'would in large part represent a consolidation of existing practices'.[1] They would, he suggested, turn out to be less important than requirements arising from Clause 7 of the Bill. To judge by the time and effort the companies and their spokesmen in the event devoted to it, this view of Clause 7 came to be theirs also.

Yet company opposition to the proposed levy (or secondary rental) started off from a basis different from that by now adopted by the Authority. The latter, unhappy as it was with the role of tax collector, had nevertheless already conceded to Pilkington that some means had to be found of reducing excessive company profits and had accepted, however reluctantly, the principle of a special impost on the profits of ITV companies. Its concern therefore had been to get, in negotiation with the Post Office, a measure that would be fair and efficient, flexibly adaptable to varying financial circumstances and not damaging to the range and quality of the programme service. Hence the dismay felt at the unexpected switch away from the scheme carefully worked out, presumably with Treasury knowledge and tacit approval, between Post Office and ITA officials for a graduated levy on profits; and which, moreover, had already been printed in the Bill.

The companies for their part took their initial stand on the basic principle of opposition to any form of discriminatory taxation; and more especially to the apparently uncontrolled and arbitrary powers the original Clause 7 gave to the PMG 'to impose a levy of any size on any or all of the companies'.[2] In Bevins' own words, it was 'widely criticised' because 'it gave excessive and arbitrary powers to me'.[3] The companies (although mostly un-enthusiastic about increased competition) had been piqued by the decision in the White Paper, following upon Pilkington's verdict on the respective

merits of the two services, to allow BBC 2, whilst leaving ITV 2 a vague
promise. Some of their friends felt ordinary fairness demanded simultaneous
licensing of both second channels so that the two services could continue to
compete on an equal footing. With an audience divided between four
channels revenue would fall and, so they argued, the case for a levy on excess
profits would disappear. This was the position of the National Broadcasting
Development Committee (successor to the Popular Television Association)
and of its spokesmen in Parliament, notably its Chairman, Sir Harmar
Nicholls and such survivors of the 1954 anti-monopolists as Captain Orr.
Others, aware of a recent marked fall in advertising revenue, saw in coming
competition from two complementary BBC services a serious threat to the
continuing commercial viability of ITV. To impose a levy, however
calculated, on top of this would not only render the eventual introduction of
a second service less feasible, it could well also jeopardise the profitability
and therefore the future of the ITV system as it stood.

Of course, the companies did not like the existing Television Advertising
Duty, itself a discriminatory tax. But the extra cost had been successfully
passed on to the advertisers and had not so far proved much of a burden, at
least for the major companies. Indeed it probably favoured them at the
expense of the smaller regional companies because increased advertising
rates would tend to cause a higher proportion of advertisers' budgets to be
spent in areas with more potential viewers. This was one of the reasons why
the Authority had strongly urged the abolition of TAD on the PMG and his
officials at the same time as it was reaching (so it believed) final agreement
on the terms of the levy on profits. But it was not until the Minister broke the
news on 6 February to Carmichael that he virtually promised an end to TAD
in 1964.

On one version of events the amendment to Clause 7 had been in large
part provoked by ill-considered agitation by the major companies and their
friends in the press and in Parliament against the whole notion of a special
levy. Early in February, records Bevins, he was told by Iain Macleod, then
leader of the House, that the Bill was unpopular with Government back-
benchers and heartily disliked by the Big Four companies.[4] Nevertheless, as
we have seen, the Second Reading, including Bevins' announcement of an
amended Clause 7, passed without incident.

In the event, as a result of procrastination by members of all parties, the
new clause was not reached in Standing Committee until the fourteenth
sitting, on 25 April, and it occupied the next four or five sittings before it was
added to the Bill on 7 May, leaving just one further (the twentieth sitting)
for the remaining seventeen clauses. In the meantime, according to the

Bevins' account,[5] approaches had been made to the Prime Minister and Butler and he was urged to discuss with representatives of the four major companies their anxieties over the likely effects of his levy proposals. He saw Sir Edwin Herbert, who was accompanied by an accountant from the firm of Messrs Binder, Hamlyn & Co. They put to him figures[6] indicating a far more drastic effect of the levy on company incomes than either he or his Post Office officials were prepared to accept. The latter had in fact already seen the companies' figures and had drawn attention to certain discrepancies. They had assumed that the levy would be payable on discounts to advertisers, even though this was money never received, and they had also assumed that the promised remission of TAD would not lead to a corresponding increase in time sold. Bevins contradicted both these assumptions. He also pointed out that the companies had left out of their calculations of future income, their earnings from *TV Times*, though these clearly derived from their television concessions. Thus the companies had been able to show a probable surplus after levy of about £6 million compared with a Post Office estimate of more than twice that amount.

At the same time the memorandum giving the company figures was circulated to the press and to Tory back-benchers. Harold Wincott wrote an article in the *Investors Chronicle*, entitled 'The Great TV Muddle', in which he said that if the figures in the memorandum were correct then 'the commerical television industry will lack the financial resources to provide effective competition with the BBC'.[7] The article was accompanied by a table taken from the companies' memorandum, showing that total ITV profits for distribution to shareholders, after the incidence of levy (at £15.7 million) and normal taxation (at £3.4 million) would be no more than £2.9 million on gross advertising receipts of more than £74 million. 'Most of the regional contractors, it is thought, would be losing money . . . and out of the four major concerns, two – ABC and ATV – would do little better than break even.'

In the first weeks of March the Authority too was in touch with the Minister. The emphasis in its representations was naturally enough on the feared effects on programme expenditure and the future health of the ITV system, as well as on the greater fairness in principle of a levy on profits. Bevins replied by doubting that there would be economies on programmes or that advertising revenue would continue to fall. He also asserted that the Chancellor's agreement to abolition of TAD had been dependent on creation of an alternative firm source of income; hence the decision to put a levy on advertising revenue. With a levy on profits, TAD would have had to remain.[8]

Carmichael saw Bevins on 19 March, first alone and later with German and Caine, when the discussion centred on Clause 7 without much tangible result apart from a commitment to allow direct talks between Authority spokesmen and Treasury officials. During the first half-hour Carmichael made his protest against the somewhat cavalier fashion in which the Authority was being treated, saying that there was evidence of some basic hostility in the Post Office. Bevins said he had been defending the Authority in the Standing Committee. 'I said the Authority had not been impressed,'[9] Carmichael reported.

The promised meeting with Treasury officials took place on 27 March. It was attended by Boyd Carpenter, Chief Secretary and Paymaster-General, as well as Bevins, Carmichael, Caine and the officials from Treasury and Post Office. The meeting got nowhere. Boyd Carpenter, according to Carmichael, made no serious attempt to deal with the Authority's case for a profits-based levy. The Treasury were undoubtedly looking for a fairly steady source of income, and they were not even prepared to concede any significant reduction in that income with the advent of a second ITV service. Boyd Carpenter had expressly said that the Government 'could hardly be expected to contribute towards the cost of a second service'.[10] Little enthusiasm was shown for an alternative scheme put forward by the Authority under which it would contribute a sum at least equal to TAD revenue by raising basic rentals and adding a flat percentage levy on profits according to its own assessment of the value of the individual franchises. The meeting lasted less than three quarters of an hour.

The frustrating interview with Boyd Carpenter left the Authority unsatisfied, not to say resentful. Carmichael sought the advice of Lord Woolton who recommended a letter to the Prime Minister, explaining the Authority's belief that the new proposal would cause serious damage to the financial structure of commercial television in a manner that might well cause both the industry and the State to lose considerably, but adding that it certainly accepted that ITV companies should pay more for the concessions they enjoyed and saw no difficulty in achieving this through a levy on profits which would be both fairer in principle and less damaging in practice.

Before it was sent, the letter to the Prime Minister went through three drafts, the final one having been reduced from close on 1000 words to about 350. On 23 April Fraser told German about the letter, explaining that Carmichael had intended to tell Bevins himself but had been unable to reach him. Bevins telephoned that afternoon to say he hoped very much that the letter would not be sent. The timing was 'absolutely dreadful' and might have 'all sorts of unfortunate consequences'.[11] He asked that in any case Carmichael should see him first. Whether this meeting ever took place is not recorded, but the letter certainly went on the very day the amended

Clause 7 was debated by the Commons Committee. It made the points suggested by Woolton, adding that it was the apparent threat to the fulfilment of the Authority's statutory obligation to provide a public television service of 'a high general standard' that had inspired this approach.

The Prime Minister's reply, dated 4 May, set it beyond doubt that the levy decision was a Cabinet one. It found nothing wrong in principle in a levy on income, which included a free slice and a sliding scale, and reaffirmed a commitment to possible future adjustments to meet possible changes in circumstance. The Authority was left to draw what comfort it could from a final paragraph which acknowledged that the ITA and the companies must be in a position to provide a first class television service and to compete with the BBC. 'We naturally intend that independent television, which we created, should continue to have adequate resources to do this and to secure satisfactory margins.'[12]

In the meantime on the companies' front, matters had not been changed by a further memorandum dated 4 April from Binder, Hamlyn and Co. followed by another meeting between Herbert and Bevins to discuss it. When analysed and compared with Post Office figures the difference between the two estimates of profits after levy but before tax that emerged from this second memorandum had been reduced from over £3 million to little more than £$\frac{3}{4}$ million, and this was more than accounted for by the disagreement over inclusion of profits from *TV Times* of approximately £1 million. Consequently the points of disagreement between the companies and the Post Office were reduced to two: the inclusion of agents' commission but exclusion of advertisers' discounts in estimates of advertising income; and the assumption that all of the remitted TAD would be spent on TV advertising. In support of their judgement on the latter the companies quoted the President of ISBA to the effect that 'certainly the whole of the £8 million released by the elimination of the duty would not be spent on TV'.[13]

The companies' position therefore was substantially reduced to the overriding issue of principle which it shared with the Authority: that a levy on gross income was wrong and likely to be inequitable in practice. Thus yet another memorandum from the accountants developed the case further, forecasting a 'drastic and possibly disastrous'[14] reduction in company profits and a reduction in programme expenditure. It argued that the possibilities of tax avoidance in an alternative profits-based levy had been greatly exaggerated and went on to explain measures whereby it could be effectively forestalled. Finally, it showed that on 1962/3 estimates, the proposed GAR levy would take £13.89 million out of the £19.06 million profits of the Big Four; and that not improbable increases in costs of 10 per cent or 20 per cent would reduce those profits after levy to £2.83 million and £0.49 million respectively. If costs were to go up by 25 per cent then the Four would make a loss, after levy, of £0.66 million.

However, when the Minister spoke at a Conservative Party Committee on 24 April, he did not have much difficulty, he claims, in persuading them that the published figures, press criticisms and other representations they had received from interested parties were all ill-founded, not to say hopelessly wrong; and that the Government's proposals were reasonable. He repeated his arguments in some detail on the following day when he introduced his new Clause 7 to the Parliamentary Standing Committee.[15]

He said he was confident that companies would still have enough to produce first class programmes and earn reasonable profits. There would be a 'free slice' of £1¼ million; on the next £8 million, the payment would be 22½ per cent and any gross revenue above £9¼ million would be charged at 40 per cent. There would be provision for these levels to be varied by the Minister in the light of changed circumstances, subject to Treasury agreement and an affirmative resolution on a draft order laid before Parliament. The £1¼ million 'free slice' would mean that the small regional companies would probably not pay anything; and the relatively low charge on the next £8 million should leave companies no excuse for economising on programmes, as some critics feared. Indeed the effect of the proposals in the financial year 1962/3 would have been to reduce company net profits from £23.8 million to £13.6 million and not to the £6.3 million given in the first memorandum which had been circulated to the press and others by the Big Four, a document from which – incidentally – the regional companies had been anxious to dissociate themselves when they met him. He thought that most of the money taken by TAD would continue to be spent by advertisers. Further, his departmental advisers had also assured him that on the best available information television advertising expenditure would not fall – as the companies were saying – but would continue to grow, reaching some £80 million in 1964/5. The companies should be in a position to spend more – not less – on programmes; and still earn reasonable profits.

As might be expected, the Minister got more support for his amended Clause 7 from Labour members of the Committee than from Conservative ones. Fred Willey thought his approach was right, although he did ask that it be kept in mind that ITV like the BBC existed primarily to provide a programme service, not revenue for the Exchequer. Captain Orr, veteran of the 1954 debates, added a characteristic note. The Committee should first be discussing, he said, whether there need be a levy at all. The public concession for which an economic rental was being required was not, as the PMG claimed, one for TV broadcasting, it was a concession for the monopoly sale of TV advertising. He did not believe any monopoly could be justified, simply by demanding a high price from those who enjoyed it. Such a monopoly, which had given rise to scandalously high profits, ought not to exist. The proper Conservative answer to the question was to end the monopoly by the introduction of competition. It was wrong to blame the ITA for the excessive profits; the fault lay with Government for not allowing them another channel. He was not surprised that Labour members were supporting the PMG because the levy proposal was in line with their Socialist philosophy.

The Socialists for their part were quick to point out that Tories who had taken little or no part in the Committee so far while programme standards and the interests of viewers were being discussed were suddenly prominently vocal in defence of big business and threatened profits. But there was cross-bench agreement, albeit for contrasting reasons, that Clause 7 was the heart of the Bill. A new element had been introduced into the debate in a fighting speech from the miners' MP, Roy Mason. While expressing support for the Minister and his scorn for the machinations of the Big Four ('They are like a big fat pig . . . squealing loudly in the hope the blow will be softened')[16] he drew attention to the multifarious representations he and his colleagues had been receiving from the craft and technical trade unions in ITV. In particular, a letter from Sir Tom O'Brien of NATKE suggested that 'there are going to be acute redundancies in many studios if this Clause goes through'. The Variety Artistes' Federation and the ACTT had also written, the latter referring to 'the disastrous effect it [the Clause] would have on the volume and quality of programme content and on employment'. Likewise, Equity and the Screen Writers had claimed that the levy would affect their livelihood by causing companies to cut programme budgets; and the Radio and Television Safeguards Committee also feared that cheapness would take over from quality in programmes. This theme was to recur at intervals throughout all subsequent stages of the Bill.

Most Labour members interpreted these representations as an indirect manoeuvre by ITV company managements to enlist their employees in an attempt to influence the attitudes of Labour spokesmen towards the levy by playing on their trade union sympathies. They suspected that the likely effects of the levy on employment had been overstated to the unions; and continued to find more convincing the Minister's assurances that, even after levy, companies would still have ample funds to sustain a full programme output of the quality and variety required by the Bill.

Meanwhile, simultaneously with the Parliamentary process, the behind-the-scenes manoeuvres continued. In between the first two Committee discussions of the Clause on 28 April, Bevins tells us he spent an uncomfortable Sunday at Chequers – 'I did not enjoy that Sunday. I felt some of my colleagues were out of touch with reality.'[17] At lunch he was seated next to the Chief Whip, who at once got on to television. He says he rejected Redmayne's suggestion that he should cut the amount of the levy by about £4 million; and was amazed to be told that the Chancellor, Reginald Maudling, had agreed to that reduction. He was determined not to give way. Next day, Monday, he and Maudling, he relates, had yet another discussion on figures with company accountants after which he made clear to Maudling that he, for one, was not going to budge. Later that afternoon they both met the anti-levy back-benchers led by Harmar Nicholls. The Chief Whip was naturally also present, and in Bevins' own words, 'squirmed'[18] when these members were heard to say that they might have to vote against the Government. 'I judged the Chancellor was getting near to saying he was prepared to reduce the levy. I wrote on a bit of paper, "You must *not* give way" and put it under his nose. He took my advice.' The consideration put to Bevins after the Party meeting by fellow Ministers that it would be politically damaging to the Government to carry Clause 7 'with the support of the Labour Party in defiance of a minority of our own Party' also left him unmoved. His account of the following day's committee session relates triumphantly how he decided to 'play it by ear', and did so with success, securing agreement to the Clause imposing the unaltered levy without a vote.[19] It rather overstates the ease of his success.

There was in fact prolonged examination of the respective merits of profits as against gross revenue as a basis for the levy. Various amendments were moved. David James, a new Conservative member from Brighton, introduced a whole group of amendments favouring a profits levy. He rejected as absurd the suggestion that men like Tom O'Brien and George Elvin (of ACTT) were 'party to a plot'. They had behind them memories of the 'bitter experience of the film industry about ten years ago' when producers, directors, script writers, first class camera men and some of the finest possible technicians were 'thrown on the scrap heap . . . until they were saved by independent television'.[20] He, in common with other Conservative speakers, was sure that a scheme for a profits levy could readily be devised that would be foolproof against evasion – to say nothing of the ITA's watchdog powers. He thought it quite wrong for the Treasury to expect an assured return from an industry like the entertainments industry which 'since the beginning of time has been of its very nature a knife-edge industry'.[21] Some of the Opposition saw this talk of a 'knife-edge' industry as an unwarranted assimilation between television and the theatre where risks of a flop were admittedly very real. They believed that the monopolist sellers of TV advertising ran no such risks and they continued to rely on the Minister's figures showing that the ITV companies as a whole would have ample funds even after payment of his levy. They refused to succumb to the 'veiled threat that if the companies do not get what they consider a reasonable return, the programmes will suffer'.[22]

It was a topsy-turvy situation. Not all Labour speakers favoured unreservedly the principle of the new Clause 7. Even Ness Edwards wondered whether there might not be better ways of assessing the value of the company franchises. Nor yet was Bevins by any means without support from members of his own party. Both Stratton Mills from Northern Ireland and Arthur Tiley from Bradford thought his approach was the right one. As so often with the country as a whole, Standing Committee B was subject to a complex area of low pressure; the winds were variable and the outlook was uncertain.

However, the £13.6 million which the Post Office estimated would be left with the companies after levy applied to ITV *as a whole*. In spite of the Minister's belief that the small regional companies would be better off than they had been, with the abolition of TAD and the proposed £1¼ million 'free slice', it was by no means certain that medium-sized companies would not be much worse off. Companies such as Anglia. It was Labour member Donald Chapman who first raised that problem.[23] If Anglia's estimates were correct, then their advertising revenue would be just over £2 million and their profits £334,000. Levy at 22½ per cent after taking into account the 'free slice' would take £210,000 which would leave relatively little to finance the worthwhile and ambitious programmes that the company provided for the network. Chapman asked whether the Minister could not adjust this sliding scale so that the maximum levy of 40 per cent was approached by more gradual steps. Bevins doubted the accuracy of the figures supplied by Anglia but did not show himself unsympathetic to the possibility of a variation in the 'free slice'; he also promised to look again at the possibility of excluding the 15 per cent commission paid to advertising agencies from the revenue chargeable to levy.

And so what had by now become the best known and most discussed clause of the Bill completed its ordeal by Committee on 7 May, unchanged from the form in which it had first appeared on the Order Paper. 'Rebels on ITV rental beaten' headlined the *Daily Telegraph*.[24] But the battle was still not won. The Whitsun recess was not far off and Bevins says he realised he was battling against time.[25] On 24 May the *Guardian* reported a statement by Geoffrey Hurst, one of the Conservative back-bench rebels, that the report stage had been deferred as a result of prodigious activity behind the scenes. 'If the Bill's further progress is postponed' commented the newspaper, 'after a rancorous committee stage, the group will regard it as a considerable victory in its campaign to make the Government pause before imposing what Mr. Norman Collins . . . has described as "a licence to lose money". It is not at all certain that the Government will stick to the Bevins scheme.' Bevins wrote that he at once saw the Chief Whip, who assured him there was no intention of dropping the Bill through shortage of time.[26]

With the Whitsun break came also the Profumo scandal which did nothing for the Government's sense of security. At about the same time, Norman Collins had said publicly that ATV would have to go out of business if the levy were accepted, and Lord Beaverbrook said the Express group would gladly take over the franchise if they did. According to Bevins he was pressed more than once by Butler to make some concessions. He also had talks with the Chief Whip who, he says, told him he was not prepared to risk further Government unpopularity 'by a hostile demonstration by our back-benchers in the House' against this 'bloody awful Bill'.[27] Apparently, there was even talk by Redmayne of going back to Cabinet and a counter threat of resignation by the Minister should they reverse their earlier decision.

The disputed Clause eventually reached the full House on 24 June. Roy Mason pointed out that it was seven weeks since the Bill had left Committee, and calculated that obviously this was due to behind the scenes pressures of the nauseating lobby still anxious to defend the profiteers. They had even brought in the much respected elder statesman Selwyn Lloyd to help them, he noted. Bevins at once announced two concessions. He had accepted the arguments for ignoring the 15 per cent agents' commission from calculation of advertising revenue. Gross Advertising Revenue (GAR) was now to become Net Advertising Revenue (NAR). This would, however, mean an alteration in the levy scale so that approximately the same amount was yielded. Secondly, he proposed increasing the 'free slice' from £1¼ million to £1½ million, which should, he thought, be helpful to the regionals. On the next £6 million there would be a charge at 25 per cent; and above that at 45 per cent. That would mean on current estimates a yield for the Exchequer in the first full year after July 1964 of about £17 million (about £1½ million less than previously estimated) and a total before tax profit for the companies of about £15¼ million. On that basis he did not think any company would have a 'licence to lose money', or be unable to produce network programmes of high standard and cost.

Both Chapman from the Labour side and Ian Gilmour from the Conservative raised again the problem of Anglia, a company with an excellent programme record – both regionally and on the network – but which seemed likely to suffer unduly, because with an advertising income of around £2 million it was on a level in between the smaller companies which the Government wanted to help and the larger ones which were to be made to pay more. The case was also supported by Peter Walker and Dingle Foot as well as by Selwyn Lloyd himself, who also re-emphasised Chapman's point that any amending broadcasting legislation should aim at improving the service to the viewer, not at providing revenue for the Exchequer. Bevins did not show himself unsympathetic. If there were good reason to believe Anglia were right, he would be disposed to help. There was a flexibility provision in Clause 7; and he could discuss with the Authority the possibility of a rental revision. But he did not think the case was proven.

On the second day of the debate, David James, once again protesting his desire to help the workers in the film industry, moved an amendment to give companies (like ATV and ABC) with a dual franchise and two production centres, a double free slice. James' concern for the workers (who were, he thought, being let down by the Labour members) provoked a vituperative outburst from Roy Mason. The Big Four lobby were hypocritical in their claim to speak for the workers, he said. Across the floor a Conservative, William Shepherd, also expressed his distaste for the way the major companies had generated groundless fears in the minds of the workers. 'It is one of the most despicable and unedifying examples of private enterprise I have had the misfortune to witness.'[28] But the Opposition leadership could not bring themselves to agree with Shepherd (or Mason for that matter) that responsible trade unionists had been hoodwinked and that their fears were groundless. Having made such public declarations of imminent bankruptcy the companies might feel a commitment to conduct their affairs in that expectation. Mawby, replying to the debate, agreed that it was natural to feel concern over the demonstration by the TV unions in the Central Lobby earlier in the week. 'They are afraid they will lose their livelihood . . . and they came to this House because they wanted Parliament to do something about it.' But 'we believe that this fear is needless . . . all the Jeremiahs will be confounded'.[29]

Bevins' concessions defused the situation. The dissidents resigned themselves to acceptance of the Bevins levy and were now concerned to do what they could to ensure that its effects should not be too harmful. The

Authority's own reaction to the two concessions was, as expressed by Carmichael: 'it could not now be claimed that the incidence of the levy would be unduly onerous given the continuation of present trading conditions'.[30] It was in the same debate that Bevins made the declaration, somewhat conditional though it was, about ITV 2 (Chapter 24). On 4 July at the first meeting of the Authority attended by the newly appointed Chairman, Lord Hill suggested 'that the Authority should accept the Postmaster-General's statement as a decision, committing the Government to the introduction of a second ITV service'.[31]

Although Bevins had repeatedly said that the levy was not a tax, the Government spokesman in the Lords took the line that it was and that Clause 7 could not therefore be amended. This provoked argument, but eventually their Lordships accepted the view of Lord Morrison that 'this might be called a levy but in principle, in practical effect, it is not much different from taxation'.[32] In the event, it proved that all the issues raised had been dealt with in the Lower House. The possibly damaging effects on employment and programme standards were deplored by Lord Archibald and Francis Williams. What we may legitimately call the 'Anglia Lobby' were again vocal, this time under the leadership of Lord Gladwyn. But the Earl of Dundee, for the Government, was able to persuade him to accept an assurance that the Government would be very prompt in applying the flexibility provisions of Clause 7 should need arise.

That was the end – for the time being – of a long drawn-out tussle. But it was a lost battle rather than a lost war. Argument over the respective merits of a profit- or a revenue-based levy was to continue for many more years. If there is any moral to be drawn from the episode it is perhaps in the evidence it offers against the thesis of those who, following on Professor Wilson, see ITV as the offspring of a commercially-motivated pressure group. In the story of Clause 7, pressure groups at work there certainly were, and none were more skilful than Anglia's. There is no valid reason why in a democratic society organised groups of committed people who care about a particular issue (not excluding those with material interests) should not seek means of propagating their views and influencing decision makers. One can justifiably add that there could be nothing harmful in pressure groups so long as people like Roy Mason were around to denounce them and Ministers as tough as Reg Bevins to resist them. The important thing was that the power of final decision lay with Parliament.

26

ENTER LORD HILL

On the last day of July 1963, the new Television Bill received the Royal Assent. On the first day of that month Lord Hill entered the headquarters of the ITA as the Authority's new Chairman, equipped, as he himself asserts, with a knowledge of broadcasting that was 'slender'.[1] He soon gained the impression that changes were needed at Brompton Road. Listening to fellow Members of the Authority 'I found a feeling of something akin to guilt that they had exercised too little influence on the service . . . There would have to be changes in the Authority's procedure; programme policy would have to be more positive; public relations needed a new approach.'[2]

So an early task given to ITA staff by their new Chairman was the preparation of a memorandum 'analysing the statutory changes in the Authority's responsibility for programmes and comparing the new requirements with current practice'.[3] This document was later presented in modified form to the companies at the meeting in September of the Standing Consultative Committee.[4] Hill had made up his mind that the Authority Members should be able to give more time to programme policy in order to assume that 'commanding position' which they, rather than their senior staff, were expected in future to have.[5] 'Development of adequate control arrangements and the organisation of the Authority's advisory committees in accordance with the requirements of the new Act were more important tasks to which the Authority would have to address itself as soon as the immediate contractual matters were settled.'[6] That the memorandum on new programme responsibilities revealed to the companies no very great changes from the current *de facto* practice of the ITA staff was almost beside the point. Under the new regime there were going to be no more feelings of guilt on the part of the masters over inadequate exercise of influence and control. That was the resolve of Lord Hill.

Both versions of the memorandum pointed out the new statutory provisions determining the Authority's programme powers. The specific mention of schedules 'drawn up in consultation' did seem to imply more than the formalising of existing practice. The Second White Paper (though not the Act) had said that the Authority would be in control of networking and to that end would take the chair of a 'committee representing all the companies'.[7] The staff had proposed to achieve this control partly by making the existing scc into more of a committee of programme review at which output as a whole would be discussed more often and more systematically than hitherto; partly by having an Authority staff presence at those inter-company committees which put together the programmes provided for networking by the Big Four; and partly by ensuring schedule consultation between regional companies and ITA regional officers. But the paper presented to the scc went further. It said the Authority favoured creation of an additional committee for schedule consultation 'composed on scc lines' and with an Authority chairman; and in addition to an Authority 'observer' on inter-company programme planning committees, it proposed also similar representation on their various sub-committees, e.g. the Network Education Sub-committee. At the scc meeting, however, Fraser emphasised that such Authority representation on programme planning and scheduling bodies would not dispense any company from the need to have separate Authority clearance of its programme schedule. As for the new committee, Fraser told his attentive audience that the Chairman of the Authority saw himself as occupying the chair. And so it was to be both for Hill and his successors.

Significantly the scc version of the document included none of the references in the Authority's version to one of the presumed reasons for the Act's very specific new Authority power – that of demanding the exclusion of any programme from a schedule and the inclusion of any programme or *kind* of programme in one. The reason, so the paper suggested, was the belief that the Four had made insufficient use of the programmes of the Eleven, and that belief was also behind the other new requirement to secure 'a wide showing for programmes of merit'. Accurately, the paper reported: 'We tried to resist the acquisition of this power . . . to order all, or some, companies to show a particular programme that, left to themselves, they would not propose to show'. Pilkington had certainly been told that the Authority would like to help get a freer circulation of programmes. But that, the Authority then believed, could be done by changing the terms of the networking and affiliation agreements. 'We always thought the utility of locally produced programmes to other companies, not only to the Four but to others of the Eleven, was vastly exaggerated'. All this was now water under the bridge, and the companies were not to be reminded of it. There was a new Act and the slate had been wiped clean.

Both versions noted that, in future, programmes would have to conform with an Authority 'code' – a term that had not appeared in the 1954 Act. At the same time it was again observed that practice had anticipated prescription. What were to all intents 'codes' were already in regular use, governing, for example, amounts of imported material, advertising, due impartiality, programme prizes, the amount and timing of the news, and so on. Now, however, the Authority had no option but to produce a formal written code on violence and possibly, though not necessarily, on offences to good taste – something it had hitherto been loath to do. The scc paper then went on to say that a consolidated rule book was being prepared which would collate rules and practices agreed upon at scc over the years with additional material concerning violence and other matters.[8]

Finally both papers reported intended Authority action on its new statutory duty to make 'arrangements for bringing the programmes (including the advertisements) . . . under constant and effective review' and for 'ascertaining the state of public opinion concerning the programmes'. A General Advisory Council was to be appointed; and regular audience research surveys would be commissioned.

Similarly a paper on changes arising from the Act in the machinery for advertising control was considered by the Authority in July and presented to the companies at scc in September.[9] The Authority would be exercising more formal and direct control of the executive decisions relating to advertisements. Hitherto the machinery of control, though effective, had lacked the appearance of strong control by the Authority itself. In future Authority staff would see scripts, consultant comments and finished films at the same time as the companies' copy committee; and they would take part in discussion of any aspect of any advertisement before its acceptance for broadcasting. In addition to the Advertising Advisory Committee a panel of medical consultants such as already existed (on company initiative) would be made mandatory, its advice and comments being equally available to companies and Authority. There would also need to be a joint executive control committee for formal discussion and resolution of general questions arising out of the day-to-day consideration of advertising problems.

There was no indication that the companies saw these new arrangements as likely to be particularly burdensome or inhibiting to the continuing success of the ITV service – at any rate so long as Fraser and the staff around him remained more or less the same. They could be less sure about the new Chairman's intentions and the award of future contracts. A *Financial Times* leader of 1 August remarked that British Television, after a second period marked by 'the arrival and dynamic progress of commercial televison', was now about to enter its third stage. 'Several unknowns remain . . . Most important is the way the ITA will function. Lord Hill has huge powers in his new job and he will have to guard on the one hand against the relative inaction of his predecessors and on the other against the heavy hand that would take the sparkle out of the commercial system.'

On that same day, 1 August, Hill held his first ITA Press Conference. He made known his plan of work for the Authority in the coming months. Its first overriding task was dictated by the fact that existing company contracts would end in twelve months' time. Decisions would have to be made on the form of the new contracts before applications could be invited from sitting or would-be tenants. This meant, *inter alia*, re-examination of an existing pattern, the number of companies, the size and boundaries of their allotted service areas. Important new factors in this re-examination would be the change to 625 UHF and in the longer term the promise of a second ITV service. 'The Authority's planning for the future must be based on the assumption that there is to be a second ITV service over much of the country.'[10] One thing, said Hill, the Authority had already resolved in this connection. This was that there should be, in each of the main areas, *two competing seven-day companies*. The immediate contracts would thus clearly have to end when the second service started, which would, in the Authority's judgement, be in about three years' time. In the meantime, with certain modifications, the existing pattern of days and areas – but not necessarily of existing companies, would continue. On finance, two main issues were claiming Authority attention. Faced with additional expenditure for the change to UHF, it would need an increased income of some £8 million. So new company rentals would have to be worked out, taking into account the relative profitability of the franchise areas. Secondly, attention would have to be given to the new arrangements for the sale and purchase of programmes, with the aim of encouraging greater freedom of movement not only from the central companies to the regions, but also from one region to another, promoting a healthy measure of competition in the provision of programmes.

On programmes, Hill told the press three things. The Authority would faithfully apply the standards laid down in the Act; and this would mean rules. No one could work well in ITV unless they accepted and honoured the rules. At the same time care would be taken not to inhibit the creative impulse. 'We shall observe Parliament's instructions – without hamstringing creative artists.' Thirdly, he looked forward to a growing contribution by the television services to the widening of the knowledge, interests, appreciation and understanding of the viewing public. 'Television has a role in exploring us as well as helping the social transformation of which it is a part.' It was an upbeat but not too grandiloquent note on which to herald a new phase in the life of ITV.

Part IV

YEARS OF ADAPTATION: 1963–8

27

NEW INSTITUTIONS: NEW CONTRACTS

The second half of 1963 was a busy time at the ITA. It would be easy to attribute this to the energising impact of a firm-willed, strong and clear minded new Chairman – all of which Lord Hill certainly was. However, significant as the contributions of certain outstanding individuals have been, the development of the ITV service is more accurately seen as a continuous process of evolutionary change in which television people, public opinion, advertisers, audiences and legislators all have played a part. In some ways these months leading up to new contract awards had the characteristics of an operatic overture in the course of which themes were stated that were destined to be heard again and again in varying forms during the next two decades.

By July 1963 the Authority had two pressing tasks. It had to prepare for the award of new contracts to run from July 1964; and as a consequence of the new Act give a more formalised institutional character to its programme control arrangements. Sir John Carmichael recalls how some Authority Members had become restless at the way in which many day-to-day decisions on programmes, some of them involving policy,[1] were apparently made on their behalf by the staff and reported to them by the staff as *faits accomplis*. At a time when as a body they had come under public attack for alleged failures of responsibility they felt the urge to play a more active role. It was therefore proposed to establish small committees of Authority Members to give detailed specialist attention to particular areas of policy. This chimed exactly with Hill's own ideas and he reports in his memoirs that he lost no time in having the proposal realised. But a Programme Schedule Committee was not, as the memoirs imply, among those established in his first months. It did not meet for the first time until November 1964.[2]

The Committee that had been set up under Sir Sydney Caine to deal with the contracts was ready with recommendations. Because of the Government's apparent commitment to an ITV 2 within three years, it recommended that the new contracts should run initially for three years and that no changes should be made in either the central areas or in the regions (save, for obvious reasons, in Wales) for which these contracts should be awarded. It also said, however, that the intention should be made known to have two parallel competing companies in the three central areas as soon as possible after the ITV 2 go-ahead had been given. Further thought was proposed on the possibility of relating company rentals more directly to their revenue and a provisional timetable was put forward, requiring consideration of draft contracts and immediately afterwards their public advertisement before mid-September; closing date for applications by end October/early November and allocation of contracts in December 1963 or January 1964. The timetable was promptly adopted. To meet the ITA's needs it was decided that the new rentals should bring in some £8 million instead of the current approximate £5.5 million. It was obvious that this 47 per cent increase could not be applied uniformly. The rentals of the three smallest franchises, those of Channel, Border and Grampian, were to be reduced by more than half; and out of the six smaller regions only the South West was to have a significant increase. The largest overall group increase (of 66 per cent) would come from the four middle regions, especially in the cases of Central Scotland and Southern. In the four central areas there were to be very big increases for the A-R and Granada franchises, whereas the ABC franchise rental was to rise by about one third and the ATV one actually fell in order to take account of the greater capital costs of the dual area operation. The overall aim was to bring about for all companies an approximately uniform return on capital employed of about 33 per cent. In the recent past some middle-sized companies had been achieving returns on capital as high as 52 per cent (STV) and 70 per cent (Southern) compared with ATV's 18.1 per cent and Granada's 43 per cent.

Clarification of networking arrangements was a precondition of any negotiation of new contracts, and throughout the summer months a series of discussions with and amongst existing contractors had taken place on future networking arrangements. The course of these will be described in Chapter 33.

The additional external guidance the Authority was required to secure included the appointment of an education committee. In fact three came into being. There was an Educational Advisory Council concerned with broad educational policy and under it a new Schools Committee as well as the existing Adult Education Committee. Although it had been left the option not to do so, the Authority also appointed a General Advisory Council. Within the system itself there came into being, in addition to the Programme Policy Committee, to which we referred in Chapter 26, an inter-company Network Planning Committee (NPC) on which all regionals as well as the four network companies had representation and at whose meetings there was an observer from ITA staff.

With these matters settled the way was clear for the contract competition for the short post-1964 period. There were reasons why some existing contractors expected this to be a perfunctory affair. Pilkington had said, as we saw in Chapter 15, 'the appointment of a programme contractor is virtually irrevocable',[3] and this was one of the Committee's reasons for advocating 'organic change'. If that was what the Committee thought, how much more significant was it that Bevins should have said in the course of his speech on the second reading of the 1963 Television Bill: 'I hope the House will remember that the risk of non-renewal of a contract is very slight unless the company has completely failed to make the grade'?[4] Such a seemingly considered pronouncement by the responsible Minister could not fail to impress some company chiefs who found it hard to believe that the Government could not in practice place the Authority under such a commitment. But in fact the competition was conducted with great thoroughness and with every indication that the ITA saw itself as completely free to make whatever decisions it thought necessary.

The advertisement inviting applications appeared in the press on 16 September 1963. The closing date was 18 November. By then all the existing programme companies and eight new groups had applied. Several of the applicants asked to be considered for more than one area contract. Only the Northern Ireland (UTV), North East Scotland (Grampian) and Borders (Border) franchise holders found themselves unopposed. Even Channel had a competitor. There were five applicants for the London weekday contract and three each for the North weekday, London weekend, Midlands weekday and Southern England contracts. For the South West there were four; two each for the remainder. The statement which had been issued on 16 September had explained that three-year contracts beginning at the end of July 1964 would be offered, with the possibility of earlier termination should a second ITV service begin before the three years was out. Were the announced date for the start of a second service to be after July 1967, the contracts would be extended up to a maximum of six years until the second service arrived. Should it, however, become apparent that there was no prospect of ITV 2 before 1970, the three-year contracts would not be extended. The Authority would instead re-examine the whole pattern on the basis of a single service.

The rentals for the new contract period would have to include the new levy on advertising income and the statement included a table showing what levy payments (or 'B rentals' as they came to be called) would have been had the Act been in force during the financial year 1962/3. The table also showed (as 'A rentals') what sums the Authority would be taking from contractors to meet its own costs. These had been fixed, it said, in order to give efficiently managed companies the prospect of a reasonable return on their necessary investments; and they took into account the varying costs of operation as well as the varying sizes, populations and advertising rates in each of the areas. Not stated, but quite evident from the figures given, was the fact that these 'A rentals' did not significantly reflect the cost to the Authority of the services it provided in each case. There was to be a large element of cross-subsidisation.

Special reference was made to the Wales and West of England contract (which in future would include the region that had been served by the unfortunate WWN company); 'The Authority intends to see that the contractor appointed will pay full regard to the needs and interests of Wales'.[5] To facilitate the fulfilment of this duty the PMG had been asked to provide a second VHF channel in South Wales so that the company appointed could transmit simultaneously to English viewers south of the Bristol Channel and Welsh ones north of the Channel their own different 'editions' of the ITV local service. There would be extensions of several other areas in England and Scotland by the construction of additional transmitters.

This was the first time that contracts were being awarded simultaneously for all parts of the national ITV system. Lessons learned over the past six years in the negotiation and operation of the successive company contracts had to be taken into account in the drafting of new agreements. All would-be applicants, including the current contractors, were told they would be required: to establish their principal offices and studios in their respective franchise areas; to include not less than three weekly hours of national news from ITN (with a twenty-minute daily minimum) plus twenty-five minutes a week of supplementary ITN material; to include in the statutorily prescribed 'proper balance' of their programme output regular religious programmes, school broadcasts and adult education programmes, all these being planned and produced in the light of appropriate advice; to include also in the schedules reasonable proportions of talks, discussions and documentaries, plays and serials, variety and light entertainment, sport, entertainment films, and programmes on the arts. Much specific detail was sought about applicants' intentions and resources and about any connections between the financial interests of one applicant and any other, i.e. cross-holdings. They were to describe their plans for local studios, their general programme policy, the quantity and nature of the local programmes they hoped to produce and what changes, if any, they would like to see in the current programme output of ITV. Finally, existing companies were asked what preparations they had already made in anticipation of the proposed change to UHF in 625 lines and what effect for their own operation they anticipated from the advent of BBC 2.

The Authority was all too well aware that new contract awards in the wake of Pilkington, two White Papers and prolonged Parliamentary debate leading up to a new statute would be subjected to close public scrutiny and comment. That *arrière pensée* was obviously present in the formulation of the particulars supplied to applicants. It was a document which could not fail to become publicly known. The Members also felt a need to have clarified for possible later publication a statement of the principles and criteria of judgement which a chosen programme contractor would be expected to satisfy.

Three principles were stated. First, effective control of a programme company – as indicated by voting shares – should not be concentrated in the hands of one individual or of one closely knit group of relatives or business associates, or of newspaper interests. Three existing companies at least (Granada, Scottish and Southern) did not conform with that requirement. Secondly, shareholdings, including non-voting equities, should be widely spread and, in the case of regional companies, have significant local participation; and this should mean a reasonable proportion available to individual members of the general public for direct investment. At least five of the fourteen existing contractors (the three already mentioned plus A-R and ABC) would not meet this requirement although the shares of the holding companies of both A-R and ABC were themselves quoted. Thirdly, boards of directors of programme companies should include adequate representation of the communities in which they operated. This was presumably meant to apply chiefly to regional companies and here both STV and Southern were clearly vulnerable.

Yet when, after holding twenty-two interviews with all aspirant groups, followed by seven second interviews, the Authority finally made known its decisions on 8 January 1964, all the fourteen existing companies found themselves reinstated. But careful thought and close interrogation had

preceded the decisions. The Authority had not concealed its critical opinion
of the internal structure, ownership, operation and programme performance of some of its contractors and their offers of contract renewal were all
conditional on changes being made. But it could not be claimed that more
than two or three of the eight new applicants were offering anything
particularly promising. The fact that four of them originally put in
applications for more than one area was in itself not encouraging. The
'Freedom Group' of Edward Martell, the right-wing campaigner against
the closed-shop, had applied for no fewer than five regional contracts.
Another applicant, seeking to replace ABC at weekends, appeared to have a
link-up with the Mormon Church. Three of the newcomers were taken more
seriously.

Lord Hill has recorded his own first liking for the contender for the North
East franchise for which the spokesman was Morris Finer QC.[6] This group
aimed to be a kind of producers' and educationalists' cooperative, paying a
fixed maximum of $12\frac{1}{2}$ per cent to its investors and ploughing back all
further profits into programmes. But the interview led the Authority to
conclude that they had not done their financial homework with sufficient
thoroughness, could offer no guarantees of access to adequate start-up
capital and were insufficiently representative of the region.

Stronger attractions were found in a group, headed by the film producer
Sydney Box (responsible for some of the most successful British feature films
in the forties), applying for the London weekday franchise. This group had a
small board of directors including Box, Norman Fisher (of BBC Brains Trust
fame), Ted Willis, James Carr of World Wide Pictures and the deputy
chairman, former managing director of Ulster Television, William
MacQuitty. In addition there was to be a Board of Governors to advise the
directors on matters of policy and a group of some one hundred associates
who, although not in many cases intending to become members of staff, were
bound to it by their enthusiasm for its general policy and had pledged
themselves to provide special programmes at intervals on a fee basis, without
any sort of retainer. These associates were mostly very well-known film and
television producers and directors, performers or writers. The group also
intended to have their own symphony orchestra.

The emergence of this star-studded group was seen by the *Observer* as a
'revolt of the intellectuals' showing the dissatisfaction of creative people with
the way things were run. Ted Willis was quoted as saying: 'There's
continual conflict between us and business executives in which we get the
worst of the deal. Decisions are taken without reference to us'. Such a 'new
and more equal partnership between producers and management . . .

might disrupt the established order . . . in a way the tycoons could not ignore'.[7] It may have been over-confidence that led Box, at the very time when the ITA was considering his application, to start negotiations for acquisition of the British Lion Film Corporation. It was clear, however, that this move had the backing of the Department of Industry and Trade.

Lord Hill certainly had the concurrence of his colleagues when he said that the Box application for the weekday London contract should be taken seriously, showing on its programme side 'a vigour and freshness of approach and a liveliness of imagination'. On the financial side, however, he thought it was weak, in contrast with the incumbent contractor A-R, which he thought strong on the business and financial side, although in some respects deficient in vigour and sparkle. 'Can we in some way secure the best of both worlds,' he asked his colleagues, by requiring 'A-R to share fifty-fifty with Box the equity and the control?'[8] The Members were in cautious agreement, and resolved to consider the incorporation of elements of this applicant group in one or more of the successful central programme contracts.

When the A-R contingent came for a second interview on 2 January 1964, Hill put to them the Authority's interest in securing the introduction into this major company of a new element from the communications field, *possibly of a film character*. Wills responded with a positive rodomontade. He asserted that of all the contractors who had served the ITA, A-R had the greatest claim to a renewal of their contract, and went on to argue the difficulties that would be created for his company and for ITV by the introduction of a minority interest, particularly if it was associated with film. John McMillan (who had just been appointed A-R's General Manager) added that the current productive relationship between board, management and creative staff would be seriously jeopardised if they were to bring in someone with limited television experience from the film business.

It is difficult to say whether the Authority was finally persuaded by these arguments. It certainly knew the differences between feature film production and television programme production. Probably the Members were influenced by their continuing concern about finance, their fears that Box would be overreaching himself if he were to take on both British Lion and a major ITV contract; and most especially they shied back from the complicated and time-consuming negotiations that would have followed on a decision to require a forced marriage between the Box group and a major ITV company which was itself already part of a financial and commercial conglomerate. However that may be the recorded decision showed that, of the four central companies, only A-R were to be offered a new contract subject to no conditions other than those already contained in the particulars supplied to applicants. Sydney Box for his part declared on 9 January (the day after the decision had been made public) that he and his colleagues would now concentrate their efforts on obtaining a contract if and when any second commercial television channel, ITV 2, was introduced.[9]

In the event the final contract offer to A-R proved to be not totally unconditional. The Authority had made known to applicants at their interview its wish to see wider participation by members of the general public in the shareholdings of ITV contractors. In the case of A-R it did not think it enough that any private investor in BET and Rediffusion also had an indirect interest in the television company. During their two interviews Wills had explained his board's intention to reorganise A-R so as to split the television and non-television interests, making the former the concern of an exclusively television company, to be called Rediffusion Television Limited. This was to be done by reducing the equity capital held by the existing shareholders in A-R from £½ million to £340,000 voting and from £7 million to £4,760,000 non-voting Ordinary shares. Instead £2 million of non-voting Preferred shares were to be then issued to a Harley Drayton company, Cape and General Finance Ltd. These Preferred shares would have rights to priority in eventual return of capital at paid-up value and dividends guaranteed to be not less than 9 per cent. One consequence would be to reduce the tax payable by the new company (Rediffusion Television Ltd) by about £1½ million while still keeping the television contract profits in the BET – Rediffusion family. The Authority disliked this plan, which did not satisfy its wish to get wider direct public participation in the London weekday television company. On 1 June 1964, a formal request was made by A-R for its approval of a revised scheme whereby the £2 million non-voting Preference shares would be offered for public subscription instead of being issued to Cape and General Finance. That approval was duly given.

Central Scotland was another ITV region where the possible claims of a rival contract application had to be seriously considered, although it must be admitted that in this case the reasons were largely negative. STV's programme performance had not been outstanding, and the over-concentration of power in few hands, the dominant press interest and the inadequate representation of the region among STV's directors were clearly all things the Authority was not going to continue to accept.

The competition came from a group (the Central Scotland Television Company Ltd) headed by Max Aitken of Beaverbrook Newspapers, which had for long been among the most virulent public critics of Independent

Television. This group did have the distinct advantage that eleven out of the proposed fifteen members of the board were eminent Scotsmen, resident in Scotland. Even the eighty-one- year-old Lord Roseberry was among them. Whether the late addition to the consortium of the British Lion film company[10] was inspired by the desire to add elements of experience and achievement from the field of visual entertainment or whether it was more an attempt to get television profits to bolster up the film industry, it did not in the event do the group much good. A proposed shareholding of 28 per cent for the film company was no way of ensuring wider public participation and it was not effective in convincing the Authority that the Beaverbrook company would have a notable new contribution to make to ITV's programming either at national or regional level.

Consequently the Authority had to turn to the task of seeing what changes it could get in Scottish Television as conditions for the award of a contract. In this it was helped by Roy Thomson himself. Having been reminded during their interview of the Authority's concern, he wrote on 6 December 1963, forwarding a suggested plan for the reorganisation of shareholdings. Not less than three, possibly as many as five, prominent Scotsmen would join STV's board, in addition to Dr Curran, Principal of Strathclyde University, who had recently become one of their new directors. Thomson's 88 per cent of the voting shares would be split between the Thomson Organisation (55 per cent) and the new directors (33 per cent). The Thomson Organisation's 100 per cent of the non-voting shares would be reduced to 55 per cent, and the remaining 45 per cent issued to the public, preference being given to subscribers in Scotland. The ultimate control of the company would still rest with Thomson through the 55 per cent voting shares held by the Thomson Organisation which he indirectly controlled. But instead of all the profits flowing to the Thomson Organisation, some 45 per cent would go to members of the public (40 per cent), the new directors (3.3 per cent) and other small shareholdings (just over 1 per cent). The Authority would certainly have liked to achieve even more drastic changes in the structure of STV. But after hearing Thomson again at a second interview on 2 January, they decided to grant the company a new contract substantially on the terms he had proposed.

Southern Television were another existing contractor called for a second interview. Although their programme record was a good one, their internal structure (which initially had commended itself to the Authority) was now in clear conflict with the principles which were coming increasingly to be regarded as necessary criteria in the selection of contractors. Their £100,000 capital consisted of voting shares held exclusively by three firms outside the region, Associated Newspapers, Rank and D. C. Thomson. The first and third of these were press interests, making up between them a clear majority (62 per cent) of press holding. There was no significant element of local representation among the directors of Southern Television. John Davis' statement at the time of the additional allocation of the South East contract, that he intended to associate prominent people from the area with the company, had not been forgotten. However, Davis – well aware of the feeble competition his company had to face – stood firm. Neither on the question of wider public participation in shareholding nor on that of over-large press interests did he give any ground. On the suggestion that more local persons should be on Southern's board he showed a more compliant spirit. The Authority accordingly decided to award Southern a contract on the one condition that two additional directors were appointed: one from the world of agriculture, the other from education. Captain Harry Tupper, a member of an old Bognor farming family, and Asa Briggs, at that time Professor of History at Sussex University, were duly invited, and both accepted.

Not much need be said about the contract awards to ABC and ATV, although both were interviewed a second time. Little was made of the fact that ABC Television was a wholly-owned subsidiary of Associated British Picture Corporation and the question of direct public participation in the television company was raised more as a matter that was likely to be discussed again with the company at some unspecified future time. It was known of course that the Corporation's shares were very widely held both by institutions and members of the general public. The Authority Members also recognised the difficulty of establishing a clear regional identity for a company operating for two days a week in two different service areas. However, the contract award was made conditional on the appointment to ABC's board of a director 'drawn from the life of the areas'.[11] In April an invitation to join ABC's board was extended to the distinguished Merseyside doctor, Lord Cohen of Birkenhead. However, after attending two or three meetings to see what was involved, he came to the conclusion that he was not able to contribute much and withdrew.[12] No further moves were made by ABC or asked for by the ITA.

Lord Hill did not have a high opinion of ATV. He and his colleagues gave scant consideration to the company's application for the London weekday franchise, despite Renwick having stressed their eagerness for it because they considered it the most important concession the ITA had to give. This preference, together with the fact that their main production activity was concentrated in the Elstree studios, had tended to reinforce the feeling that the company did not regard themselves as wholeheartedly committed to the

Midlands. Successful as their networked offerings undeniably were, the output for the region had consistently attracted adverse criticism on grounds of quality, quantity and relevance to local interests. Their application promised to remedy that situation. A new TV centre in Coventry was tentatively proposed. A Midlands Advisory Board would be established and the whole Midlands operation would be the responsibility of a resident director. On the question of the machinery for programme decisions and planning, it emerged that the traditional Programme Controller role was mainly centred on the Managing Director, Lew Grade, with the support of Bill Ward, Production Controller at Elstree.

The decision to renew ATV's Midlands contract was in the event made conditional on the appointment of an extra member of the board drawn from the life of the Midlands, in addition to the proposed resident executive director who would have charge of the programme effort there. It became known by the following April that Sir Eric Clayson had become a member of the ATV board, and that Robin Gill, erstwhile Managing Director of Border TV, had been appointed to the board as Grade's deputy with effect from 30 July 1964. Gill would have special responsibility for the Midlands operation and it was intimated that he would spend two or three days a week there. Although this latter arrangement fell short of the terms on which the contract offer had been made and accepted, the Authority accepted the change. By the following year, the Midlands programmes had so far improved, and the whole organisation of the operation had been so far tightened up, that the Authority declared itself ready to overlook yet a further departure from the contractual agreement – the fact that Gill was not frequently in Birmingham. But it did seem to Fraser, and apparently also to Hill, that once the intended end had been achieved (i.e. improvement in Midlands output) it was reasonable to be clement over strict enforcement of the agreed means.

The reassurances which the Authority felt it necessary to seek from Granada before offering a new contract were different from those they sought from other contractors. Although questions of concentration of financial control, absence of regional representation at board level, the imbalance between the two sides of the Pennines in local programme coverage were all touched on in the interview, they do not seem to have been pressed. The Authority's major preoccupation was the nature of the day-to-day relationship between the company and the staff of the Authority; and this related both to the regular supply of programme information and the extent to which the programmes themselves might be in conflict with the Authority's responsibilities under the Act. The quality of Granada's programmes was not put in doubt but there had built up in the Authority, as Hill put it to Sidney Bernstein, 'a conviction . . . that, although always courteous in exchanges with the Authority, you are less co-operative, less understanding of the Authority's role and responsibility than any other company . . .'[13]

The Granada representatives put up a robust defence against the implications of these remarks. Their board took very seriously their programme responsibilities and, in doing so, took equally seriously the significance of the word 'independent' when applied to the ITV service. They were prepared to tackle in the documentary and current affairs fields topics which could raise problems of impartiality or offensiveness to public feeling – what Bernstein called 'hot' subjects. The care they took in reaching decisions on such programmes sometimes meant that information reached the Authority late and in a manner that seemed to challenge the right of the Authority to re-examine for itself the legality of those decisions. Moreover, because programme decisions had been taken at board level, exchanges about them between Authority and company had to take place, Granada maintained, at the same level, in other words between the Director General or his deputy and the nominated Granada director, Victor Peers, who was not in the main stream of company programme activity. The Authority did not think that this situation was compatible with its new statutory programme responsibilities. The outcome was to offer the contract to Granada subject to assurances that the company would establish with the Authority and its officers a working relationship appropriate to the respective functions of the Authority and the company; that the company would take steps to establish effective contact between its staff at various levels, and in particular the staff primarily concerned with programme planning, and designated ITA officers; and that the company would make effective arrangements for the full, prompt and regular provision of programme and other information to the Authority. The assurances were given. How far a less difficult relationship ensued will be seen later, particularly in Chapter 32.

Different problems arose over the allocation of a contract for the Wales and West of England area. This was not because of any doubts over who the successful applicant should be. TWW had been virtually assured of a renewal of their franchise when they came to the rescue of WWN. Their offer to WWN shareholders went out within a few days of the ITA's advertisement inviting applications for new contracts. The formal take-over took place again within days of the Authority's public announcement of its contract awards on 8 January 1964. With the amalgamation of the two service areas the

Authority was concerned that the purpose for which WWN had originally been set up as a separate contractor should so far as possible continue to be served. 'Full regard', it said, would have to be paid to the 'needs and interests of Wales'.[14] Moreover, by the time TWW representatives came to the ITA for their interview it was known that the request to the PMG for an extra VHF channel to carry Welsh language broadcasts in South Wales was to be granted.

The application was made in the names of both companies, TWW *and* WWN. TWW wanted to keep WWN in existence as a trading company in order that they might legitimately reap a tax advantage from the latter's accumulated losses. Although the Authority was unwilling to consider a contract award to the two companies jointly, a compromise was reached under which TWW alone would be party to the contract but that would contain a provision recognising TWW's right to obtain some of the services necessary for it to comply with its contractual obligation from WWN which would therefore be in the position of a subsidiary company.

Further discussions between TWW and the ITA concentrated on two matters: the representation of Welsh interests on the TWW board, and the total amount of Welsh language broadcasts to be provided. The board of TWW had seventeen members of whom five were Welshmen, resident in the company's original area, and Lord Derby expressed unwillingness to increase the size of an already large board. Yet it seemed to the Authority that, since TWW were actually making an application in the names of both TWW and WWN, it would be reasonable to expect some TWW board members (perhaps former directors of WWN) to be appointed to represent the interests of the people that the latter company had been set up to serve.

The idea of taking on WWN directors was rejected out of hand. To TWW it seemed that these were the people whose lack of business sense had been responsible for their company's failure. Eventually Hill and Derby settled the matter between them. The requirement of an appointment to the main board was withdrawn. Instead TWW's Welsh Committee was to be re-named the Welsh Board and the Authority's new condition was that there should be added, either to the main board or to any subsidiary board to which it would delegate full responsibility for Welsh programmes, three individuals drawn from the WWN service areas. This responsibility would include control of publicity for the Welsh programmes, development of Welsh educational programmes and grants within Wales to the arts and sciences. The Authority also expressed the wish that the three persons should be Welsh speakers, at least one of them from South West Wales and one from North Wales. Lord Derby was relieved and grateful, and hastened to assure Hill that the new Welsh Board would have *all* the powers the ITA required.

Less difficulty was found in reaching agreement over the hours of local origination. In anticipation of the ITA's requirements the company were already planning for a Welsh news service and a Welsh magazine programme which together would fill five hours a week and they hoped to be able to increase that by at least one hour in time for the opening of the new VHF channel from St. Hilary. Embodied in the final offer of contract was a provision that within twelve months of the opening of the new South Wales Channel 7 total local programming would average twelve hours a week, of which five hours on average would be in Welsh, one hour of specifically Welsh interest either in English or in Welsh and six hours a week on average, all in English, of which broadly three would be of Welsh or mixed Welsh and West of England interest, two of primarily West of England interest and one of primarily Welsh interest. These totals were to be reached progressively over the period until transmission started on Channel 7, which would carry from the start all programmes of Welsh or mixed Welsh–West interest in good mid-evening viewing times. These same programmes would also be shown, though not necessarily at the same times, from the three stations outside South Wales.

The question that arises in relation to the 1964 competition is why the velvet glove did not conceal an iron hand. The Authority had been severely criticised in the Pilkington Report, in Parliament and even by its Minister. It had been stigmatised as being a public relations spokesman for greedy company tycoons instead of the regulator and controller of their operations. Ostensibly, Lord Hill was appointed to change all that; and, armed with a new Act, he had sought in discussion with his fellow Members to establish new rules of the game designed to ensure tighter control of the nature and activities of the companies. Yet when decisions came to be made, when faced with spokesmen for companies whose structures were patently at variance with the very principles it had set itself to observe, the Authority compromised.

Some explanation for this inconsistency lies perhaps in the personalities chiefly involved, in particular Hill and Fraser. Hill was ever a man for the dramatic, attention-arresting gesture; Fraser one for cool, quiet, reasoned persuasion, content unobtrusively to leave public credit for success to the one persuaded rather than to the persuader. Hill was believed to have gone to the ITA with a remit to bring about change. Once there and able to take stock he was bound to observe that the over-simplified, politically-motivated and press-promoted image of the ITA and its activities did not wholly correspond to reality. A new national broadcasting service had been created by his predecessors that gave the British public something they had not had before and which they found worthwhile and duly appreciated. Fraser, in the new situation which Hill's arrival created, in which he saw himself rather as the civil service mandarin to Hill's Minister, proved able to persuade his new Chairman of the reasonable acceptability of certain situations which were theoretically incorrect but which, in practice, were not harmful. Carmichael and Caine would have seen the situation in much the same light.

Factors in the situation were not only the relatively smooth working relationship which existed between Authority and contractors and the far from unsatisfactory programme service that this relationship had brought about, but also the absence in 1963 of any more than one or two credible competitors for the new franchises. And once it had been decided – pending ITV 2 – to review contracts in 1967, serious practical doubts were inevitable about the possibility of any newcomer being able to take over so soon as July 1964, with no certain prospect of being a contractor for more than three years. However, changing contractors was one thing, imposing strict conditions on renewal of contracts quite another. Since the conditions were in general none too strict and were in a number of cases allowed to remain unfulfilled, Hill's medicine was certainly mild. On this occasion the Authority seemed more concerned with making its points than with actually enforcing them.

A clear indication of the erosion of Authority intentions came in Hill's press conference on 8 January 1964 announcing the contract awards. What originally was to have been a public statement of the principles which guided the Authority in selecting programme companies, was now delivered, after the event, as a look to the future. 'Now that ITV has come to stay,' he said, 'it may be helpful if I indicate, in a general way, the Authority's thinking on some aspects of programme company structure.'[15] The statement then went on to speak of the need for the direction of the companies to be spread among a number of persons and a variety of interests; and for beneficial ownership to be widely spread, including in the case of the regional companies residents in the region. 'In many cases the present company pattern satisfies these criteria: in others progress towards them is being made. I mention these objectives now so that present companies and future applicants may take them into account when the time comes in three years or so to formulate applications for the next phase . . .'

Press comment on the 'no change' decision was singularly muted. It tended to focus on the plans Hill had judiciously added to his announcement that 'in no case had the Authority been persuaded that appointment of one of the new applicants would improve the service.'[16] These included, in addition to the proposals for the restructuring of stv, the creation of a Programme Policy Committee linked with greater involvement of the Authority in scheduling and networking; changes in networking charges; the establishment of an ita Research Department under Sir Harold Evans; and the appointment of a General Advisory Council, with members drawn from the general public. This last new body would be holding its first meeting very soon, in early February, with a remit to keep programmes under review, proffering their advice to the Authority on their general pattern and content. 'We shan't muzzle that Committee, if in disagreeing with us it wants publicly to express that disagreement. We shall do our utmost . . . to make it live and effective.'[17] Even the normally critical *Daily Express* supplemented its 'Same Old Bonanza'[18] headline with an enumeration of the various ways in which the ita would in future, it said, be exercising 'tighter controls' and 'a closer watch'.

28

COLLECTIVE PROGRAMME POLICIES

Although history is, or should be, a narrative of events, it is rarely possible to observe a simple, chronological sequence because so many events overlap and often interrelate one with the other. Selection and classification are unavoidable. This is particularly so in relation to the developments in ITV programme policies between 1963 and 1968, and in this chapter the narrative proceeds under a number of separate headings.

(i) THE '8 O'CLOCK LINE'

The Authority's newly-formed sub-committee on Programme Schedules met for the first time on 12 November 1964. Hill had decided that he would himself be the chairman of this particular committee, just as he had also decided that he would take the chair at the quarterly meetings of the new Programme Policy Committee, on which the ITA and each of the companies were represented at the highest executive levels. As it turned out the sub-committee's very first recommendation launched the ITA on a course which involved tedious difficulties over the next three years; and the advantage gained was scarcely commensurate with the trouble it occasioned. It was a case-history in the problems that could arise when the programme planning of a diversified television service was subjected to control from on high that, however worthy its objectives, paid scant regard to problems of implementation at working levels.

It had been emphasised by both the Government and Parliament that the new Act was supposed to involve the direct supervision *by the Authority itself* of the planning of ITV schedules. Only trial and error was to show how far this could be effectively achieved by a body of part-time non-professionals. Was it possible to regulate this activity by issuing, when necessary, directions applicable not just to *ad hoc* issues as they surfaced but to a continuing situation recurring as schedule succeeded schedule; or was it that, as Hugh

Greene wrote in 1965, the only sure way of exercising control is to proceed by persuasion and not by written directives,[1] an approach which hitherto had characterised Fraser's activities under the previous legislation?

The committee noted a lack of home-produced material 'of good quality'[2] in the period between 8 and 9 p.m. on weekdays, and recommended that the companies be asked to study ways of improvement and to make proposals in their next quarterly schedule submissions. It was a fair point, because many producers had little taste for working within the constraints of 'family viewing', and it was put at the next meeting of the Network Planning Committee on 7 December. Discussion proceeded at various levels, but, by the spring of 1965, it had become abundantly clear that the three major companies concerned were reluctant to contemplate any radical change and sincerely believed that the mixture of crime, adventure and westerns being supplied between 8 and 9 p.m. on the five weekdays was successfully satisfying an evident public appetite for good but 'undemanding' entertainment. Certainly it was handing over to the ITN news at 8.55 p.m. a substantial majority share of the viewing audience. When the Programme Schedule Committee came to examine the autumn schedules of these companies on 12 August it noted that this period continued to be dominated by programmes falling within the general description of crime and westerns, and a high proportion of these were American. In the absence of an August meeting of the Authority it ruled that all companies should submit new proposals for this part of their schedules.[3]

By this time provisional schedules were already in the hands of advertising agents. August holidays were in full swing, and, for the newspapers, it was the silly season. Inevitably, with no time to lose, those in the company managements who had been left holding the fort wanted to be told what were the changes which would ensure ITA approval. With Hill's agreement Fraser told them that not more than two of the five programmes a week should be American and that not more than three of the five should be crime stories or westerns.

For the companies to come into line with this requirement presented no great difficulty – although A-R in London were short of suitable material because they had no access to Lew Grade's ITC series – currently *Danger Man* – since these were withheld for use by ATV at the weekends. But the story reached the press, for whom it was manna from heaven. Here at last was some evidence – and they had been waiting two years for it – that the doctor was asserting his commanding role. It received lead-story headlines in the popular press: conflict between the ITA and the companies was a useful topic when news was in short supply. Especially as the tenth anniversary celebrations of ITV were pending.

Having found itself driven into making – or at any rate endorsing – a precise and highly publicised ruling about one particular hour in the day, the Authority had little option but to stick with it. A very plausible request from Granada and ATV to exempt westerns from the ruling was twice rejected. Such an overt and unprecedented restriction on American material in British television aroused resentment on the other side of the Atlantic and its compatibility with the multilateral international agreement aimed at the reduction of tariffs and import quotas known as GATT (General Agreement on Tariffs and Trade) was seriously questioned at governmental level. Nor was its maintenance made any easier when, within a year, the BBC was found to be scheduling at 8 p.m. a western on Mondays and crime series on Tuesdays, Wednesdays, Thursdays and Fridays. The companies were far from pleased, but they conformed. Under the new Act and contracts they had no option.[4]

The restriction was eventually withdrawn in 1967 as part and parcel of the revised pattern of programmes put into effect in July of that year which is described in the following section. It had been widely stigmatised as clumsy and negative, but at least it underlined the need for a new style of home-made drama not unsuitable for the family period. *The Power Game* series was one such product.

(ii) THE PATTERN OF PROGRAMMES

It was taken for granted when Lord Hill became Chairman of the ITA in 1963 that his intended role was so to reform the whole programme performance of ITV as to remove for ever the possibility of it suffering again such an onslaught as had been made by the Pilkington Committee. There was widespread expectation of a sweeping use of the new powers that Parliament had thrust upon the Authority in the new Act. The strong man, so often heralded by Bevins during the debates, had arrived. These over-wealthy and complacent companies were now to get their come-uppance. It did not happen. Not only – as we have seen – were they all given renewals of their contracts, subject to some not very arduous conditions; not only did their 'friend and partner', Robert Fraser, continue in his post; but Hill in a variety of ways commended himself to ITV at all levels by his seemingly realistic and earthy understanding of the ITV ethos and by his readiness to spring robustly to its defence when it came under attack from critics with a Pilkingtonian turn of mind.

Certainly from September 1963 onwards there was a marked increase in the number of ITA 'programme interventions', and Hill referred to these in his subsequent memoirs.[5] We shall be examining some of them later in this chapter and in Chapter 32. But there is nothing to suggest that at this juncture Hill had formed a master-plan or acquired any great sense of mission. It would certainly be true to say that he arrived at the ITA in 1963 with fewer preconceptions than when he arrived at the BBC four years later. He was a pragmatist and his main aim was to do all he could to make the new deal introduced by the Government and Parliament work. More relevant to this task than his recent experience in government was experience *fighting* government as Secretary of the BMA back in the forties. The Radio Doctor was to assume a new role as Independent Television Doctor, and it was in character that he should concentrate in the first instance on getting the kind of organisation within the ITA that suited his concept of sound administration; and also establishing the machinery of relationship between Authority and companies which was consistent with the requirements of the Act. The time would then come when his energies could be further applied to the strategic aspects of programme planning, but he would allow himself and his Authority colleagues ample time for running-in. The flurry over the 8 o'clock programmes in 1965 was but a part of that process. Meanwhile individual problems and issues would inevitably arise and these would be dealt with in a manner which accorded with his reputation for sound common-sense. His colleagues and his staff warmed to this approach and the attitude of the companies changed from one of initial apprehension to one of increasing confidence and respect. He could be brusque and did not hesitate on occasions to emphasise where the ultimate power resided, but he responded to frankness and candour; and if there were difficulties, well then there was the fatherly Fraser to smooth them out. ITV 'never had it so good'. Nor, as his memoirs readily admit, did Lord Hill.

As we saw in Part V of Volume I, ITV had by the early sixties achieved both success and distinction in certain of the main sectors of television programming; and the facts belied the image of the service presented to readers of the Pilkington Report. Hill and his colleagues were only too glad to acknowledge this and to have it demonstrated in annual reports and year-books. But they were also aware that, as we saw in Part II, the Pilkington charge was given credence by the irregularity of the prestigious, 'worthwhile' offerings in the main viewing hours. Long after it was first made in June 1962 this charge still stuck. A memorandum circulated to company members of the Programme Policy Committee on 15 August 1966 – three full years after Hill had assumed the chairmanship – said:

> In general, Independent Television has a very good record. Taken as a whole our programmes embrace the serious as well as the light; informing, stimulating and entertaining most groups in the community. Minorities do not go to the wall in Independent Television. We prove this by an analysis of our total programme output.
>
> Yet despite the validity of our rejection of the criticism that a commercial service can never be a public service, the charge sometimes made that the one motive behind our service is numbers, and so profit, might be held to find some semblance of support from a scrutiny of our offering which is limited to peak hours . . . What then are we after? Quality, of course, at all times – there will be no two views about that. But also at all times – sufficient variety . . .
>
> The Authority asks all companies to take a fresh, hard look at the make-up of their schedules between 7 and 10.30 p.m. with a view to securing within these times a generally wider range of programmes.
>
> The aim should be to whet the appetites of the more intelligent viewers by providing more variation from the standard fare . . .[6]

The document went on to refer to some specific programme categories – drama series (inadequate variety), light entertainment (no longer a category of marked strength compared with the BBC), children's programmes (hoping to see a change for the better), feature films (need for more careful selection and editing) and serials (need for a more consistent standard of quality).

This memorandum seemed to bespeak the long-awaited exercise of the commanding role of the Authority in programme affairs. As such it was respectfully but cautiously received. How to meet the principal request was something about which the three major weekday companies did not easily agree – and without their collective lead the regionals were helpless, and prone to succumb to whichever of the three they most feared. Their attitude was characterised by reluctance to incur the risk of offending Lew Grade, who could be a formidable adversary just as readily as he could be a benevolent friend. The schedules for January 1967 revealed no radical change, and it was noteworthy that there were unusually marked differences between the peak-time offerings of each of the three majors – a situation which in earlier days the ITA would have welcomed as evidence of competition, but now that it was, as it were, in command of the scheduling, this seemed to be less of an attraction. It became increasingly restless at the lack of a positive and concerted response to an initiative by which it had set much store.

On 9 February 1967 the Authority's Programme Schedule Committee received a staff paper which was destined to have quite far-reaching consequences. It reported that there was no sign of 'a recognisable new look in Independent Television' and it went on:

> The staff have become impressed by the need to seek from the week-day companies during the period 7 p.m. to 10.00 p.m. a basic network schedule which is broadly identical for all areas and which is planned on entirely new lines. This should be accompanied by the renovation of the 5-6 p.m. hour of children's television. As now, 6-7 p.m. would be 'local', carrying the successful regional news and news magazine programmes after the 5.55 p.m. national news. After 10.30 p.m. the system could go 'local' again, with a variety of local and network programmes more loosely arranged. The argument rests on the premise that if there is to be a major shake-up in the period from 7 to 10 p.m. it must be a collective one. It is felt by the staff that the main evening news at 8.55 p.m. may have become a constricting factor, leading to stereotyped programming during the two hours that precede it. Keeping in mind the case that is being argued in ITN for a longer news bulletin (ITN's Board will be considering this at its meeting in March), we think the week-day companies might be invited by the Authority to prepare and put up for consideration at the April meeting a draft network schedule for the summer, covering the period from 7 p.m. to 10.00 p.m. on the assumption for planning purposes that the main evening news will then begin at 10.00 p.m.[7]

This proposal for the main evening news to be at 10 p.m. received a welcome from the committee. It was, however, only one stage – though perhaps the decisive one – in the long campaign that led to the introduction of *News at Ten*, which subsequently became perhaps the most majestic pillar in the edifice of ITV programmes. The idea of a half-hour news had been one of a range of alternatives put forward by the ITN Board to the NPC in the summer of 1964. It had been rejected, and so too had an alternative plan for the networking of *Dateline*, which would have given ITN in effect a two-tiered evening bulletin, with one segment in peak hours and another around 11 p.m. When a year later the Early Bird satellite made satellite transmissions available eighteen hours a day, Cox returned to the attack with a proposal that *Dateline* and *ITN Reports* be merged with the bulletins to form a nightly half-hour news – the procedure ultimately adopted for *News at Ten*. This too was rejected. Having lost this frontal assault, Cox decided that his best hope lay in waiting until the companies' contracts came up for renewal, and then pushing hard for half an hour of news. Until then he thought it important to lie low, in order not to alert the current affairs producers within the companies who would tend to regard a longer news as a threat to access for their programmes to good viewing times.[8]

However, as an old war correspondent, Cox knew only too well that a campaign, however carefully planned, needed to be adapted to changing circumstances, and in the event the build-up towards the introduction of a half-hour news around 10.00 p.m. moved rather ahead of his schedule. The main reasons for this could not have been better put than in an article he wrote on the occasion of the ITV's tenth anniversary in September 1965:

> We are about to enter the satellite age, which can bring a new dimension into news coverage by linking the whole world into one close knit immediate news gathering operation. I know that Early Bird at first sight looks like a television flop, because it has been smartly and effectively priced out of the reach of television stations. But there will be other Early Birds, which will hover not only over mid-Atlantic but over region after region of the globe, and which will work at reasonable prices. This will make it possible to bring news from the Middle and Far East, from Africa and Australia, New Zealand and South America as rapidly as we can now from Europe, via Eurovision, or from America on the occasions we use Early Bird. This flow of more news towards our screens must carry news on television into an even more significant place in the structure of daily journalism.[9]

If the high expenditure involved in the use of satellite communication across the Atlantic was to be justified, ITN's news service had to occupy more time, be placed relatively late in the evening and be transmitted over the whole ITV network.

Consequently, when the ITA held a consultation on News and Current Affairs in January 1966 Cox could neither restrain Alastair Burnet (then Editor of *The Economist* and a guest speaker) nor restrain himself, despite the risk of hardening opposition in the companies, from bringing into a wider forum arguments which had so far only been expounded behind the closed doors of programme meetings. These arguments did not go uncontested by those present, who saw in the possible invasion of the hour between 10 p.m. and 11 p.m. by a network service from ITN a serious threat to the secure development of topical regional programmes which depended upon inheriting large audiences from the main peak time network fare between 7 and 10 p.m. It was probably for this reason that neither within the collective council of the companies nor within the ITA itself did the Cox/Burnet *démarche* make much apparent impact in the course of 1966. Hill, whilst sympathetic, told Cox that the ITA could not impose the development on unwilling companies by directive: he would have to plough his own furrow until such time as a significant element within the companies would support him. At this juncture, ITA could move in and rule in his favour.[10]

However, the fact was that by February 1967 none of the three major weekday companies was yet in favour of a half-hour news. A-R were strenuously advocating a news at 8.40 p.m. in order to be, as McMillan put it, 'first on the streets',[11] whilst Granada and ATV had come together on a proposal for 9.25 p.m.; but news slots of half an hour in length were not in contemplation.

By now Hill recognised that a solution to the seeming impasse required a strong ITA initiative and he was prepared for it to be taken. With his blessing Fraser and I met Bernstein, Grade and McMillan on 15 February[12] and pushed hard for urgent collective action to establish an entirely new pattern, including a longer news. On 21 February they were back to present us with a plan, and it was one which the Authority received with gratitude. It included provision for a news at 10.00 p.m. together with a number of other welcome changes. The regional companies heard of it in letters written on 1 March:

. . . we have agreed with the three companies that they will now prepare their own draft summer schedules on the basis that each will contain a number of fixed common elements which would no longer be variable as regards day of the week or hour of the day. These common elements will be:
1. A main evening news at 10.00 p.m. Monday through Friday,
2. *Monday*: at 8.00 p.m. the Granada current affairs programme and at 8.30 p.m. the principal play of the week,
   Tuesday: from 8.30 p.m. to 9.30 p.m. the feature/variety programme formerly slotted at 9.40 p.m. on Wednesdays,
   Thursday: from 8.30 p.m. to 9.00 p.m. *This Week*,
   Friday: from 7.00 p.m. to 7.30 p.m. the ATV sports programme, *Sportsweek*.

When the remainder of the three schedules come to be filled in there will probably be several other instances of simultaneity, e.g. *Coronation Street* from 7.30 p.m. to 8.00 p.m. on Monday and Wednesday, but it is the programme slots described above to which the Authority attaches particular importance and which form the essence of the plan which we are asking should be adopted in the summer schedules . . .

Finally, a word about the news at 10.00 p.m. A firm decision about the nature and length of it will depend upon proposals coming from the Editor, who has, of course, been fully informed about this development. If, as we are hoping, these provide for a new-style news occupying the whole of the 10.00 p.m. to 10.30 p.m. period, then we would expect that neither *Dateline* nor *Reporting '67* would continue to be available.[13]

ITA hopes were fulfilled and the result was *News at Ten*.

The programmes thus designated for full, simultaneous networking came subsequently to be known as the 'mandated programmes'. Actually this was a misnomer: in theory, and sometimes in practice, the ITA would (saving for the news) allow alternative programmes to be shown locally, provided they were of the same kind and quality as the network offerings. The doctrine of 'mandating' related to 'slots' rather than individual programmes. An example of the niceties of internal ITV politics was the presence in the package of the rather undistinguished *Sportsweek* from ATV: it was recognised as necessary to concede to Grade his due place in the sun if his agreement with a plan for which he had no personal liking was to be secured.

Hill was pleasantly surprised by this collective action and duly grateful, but, characteristically, he saw it as a reason for renewing rather than relaxing the pressure. Consequently on 29 March the companies received another missive for the PPC comparable in character to the one of the previous August saving that it was noticeably sharper in tone.[14] It pointed out that over the intervening months quite a lot of public comment had contained criticisms along the lines of those previously made, which were recapitulated. But it did not fail to acknowledge that on the credit side substantial fresh efforts were now being put into the production of comedy; in children's television there were welcome signs of awakening vitality; and that ITV remained strong in news and news magazines and in documentary and current affairs. The audience for *World of Sport* had been picking up. And deserving of special note in any review of this period was the phenomenal *Frost Programme*, although its transmission had (to the astonishment of the outside world) been confined to the London, Border and (latterly) Anglia areas. *The Frost Programme* came from Rediffusion.

The 'new look' pattern already described (which by this time had been publicly announced by Grade who in February had taken over from

Bernstein as chairman of the Network Planning Committee) also received acknowledgement. The remainder of the document contained comments under three heads:

Children's Television
After exhaustive consideration the Authority has concluded that the arguments against centralising production in this field outweigh those in favour. It bases its expectations on the individual initiative of the companies, supported by energetic co-operative planning and, where appropriate, co-production arrangements between groups of companies. There is a pressing need for increased specialisation in this field within the larger companies.

The Problem at Weekends
We do not succeed to any extent in giving satisfaction to that small but highly articulate and influential section of the audience which only makes use of television with regularity on Saturday and Sunday afternoons and evenings. For these people, and indeed for many more intelligent viewers, we do not provide properly balanced programmes on these days . . .

Network Planning Machinery
. . . The Authority is not in favour of frequent meetings of large committees and sub-committees: but it believes that the proper way of obviating them in such a fast-moving industry as Independent Television is by arrangements which ensure for these committees adequate advance preparation of the issues for consideration and decision, and effective follow-up action on the matters that have been dealt with. By any standards the Network Planning Committee seems to lack such necessary machinery. The diversity which, as has often been said, constitutes the main strength of Independent Television does not preclude the central execution of collective tasks. The need for this has already been recognised in certain areas, as may be seen in the establishment of a Central Schools Secretariat and the agreement to set up a Central Sports Unit . . . If a proliferation of *ad hoc* centralising measures is to be avoided, the Authority considers that the companies should take steps to establish under the Network Planning Committee a central secretariat and planning executive which can provide the necessary supporting services for itself and those of its subordinate committees . . . which are, or should be, regularly concerned with the planning of collective programme action.

When the paper came to be discussed in April there were two concrete developments to be reported – very different in kind one from the other. The first was the decision to establish forthwith a central secretariat and planning executive under the NPC, and the second was the impending reduction in the number of episodes of the popular early evening serial, *Crossroads*, from five to four a week. The former heralded a transformation in the collective arrangements for programme planning which was of very great significance for ITV in the years ahead. The second was intended to help enhance the quality of the serial by relieving its production staff and cast of the pressure generated by five episodes a week. It was a concession wrung from Lew Grade with the utmost difficulty.[15]

Beyond these two matters emphasis was placed on the time needed to effect changes which would be apparent on the television screens.[16] This was the last of the collective discussions on programme plans in which Hill took part. The initiative he had begun to take in August 1966 undoubtedly yielded beneficial results. Without his particular flair for choosing his time and pressing home an advantage, less might have been gained. As it was, the ground was prepared for programme achievements over a period lasting a good ten years. Finding the way to make the new statutory relationship between Authority and companies work effectively was perhaps his most solid achievement.

News at Ten was first transmitted on 3 July 1967 and was from the beginning a considerable success. By November it was being described in an ITA paper as having become 'the most important news programme on television'.[17] It generally secured a majority of the audience between 10 and 10.30 p.m. and a larger audience than the BBC main news at 8.50 p.m. But doubts were still harboured in some quarters of ITV. The audience measurements could be read in different ways, and it was thought that the situation could change if the BBC were to place more popular programmes against it. However, whilst there was no evidence that the ITV audience at 10 p.m. had diminished on account of *News at Ten*, there was by the autumn of 1967 a trend showing a decline in the relative popularity of ITV programmes in almost every category. Some were inclined to attribute this to the structural changes in the schedules introduced in July; others pointed to a failure to match the BBC in producing popular entertainment. Ten years previously it had been a very different story.

Successful as *News at Ten* was *per se*, the belief that placing it at 10 p.m. would 'open up' the evening was never fully borne out. Before long, there was talk of it being a 'ceiling'; that is to say it obstructed the natural extension of the concept of peak time into the hour between 10 and 11 p.m. The dilemma became all too clear. Many 'prestigious' programmes – documentary or serious drama – did not stand up well in audience measurement terms against the popular fare supplied by BBC 1 after their mid-evening news. It could be argued that more viewers overall would be secured for them if they were placed at 10.30 p.m. Yet if this was done a sector of 'informed opinion' (of the kind which had influenced Pilkington some years earlier) was apt to condemn it as a commercially-motivated abdication of responsibility. For them 10.30 p.m. was a late night ghetto – contemptible and derisory timing for anything really worthwhile. It was a complex issue with which programme planners were to wrestle for many years to come.

In 1968 Thames, inheriting Rediffusion's last prestigious offering, the series on the *Life and Times of Lord Mountbatten*, decided on a bold move and firmly proposed it as a series of twelve hour-long episodes to be scheduled at 9 p.m. as an addition to the normal 'Tuesday feature'. ATV with equal firmness advocated 10.30 p.m. as the proper placing. Not wishing to be dogmatically authoritarian, the ITA allowed the option, so that one part of the network followed Thames and the other ATV. In the event, as the ITA bleakly recorded in its Annual Report for 1968/9, the series 'attracted a large audience, particularly in those areas where it was screened in peak time'.[18]

This event highlighted the continuing dilemma created by the presence of *News at Ten*. On this occasion the ITA's tolerant – perhaps excessively tolerant – respect for conflicting views met with contemptuous criticism in the press: as so often in such matters it was seen as the pig in the middle.

There is no better illustration of the flair Howard Thomas, by then Managing Director of Thames, always possessed for spotting a classic winner and backing it heavily: in a different field he had previously done the same with *The Avengers*. (Later we shall find him doing the same again with *World at War*.) On each of these two occasions he came into collision with Lew Grade, who was seldom disposed to take risks where audience ratings were concerned. By providing only muted backing for Thames' bold move, the ITA missed a good opportunity of demonstrating its power at the outset of a new contract period, and appeared to display the kind of weakness of which it used to be accused before the era of Lord Hill.

Thomas was now for the first time in his ITV career involved in the shaping of the weekday schedules, and in Brian Tesler as his programme controller he possessed one of the most skilful programme planners ITV has ever had.

The removal of ATV from the London scene marked the beginning of the gradual withdrawal of Lew Grade from his life of almost total preoccupation with the affairs of ITV. Many people have paid tribute to his brilliant showmanship, to his astonishing industry and to his being invariably a man of his word. His drive and energy sometimes outstripped his judgement. It was Hill who remarked upon one rare attribute – his willingness to admit when he was wrong. During the sixties his personality was built into the corporate persona of ITV – so much so that for many people the image of Lew Grade seemed to personify all that ITV stood for. Essentially, however, he was a solo performer and he had no enthusiasm for the give and take of collective planning. His occasional blockbusters, whether in show business or Shakespeare or the highly idiosyncratic *Golden Hours*, have to be set beside much safe but successful mediocrity. Such was the force of his personality that whatever he chose to offer, the rest of ITV did not usually think twice about taking – and even taking twice! There were, however, occasions when ABC or Granada or Rediffusion or even a regional company would steel themselves to the exhausting process of deviating from his wishes. Those were truly titanic battles.

When it was necessary to reconcile Grade's ideas with those of other network colleagues, the task invariably fell to Cecil Bernstein of Granada, for the two men had a close rapport. Bernstein was ITV's great go-between, and he combined exceptional skill as a conciliator with powerful advocacy of Granada's own distinctive views. He was much helped by the emergence within the ranks of the company of the able managerial figure of Denis Forman, now Chairman of Granada Television. The two new network companies, London Weekend Television and Yorkshire Television, were as yet unknown quantities, and how they fared under managing directors Michael Peacock and Gwyn Ward Thomas respectively will be described in Volume 3.

But it was by now no longer possible to regard the major network companies as having a monopoly in ITV statesmanship. Experienced and resourceful men had emerged amongst the regionals. Hitherto the passivity and reticence of the Ten in such collective forums as the PPC, SCC and NPC had been a source of disappointment, not to say irritation, in the ITA itself. Such men as Aubrey Buxton of Anglia, David Wilson of Southern and William Brown of STV had behind them the strength of very substantial and prosperous companies which had secured renewals of their contracts on two occasions. In the eyes of the ITA they had the status to exercise a significant influence over the course of events. By the end of the period covered by this volume it still remained to be seen what share they would eventually succeed in securing in the overall distribution of power within the system.

(iii) INDEPENDENT TELEVISION SPORT

There has been no area of programmes in which it proved more difficult to operate the plural system of ITV than that of sport, and it was a continuing problem throughout the period covered by this volume. Lord Hill met it when he arrived, endeavoured to grapple with it in so far as this lay within the Authority's power, but left it behind, still unresolved, when he left. In organisational and institutional terms the dice were always loaded in favour of the BBC, and it is not by chance that they elected to place the coverage of sport in the vanguard of their counter attack against the forces of their competitor.

There had been almost continuous concern about ITV's coverage of sport since the summer of 1962 when serious attention had to be given by ABC and ATV to the failure of the Saturday afternoon sports programmes to compete with any success at all with the BBC's *Grandstand*. Eventually, ABC came forward in 1964 with plans for a new approach which led to the launching in association with ATV of *World of Sport* in the autumn of that year.

These plans preceded by only a month or two the presentation of a report by a Sports Working Party which had been set up by the Network Planning Committee 'to investigate the acquisition and coverage of sport'. This working party, which was under the chairmanship of none other than Tim Hewat, the Granada current affairs producer, recommended the setting up of a 'Central Sports Team' – producers, directors, commentators and others – responsible to the NPC. This team would 'acquire and present all the network's sport'[19] on a seven-day basis. Because of the new ABC plan, the NPC did not adopt this recommendation, merely recording that 'the arrangements for Saturdays during the autumn would be carefully watched with a view to further development along the lines suggested in the working party's report'.[20]

In February 1966 the Authority reopened the question of sports policy at the PPC when it was agreed that the quality and organisation aspects of sports programmes would be further examined on an industry basis. Hewat's working party was reconvened and promptly re-affirmed its original recommendation saying:

It is absolutely vital to have one staff with a pre-determined· annual budget to handle all ITV sports, thus giving it continuity and style; thus enabling decisions to be made quickly; thus making it possible to improve the quality of sport covered without pushing costs up astronomically.[21]

Once again, however, the Committee deferred a decision, electing to await a Consultation on Sport which had in the meantime been arranged for June.

The Consultation came to be dominated by three factors. First, the vigorous advocacy by a number of influential programme practitioners of the case for a Central Sports Unit as the only means of ensuring a consistent and coherent policy for sports coverage and its efficient execution technically, creatively and financially. Secondly, the presentation by ATV of their case for a new, experimental approach to sports coverage at the weekends – an approach already embodied in their draft autumn schedule for the London area. This would involve the reduction in the amount of live sport on Saturday afternoons by about $1\frac{1}{2}$ hours and the scheduling between 3 p.m. and 5 p.m. of ordinary entertainment programmes, sports programmes being resumed with the wrestling at 5 p.m.; and the introduction on Sunday afternoons of a new $1\frac{1}{2}$ hour programme of recorded sport in a magazine format. Thirdly, the presentation by Market Investigations Limited of the findings of a survey on viewer attitudes to televised sport undertaken for the ITA. The principal finding of this survey was that Saturday daytime viewers preferred sport to any alternative programmes and that there was a relatively low interest in the possibility of regular sports programmes at other times, as well as a low interest amongst non-sports viewers in the possible introduction of other types of programmes on Saturday afternoons.

There emerged a radical division of opinion between those who wished to develop a comprehensive live sports coverage based on the retention of *World of Sport* on Saturday afternoons and backed, if necessary, by a centralised sports unit as advocated by Hewat and others, and those who wished to abandon the Saturday afternoon routine, distributing roughly the same amount of sport on a Saturday and Sunday, offering two hours of entertainment programmes on Saturday afternoons and recorded 'highlights' of sport on the Sundays.

The case for a centralised sports organisation, as vigorously expounded by Hewat, took as its starting point the fact that the machinery for coordination was widely regarded as inadequate. It was claimed that it could serve the whole network seven days a week and act quickly to secure contracts, provided it was adequately supported financially, and that it could give an *identity* to all ITV sport which had always been lacking by comparison with the BBC. Moreover, it could greatly improve the technical quality of sports coverage by having complete control of outside broadcast equipment specially designed for the job.

The argument against it was that it conflicted with the federal character of Independent Television, deliberately geared to facilitate the maximum diversity within the system and to encourage regional enterprise and decentralised programme planning. A decision to proceed with the establishment of a centralised sports unit did not necessarily preclude a short-term experiment in a new pattern for weekends as advocated by ATV and supported in several regions. Despite the gloomy prognosis of the Market Investigations research, it was difficult to dismiss the ATV concept before it had been tried. It was claimed that it would make possible the elimination of miscellaneous minor sports on Saturdays and the introduction on Sundays of selected recorded sport of a much higher quality; that four hours of continuous sport on Saturdays was an awful lot and Saturday afternoon would offer a more attractive and balanced fare if the sequence were two hours of live sports, two hours of family entertainment and an hour of wrestling, and similarly that on Sundays the introduction of recorded sport would add variety to the afternoon. There was not much sense in the offer of nothing but continuous sport on both channels for four hours on Saturday, and the introduction of entertainment programmes would offer viewers the choice without depriving them of continuous sport if they preferred it, for that would still be available on BBC 1 or by a combination of watching ITV for part of the time and BBC 1 for part of the time.

The main objection to such an experiment was that, even if it was clearly limited to a thirteen-week period between October and December, the strength and resources of *World of Sport* might be so diminished by the lack of an adequate outlet in London and the other areas making the experiment that ITV would emerge from the experimental period in total disarray so far as sport was concerned.

When these arguments were put before the Authority in July it was so far impressed by the case for a central unit that it decided to request the companies to work out definite plans for one, and at the same time to give a compromise ruling on ATV's proposal for non-sporting entertainment on Saturdays, agreeing to one hour of it but not two. Such a furore of well-publicised excitement was generated by these two decisions that Hill found it necessary to make a public statement on 2 August explaining what they were and why they had been reached. The more formal note to the PPC despatched the next day contained a touch of asperity:

> The Authority now . . . asks that the companies should as a matter of urgent policy consult together with a view to making concrete proposals for the centralisation of ITV sport services either on similar lines to that adopted for the supply of national and international news, i.e. the establishment of a central sports unit, separately managed and financed,

and having a direct relationship as regards programme planning with the Network Planning Committee; or in some other way.[22]

A period of intensive consultation and negotiation followed lasting right into November – consultation between the companies, involving both 'the Four' and 'the Ten', and negotiation with the ITA in which Cecil Bernstein, as chairman of the NPC, took the lead. It was a major test of the capacity of ITV's 'two-tiered' system to reach a collective decision about organisation and structure. The Authority had left open the possibility of achieving the central direction of ITV sport by 'some other way' than the establishment of an ITN-type organisation. The companies clutched at this alternative because, as a memorandum first presented to the Authority on 19 October put it, they 'decided to respect the established practice of networking and incorporate a new sports organisation into it rather than create an autonomous unit outside it'.[23] There was to be no surrender of NPC control over sport and no allotment of separate equipment and other resources to the 'Unit'. What mainly justified the continued use of this word was the proposed appointment of a Chief Executive, having the status of a member of the NPC, together with an administrator and an executive producer. They would be financed in the first instance by the Four, and all companies would put outside broadcast units at their disposal. They would make a sustained effort to acquire for ITV certain of the major sporting events currently exclusively contracted by the BBC.

Hill and his colleagues didn't say 'yes' but they didn't say 'no'. They sought assurances – assurances about finance, about the availability of technical resources and about the status of the new chief executive. They wanted the latter to be empowered to 'negotiate and settle deals with sports organisations',[24] and it seems clear that the assurances they duly received, and on the basis of which the plans of the companies were approved, included none precisely in these terms. When on 29 December 1966 Cecil Bernstein announced the intention to set up a Central Sports Unit it was said of the Director of Sport that he would receive full powers within the approved Budget to negotiate and secure (not 'settle') contracts with relevant sporting bodies. The executive producer would establish and supervise the standards of a broadcast presentation of all network sports programmes by all companies and secure (that word again!) and maintain a common identity for all such programmes, harmonising their style and continuity. The collective technical resources of all companies would be available to support the plans of the Unit as agreed by the Network Planning Committee. Applications for the appointment of Director of Sport were invited by public advertisement at the beginning of February. At a meeting of the PPC on 8 February, Grade, on behalf of the NPC, assured the Chairman, Hill, that the companies were seriously and vigorously progressing the establishment of the Unit.[25]

Whatever else it was, this arrangement, negotiated laboriously – and with great mutual goodwill – between the ITA and the companies, was not the new, self-contained central force in ITV sport so eloquently and passionately advocated by Hewat back in January 1966. But Hill felt satisfied that the Authority had ensured for the Unit 'real power to negotiate sports contracts'.[26]

In the meantime the limited experiment which ATV had entered upon was not doing too well. In the Midlands and North, where ABC adhered to the established practice of presenting uninterrupted sport between about 1 p.m. and 5 p.m., the ITV share of audience was higher than in London, where, after the experiment was introduced, the percentage share fell substantially. At this stage, the spotlight moved from ITV's sports problems to the more sensational matter of the new contract decisions.

When August provided a little breathing space there was a bright idea. It had become clear that the new arrangements in London (see Chapter 36) would leave no room for the experienced and resourceful General Manager of Rediffusion Television, John McMillan, and all were agreed that somehow his talents should be retained in ITV. Accordingly Bernstein and Grade offered him the post of Director of Sport, even though he still had the best part of a year to run in his existing post. It was announced on 17 August that he would take on the job, and that additionally he would become chairman of the 'Special Events' Committee and the companies' representative with the European Broadcasting Union (EBU). The arrangement was warmly welcomed by the ITA. It was, however, now recognised that the upheaval over the weekend contract in London, meant that the new arrangements for sport would not now take effect until the new contracts came into force at the end of July 1968, and that in the meantime network sport would be provided on much the same basis as that established in 1964. To a reminder that the arrangements were still outstanding business, Grade replied on 27 December stressing that this was but one of many matters that had to be finalised and adding that 'the very important issue of which company is to be responsible for the output of sport, particularly over the weekend, is now on the agenda for discussion between the five companies'.[27]

So far as weekend network sport was concerned the old firm of ABC/ATV would be going out of business at the end of July 1968; but, whatever its shortcomings, *World of Sport* remained the corner-stone of ITV sport. Now a new company, London Weekend, were coming on the scene and they claimed the inheritance. For them it was vital to have it as a programme exclusively their own, however much it incorporated items supplied from elsewhere in the network. Without the 'hourage' it provided their slice of the network cake would be too small to substantiate their status as a network company. Besides, if they could make a success of it, the kudos it would bring them could be substantial. The three seven-day companies were not readily persuaded that this claim was a rightful one; but the ITA ruled that it was and the ruling was accepted. Where then did this leave the Director of Sport and his so-called Unit? It was a difficult question, which generated much argument and some heat. LWT's thrusting new Managing Director, Michael Peacock, was resistant to rule by committee, but, as we have seen, it was in effect such a system of government which the companies had successfully stood out for in their dealings with Chairman Hill and his colleagues in the days before the contracts deluge.

Eventually Fraser himself had to take a hand. The facts of life were that neither the Sports Unit nor LWT were going to disappear; a *modus operandi* had to be agreed. It must not be allowed to go so far in one direction as to destroy the significance of the Unit as the central planning and purchasing agency for ITV sport nor so far in the other direction as to invade the responsibility of LWT in the production of *World of Sport* as an LWT programme. The Unit had to be a special agency of the NPC and its Director must be ex-officio chairman of the NPC's Sports Committee. All this Fraser made clear. Implicit in his reasoning was the fact that the 'Unit' was now a misnomer and it soon fell out of use. For, though the Director of Sport had responsibility for important aspects of policy, he was not in charge of the production of any sports programmes. He was a characteristic product of ITV compromise – part negotiator, part trouble-shooter, part custodian of standards. He was located at the central headquarters of the Independent Television Companies Association (ITCA), but in practice he had one foot in the ITA itself, which did not now need to have a sports specialist on its own staff.

Finalising McMillan's terms of references in words acceptable both to him and to Peacock required the rare talents which only Fraser possessed, and behind the scenes he exercised them to good purpose. It was agreed that the Director of Sport would take charge of all negotiations with international and national sporting bodies for the renewal or purchase of rights above an agreed figure, having the assistance of a negotiator responsible to him, and being associated in negotiations, where agreed at the Committee or on his initiative, with a representative or representatives from the companies. He would be responsible for ITV's relations with the international and national sporting bodies, and the national sporting bodies would deal with him, and in all cases be directed towards him, should they wish to make representations on any matter to ITV. He would have the power to make representations to individual companies should the television coverage of any event be so conducted as to threaten to impair ITV's relations with any of the sporting bodies. After consultation with the Sports Committee he would submit proposals for the scheduling of ITV network sports programmes for the approval of the Network Planning Committee. But the production or direction of any network sports programme would be the concern of the relevant producing company.

It was a creditable end to a tortuous course of events which punctuated a period otherwise dominated by the changes in the pattern of programmes and the new contract decisions; and it had implications of lasting importance in the structural development of Independent Television. Although, as we shall see in Volume 3, the institution did not survive very long into the seventies, the concept of ITV sport as a centralised element in a plural service remained and the ultimate gain in programme strength was considerable. One of ITV's long-standing areas of weakness was at last on the way to attaining the robust health necessary to confront the BBC in the ongoing competitive struggle.

(iv) THE NETWORKING OF REGIONAL PROGRAMMES

We have seen both in the previous volume and earlier in this one that the lack of opportunity for companies other than the Big Four to secure a national showing for their programmes was widely regarded as a disappointing aspect of a television service which took pride in its plural structure. Certain features of the networking system acted as a disincentive to any regular contributions from the smaller companies to the network schedules, but over and above this, there was confusion of thought within ITV about the extent to which the regional companies should be even trying to provide programmes for viewing outside their own frontiers.

Up to the mid-sixties no more than about 3 per cent of the transmission time in the four main areas was normally occupied by material from the Ten, and much of that consisted of items provided for insertion in *World of Sport*. In 1965 there were some promising signs. To add to Anglia's break into network drama, the regional companies had secured a foothold in children's programmes with their collective series *Go* which was due to replace ATV's *Seeing Sport*; Southern's special effort in children's series also seemed to be paying off; some network features had come from regional sources and so also had some of the Sunday religious services. By this time Anglia's *Survival* could be fairly sure of a ready acceptance whenever a sequence was available, and Tyne Tees were contributing to weekend adult education with *Say it in Russian*. But it could not be said that these were indicative of continuing growth. If some concrete way of further strengthening the position of the regionals on the network was to be sought the only thing that suggested itself was the creation of a weekly half hour network slot available to the Ten collectively in the same way as in practice regular slots were available to each of the Four. Ideally such a series should possess some kind of regional flavour. Cecil Bernstein had made such a proposal to the regionals some years earlier but they had looked askance at it.[28]

It was this proposal which Hill resurrected at the PPC in September 1965. This led to a paper on the subject agreed by the companies' Network Planning Committee. It explained that, under a procedure established a year earlier, regional companies wishing to make an offer to the network notified their proposals to a sub-committee of the NPC the composition of which was balanced equally between the major companies and the regionals, with one of the ITA's staff in attendance. A representative of any company making an offer was present when the programme was screened. So far the sub-committee had normally met monthly and had considered forty proposals, taking as its criterion the standard of quality achieved by the programmes on offer and their suitability for network showing. The procedure was thought to have worked well both by the major companies and – at management level – the regionals, and most of the programmes recommended as suitable had subsequently been seen by viewers in many parts of the country, either simultaneously on the network or as a result of separate transmissions.

But although these programmes had been produced by regional companies in regional studios, most of them did not have any specifically local content or appeal. For example *Survival* (Anglia) and *That Show* (Southern) were only regional programmes in the sense that they happened to have been produced by a regional company and not by a major. Few programmes were coming forward which were both local in flavour and possessing a wider appeal. Programmes like *Three Squires of England* (Westward) and *Singapore Calling* (Tyne Tees) were strongly local in flavour, but lacking in interest to a wider audience. That was the heart of the problem, apart from some more general considerations, such as the limitation of hours of broadcasting, the need for the major companies to maintain a level of production to which their studios and staff were geared and the contractual obligation of the major companies to provide a guaranteed number of hours weekly to the regional companies.

It was reported that the proposal for a regular weekly programme, consisting of regional contributions with a national appeal, had been discussed by the regional companies at a meeting of their own association (BRTA) which was unanimous in its opinion that this type of programme would not serve the best interests of ITV. It seemed too much like a ghetto. The NPC had therefore concluded that it would be best to allow the existing procedure to continue unchanged for a further year, whilst bearing in mind the Authority's desire to see more programmes being put forward that possessed both a local flavour and an appeal to a national audience.[29] As it happened a proposed serial, *Weaver's Green* had recently been put forward by Anglia and was thought likely to possess just these characteristics. There seemed to be the possibility of a companion piece to *Coronation Street*. It had been agreed to underwrite the production of an initial fourteen episodes on a network basis. The subsequent failure of this serial to retain a place on the network was to provoke some bitterness and also some cynicism from professional critics.

Hill returned to the charge in April 1966,[30] stressing that expectations had been built up that the amount of regional contributions would grow. Once again the companies undertook to consider setting aside a proportion of network hours for regional programmes having a distinctive flavour. But this device clearly still lacked real support amongst those it was designed to benefit – the regional companies themselves. All that came out of the new exercise was a resolve that regional companies and major companies should consult with each other at the earliest possible planning stages of programmes thought by the former to have network potential.

Hill acquiesced. No slick device was to be found and 'network itch' was destined to remain an irritant for some years to come. The easing and eventual removal of the controls on television hours were an emollient, but, as will be seen in the next volume, the best answer lay in the evolution of more sophisticated machinery for collective programme planning.

(v) TELEVISION INTERVIEWS

The interview in one form or other is an essential ingredient in all informative, factual broadcasting; and 'immediacy' is usually claimed as its distinguishing merit. The emphasis tends to be not so much on the creation of opportunities for self-expression by the interviewees, but rather on eliciting from them, on behalf of the viewing or listening public, the information that that public is assumed to want or need. Much depends on reasoned judgement in the selection of those interviewed and – given pre-recording – the degree of integrity demonstrated in the presentation in programme form of the interviewee's responses.

It was natural that the ITA's new General Advisory Council should have shown interest in interview policy. At their third meeting on 14 July 1964, one member expressed his distaste for a recent ITN interview with the grandparents of a murdered girl. ITN's Editor, Geoffrey Cox, agreed that, as a matter of general policy, interviews with persons recently bereaved in this way should not be used; he justified that particular case on the grounds that the grandparents had themselves wished to communicate their views about the climate of public morality in which such a crime could occur.

That was a complaint about the choice of person to be interviewed, and the history of ITV is dotted with incidents of public outcry over such choices, over the showing of interviews, for example, with victims of disaster or crime, with criminals, with terrorists, with spokesmen for political extremism or other forms of heterodoxy. More persistently recurrent difficulties have, however, arisen over the actual mechanics of programme use of interviews: with, that is to say, the initial briefing of the interviewee, the manner of the interview itself and the way in which what was said had been incorporated into the programme. In February 1962, Fraser had felt moved to remind company managements at the SCC of the need always to inform those invited to be interviewed about the general nature and shape of the programme in which they would be seen, to tell them in what context their contribution would be presented and how far what they said might be edited or cut about. This did not necessarily imply advance warning in detail of all questions to be asked. A zealous television journalist would naturally feel he might give viewers something nearer the truth by seeking unrehearsed replies to awkward questions rather than by relying on self-justificatory statements, especially from politicians and other public figures. In January 1966 he was telling the GAC that the editing of interviews was usually done fairly and impartially on ITV. There were few occasions when it had been done in such a way as to make them fit in with the view the producer wanted the audience to accept.

Neither he nor his listeners could know that, scarcely a month after this meeting, precisely that criticism was to be levelled against a Rediffusion *This Week* programme and that the furore that it provoked was to continue to reverberate for the best part of the remaining year. The programme was the first of a proposed series on the law in action and it took as its subject the work of the police. It was shown on 3 February 1966. The producer was Alasdair Milne and the reporter Ludovic Kennedy. The thesis of the programme was as follows. Crime was on the increase. The law seemed to afford too much protection to the criminal: too many of the undoubtedly guilty were being acquitted. Frustrated in their fight against crime many policemen were therefore bending the rules. This was bad. Therefore, the law should be altered.

It was the implication that rule-bending by the police had become normal practice that provoked the strongest protest about programme content. Complaints came from members of the public as well as the Commissioner of the Metropolitan Police and the President of the Police Superintendents' Association. But there were also protests from those who appeared in the programme. Two of the main contributors, Lord Shawcross and the Chief Constable of Leicester, Robert Mark, wrote to *The Times*[31] complaining that their interviews for the programme had been grossly distorted. A considerable correspondence on the pre-recording and editing of interviews developed in the Letters to the Editor columns. Sir Lionel Heald MP wrote saying that when he saw the programme he had been 'effectively deceived' into thinking that the participants were speaking in each others' presence. It was, he said, as much an example of 'manipulation and faking' as had been the Granada *21 Quiz* which he had investigated some years ago.[32] He subsequently put down a Parliamentary question to the PMG asking him to require the ITA 'to refrain from broadcasting any matter and from using or adopting any technical measures or processes which may involve the manipulation of recorded television interviews'. A question put down by William Deedes went even further, calling for a total ban on 'recording, arranging and cutting interviews in public affairs programmes'.[33] There were also letters from Ludovic Kennedy and Alasdair Milne, and from the Chairman of the Guild of Television Producers and Directors defending the professional integrity of television journalists in general and the impartiality of this programme in particular. Strong exception was taken to the use of terms like 'fake', 'suppression', 'deceit', all seeming to imply a deliberate intention to mislead.

Lord Shawcross in a *Times* article was less immoderate than his legal colleague Heald. He was sure the programme was 'an honest programme and that no attack whatever can be made on the integrity, as distinct from the opinions, of those who produced it'. He was all for robust controversy on public issues: programmes need not be so nicely balanced that they suggested no conclusion at all. The conflicting arguments should be set out fairly. 'All one can insist on is that those responsible for a particular view are indicated and that those who disagree with it should have an opportunity to say so'. The participants, however much their own statements are edited or juxtaposed, should all know what the programme as a whole is trying to say. For his own part, he had known that one of the propositions in the *This Week* programme, the one in fact to which he lent the weight of his authority, was that the existing law should be changed. But he had been unaware – as were others heard in the programme – that it was also asserting habitual malpractice by the police, something he did not accept. As presented, his statements could well have been taken by some viewers to suggest that he agreed there was malpractice and was suggesting a possible cure. One person heard in the programme, an ex-policeman, had not in fact contributed to it at all. He had declined an invitation to do so. So an extract from an interview he had given in a BBC *Panorama* programme three years previously had been taken and used without his knowledge. Speaking for himself Lord Shawcross said that if ever asked again to take part in a pre-recorded programme of this kind, he would always insist on seeing a final script of what was to be broadcast.

ITA Members met to view the programme together on Tuesday 8 February. Their conclusion was that, although no doubt intended to be impartial, the programme 'failed in fact to achieve a due and reasonable balance, and in particular to represent accurately the views and attitudes of the police themselves'.[34] A public statement to that effect was issued. It said nothing about the general problem of edited interviews. Rediffusion were told of the Authority's decision that a breach of the Act had occurred. The company Board accepted the reproof and apologised. A further programme was arranged in which the police had the opportunity of giving their point of view.

Although this Rediffusion programme had raised quite a storm of public protest, it was by no means the only instance of expressed concern and complaint about distortions and misrepresentations in the use of recorded interviews. It was patently necessary to do two things. Firstly, a further public statement had to be made declaring the Authority's own attitude, as the responsible public body, towards the editing techniques used. Secondly, early consultation must needs take place with those companies mainly concerned with major current affairs programmes in order to arrive at agreed guidelines for the assistance of producers engaged in the preparation of programmes in which extensive use of interview material was likely.

The Authority had clearly seen, as Lord Shawcross had done, that the editing and interleaving of statements given in interviews did not of themselves inevitably cause distortion and bias. Hill made the point in an address to the Luton Rotary Club on 17 February:

> Both television and newspapers have to cut their material to fit the time and space available . . . Often television cuts from one speaker to another – neither of whom may have met the other – in order to emphasise different points of view. There is nothing wrong with this technique of arranging pre-recorded material into a coherent pattern, provided that it does not result in a biassed presentation or any impression that a contributor is supporting a point of view not his own.[35]

But, he continued 'the hazards are great'.

With the aim of drawing programme makers' attention to these hazards, it was agreed, after preliminary discussions with Rediffusion, Granada, ATV and ABC representatives to set down on paper the principles to be kept in mind. The task of drafting this document was remitted to ITA staff. It went through several changes arising from comments by the four majors and a subsequent discussion at PPC before it was shown to the Authority on 28 April 1966. The revised version was circulated to all members of PPC on 9 May. Company reservations, most cogently argued by Denis Forman of Granada, had attached mainly to the idea of a set of rules that could be seen as a restriction on a programme maker's own freedom of decision and consequent sense of personal responsibility. It had already been conceded by Hill himself that manipulation of interview material did not of itself necessarily lead to bias and partiality. Theoretically at least such procedures could (like 'bugging' or illegal telephone tapping for example) sometimes even lead to a revelation of important truth.

The final document, as circulated to the companies, placed its main emphasis on protecting the rights of those contributing to programmes in unrehearsed interviews. The cutting and rearranging of interview material was accepted as *in itself* quite proper. But 'quality and validity of editing depend on the producer's general competence and integrity'.[36] The interviewee should be told in advance the nature and shape and purpose of the programme, the way and the context in which his own contribution was going to be used. Any significant later change in these plans should also be conveyed to him. He should be warned that all he said would most probably not be used. After he had agreed to participate in full knowledge of those facts, it remained the producer's responsibility to ensure that the interviewee's statements were not in any way misrepresented.

Qualifications to expressions of opinion should not be suppressed. Juxtapositioning of extracts from interviews should not be so used as to give an impression of a discussion or conversation between the speakers together at one time in one place, or to imply by such juxtaposition, and without corroboration, that the speaker of one edited extract necessarily accepted without qualification statements made by others in extracts placed before his own. A caveat was also inserted against the use of extracts from recordings of interviews made some time ago for other purposes.

Probably because of the number of different hands involved directly and indirectly in its drafting, this final document turned out to be verbose and repetitive. It was given the status of an internal ITV confidential document; and no steps were taken to make it public. The assumption must have been, however, that company managements would at least make the main substance of its contents known to their senior production staff in current affairs. A full six months later, on 12 December 1966, *The Times* carried a story on its main news page saying that 'Independent Television has agreed on a code of practice to govern the editing of current affairs programmes'. The report referred specifically to the correspondence following on the Rediffusion police programme. It summarised the main recommendations of the paper and mentioned that the 'notes on editing' were regarded as a private document not for distribution outside the industry. As a result, it said, Ludovic Kennedy had neither seen nor heard of it; and programme editors 'do not know their newly agreed duties and contributors are ignorant of their newly agreed rights'. Since the document had aimed to do no more than formulate what was believed to be already generally accepted practice of all responsible television producers of integrity, this article was not altogether fair. Nevertheless the Authority was sufficiently impressed to ask for the paper to be circulated once again to all ITV companies.

The ITA recognised that public criticism by public figures in the columns of *The Times* was not necessarily an accurate reflection of the reactions and opinions of the viewing public. Awareness of the distinction was doubtless a motive behind the commissioning in late 1966 of a special research project in order to get evidence of general audience attitudes to television interviews. It was reassuring that a large majority of those questioned agreed that TV interviews (both BBC and ITV) usually helped them to understand the subject discussed.[37] Nevertheless a sizeable minority (25 per cent) agreed there were too many interviews on television and about the same proportion claimed that interviewers were occasionally too aggressive in their questioning. Many more, a majority in fact, went so far as to agree that interviewers were sometimes too intrusive, putting questions that were too private and personal; and this failing was attributed more often to ITV than to BBC programmes.

This last criticism was assuredly provoked by memories of the television coverage by both services of the recent tragic disaster at Aberfan. On Friday 21 October 1966 a pit slag heap slid down the mountainside overlooking this small Welsh mining village. It engulfed and destroyed several buildings, among them the village school which at the time was occupied by children at work in their classes. The early evening ITN bulletin at 5.55 p.m. carried six minutes coverage from TWW. It included four interviews with anguished parents. Much fuller coverage was given in the specially extended bulletin at 8.55 p.m. This had interviews with parents and also with children who had narrowly escaped death. On the Sunday *The Mountain that Moved*, a special programme prepared in haste by ATV, was shown. It was transmitted in the 'Closed Period', that is in the network time slot usually reserved for religious programmes at 6.55 p.m. This departure from the advertised and customary programme schedule had been approved on the understanding that the programme would be in the nature of an outside broadcast and would concentrate on more positive aspects – on brave, active response to disaster, rather than on the agony and heartache of families whose loved young ones had been buried alive under a river of sludge. In this purpose the programme failed. There were prolonged and painful interviews with tearful parents and frightened young children. There was a lapse of taste in the selection of material for transmission. Much of what was shown was 'offensive to public feeling'. A swift reprimand to ATV's management (who admitted error) anticipated the complaints from ITA Members and a stream of letters and phone calls from viewers, to say nothing of articles and readers' letters in the press, national and local. ITN defended themselves. They claimed, with some justification, that their coverage had avoided exploitation of grief, using interviews either to illustrate the fortitude of the bereaved or to extract information on what had actually happened.[38]

To some extent the widespread protest and criticism of BBC and ITV coverage of this unparalleled disaster was certainly a case of blaming the messenger for the bad news, transferring to the reporters the feelings of horror and distaste evoked by the harrowing scene displayed. The *Daily Mirror* shrewdly underlined the risks inherent in such situations for the television interview in particular:

> Where a newspaper reporter interviews somebody deeply concerned in
> the tragedy . . . it is a private discussion . . . but when people are
> interviewed 'live' on TV . . . not only is the interviewer himself intruding

on a deep, private grief, but he is doing so in public . . . inviting millions to look through the same keyhole. Aberfan has spotlighted all the hazards in reporting human drama and heartbreak fairly, fully and sympathetically.[39]

There were some who were prepared to defend television's general coverage, saying it was right to show the sorrowing and right to invite the viewing multitude of strangers to witness and share the grief of the afflicted, so that they might acknowledge through compassion and more material aid a common social responsibility for the victims of disaster. More cynical observers might even have seen in Lord Robens' strongly worded complaints, in a letter to *The Times*, of 'callous reporting' and 'a cruel attempt to make a public spectacle of private grief'[40] a half-conscious attempt to try to divert attention from the special responsibility of the Coal Board of which he was then Chairman. But, remembering earlier public criticisms of interview editing, it is worth noting his comment that 'live interviews with the sufferers should never have been permitted. Editing provides a vital opportunity for second thoughts . . . ' One wonders whether 'second thoughts' might not be a euphemism for 'modifying the truth', the very charge levelled by the critics of interview editing.

Hill, on behalf of ITV, and Huw Wheldon for the BBC, both replied to Robens. Both in their different ways asserted the right and duty of the medium to bring to viewers the dimensions of the disaster, that live coverage was necessary and unavoidable in the circumstances even though the appalling conditions on the site gave rise to occasional lapses which were regretted.

There was no formal discussion with the companies on this occasion and no new document of policy guidance was issued. The event had nevertheless served to underline once again the difficulty of striking a middle way between obligations of accuracy on the one hand and avoidance of offence on the other. Once again there had been made clear the real though ill-defined limits to the unrestrained pursuit of truth and its uninhibited proclamation to the world. Often, it was all too evident, there would be large sections of the public unwilling to accept the full unpleasantness of unvarnished truth. Yet the evidence of similar incidents in the years since Aberfan testifies to the continuing undiminished strength of the broadcasters' conviction that their duty lies in judging how much truth they can defensibly give – not how little.

The recurrent moral dilemma of 'ends and means' arises in a different, but no less acute, form when an interview is recorded for programme purposes without the knowledge of the person interviewed. At a meeting of the PPC in April 1967 company representatives for their part, while accepting a general principle condemning the practice, did not favour a complete veto. Exceptional circumstances could arise, they said, in which service of the public interest might justify such methods. It was, however, agreed that before employing them in any particular case Authority advice would be sought. Consequently when Granada consulted the following October about their intention to include in a *World in Action* programme on Rhodesian sanctions-busting a secretly-made recording with an employee of the shipping company involved, a compromise solution was adopted. This involved reconstructing the interview using the actual words spoken but not their recorded sound. When this was reported to them, the Authority Members remained most reluctant to concede the validity of exceptions to a generalised ban. Even after consultation with Geoffrey Cox at ITN and with the Press Council had elicited the information that both bodies would countenance exceptions in rare cases, they declared themselves against acceptance of any recording of a telephone interview for television use, unless the interviewer had first identified himself as from ITV and had got the consent of the interviewee to the recording. The companies continued to demur. They foresaw insuperable difficulties for current affairs reporting if no flexibility at all was to be permitted.

A paper specifying these difficulties was prepared by Denis Forman and Michael Peacock.[41] Even the most responsible, ethically self-conscious journalist could not do his job, they asserted, if he were obliged always to reveal his identity when seeking information. They agreed, however, that the surreptitious recording of such interviews, whether in sound alone, or with hidden cameras, should be practised only as a last resort when the information was of major public importance and there was no other way of proving its authenticity. Examples were given. They included a *World in Action* programme in which reporters had themselves masqueraded as arms dealers in order to get information about illicit gun running to Biafra; and a BBC *Panorama* investigation of 'switch selling' in which the peccant doorstep salesman was filmed without his knowledge. Whether in such cases the persons involved should then be told about the recording and asked to consent to its use, should (so argued the Forman/Peacock paper) depend on the nature of the subject matter. Sometimes, as for example with cases of alleged unethical behaviour, there could be programme advantage – and fairness – in persuading the interviewee to appear in the programme and comment on what had been recorded. But when illegal activities were involved, those concerned would seize any opportunity of preventing their public exposure. The paper concluded by asserting sensitive company awareness of the ethical question. Use of underhand methods of gaining information would be countenanced only in 'cases of criminal issues, security matters or other similar situations'. Even then producers would have permission to proceed only after careful deliberation at top management level; and before the final decision was reached ITA officers would always be consulted.

This paper having been fully discussed and accepted by all companies represented at the SCC, the Authority was persuaded in February 1968 to relax the rigidity of its previous ruling. It agreed that there might be valid exceptions to the principle that interviews or telephone conversations should not be recorded for possible use on Independent Television unless the interviewer had identified himself as being from ITV and the interviewee had given his consent.[42] There, for the time being, the matter was to rest. But it could only be for the time being. The reference to illegal activity in the Forman/Peacock paper was significant. Such cases inevitably give rise to problems associated with contempt of court and what came to be known as 'Trial by Television'. Before long the new London Weekend company's programmes with David Frost, with their use of live interviews before an invited studio audience, were to bring these problems once again to the fore.

29

PROGRAMMES AND PUBLIC ATTITUDES

In the previous volume (Chapter 34) an attempt was made, by using a random dipstick, to convey an overall impression of the ITV programmes which by sheer novelty captivated viewers in the years following the introduction into Britain of competitive television. By the sixties ITV had become a normal part of most people's lives, providing frequent pleasure and occasional offence to millions, and programme references in this volume are related more closely to developments which occurred in ITV policies as the system evolved. An illustrated book charting the general programme story of ITV in chronological sequence was published in 1980 entitled *25 Years on ITV 1955–1980*[1] and makes evocative reading.

An inevitable consequence of Pilkington and the debates leading to the 1963 Act was that the term 'People's Television' acquired a pejorative connotation. More of ITV in the sixties, whilst remaining generally popular, was slanted towards opinion formers whoever they might be and wherever they could be identified. A successful contract application in 1967 was to speak, critically, of 'Producers' Television' (Chapter 36). Its character was also much more regularly debated within the service as a whole than it had been in the days of the network carve-up.

Apart from the formal committees established by the ITA and the companies, a principal focus of internal debate was the various 'consultations' to which reference has already been made both in this volume and the preceding one. With the exception of two about religion, the reports on them were not published; today they provide a fertile source for discerning the trends in programme thinking within ITV. Some consultations were serviced by research studies into public attitudes, round which discussion centred, and these also were generally kept within the ITV family. In consequence attitudes towards, and opinions about, Independent Television during the decade tend to fall into two sectors, the disclosed and the undisclosed. The growth of an increasing range of *public* voices, some strident, some less so, was a television phenomenon in the sixties.

As we have seen the new Act continued to require the Authority to secure the exclusion of programmes 'offensive to public feeling'. Under Lord Hill it soon extended and elaborated its invigilation over the output. Its vigilantes worked as a team and there were few company managements which escaped having their noses rubbed in occasional irregularities by their programme makers. The ITA programme staff strove not to be capricious in their judgements; there were continuous consultations with companies and amongst themselves, and regular references to the Members. Judgements of Solomon had to be made, and they were not blatantly arbitrary: nevertheless there were occasions when, even though there was no separate appellate body, the Authority's rulings were successfully contested and either reversed or modified.

In his broadcasting memoirs, Lord Hill referred to a programme which at a preview in April 1964 the Authority deemed to be obscene in two of its scenes but which nine months later on a second look it considered entirely acceptable. He saw it as an instance of how swiftly standards of taste could change.[2] The programme in question was *The Entertainers* devised and produced by Denis Mitchell. It was highly experimental, being shot and edited entirely on mobile videotape. Hill called it a play, but it was also a documentary because, as Norman Swallow has pointed out, not only the dialogue but also the developing relationships were improvised and spontaneous.[3] It depicted both the private and the public lives of a group of entertainers working the North Country clubs. It had complete authenticity and this is probably what misled the Authority, who viewed it initially as if it were a scripted play and concluded that two of the scenes of nudity were unduly 'gratuitous'. Granada took the view that the taste of the distinguished producer was more reliable than the taste of the censor and preferred not to transmit the programme rather than accept the cuts. When, after the change of mind, he came to defend it in reply to critical letters, Hill was calling it a documentary and saying that, having regard to the intentions of the producer and the non-erotic nature of the material, it was acceptable for showing at an adult time.

The evidence which by the mid-sixties was at the disposal of the Authority and its staff was super-abundant even if it fell short of being conclusive. There was the evidence of their own eyes and ears and of their advisory bodies. There were the views, often disparate, of company managements and programme makers. There was what the professional critics were saying and what, on the other channel, the BBC were doing and seemingly getting away with. There was the advice of various self-appointed protectors of the public interest, most of it, but not all, pointing in the direction of greater censorship. Finally, there were the attitudes of the viewing audience as reflected in audience surveys, opinion polls and other devices of social research.

Lord Hill himself was not greatly preoccupied by the censorship work; in his view it had to be done but it would never make any difference to the quality of the product. In a note dated June 1966, designed to provoke a discussion on programme quality, he said: 'We tend to concentrate on life at its oddest, searching for angle and sensation. We do too little to help people come to terms with the world.'[4] Like his predecessor, Kirkpatrick, he was less concerned with the avoidance of offence than with eliciting programmes which did some recognisable good. But for many creative people, coming to terms with the world involved making the very kind of programmes which over-zealous, self-appointed watchdogs were prone to consider reprehensible.

Amongst all the self-appointed advisers the first in the field was the Viewers' and Listeners' Association, which grew out of the earlier Sound Radio Society. Its organiser was Peter Laslett – a Cambridge don. It had submitted evidence to Pilkington over a whole range of matters and advocated the establishment of a viewers' and listeners' council to keep the authorities in line with their statutory duties. It thought that 'the services administered by the ITA should be freed from the commercial control which is now seen in the amount and quality of its advertising, and in the "market-orientated" content of its programmes'.[5] Another and more down-to-earth body was created by the National Federation of Community Associations and it was originally called the Central Committee for Television Viewing; its first chairman and moving spirit was Frank Milligan, the General Secretary of the National Federation. Milligan was prepared to take television as he found it and to work for its active use for educational and social purposes. He was ahead of his time. In 1960 his committee changed its name to the Standing Conference on Television Viewing and moved to the offices of the National Institute of Adult Education. Although well disposed towards it, ITV was insufficiently generous to offset its chronic and crippling lack of funds. It changed its name yet again to the Television Viewers' Council, whose chairman, Mrs Mary Adams, became a Member of the ITA in 1965. Sadly however, it failed to secure a substantial membership, and an opportunity for ITV to establish in the sixties the close association with community interests that eventually developed in the seventies was lost.

The field was thus left clear for what Richard Hoggart called 'the new populists' side by side with the 'old guardians'. The latter were, of course, the churches (amongst which the Church and Nation Committee of the Church of Scotland was most active) and the establishment bodies which had turned in routine evidence to Pilkington and which were in general none too familiar with the day-by-day content of television. They included the established women's organisations. The former were a new phenomenon. Principally there were the Clean Up Television Campaign and the National Viewers' and Listeners' Association (NVALA), which had nothing to do, of course, with the earlier organisation founded by Laslett. Its secretary was an ex-school teacher, Mrs Mary Whitehouse. The fact that the movement with which her name was associated was principally activated by rebellion against the new trends which Hugh Greene was introducing in the BBC did not diminish its significance for ITV. A new force had entered into television affairs. The only difference was that, whilst the BBC decided to meet its onslaught by ignoring it, ITV, whilst not exactly turning the other cheek, elected from the first to take notice of it – which was not necessarily the same thing as responding to it.

Mary Whitehouse published her book *Cleaning Up TV: from Protest to Participation*[6] early in 1967 after nearly three years of remarkably effective propagandist activity which had made her name a household word and a decidedly controversial one at that. In the meantime, counter-propagandist bodies had inevitably sprung up; first the 'Cosmo Group' founded by Mrs Avril Fox, which was unashamedly libertarian in outlook and then the more intellectually respectable Television and Radio Committee (TRACK) which received facilities from the British Humanist Association, and which was fathered by none other than Professor Hoggart (then with the Birmingham University Centre for Contemporary Studies) and whose first chairman was Roy Shaw, then head of the Department of Extramural Studies at Keele University.[7] TRACK was far more ambitious than its resources allowed: it sought to provide a consultative service on every aspect of broadcasting policy and it never came within range of fulfilling such an aspiration. Like Hugh Greene himself, they regarded the Clean Up TV campaign against 'unnecessary dirt, gratuitous sex, excessive violence and so on' as based on assumptions which were 'anti-intellectual and anti-imaginative'.[8] Mary Whitehouse's retort was that what mattered was 'moral sense'.[9]

Although the Clean Up TV campaign had been launched early in 1964, it was not until November 1965 that NVALA was established. Mrs Whitehouse claimed that in a year it acquired about 3000 paid-up individual members and block membership totalling over 100,000. It was dedicated to the promotion of 'the moral and religious welfare of the community by seeking to maintain Christian standards in broadcasting'. The motto of its first national convention in April 1966 was 'From Protest to Participation'.

The first recorded communication received from Mary Whitehouse at the ITA took the form of a telegram to Lord Hill on 24 November 1964 congratulating him on the ITA's code on violence which had been published that day, and saying that 'it could set a pattern of new thinking for television throughout the world'.[10] Following his normal practice, Hill acknowledged it personally. Thereafter, the correspondence between her and Brompton Road (usually but not always the Chairman) became extremely regular. In her book she praised the ITA for its courteous and considerate attitude, contrasted it with that taken up by the BBC and commented favourably on the effectiveness of ITA control over programme content. Within the councils of ITV there was never any set consideration of policy towards Mary Whitehouse or the campaign for which she worked. It just seemed sensible to treat the campaign with respect even when it went over the top, as it sometimes did, on some point of criticism. The range of reactions to Mary Whitehouse and what she stood for could not have been markedly different within ITV from what it was within the BBC. The difference was that the BBC had a predetermined policy of opposition, whereas ITV did not. 'We stand up' she wrote, 'as opponents of the current authoritarianism of the BBC and before we know what is happening, *we* are the culprits. They are the "emancipators". They are fighting for "freedom".'[11] For them, it was decreed that she was Mrs Grundy; for ITV she remained the persistent, sometimes obtuse, but often perceptive, Mrs Whitehouse.

In April 1967, against the background of the imminent franchise awards the committee of NVALA urged the development of 'a realistic and extending dialogue'[12] between the ITV companies and the viewing public. Hill replied on 2 May reciting at some length the range of existing contacts with viewers and concluding:

And so it seems to me that Independent Television is already well exposed to the impact of viewer opinion at quite a number of different points in its structure. I am not sure it would necessarily be an advantage if our relationship with our audience were canalised more narrowly. Public opinion expresses itself in a whole range of different ways and it is important to ensure so far as we can that we get a true 'consensus'. So far as your own Association is concerned, I think you and your committee know that we are always ready to hear its views and to consider with care any representations it may make to us. I feel sure that, in saying this, I am speaking for Independent Television as a whole.[13]

The social significance of the movement of which Mary Whitehouse was the principal spokesman is outside the scope of this history and has been examined in other works.[14] She and her associates saw the increasing secularisation of society, of which television provided many examples, as a profound threat to the survival of the Christian faith. Combating it was God's work. The BBC, so long as Greene was their dominant leader, were the main enemy; ITV, listening if not responsive to criticism and anxious not so much to avoid offence as to mitigate it when it was given, seemed far less formidable an adversary. Nevertheless, all television went into the home, the place where, even more than the church, the last refuge of Christian culture was to be found. And so it was television above all else that had to be cleansed. Where, collectively, NVALA failed was in concentrating their minds and energies on their main aim. Their leaders allowed themselves to be led by all the media into tortuous byways which were often off-course and sometimes dead-ends.

Even though Mary Whitehouse sometimes gave credit where she thought it was due, her approach was generally critical or outright condemnatory where taste, decency or that elusive thing 'public feeling' were concerned. That was only to be expected of someone who found much in television that was an offence to morality. But she and her associates might have sought to be less negative – to look for and identify ways in which television could be an influence for good.

The ITA had a good foretaste of the conflict of voices about these matters when its own new General Advisory Council at only their third meeting recorded in relation to Section 3(1) (a) of the Act (good taste, decency, etc.) that they thought the Authority 'tended to be too fastidious in its interpretation of this section, and to concentrate on observance of the letter of the law at the expense of qualitative considerations'.[15] They might have hesitated to make this criticism had they been told the following case-history.

In 1962 A-R had secured from Harold Pinter a one-act play called *The Lover*. Brownrigg wrote to the ITA about it, saying that it was a brilliant play and 'one which might well be shown on television if our audience could be restricted to married people. It is, however, in our opinion, unsuitable to televise to an audience which would include the unmarried in the age bracket 18–23.'[16] This opinion did not, however, represent the views of all concerned in A-R and certainly not of McMillan and Joan Kemp-Welch, the senior drama director. The staff of the ITA replied that if, on reflection, A-R decided to present the play, they felt they ought to support them and, if necessary, defend them. For the very reasons given by Brownrigg, they did not think it would be prudent to include the play in the regular series at conventional times; something would need to be done to indicate that it was intended for a minority taste. They therefore hoped that a later than conventional time could be found, not earlier than 9.45 p.m., and went on to say that there would be special problems of presentation which could only be solved in the creative direction of the production. It was not a script which could readily be made 'innocuous' by ordinary amendment of the text – that is, without spoiling the special quality which alone justified contemplating the possibility of its transmission.

Brownrigg conceded. The direction of the play was undertaken by Joan Kemp-Welch, who had received an award as the best director of Light Entertainment in 1958 for her work on *Cool For Cats*, and had directed the highly acclaimed production of *Electra* in the original Greek as well as Léonide Massine's ballet *Laudes Evangelii*. The play was shown twice during 1963, although on the first occasion, in March, some regional companies elected not to include it in their schedules, because they believed it would offend their audiences. It certainly gave very considerable offence on both transmissions, particularly in parts of Scotland, but it delighted the professional critics. It became ITV's first entry for the prestigious Prix Italia in Naples in September and it received the premier award amidst general acclaim from a large international gathering. In November the director and leading cast – Alan Badel and Vivien Merchant – received awards from the Guild of Television Producers and Directors; and it was shown at the First London Festival of World Television in the National Film Theatre, together with Granada's epic 2½ hour production of *War and Peace* and ABC's *Mr. Big* based on a story by Ray Bradbury. In the following March it was chosen as the best television play of the year by the Screenwriters' Guild, with Arden Winch's *Return to the Regiment* from ATV as runner-up.

The play had clarity in the sense in which Pinter himself understood the word, but whether it was one that the audience could readily understand is highly doubtful. The critics themselves were at variance; one of them said that, whilst most people seemed to regard it as a weird piece of mumbo-jumbo to be interpreted with cunning and with symbol detectors, it was in fact a straightforward and engaging slice of domestic fetishism in which husband and wife jollied their lives along by playing the roles of lover and mistress. Fraser's laconic remark was 'Garlands in Italy and Park Lane. Thought debased in Paisley – and not only there. Two worlds. I imagine the second is much the larger.'[17]

The professional television critics really constituted a third world rather than being members of either of Fraser's two. Writing about them in

Contrast, Peter Black began by quoting an observation of Kenneth Tynan's in *Encounter*: 'No man has a range of experience and interests wide enough to qualify him as a judge of television's enormously varied output'. And yet, as Black pointed out, this was just what newspapers demanded of their television critics. They did not always speak for the world of Park Lane, and a few wrote mainly on behalf of Paisley. Black described the *Daily Express*'s attitude to television as basically hostile. 'An occasional feature by *Express* writers bangs away at such subjects as violence, background music, gloomy plays, the shortage of new material, the maleficent effect of TV on children.'[18]

Of particular interest was a book published in 1964 called *Tempo* by Angus Wilson, himself a television critic for some years.[19] *Tempo* was ABC's enormously versatile weekly programme about the arts, produced by Lloyd Shirley and Reginald Collin, edited by Kenneth Tynan and presented, amongst others, by the Earl of Harewood. By 1967 *Tempo* had long been the foremost arts programme on Independent Television. Since its start in October 1961 it had presented over 150 programmes. It had ranged over the entire spectrum of the arts, and it had covered performances from a scintillating gallery of artists. It had probed the individual creative imagination at work and the personalities of artists and performers in order to illuminate the finished work. It tried always to exploit the technical potentialities of television, and occasionally in an attempt, made its own artistic contribution. It captivated Angus Wilson's imagination. He wrote:

> If, in fact, any generalisation about the effects of television is possible, it must surely be that millions more people in this country have become familiar with the arts (if only to be given the chance to reject them) than have ever been wooed away from them. Television plays, serialisation of novels, occasional concerts, or talks on painting must at the very least have converted some thousands previously living in ignorance – not all viewers switch off immediately they see the unfamiliar . . . Perhaps the successes and failures of such a programme as *Tempo* may even throw some light on whether television, apart from fostering other arts, has any creative originality to offer, is not in short only a medium but itself an art.[20]

Occupying a midway position between the public and private voices were the bodies which represented the views of creative television people. The ITA staff were never anything like so remote from the 'coal face' as Pilkington had been led to suppose (see Chapter 12), but they were chary of developing such relations in a way that would lead managements to suspect that their authority within their companies was being undermined. However, in one case in particular a formal relationship was established in the sixties with the knowledge and assent of the managements. In 1963 the Screenwriters' Guild (later called the Writers' Guild of Great Britain) established a Television Censorship Appeals Committee and an arrangement was made which enabled it to make direct representations to the ITA, so long as the managements concerned were kept informed. It was an effective voice in making known to the Authority the viewpoint of writers generally, and in particular of the authors of plays which in one respect or another created problems under the censorship provisions of the Act.

In 1966, Granada had a play called *The Division* written by Bill Meilen and produced by Derek Bennett and it dealt with life in a nautical approved school run by ex-naval officers. Three, and only three such schools existed, operating under the auspices of the Home Office. The ITA found the play unacceptable in view of what it described as the 'prolonged scenes of violence and brutality'[21] which it contained. Granada's Programme Committee found the ruling incomprehensible and appealed against it. The question arose whether the ITA's attitude should be one of intransigence or whether it should believe it possible that it could have been wrong. The play was viewed again – this time by Authority Members in the presence of a strangely tongue-tied representative from Granada – and the decision was upheld.

But Granada were not alone in their opinion. Much upset by the decision, the author, Bill Meilen, obtained permission to show the production to colleagues in the Guild and in consequence, the Television Appeals Committee received a remit which they saw as highly important. By this time the banning of the play had become something of a *cause célèbre* and the ITA was at the receiving end of much adverse comment. After correspondence with Vernon Beste, the Committee's ever-courteous chairman, ITA staff found themselves involved in a mini-confrontation, when my colleague Stephen Murphy and I had what in our report was accurately described as a 'conversation' with Beste, Philip Mackie (already a writer of wide experience and distinction) and the author of the play.

We learnt for the first time how much of a drama-documentary the play was. Meilen had himself been in an approved school and had undergone each of the punishments depicted in the play. Every punishment officially given was on the Home Office list of approved punishments; every unofficial punishment inflicted was a toned-down version of things Meilen himself had witnessed or suffered. The play had been read by staff of the school which, twenty years earlier, he had attended and they had admired it. It had been intended as a case against violence – as an expression of his fervent belief that violence in any community always corrupts. To this we made the obvious reply that the ITA had to concern itself primarily with the programme as we believed it would be received by many viewers. There had been the recent experience of well-intentioned television coverage of the Aberfan disaster being widely regarded as the exploitation of human grief.

In due course Authority Members viewed and considered the programme again. Not without difficulty, it was concluded that the ban could not be maintained. They were helped by an offer from Granada to provide a brief introduction which explained that the play was based on incidents that had taken place twenty years ago and that the author's purpose was to show how, within a closed community, violence could breed. When transmitted with its introduction, the play provoked no great outcry.

Public voices such as we have been describing had one characteristic in common with the more private ones monitored by means of audience research. They could tell the broadcasters about people's reactions to programmes, but they could not tell them what would be the reactions of people to programmes not yet seen or even yet made. The situation was not as simple as when the opinion polls ask voters at an election whether they will be voting for this party or that on polling day. Where audience research had the advantage over all the other voices was in its reliance on rigorously-designed statistical samples of the public as a whole. Provided the methodology was right and provided the questions asked were right it was possible to get answers which were right – in the sense that they came from the generality of viewers and not just from some viewers with an axe to grind.

Thus, at its most simple level, when Gallup Poll Ltd on behalf of the ITA in March 1968 asked respondents in their sample 'Do you personally see or hear things on television which you find offensive?' the answers in respect of ITV were:

At least once a week	19 per cent
At least once a month	11 per cent
Less often	15 per cent
Don't know	7 per cent

At least 45 per cent of viewers found some offensive material on ITV. The kind of things respondents found offensive were predominantly bad language, sex and violence in that order. Periodic surveys of this kind right through the decade had shown no marked variations.

Much could be written about the welter of audience research which developed within ITV during these years, which were also years when television became a dominant topic for academic social research.[22] Trends in public attitudes were identified, the relative popularity of different programmes and categories of programme were measured and the effects both of television in general and of specific programmes analysed. Programme planners were both stimulated and goaded by it, and some of it rubbed off. But, with extremely rare exceptions, those who studied programmes lived in one world and those who planned and made programmes in another.[23] Such was the nature of television production that planners, writers, directors and producers were seldom, at any rate consciously, greatly influenced by what research had to say, and those who conducted it did not succeed in persuading them that it would be to their advantage to seek the help of research in doing their jobs.

It was, however, of greater direct value to the controlling authority and to that extent Pilkington and the legislators were right to place emphasis upon it. The ITA saw its proper role as taking the study of ITV programmes beyond audience measurement into the area of audience appreciation. During these years TAM were offering their subscribers regular measurements of appreciation under the title of TVQ. By studying these reports and by supplementing them with specially commissioned surveys of its own, it was able to identify areas of weakness and trends in public favour which were not always evident from audience measurement data. The findings were put before the companies at the PPC and at the consultations. Research should have been, but somehow wasn't, the most powerful of the voices to which this chapter has referred.

The role of the academic researchers was to endeavour to discover and establish valid truths about the social impact of the medium. They found the going tough. The Television Research Committee, which was set up in 1963 by the Home Secretary and was financed by the ITA's grant of £250,000, was by 1968 nearing the end of its natural life. If the ITA's gesture had been seen as casting bread upon the waters it was not to be found again within many days or even years. The original aim of the grant had been to ascertain the relationship, if any, between television and delinquency, but the theme became broadened and generalised to include all forms of attitudes and behaviour and all media of mass communication. It was considered that television could not be examined in isolation from other forms of communication, but the widening of the field of enquiry meant that simple, quick research results were as impossible as they would have been unrealistic.

As in America and elsewhere the place of television in society remained an issue surrounded by controversy. Peter Black said that belief in television's influence was rather like belief in life after death. 'Most of us would like to be able to prove it, but the evidence is inconclusive.'[24]

30

POLITICAL TELEVISION

In 1963 the ITA gave a formal assurance that the annual series of party political broadcasts would be transmitted by Independent Television, and so avoided a requirement being included in the new Television Bill. Wheeling and dealing between the political parties and the two broadcasting bodies about them proceeded wearily through the sixties without effecting any major changes in the established pattern. Arguments revolved around the total amount of time to be made available each year; the number and length of the individual broadcasts within this total; whether or not these should be delivered simultaneously by both services (including BBC 2); at what time of the evening they should be shown; and whether the broadcasts should be wholly or partially regionalised so that viewers, for example in Scotland, should not be addressed on subjects almost exclusively relevant to the English political scene. On the whole BBC and ITV were more successful in holding a common front than were the political parties, whose views tended to vary according to whether or not they were in office and to the changing tactical situation in party conflict. In the formal meetings of the Committee on Party Political Broadcasting the parties could only find permanent common ground in regarding the broadcasters collectively as mean and grudging in their attitude and as lacking in proper awareness of the high importance of these party pronouncements in the political life of the community.

Less formally the situation was rather different. The broadcasters never made any secret of their view that, between elections, this type of broadcasting was an encumbrance, to be removed if ever the hard realities of relations with Westminster would allow. It was evidence of the growing sophistication in the relationship between the ITA and the fourteen companies that widely varying attitudes towards such issues were always reconciled so that in negotiation with the BBC and the parties a common front was preserved. Over most of the period the task of speaking for the ITV federation was in the joint hands of Fraser and Cecil Bernstein. As for the parties the private views and the public stance of some of their leaders were markedly different. In October 1964 (after the Conservatives had lost office) R. A. Butler was heard to say 'Television politics prove to be a great *bore*' and his audience – all experienced in decoding Butlerisms – knew he was referring to party broadcasts.

Throughout this period the prospect of relief for the broadcasters hovered tantalisingly on the horizon. At a meeting of the PPC in November 1964 Hill could say that 'the climate of opinion in the political parties towards Party Political Broadcasts might well be changing, at any rate so far as the period between general elections was concerned'.[1] Three years later one of the leaders of the Conservative Party was telling Lord Aylestone, Hill's successor, that a number of his colleagues were of the opinion that party politicals should end and be replaced by additional current affairs programmes in which the parties would be represented. It was abnormal to hear such views being expressed by the party in opposition. Progress went so far as for it to have become possible in 1968 for serious, if informal, discussions to take place about an idea that the parallel institution of 'ministerial' broadcasts should be modified and extended so as to absorb party broadcasting between elections. But when attitudes were struck in the relatively open forum of the Committee on Party Political Broadcasting the hopes of the broadcasters were seen to be illusory and old themes were constantly being replayed with occasional variations.

In the end the year 1968 was a fairly disastrous one in which progress in any useful direction was notably absent. A meeting of the Committee on 19 March was so stormy and unproductive that no attempt to reconvene it could be made for the rest of the year. The trouble on this occasion arose from several failures on the part of the Conservative leader, Mr Heath, to achieve his objectives. He wanted regionalisation of the broadcasts in Scotland but got no support from the Labour and Liberal parties and encountered a recital of difficulties from the broadcasters which seemed to him little short of tiresome. He also proposed, to the horror of the broadcasters, that parties should be free to divide the whole of their time, if they wished, into five-minute broadcasts, thus opening up the possibility of a total of no less than twenty-eight party broadcasts in a year instead of eleven or twelve. The broadcasters stone-walled. Finally his desire to depart from the traditional simultaneity in the case of these shorter broadcasts was blocked by Mr Crossman on behalf of the Labour Party. It was not Mr Heath's day, and the full force of his impatience and frustration was vented on the representatives of the broadcasters.

Force of necessity impelled the two competitors to work together and to reconcile their own differences, which were sometimes substantial. Such experiences taught them where were the areas in which competition served the interests of neither, and certainly in the area of party political broadcasting the precept that dog does not eat dog came to prevail. The full story of the relationship between broadcasting and the political parties is outside the scope of this history; but the period covered by this volume was certainly one in which ITV and BBC acquired a more sensitive awareness of each other's problems and benefited from each other's experiences. This development had constitutional significance. In August 1964 the PMG had, despite protestations, insisted on describing party politicals in a formal directive as 'based on an offer of time made by the British Broadcasting Corporation after consultation with the Authority'.[2] By 1968 this pride of place officially conceded to the BBC no longer had substance. For good or ill ITV had become part of the broadcasting establishment.

The General Elections of October 1964 and March 1966, both in their national and regional aspects, received extensive coverage on Independent Television. It was provided in the following categories of programmes.

Formal Party Broadcasts. All Independent Television stations, with the exception of the Channel Islands, carried the thirteen programmes in the agreed series of party election broadcasts. There were five each for the Labour and Conservative parties and three for the Liberals. They were broadcast on agreed days simultaneously on Independent Television, BBC 1 and BBC 2 at 9.30 p.m. on the first occasion and 9.10 p.m. on the second. In 1966 there was in addition a five-minute broadcast for the Communist Party shown simultaneously at 6.30 p.m., and there was one regional broadcast of five minutes each for the Scottish and Welsh Nationalist Parties, also shown simultaneously.

News Programmes. In addition to reporting the campaign extensively in their regular news bulletins, ITN produced a twenty-minute late-night news round-up each weekday during the campaigns. Regional companies also included election news of particular interest to their areas in local news bulletins. Throughout polling night and much of the following day in 1964, ITN provided an election results service and analysis – and this was repeated in 1966 except that live coverage was interrupted between 3.30 a.m. and 6.30 a.m. Each occasion was a masterpiece of sustained reporting on the part of Alastair Burnet and a skilled team of commentators.

Descriptive Programmes. On Dissolution day on the first occasion and the day after on the second, ITN produced a special half-hour programme giving the background to the forthcoming election.

Regular Current Affairs Programmes. In contrast to 1959, when, like other similar programmes, it was taken off for the three weeks before polling day, *This Week* was produced throughout the 1964 and 1966 campaigns. Opening on the day of the election announcement with a special edition in which the leaders of the three main parties were interviewed, the series dealt in successive weeks with the major election issues.

Special Local Programmes. Programmes with local candidates were produced in all regions except London. There were the 'constituency programmes' in which all candidates in a particular constituency appeared and also, in 1966, 'constituency reports' in which individual constituencies were the subject of filmed descriptive reports. There were programmes in which party representatives explained and debated their policies. There were discussion programmes on topics of special regional interest, involving party specialists. Of particular interest were the 'Marathon' series presented in their respective regions by Granada and (in 1964 only) Tyne Tees Television, in which candidates of all parties from all constituencies in the service areas were invited to appear and address the electorate. In the event Granada were able in 1964 to cover 77 out of 160 constituencies and Tyne Tees 30 out of 35; in 1966 Granada covered 57.

In all, during the twenty days from Dissolution to the eve of polling day in 1964, Independent Television, in addition to normal regional and national news bulletins, broadcast 3 hours 15 minutes of party broadcasts, 5 hours 30 minutes of special election news and feature material from ITN, 2 hours 25 minutes of regular national current affairs programmes and 42 hours of regional programmes on the election – a total of some 53 hours. In 1966 the respective figures were somewhat lower, the total hourage being 44. There were also the programmes of election results and analysis on election night and on the following day.

Behind these arrangements lay an immense amount of discussion and planning. First there were negotiations at top policy levels with the main political parties resulting eventually in an understanding, not markedly precise, as to the extent of the cooperation at both national and local levels which the two broadcasting organisations could expect to receive from the party organisations. Within the parameters of this understanding there was still scope, although less than ITV would have liked, for independent initiative on the part of the broadcasters. The free rein of competition was in practice restricted by the fact that both BBC and ITV were represented at collective meetings with the parties and there was no way in which the plans of the one could be concealed from the other. For ITV these occasions were tests of the ability of a controlling authority plus fourteen companies so to coordinate and collate their plans as to keep abreast of the more centrally controlled plans of their competitor. On the other hand, the regional strength of ITV provided more opportunities for covering the election campaigns with due regard to local issues and the very real variations in outlook between party area organisations. Experience showed that the writ of party headquarters was not always sacred in areas away from the centre, and regional companies were occasionally able to secure a degree of cooperation which was denied to their big brothers.

A report on the state of play shortly before the 1966 Election campaign listed three rules which the parties were imposing. First, party spokesmen would not agree to appear in programmes arranged to include audiences. Secondly, where programmes on *selected* constituencies included discussions between the candidates, the selection had to be agreed with the parties. Thirdly, where party policy was to be stated or discussed by party spokesmen, the choice of the party representative had to be agreed with the respective party. These limitations, though severe, were understandable. One concession had, however, been negotiated which turned out to be valuable and to make coverage of the 1966 campaign appreciably less troublesome for ITV than it had been in 1964. Consultation could in all cases take place with the regional party headquarters rather than, as previously, at the national level.[3]

The antipathy of the parties towards programmes with audiences was based primarily on the belief that they would be unreal in that the audience would, for reasons of 'balance', be artificially assembled by securing from the party agents the names of those who would attend, so that it would not be genuinely an audience at all but an assembly of three rival groups. At that time nobody believed there was any other way of assembling an audience of which the balance could be guaranteed. They also thought that such programmes could degenerate into a hecklers' outing or even into a shouting match.[4]

As if the strict impartiality requirements of the Television Act were not enough there was the looming presence of Section 63 of the Representation of the People Act, 1949, which, *inter alia*, provided that 'no expense shall, with a view to promoting or procuring the election of a candidate at an election, be incurred by any person other than the candidate, his election agent and persons authorised in writing by the election agent . . .' and from which broadcasting, unlike newspapers and periodicals, was not exempt. Late in 1965 a Speaker's Conference on Electoral Reform was informed that the statutory obligations and duties of the Authority in relation to political programmes were sufficiently clear as they stood and that ITV's duty to provide news and an informed coverage at elections ought not to be restricted by conflicting requirements or uncertainty as to the interpretation of the Representation of the People Act. In so far as it placed duties on ITV different from those in the Television Act, it was unsatisfactory and Parliament should legislate to bring the two statutes into line with each other.[5] In the meantime, however, ITV had to live with both statutes as they stood and a revised Representation of the People Act did not reach the statute book until 1969.

Considering all the difficulties, which by reason of the statutory basis of ITV were somewhat greater than those experienced by the BBC, it must be judged remarkable that the coverage of both elections was an acknowledged success, as had indeed been the coverage of the election of 1959. The three weeks of General Election campaigns came to be accepted as necessary but inevitably traumatic upheavals in the flow of television broadcasting. Cynics could say – and they did – that the coverage provided more stimulus and excitement for the broadcasters than for the audience.

In 1964 it was the so-called 'controlled' programmes – the ones that had to be arranged with the parties – that proved the least satisfactory. In general, it was found that the parties were often taking into account factors that did not make for the most informative television. For example, if the spokesman of one of the parties came from a marginal constituency, the rival parties were tempted to approve no spokesmen other than their candidates in the same constituency. As regards the constituency programmes intended as such, constituencies likely to provide lively television because the candidates were famous, or because some issue had a particular interest, or because the result was in doubt, might be ruled out by one of the parties because of some disadvantage to itself which it feared from that particular choice.[6] In 1966 relations with the parties were in general considerably easier and the companies experienced little difficulty over the choice of party spokesmen or of constituencies.

Perhaps the most interesting development in 1966 was that ITN carried for the first time speeches by party leaders made within their constituencies – a practice which had hitherto been assumed to be contrary to the Representation of the People Act. They took care not to identify them as candidates and not to state that they were within their own constituencies. They also interviewed the party leaders on the eve of the poll, hitherto regarded by convention as a 'closed day' for broadcast coverage of elections. They held such interviews to be strictly news, but the BBC considered them a regrettable, even dangerous breach of a salutory precept.[7]

31

SPECIAL CLASSES IN THE SIXTIES

As we saw in the previous volume, the term 'special classes' covered certain categories of programme which deserved a place in the schedules by reason of their public service value but which could not be accommodated within the limited ration of television hours originally allowed by government without displacing programmes of popular appeal and consequently involving an appreciable loss of the advertising revenue from which ITV had to finance itself. From the outset religious programmes were, as we saw, considered to be off-the-ration so far as transmission hours were concerned, and from 1957 onwards so also were programmes for schools. Programmes in the Welsh language soon joined this exclusive club but attempts to extend its membership to other categories met with stout resistance from the Post Office which continued to administer the state policy of precluding more television than was considered socially acceptable.

(i) ADULT EDUCATION

The emergence of a category of programmes specifically designed for the education of viewers no longer at school was inevitably bound up with this control over hours of broadcasting. Inevitably, because, whilst it was relatively easy to identify a schools or religious programme, it was much less easy to distinguish between an adult education broadcast and one intended seriously and authoritatively to inform on any matter of factual interest such as was expected to find a place in a 'balanced' programme output within permitted hours.

There is little doubt that it was the 'unrelenting opposition of the BBC'[1] that strongly influenced Post Office resistance to the creation of a new special class. More television hours meant more earning power for ITV, but for the BBC just more expenditure. Yet when in November 1961 the dog came out of the manger and the Corporation made public their intention to supplement existing educational television output with series for day release students attending technical colleges their request for extra time was not immediately approved. They were told that if their proposals proved to be compatible with the Pilkington Committee's eventual recommendations on educational broadcasting then their request would be granted. This led the Authority to suggest to companies that they too might consider preparing plans for televised courses clearly related to further education or similar vocational instruction in anticipation of a grant of extra time by the following autumn 1962 when Pilkington would almost certainly have reported and their recommendations been considered by the Government.[2] The response was immediate. At the scc meeting on 10 January Norman Collins and Howard Thomas exposed their companies' joint plans for one hour of weekend education on either Saturday or Sunday mornings. The hour would be made up of three twenty-minute programmes.

In the meantime, the ITA was establishing contacts with appropriate sections of the educational world with the aim of formulating a policy against which any future programme proposals could be judged. If, as had been virtually promised, the Government were to accept Pilkington's anticipated recommendation of a protected place for adult education on television then the Spring 1962 was not too soon for consideration of plans for programmes to be shown that Autumn. The BBC was known to be busy already on the task. Companies were asked to put forward their plans, however tentative, as soon as possible.[3] Advice from spokesmen for the Universities had drawn attention to a relatively large clientele for adult education outside the relatively restricted field of vocational training and study. Companies were encouraged to include such non-vocational (e.g. liberal arts) topics in any plans they might make. This extension of the possible areas of programme content made further steps patently urgent. Firstly, a new group of professional advisers would be needed. There was little likelihood that the PMG would grant the extra hours without a stamp of approval similar to the one already expected for religious and schools broadcasting. When the ITA held a meeting in May with spokesmen from the University extra-mural departments, the local authorities, the WEA, the National Institute of Adult Education and the parallel Scottish interest groups, it was overwhelmingly apparent that any new advisory body would have to work with some clarifying definition. As we saw in Chapter 20, this need was clearly stated in the first White Paper following on Pilkington.[4] A tentative formula was discussed with the companies in July.

ABC and ATV continued to make the running. The former suggested that similar advisory arrangements to those already obtaining for religious

programmes might very well serve, a view which was shared by the
Authority. Even if there did not turn out to be a committee – like CRAC –
common to both BBC and ITV, given the multiplicity and variety of bodies
officially concerned with adult education, a fair degree of overlap in
membership between BBC and ITV committees seemed desirable. By the end
of July agreement had been reached with the BBC on a proposed 'formula'. It
ran:

> Educational programmes for adults are programmes (other than school
> broadcasts) arranged in series and planned in consultation with appropri-
> ate educational bodies to help viewers towards a progressive mastery or
> understanding of some skill or body of knowledge.
>   This definition shall be held to include programmes primarily designed
> for class use (e.g. in technical colleges or in centres for adult education)
> and also programmes primarily designed for the home viewer.[5]

Recruiting membership for the proposed Advisory Committee was
complicated by the profusion of specialised bodies concerned with adult and
further education, all of which were in a state of some rivalry. It would not
be easy to avoid an over-large and unwieldy committee; or to find a suitable
chairman. Time would be needed. To cover the interim period, a small
'panel' of three adult educationists was set up: Asa Briggs of Sussex
University, Maurice Bruce of Sheffield University and Werner Burmeister
of London University (the 'three B's').[6] This group set to work immediately
and met at regular intervals until the final establishment of the full
committee in February 1963. It was largely on their advice that the then
Dr John Fulton, Vice Chancellor of Sussex University, was invited (and
agreed) to become chairman of both the BBC's and the ITA's Adult Education
Committees.[7] He was not the only member of both bodies.
    While the 'three B's' were discussing the terms of a policy statement by the
ITA on adult education, a letter from the Post Office of 4 October 1962
intimated Ministerial acceptance of the 'agreed formula', after due
consultation with the education departments. The PMG was therefore now
ready, the letter went on, 'to consider any application . . . for additional
television hours to be used for broadcasting programmes covered by this
definition'.[8] On 15 October a formal application was submitted by the ITA
for one extra hour on Sundays between 10 a.m. and 11 a.m., beginning on
25 November 1962 to accommodate three series of twenty-minute broadcasts provided by ABC and ATV.[9] These were the series for which the two
companies had made known their plans as long ago as the previous January.

From ABC: *You Don't Say*, a series on spoken English, and *Don't Get Me Wrong*, a similar series on written English, and from ATV: *Mesdames, Messieurs*, a brush-up-your-conversational-French series.

This swift response seems to have shocked the mandarins of St. Martin's-le-Grand by its failure to observe the customary decorum of slow and deliberate bureaucratic decision. 'We have been a little taken aback by the speed with which your application followed my letter of 4 October.' It was agreed, however, to treat 'the present proposal as a kind of operational trial run, carrying no commitment . . . for the future';[10] and the one hour extension was conceded. It was clearly hinted that a master plan for televised adult education should be devised in which ITV's programme contribution would be dovetailed into that of the BBC.

If this reflected the Ministerial hope to impose some system of order, through television, on the confusion of British adult education, it was doomed to failure. Apart from the fields of vocational further education or training, so long as public participation in adult education remained on a voluntary basis, the courses offered would depend to a large extent on the varieties and vagaries of public interests and tastes rather than on any centralised master plan for public enlightenment. Educational courses offered to the general public, whether in institutions or on television, do not have a captive school audience. They have to attract and hold an audience just like any other broadcast. In the very nature of the case the first ventures into this field by the broadcasters would have to be trial runs, testing the market, as it were. Coordination with the BBC was in the long run not likely to add up to much more than avoidance of unnecessary duplication.

By the end of 1962, the ITA had completed membership of its Advisory Committee and, aided by the three-man panel, had drawn up a policy statement and brief to which that committee could work; and it continued to urge companies to put forward proposals for the committee to consider. On the question of the terms on which additional time would be granted the Post Office position remained defensive, if not downright obstructive. It was intimated that the PMG wished to be satisfied that the Authority's policy and general plan was 'on the right lines' before future proposals could be accepted without question, once they had been certified by the Advisory Committee as conforming to the agreed formula. ITV spokesmen might well have riposted that the Minister and his officials should not have accepted the formula in the first place if they could not agree that programme proposals certified by competent educational experts to be fully in keeping with its terms had a legitimate claim to extra air time.

These early experiences in the field of adult education reflected the attitude that PMG Bevins apparently felt called upon to display towards ITV. As in the case of Wales (West and North) this Minister and his staff tried, in consideration of favours which it was undoubtedly in their power to grant or withhold, to exercise a degree of pre-emptive control over programme matters which exceeded their statutory right. As a result, for some years to come, all adult education proposals from ITV companies were to be submitted in full detail, covering proposed content as well as length and timing (after they had been examined, discussed and not seldom modified by a committee of practising educators) for further scrutiny by Post Office officials before they could be accorded the boon of the necessary air time. They seemed to be obsessed with the fear that one or other of the ITV companies might get away with extended – revenue earning – hours for a programme that it could just as well have transmitted within the basic fifty-hour allowance. The consequent bureaucratic officiousness sometimes went to absurd lengths. Every individual company's showing, and even repeat of a previously approved series, had to be submitted for separate approval. On one occasion even a change in the running order and title of a series, after the time extension had been granted, was made the subject of critical correspondence and implied reconsideration.[11]

The policy paper[12] which the Adult Education Advisory Committee had before it on its first meeting foresaw a three phase development. The first covering the first half of 1963 was to be devoted to experiment, trying out different topics, addressed to different audiences. The second from October 1963 to July 1964 would attempt to achieve a more coherent pattern 'covering . . . a number of different potential audiences'. The third phase would be based on lessons learned in the first two and the consequent understandings reached in the course of negotiation of the new contracts on the appropriate amount of adult education to be included in a week's programme output. The policy statement showed little recognition of the weight and importance of unpremeditated and indiscriminate viewing in the mass medium. Three broad programme categories were envisaged: specialist courses which would be linked either to classroom groups or correspondence courses; liberal adult education such as practised by the WEA and University extramural departments involving study of a chosen subject 'for its own sake'; and treatment of leisure pursuits, including hobbies, homecrafts and other do-it-yourself activities.

The actual programme proposals put before the new committee at its first meeting were the ABC/ATV Sunday morning package in future to be known as 'Sunday Session'; a highly specialised series from STV aimed at the professional up-dating of medical practitioners; and a proposal submitted to

Anglia by Peter Laslett on behalf of the Cambridge University Educational Television Committee. This was to be an experimental week of early morning undergraduate level broadcast lectures on the model of the 'sunrise semesters' currently in vogue in the United States. The Scottish medical series clearly fell within the 'specialist' audience category; and the Cambridge one might be thought to do so too because of its assumed educational level. The Sunday Session proposals however – coming as they did from experienced broadcasters – had the advantage of both vocational utility and wider general audience appeal. The Committee noted that the two other major companies, Granada and a-r, were showing little disposition towards any adult education programme commitment at that stage. Their hesitations eventually evaporated in the new contract period after 1964. What was to be notable over the years ahead was not only the number and diversity of programme projects but also the regular participation of all iTV companies, large and small, in the production – as well as transmission – of designated adult education series.

The ABC/ATV weekly Sunday Session quickly established itself as the central pillar of iTV adult education. ABC's first term series on spoken and written English was followed in the Summer of 1963 by *Clear Thinking* and *Your Environment* (town planning, local government). ATV's brush-up-your-French *Mesdames, Messieurs* continued through both thirteen-week terms and into the following (1963/4) academic year when the 'Session' expanded to a four series package. There was nothing particularly vocational about the other three offerings, a popular science series on meteorology from ATV, and, from ABC, a series describing the English educational system together with one offering guidance to the home motor mechanic. In 1965 a regional company's series, Tyne Tees' Russian language course, was included in Sunday Session; 20,000 copies of the accompanying booklet were sold. Outside the Sunday Session frame four regional projects emerged in the first year. STV's highly specialised Post Graduate Medicine, Tyne Tees' *Looking Back to Tomorrow*, a look at the social and economic scene past and future in their own region, and Ulster Television's *The Enquiring Mind*.

Predictably perhaps, most public attention was drawn to the *Dawn University* experiment. The six broadcast lectures by Cambridge dons of considerable academic distinction (including three Fellows of the Royal Society and one Nobel Prize winner) were in fact part of a larger plan to demonstrate the potential of television as a teaching medium for university degree courses. There were also a closed circuit link between lecture rooms in Cambridge and Norwich and a two-way video linked research colloquium between participants in Cambridge and Imperial College, London. Added publicity was undoubtedly given to *Dawn University* because the broadcasts took place only a few weeks after Harold Wilson's first public statement in September 1963 about a proposed 'University of the Air', and it was no doubt a useful pointer towards what was to become the Open University.

Probably more important for ITV educational policies were the findings of the Gallup research into audience response to the first thirteen weeks of *Sunday Session*. The estimated audience for at least one of the broadcasts during an average four weeks was 1,870,000 adults (sixteen years and over), the average weekly audience being 750,000. Of these 62 per cent were younger than 45, 28 per cent had left school at 14, 47 per cent at 15/16 and 48 per cent of the viewers said they had attended no form of institutional education since leaving school.

When the viewers were asked what they thought ITV's 'main concern' should be in adult education, they divided more or less equally between 'knowledge and skills useful at work', 'hobbies and leisure interests' and cultural interests like literature and the arts. Topics in the last category were preferred by over half (55 per cent) of those educated beyond the age of seventeen. But such people were at that time no more than 12 per cent of the UK population. When asked what they themselves would prefer to see in educational broadcasts, the generality of viewers (45 per cent) were outstandingly in favour of 'hobbies, handicrafts and home decorating'. Subjects like history, the arts, literature, maths, music, geography and languages were favoured by about one quarter, sociology and economics by about half that number. It would be difficult to say how far these data influenced later the development of ITV adult education policy and practice. At all events experiments were to continue for some time with series aimed at narrowly defined target audiences, either linked with other forms of teaching or with precise educational objectives and sometimes both; and these by definition could not be judged successful or otherwise on crude global audience figures alone.

From the outset, attention was directed towards the possibilities of links between broadcasts and outside educational agencies. These it was felt could offer encouragement and help in taking things further. As the ITA's Education Officer put it:

> Even in the classroom, learning does not take place without an active contribution from the student . . . television teaching, whatever its real advantage, is similarly incomplete and similarly needs to be supplemented. Like all other forms of educational communication it is not a source of education in itself but an aid and an occasion for learning.[13]

In the case of STV's postgraduate Medicine series the target audience was readily identified. The same could be said of Westward's 1964 and 1965 *Teachers' Workshop* series designed to facilitate the work of Exeter University Institute of Education in meeting its responsibilities for in-service training at the secondary and primary schools in the area. There were twelve twenty-minute programmes on the teaching of the 'new maths' in primary schools broadcast at midday on Sundays and repeated late on Wednesday evenings. An indicator of success in this particular case was the active interest displayed by Government departments concerned with overseas aid and technical cooperation. With grants from the Department of Education and Science and the Gulbenkian Foundation some of the programmes were transferred to film for distribution overseas in developing countries.

Border Television's *Farm 65* and *Farm 66* offered further examples of a small regional company producing in partnership with a local educational institution a series aimed at specialised vocational instruction. With cooperation from Newton Rigg Farm School, a practical course of half-hour Sunday morning programmes for young farm workers was devised. In 1965 about 16 per cent of all school leavers in the area went into agriculture. Nearly all of them enrolled for the television course (on farm machinery) with the prospect of taking at its end a special City & Guilds test and receiving a certificate.

Similar experiments with the narrow target audience – defined this time by educational level rather than by vocational objective – were the 'O Level' maths and English courses produced by Anglia's *College of the Air* in 1964 and ABC's *First Steps in Physics* in 1966. Both of these were reinforced by relevant correspondence courses provided by the Cambridge-based National Extension College. The latter body, established by Michael Young in the aftermath of Wilson's 'University of the Air' speech, was to become over the following years the regular provider of the correspondence element for adult education series produced by ITV and also the BBC.

By no means so deliberately restricted in their intended audiences or educational aims were two other linked adult education projects of those early years. Southern Television's 1964 English Literature series *The Full Man* was in more than one way unique. It was presented by Dr David Daiches, of Sussex University, and was boldly scheduled at 7 p.m. on Tuesday evenings, a time deliberately chosen to facilitate viewing by organised evening classes in the company of their tutors. The Department of Education and Science made additional grants available to those responsible bodies wishing to take on extra tutors to start classes. In the sixty classes thus started in the Southern TV region – divided about equally between the LEAS and WEA/University extramural departments – were about 1100 students. The home audience, however, was estimated to have included 450,000 who had viewed at least one, 150,000 who had seen at least half and 15,000 who had viewed all twelve programmes. One programme from the series, *Araby* (based on a James Joyce short story), received a major prize at an international educational television festival in 1965 in Tokyo. Unmistakeably non-vocational in its purposes, this series was clearly more in keeping than other institutionally linked projects with the traditional missionary role of British adult education as practised by extramural departments and the WEA. The same could be said perhaps of the ATV elementary economics course, *The Standard of Living*. Devised and coordinated by the extramural department of Nottingham University under its director Harold Wiltshire, the series consisted of thirteen twenty-minute programmes transmitted in the Midlands. There was financial support from the Leverhulme Trust. The 1656 students who enrolled each received a handbook for background reading, reference papers and weekly exercises. Meetings with local tutors were arranged. Only some 300 of the students were in senior school or college classes. Of the 1347 'individual' students, 1119 took the course: and over 200 attended a closing conference at the University.[14] These figures were impressive when compared with the customary size of adult education classes in a single subject at a single institution, but as a proportion of the potential mass television audience they were minimal.

It could not therefore be long before questions began to be raised about the validity of highly specialised courses for deliberately restricted audiences within the output of an open access popular mass medium, even if the supporting apparatus of textbooks, tutors and correspondence courses were paid for by others, not the broadcasters. Such educational use of television might have been more appropriately placed in the separate ETV channel for which the ITA had argued in its Pilkington evidence. The arrival of BBC 2, and the development within the Government of plans for a University or College of the Air, using time made available in the new channel, severely discouraged further such developments in ITV's single service.

Over the years that followed there came from the ITV companies an ever increasing, richly varied output of adult education series. But the balance of effort perceptibly changed. Attention turned away from the narrowly targeted or linked courses, designed for identifiable, relatively homogeneous audiences. Not totally, of course: to the public eye such enterprises were always more obviously 'educational'. There were therefore continuing series for farmers in more than one region. Besides ATV's French courses and Tyne

Tees' Russian, there was Welsh language instruction from TWW. There were excellent series for management students from Granada (1965/6), Grampian (1966) and STV (1966/7). STV's medical series continued and there was even, from TWW, a series on preventive medicine in Welsh (1966/7). But such productions were a diminishing proportion of the whole.

As the output built up above the nineteen series in years 1964/5 and 1965/6, increasing attention was given to topics more obviously related to the character and interests of the general ITV audience. Three broad subject areas came progressively to the fore. There were those programmes which could help the average viewer as a citizen to a better understanding of his world and its happenings. There were those which dealt with concerns of his daily living as an individual or family man, helping him maybe to do better those things which he would probably do anyhow. Thirdly there were the arts, literature, philosophy and history, the traditional pabulum of WEA and University extramural classes.

The trend that these changes illustrate does not seem to have been deliberately planned. It was rather the cumulative outcome of a number of discrete decisions made by individuals working not all together in a single educational broadcasting unit but each in the mental atmosphere of more generalised programme thinking and discussion that prevailed in a typical ITV company. Their attitude towards their audience was in other words more that of mass media communicators who tend to approach their public as suitors rather than that of professional educators who are prone to regard the public as their beneficiaries. The belief that the trend in programme balance was a sensible one reflecting the interests, concerns and aspirations of the ITV audience may well have been encouraged, even reinforced, by the sales figures for some of the booklets published to accompany adult education series.

For some critics among the advisers the emphasis in the output on everyday practical activities, sports and pastimes seemed too great. The fifty or sixty programme series (including repeats) shown on ITV in a year were seen as a haphazard miscellany rather than the product of an educational policy planned to serve needs as well as wants.[15] More effort should be directed, it was thought, towards the awakening of new serious interests and stimulus to further study. Attempts were made to draw up a scheme whereby every company would be required to show and/or produce in the course of a year at least one series in each of five distinct programme categories within an average output of three hours a week. Little was achieved, and the balance between different kinds of subject matter remained much as it had been.

Inevitably, doubts about the value of the 'agreed formula' began to grow. It had become increasingly difficult for the viewer to distinguish between an approved adult education series (that earned extra time) and a similar general output on the same subject (that did not). Certainly series on kitchen or loft conversion or on dog training could readily be described as contributing to 'a progressive mastery of some skill or body of knowledge' – even if they did not altogether correspond with traditional notions of academic education. Yet only by stretching to looseness the meaning of words could the same be said about a group of Lord Clark lectures, about an account of contemporary British stage drama, or even Westward's examination of the present-day social role of the clergyman.

As will be seen in the next volume it was to come as something of a relief when in 1972 Christopher Chataway, the Minister of Posts and Telecommunications, swept away the restrictions on television broadcasting hours. The need for the formula as a qualifying test disappeared. At the same time, however, the ITA showed no disposition to disband its Adult Education Committee or to modify its view that no company schedule could be considered properly balanced without a proportion of designedly educational programmes for adults. The challenge to think out a generally acceptable, defensible policy for a distinctive programme category called *adult education* on ITV did not dwindle.[16] It was to become all the greater.

(ii) SCHOOL BROADCASTING

The two White Papers and the subsequent legislation led to two changes, one general and one specific that reflected Pilkington's thinking and were bound to affect future arrangements for educational broadcasting by ITV. As Pilkington had observed it was anomalous for an independent authority expected to play a dominant role in taking full public responsibility for a national broadcasting service to be statutorily bound to comply with the policy recommendations of one of its advisory bodies. Yet such had been its relationship with the Children's Advisory Committee. The Government agreed. It also agreed with Pilkington that it was 'incongruous' to have the same committee advising on children's programmes and broadcasts to schools.

So the early sixties saw the ITA preparing to assume a more overtly 'dominant' role in programme matters, by the appointment of additional experienced specialists to the staff of its Programme Division. The first to be appointed was the Education Officer, Joseph Weltman (whose 'office' was later to become a full-scale 'department'). The Children's Advisory Committee ceased to exist and there was created a new Authority-based educational advisory structure. It consisted of an Advisory Council concerned with overall educational policy as reflected in general output as well as in specifically designated educational programmes; a Schools Committee to advise on the acceptability of programme proposals from the companies; and the Adult Education Committee which had already been set up to do likewise for developments (most notably from ABC and ATV) in this new field.

It is perhaps arguable whether or not these largely bureaucratic dispositions helped to stimulate the period of greatly increased original creative activity in ITV school broadcasting which ensued. That growing sense of common purpose which began to emerge with the appointment of dedicated company education officers, following on the creation of the inter-company network education committee, was certainly another important factor. But equally influential must have been the encouraging evidence of a responsive audience, of changing attitudes in the educational world itself. This was nowhere more tellingly illustrated than when Sir John Newsom accepted the Authority's invitation in March 1964 to be the first chairman of its newborn Educational Advisory Council. 'Half Our Future', published in 1963, was a report by the Ministry of Education's Central Advisory Council, of which Sir John had also been chairman, on the education of children of average and below average ability. It contained the unequivocal statement that local education authorities should base their development plans on the concept of television receivers as necessary equipment for the education of our children. This was a far cry from the equivocal attitude of the 1957 Education Ministry when it grudgingly conceded a 50 per cent grant for one TV set per 100,000 of school population. The next report, in 1966, from this Central Advisory Council – by then chaired by Lady Plowden – dealt with primary schools and was equally forthright about the educational value of television, an aid that could 'enrich enormously the resources available to teachers'.

The number of viewing schools was swiftly growing. Teachers, once they were persuaded – as they now could be – of the educational credentials of the programme providers, were as ready to use programmes from the commercial TV companies as they had long been happy to do with the school radio programmes of the BBC; always provided of course that they could find programmes that fitted their own purposes. So two-way channels of easy communication between educators and ITV programme makers were more than ever necessary. In 1962 the companies supplemented the printed material they had widely distributed (and sold) about their schools series with so-called 'Out of School' broadcasts, transmitted during the Christmas holidays, showing sample programmes from new series planned for broadcast the following autumn. Cards for weekly comments by viewing teachers were complemented by regular teachers' meetings in each company area and by full reports from company education officers visiting schools to observe classroom reactions. In 1967 the Authority agreed to endow on an annual basis twelve Schoolteacher Fellowships, tenable by young teachers for a term's secondment to a university institute or department of education. The aim here was to encourage in the profession more widely informed and better critical understanding of the television medium and its potential; and simultaneously to facilitate more comparative study of its effective classroom use.

By 1963 the number of viewing schools had passed the 5000 mark. At the decade's end it was over 20,000. Inevitably this growth meant a change in the composition of the audience. As it came to reflect more accurately the whole school system, there would be an increasing preponderance of primary schools. The balance of output had therefore perforce to change. No longer was it a question of seeking an audience by offering palliatives for well publicised temporary shortages (say, in Maths or language teaching), or to serve perceived growing points or new departures (e.g. 'general science' for the secondary modern), though such pioneering, propagandist work can always be a valued function of a national educational broadcasting service. To sustain credibility the ITV service had from now on to offer a central output of programmes over as wide a spectrum of day-to-day educational purposes as available airtime could allow. In 1959, there were some $4\frac{1}{2}$ hours a week during school terms; in 1963 $5\frac{1}{4}$ hours; at the end of the sixties between 9 and 10 hours – over 12 per cent of total output in those weeks. (The comparable figure for sport was 10 per cent.) By that time almost two thirds of registered viewing schools were primaries and of the total of thirty-eight separate school series shown during the year eighteen were at primary level. And in the years ahead the balance was to shift even further.

By 1968/9 sixteen nationally networked weekly series (not all of them running for more than one term), three more than in the previous year, were being shown, produced by the four major companies: ATV, Granada, and the newly appointed Thames and Yorkshire companies. (Thames had substantially absorbed the highly professional and successful Rediffusion Schools Department.) Such an output, substantial as it was, could not of course cover the whole breadth of both secondary and primary school curricula. Priorities had to be agreed – a vital prime function of the educational liaison structures, at all levels.

Perhaps the most striking feature of this period of increasing activity in ITV school broadcasting was the part played by the smaller, regional companies. At classroom level above all, education in Britain is traditionally a local rather than a central government concern. This seemed in practice to fit in well with the decentralised regional structure of ITV. With their increasing involvement in the educational life of their respective regions companies like Tyne Tees, Grampian, Scottish Television and, of course, Ulster and the Welsh company began, in response to local advice, to provide their own local variations on the nationally networked service, both with special additional showings of networked programmes as with original locally produced series of their own devising. The Scottish companies were especially active. From very early days Grampian had a regular output of home productions for the primary school, ranging from sex education (a 'first' on British TV), craftwork, biographies of eminent Scots to an introduction to the pre-numbers stage of mathematics for five-year olds. The close links early established by this small company with its schools and local education authorities were well demonstrated during the 1964 typhoid epidemic in North East Scotland. As a precautionary health measure all schools in the area were closed. Despite objections from the BBC, Grampian were given permission to put out daytime programmes, both entertainment and instructional, for the children thus obliged to stay at home. Scottish Television had begun by contributing occasional single productions to be included in Rediffusion series shown throughout the UK. But they moved on to provide for local consumption series at secondary level on computers, civics, design and local history. Ulster sought to offer its fifteen-year olds a cool, objective look at local current affairs. Tyne Tees producers turned their hands to primary school French and elementary economics.

The ITV schedule of school broadcasts thus came to vary from region to region. In 1968/9 of the thirty-eight separate school series shown during the year over ITV as a whole, no more than twenty-nine were seen in all regions. Not only had educational broadcasting become a major constituent element of the Independent Television service: ITV had itself come to be recognised as an integrated, fully accredited partner in the national educational system.

(iii) RELIGION

The publication of Dr John Robinson's *Honest to God* early in 1963 created a considerable stir, for when a bishop of the Church of England could express his doubts so freely, the place of organised Christianity in the 'establishment' itself came into question. In the new climate of opinion, of which quite apart from the bishop's book there was now much evidence, religious television could no longer command unquestioned support. Yet the ITA continued to treat it as a distinctive category entitled to a protected place in the output.

The change of mood was reflected at the centre of the advisory system. In response to the Pilkington Committee's recommendation that the Central Religious Advisory Committee needed new blood, six lay members were added to its number.

As for Pilkington's recommendation, which the BBC backed, that the ITA should have a separate committee (as much as to say that there was a gulf fixed between official BBC religion and the more popular ITV version), CRAC itself, along with the ITA's own Panel of Religious Advisers, dug their toes in. By way of compromise, as an 'experiment' which has since stood the test of time, the ITA began meeting CRAC in separate sessions. That left room for occasional joint meetings, but what the arrangement really meant was that the 'main streams' of religion no longer regarded ITV as an awkward underling. By the end of the sixties things had moved further. Appointments to CRAC, originally the prerogative of the Corporation which the Authority was merely invited to endorse, became made jointly.

Pilkington had recommended that the Authority extend its surveillance of programmes, and one of the new posts created to do that work was that of Religious Programmes Officer, hitherto deemed to be filled 'in commission' by the Panel. There was a large number of applicants, but the qualifications of Penry Jones were outstanding. Since 1958 he had been the begetter of ABC's *Sunday Break*, the programme that had set the pace in religious television. His successor at ABC was a man of similar stamp, well in tune with the questing temper of religion. The Revd Ian Mackenzie was a music graduate of Edinburgh University who had joined the staff of the Student Christian Movement. A Highlander by origin, and by temperament, he brought to television a mind well-read in contemporary theology. He very soon made his mark on ABC's output. With BBC's *Songs of Praise* now well established, ITV broke new ground with *Hallelujah* which introduced Sydney Carter and a group of folksingers to create anthologies. In discussion programmes too Mackenzie cut through much conventional assumption, and such series as *Looking for an Answer*, presented by Robert Kee, showed that no holds were barred.

There were other ministers of religion fully employed by ITV. Later in the decade Scottish Television appointed The Revd Nelson Gray as its editor of religious programmes, the largest such output of any ITV company; and from their beginning Anglia Television had created a virtually full-time post for their 'Chairman of Religious Advisers', held till his death in 1980 by Canon A. R. Freeman. Traditionalist as he was by instinct, believing deeply in the natural hold of the things of God upon all sorts and conditions of men, 'Peter' made a unique contribution to religion on ITV. He made the most of his regional late-night programmes, and while straightforward 'epilogues' remained the norm elsewhere, Anglia introduced a range of formats. With a different sort of programme for each night of the week, under the general title *Reflections*, Freeman showed what could be done: interviews, singing, illustrated portraits of great men and women, and a weekly discussion series *Big Questions*. In the sixties it was more customary than it later became for English regional companies to opt out of part of the Sunday evening network provision and show programmes of their own. Thus Anglia's *Your Music on Sunday* was the first British television programme to present screen personalities introducing their favourite religious music and hymns. It was in the tradition of 'people's television', and a straightforward way of letting the audience see that broadcast religion was part and parcel of life.

This conviction was beginning to shape thinking about the whole of the religious television output. In the fifties ITV had made its impact as a popular service, in sharp contrast to the paternalism of the BBC, and in religious affairs it had done so self-consciously. The first religious consultation at Oxford in 1961 had been unashamed in its attitude. 'Our audience is middle-aged working-class mums,' one speaker had said. Twenty years later, we are embarrassed by the condescension implicit in that remark. In the years after Pilkington ITV succeeded in breaking through the class barrier. Those who had earlier stuck to BBC because they 'couldn't bear all those advertisements' dared to switch over. The brand loyalty of audiences that had been such a feature of the early days began to weaken.

At the second consultation in Cambridge in September 1963,[17] the Archbishop of Canterbury, Dr Ramsey, declared 'we must use every possible medium conveying the truth of God and here is a great one, and we can't help using it'.[18] But the idea of 'using television' did not appeal to everybody present. 'We cannot hand over the building up of the churches to the television box,' said Dr John Marsh, an eminent Congregationalist. For the Roman Catholic Father Vincent Whelan television was casting bread on the waters. Vernon Sproxton, a guest producer from the BBC, said bluntly, 'When I hear people ask "How should the church use television?" it sends shivers down my spine!' Dr Robinson spoke for many – clerics and laymen – when he said 'The prime purpose of religious television is *not the making of individual Christians* . . . it is seeking to communicate with the "latent church" from a fundamentally different point of view from that of the local churches'. So ITV religious producers began to think in terms of 'opening new windows of comprehension' as the BBC's Sproxton had put it.

When the third religious consultation, held at Durham in September 1965,[19] took as its title 'The Audience we Serve', it no longer just meant middle-aged working-class mums. For ABC Television had on its own initiative commissioned from Gallup a survey on 'Television and Religion', and in advance of publication made the findings available for Durham. The findings called into question the assumption, still a commonplace, of a 'mass audience'. They indicated, moreover, the great gap between profession of religious belief and any sort of church allegiance. With a succession of figures to elaborate this finding, the research cast doubt upon the widespread belief that if only Christian communicators could master the techniques of television, they could fill the pews. Instead, they focussed attention on the realities of a society largely alienated from the domain of organised religion. After all, this was the 'swinging sixties'.

One of Durham's visiting speakers, Ronald Goldman, a specialist in religious education, drove home these unpalatable realities. He demonstrated why teaching young children Bible stories did not lead to faithful adherence in adolescence, and argued instead that the natural way to religious understanding was through the senses. Programmes about bread, or water, for instance, might encourage a far more enduring religious awareness than the retelling of incidents from Scripture.

Durham made considerable impact upon the output in the following years, not least upon the provision for children. It became regular practice to give over the first twenty minutes of the 'closed period' to programmes for children, and so pose a fresh challenge to creative talent. At ATV, Michael Redington provided younger children with the song-and-story series *A Box of Birds*, and older ones with two drama serials, *The Forgotten Door* and *I am David*. At ABC a distinguished director of children's programmes, Pamela Lonsdale, in 1977 produced a dramatised serialisation of C. S. Lewis' *The Lion, the Witch and the Wardrobe*, while the following spring her colleague Voytek, a Polish director, made for the network a four-part presentation of *Pilgrim's Progress* that gave Bunyan the flavour of Kafka.

Much of the output remained bread-and-butter. For all the criticism at

Durham of 'talking heads', regional programmes in particular found their staple in discussion. A *Punch* cartoon of the time showed three men round a studio table, with the caption 'A psychiatrist, a sociologist, a parson . . . it must be a religious programme'.

Durham had steered away from heady arguments at Cambridge for abolishing the Sunday 'closed period'. The protection of an hour and a half that it had originally offered had already been whittled down, by two stages, to seventy minutes. But by the mid-sixties, religious television was beginning to feel the effects of protection in another way. With competition circumscribed, companies lacked any natural incentive to give religious television the resources that would put it on a par with other parts of the output. It was not just a matter of money. Generally budgets for programmes were adequate, and on occasion generous. Rather, with the first wave of excitement passed, religious programmes attracted few new recruits of high potential.

The BBC snapped up Penry Jones. At the beginning of 1967 he was appointed their Head of Religious Broadcasting, and his place at the ITA was taken by Christopher Martin. The newcomer looked round for signs of life. Alongside the networking companies, Southern Television had already made a distinctive mark. They were the only regional company regularly contributing to the rota of Outside Broadcast worship, thereby reflecting the origins of their Programme Controller, Berkeley Smith. Moreover it had in The Revd Bill Todd a particularly lively young Church of England adviser. So it was Southern that during 1967 led the regional companies away from the network for a time with an inter-regional religious quiz, and Southern that provided the network with *God's Trombone*, in which a light entertainment director, George Egan, had stars of stage and screen 'juggling before the altar'.

There was liveliness in Tyne Tees too. Its Head of Religious Broadcasting, Maxwell Deas, had formerly been on the stage, and if his understanding of religion was conventional enough, he had an eye to the visual. Such music programmes as *Fishermen of Staithes* and *A Steel Town Sings* brought the breath of a fresh Nor' Easter on to the screens. Further North, the Programme Controller of Grampian, James Buchan, a self-styled 'radical Catholic' seized what chances he could to network vigorous programmes. But the convention that then allowed regional companies only twelve network religious programmes a year between them did not encourage these initiatives, and tended to impose a feeling of Buggins' turn.

Not that the network companies lacked initiative. Rediffusion, with their weekday contract, had in Guthrie Moir a departmental controller of verve;

and it was on Rediffusion's *Frost Programme*, one weeknight, that Dr Michael Ramsey made himself at home with the ITV audience. The same company's serial, *Sanctuary*, set in a convent, took great pains to be authentic and not just pander to romantic notions of life in a nunnery. Granada, too, having with their five-day contract previously resisted any pressure to make programmes designated as religious, came with fresh eyes to the subject. In Norman Swallow and Denis Mitchell they had two film-makers of high distinction, and their studies of the Salvation Army in Liverpool or the decline of non-conformity in a West Riding dale deserve their place in the archives. The new contract arrangements established four networking companies operating at weekends instead of the previous two. Yorkshire and London Weekend would take their place alongside ATV and Granada to provide the network religious output.

To accommodate these new arrangements the companies themselves established the Network Religious Sub-Committee. It was chaired by Berkeley Smith, with all major companies represented and Maxwell Deas, Bob Macpherson of Scottish Television and Wynford Vaughan Thomas from Harlech on behalf of the ten regional companies. Its establishment provided a further marker for the place of religion in the total output.

Independent Television's place internationally was reflected by the election of Christopher Martin as the British member of the Central Committee of the World Association for Christian Communication (WACC), an organisation newly constituted in 1968 to serve the non-Catholic constituency. Shortly beforehand, the ITA had acted as host to a joint meeting of the Association's European committee and of its Roman Catholic counterpart, UNDA, from which came the establishment of the biennial International Christian Television Festival. One of the key figures in that initiative was Fr Agnellus Andrew, OFM, a member of the BBC's religious broadcasting department since 1941 and founding director of the Catholic Radio and Television Centre at Hatch End. In the summer of 1968 he retired from the BBC and became the Roman Catholic member of the ITA's Panel in place of Fr Geoffrey Tucker, who became ATV's adviser. Soon afterwards, with the goodwill of Dr Ramsey, Monica Furlong was appointed to fill a vacancy as Church of England member of the Panel.

The international meeting took place in Canterbury in April 1968, on the eve of ITV's own fourth religious consultation.[20] The coming of the new contract period made this consultation opportune. Its title, 'Response and Responsibility', sought to go beyond Durham's focus on the audience by examining what effects programmes have and what they should have. The ITA's recently appointed Head of Research, Dr Ian Haldane, paved the way with a fresh study of religion in Britain and Northern Ireland. It demonstrated very starkly the difference between an isolated province that took religion seriously and the mainland that was more inclined to pay it lip-service.

This was an arresting body of evidence for the consultation to digest. A dialogue between David Frost and (the then) Canon Hugh Montefiore offered little solace. A presentation of LWT's proposed *Roundhouse* by the redoubtable Doreen Stephens created a further stir. The Archbishop of Canterbury himself, the main guest speaker, said:

> Television, if it is to convey anything about Christianity, ought to consider positively and objectively what Christianity is really doing in the world as a phenomenon (and in fact Christianity is doing a very great deal in the world) . . . It includes a lot of ordinary human lives whose outlook is made totally different by their waiting upon God and taking God seriously.'

Five years after Cambridge, his notion of 'using television' had taken several steps forward.

How religion on ITV in the next contract period responded to this challenge is a subject for the next volume.

32

DUE IMPARTIALITY

In the closing stages of the Commons debate on the first Television Bill (see Volume 1) opposition speakers were unhappy about the vague generality of the programme control duties of the proposed Authority. They wanted these to be more precisely defined, and subjected to regular Parliamentary check on their proper fulfilment. The Government reply, that what was offensive to public feeling could not be other than what the Authority judged to be offensive and that 'due impartiality' would be what the Authority deemed duly impartial, left them uneasy. As with Humpty Dumpty, words were to mean what it chose them to mean. However, with the growth and spread of the ITV service it became increasingly clear that a workable interpretation of statutory duties could only be reached in *ad hoc* day-to-day dealings between ITA and companies in relation to particular television programmes and the problems that these raised in practice.

The 1964 Act repeated the 1954 Act in regard to due impartiality, but added a rider allowing a series of programmes to be considered as a whole. This fulfilled the undertaking in the White Paper to put beyond legal question the Authority's power to allow 'balance in series' (Chapter 23). Section 11 (5) of the 1964 Act empowered the Authority to require full details in advance of any programme which a company might offer for transmission, and was the basis on which the machinery of programme supervision and control was operated. It provided the sanction for the system already established of informal discussion and consultation in relation to a regular flow of programme information in the form of outline plans, synopses, scripts and, in relatively rare cases, previews. The rarity of the occasions on which ITA intervention meant actual refusal to transmit could well be taken as a measure of the success of this system. On the other hand total absence of error or conflict would be no grounds for self-congratulation. It was the more adventurous, imaginatively creative programme makers who ran the greatest risk of interference.

More often than not an intervention led to voluntary corrective action

by the programme company. Occassionally, however, there was disagreement and the dispute sometimes became public. This was almost inevitable
where a conscientious producer or reporter came to the conclusion in the
course of his investigation that one opinion or version of events was
demonstrably the right one and was able to gain the backing of his company
management. And this happened most often, as we shall see, with Granada
productions. The Authority for its part interpreted the wording of the Act as
meaning that no production could express, imply or suggest a judgement on
any controversial matter of current public concern. The fact that television
programme makers, like all other human beings, inevitably had personal
values, personal loyalties and predilections which were bound to have some
influence on their work could not justify any grinding of axes. It was the
Authority's view that in the treatment of such issues there should at all times
be exercised clearly apparent efforts to maintain, so far as humanly possible,
a carefully neutral balance. The critics of this policy – and there were
many – tended to substitute 'neuter' for 'neutral', figuratively equating
removal of bias with castration.

From the start the concept of 'balance' played a central, perhaps
excessive role in this interpretation of the impartiality requirement. It led at
times to a finicky counting of minutes given or words allowed to opposing
sides of a debate. But the rigidity was never absolute. With the passage of the
years and with growing experience, application of the control became less
crudely mathematical, dwelling more on the attitude and manner of
presentation of a programme as a whole.

Questions about lack of due impartiality were raised in their simplest
form when a single individual was given an opportunity for unchallenged
expression of controversial personal views. Thus when Michael Foot
appeared in Granada's *What the Papers Say* on 17 May 1962, ITA officers
found that he had used the programme as a vehicle for his own political
views. Although the company did not demur, their view that individual
editions of this series should not be judged separately but that one should be
taken together with a sequence of others was well-known to the ITA. 'The
essential thing is to see that alternative opinions . . . are given a hearing over
a period,' they had said to Pilkington.[1]

Within the field of political concern was an interview in the Norwich-
based company's local current affairs series, *About Anglia*. The interview,
transmitted on 22 November 1962 was with the Secretary of the Con-
federation of Health Service Employees (COHSE). It dealt critically with
the likely effects of cuts in the Health Service expenditure resulting from a
Ministry of Health economy drive. There was no spokesman for the

Government and no attempt to state the Government's case. The Ministry of Health complained that the programme was in breach of the Television Act. In reply the ITA agreed that a serious breach had occurred but explained that the matter had in fact already been taken up with the company immediately after the broadcast. Anglia subsequently tried to arrange a second programme in which the Government's case could be put, but the Ministry fought shy.

Another programme item dealing with the Health Service was one in the ATV *On the Braden Beat* series shown in February 1966. In this series Bernard Braden was cast in the role of spokesman and defender of the private citizen with a grievance against 'the system', be it tyrannical officialdom or dishonest commercial enterprise. From the standpoint of due impartiality, it was necessary to establish how far a particular grievance was legitimate, and what those accused had to say in their own defence. The item dealt with complaints against the Group Practice system as it was being operated in the new town of Harlow in Essex. A number of patients had certainly been removed from one Group Practice's list and were finding difficulty in getting on to another. Braden introduced the subject by contrasting the bright promise of a brave new world, illustrated by pictures of the New Town's hospital and medical centre, with the sense among the inhabitants that 'something is going wrong'. He quoted a few cases adding that there were many more, sufficient to fill the rest of the programme. Three doctors were also quoted as well as the local NHS Executive Council, but only selectively, i.e. in such a way as to imply that there were genuine grounds for patients' complaints. No other voice was heard in the programme. Everything was presented from Braden's point of view, seen through his eyes; and he delivered in conclusion a personal verdict that 'too many people are being dropped from doctors' lists and not accepted by other doctors'.[2]

A letter of complaint reached 'Dr the Rt. Hon. Lord Hill of Luton' from the Secretary of the local division of the BMA. This was followed by another from Lord Taylor, an eminent physician, who had played a prominent part in House of Lords debates on ITV. He happened also to be closely associated with the Harlow Medical Services, indeed had himself planned the Group Practice system in the new town. The ITA saw no alternative to an admission of fault and apology to both Taylor and the local BMA man; and, for redress, an invitation to Harlow doctors to take part in a further discussion of the group practice system in the town. It is doubtful whether later years would have seen the Authority adopting so purist a view. Of course there was something wrong with the GP services in Harlow. Nevertheless, the programme would certainly have been more defensible had the doctors been allowed to put their own case. That was what happened in the follow-up programme which ATV, in response to ITA pressure, showed on 28 May. Lord Taylor and the BMA's Essex division declared themselves 'completely satisfied with the outcome'. They were positively fulsome.

Equally vulnerable apparently were some of the early Frost programmes which were described by Rediffusion as 'programmes of comment, conversation, people and entertainment'. But their main feature was usually an interview conducted by Frost. The live interviews, before an invited studio audience, frequently with persons in the news, (and sometimes also on matters of public policy) naturally reflected that general satirical, anti-establishment, 'frondeur' mood of the mid-sixties which successive series of Frost programmes admirably exemplified. Recorded in ITA Minutes for December 1966 was the view that 'the Frost programme . . . in spite of occasional lapses and difficulties had found an acceptable format'. Nevertheless among the programme's lapses, in the Authority's view, was one shown in November 1967. It included an interview with Lord Russell of Liverpool, allowing the latter to make an unchallenged personal statement on a 'cause célèbre' of that time, the so-called A6 murders. There had been much public discussion of the trial and the possibility that the man convicted, Hanratty, was in fact innocent. Lord Russell's statement was nothing more than a lengthy attack on the recent decision by the Home Secretary not to hold an enquiry. No mention was made of the evidence given at the trial by the Crown witnesses, which had led to a conviction. The ITA staff's complaint produced an immediate admission from Rediffusion that they were in breach of the Act. They promised efforts to exact stricter self-discipline from the producers and presenters of these live broadcasts.

These were cases in which a solo statement by a single speaker was allowed to put forward a one-sided view on a matter of public policy. Often, however, the breach of impartiality could be implicit in the way in which the programme material was presented. An extended edition of Scottish Television's lively local daily news magazine Here and Now in March 1963 dealt with Dr Beeching's proposals for the future of British railways. Not only did the compere express his own critical opinions throughout without challenge, but the usual jaunty introductory signature tune of the series had been replaced by a mournful lament sounding over pictures of derelict railway yards. ITA staff remonstrance produced an STV apology and promise of tighter control. Yet the series erred again the following September in its coverage of a dispute between parents and a local education authority. The parents were refusing to send the children to school because they believed a bridge the children had to cross was unsafe. Three mothers were inter-viewed. The interviewer then drew attention to the absence of any spokesman for the local authority. They had been invited he said, but had pleaded prior engagements. While this was being said the cameras brought pictures of the two empty chairs in the studio which spokesmen for the local council and education department might have occupied.

This visual use of the 'empty chair' as an essentially rhetorical device to discredit one of the parties in a public dispute was, in the ITA's view, a clear breach of impartiality. The point had already been considered three months earlier when ATV were planning a new series *Fair Play* in which viewers were to be given an opportunity to air their grievances against authority, officialdom or traders before a sort of television 'ombudsman' in the person of lawyer and journalist Edgar Lustgarten. There had been an agreement that whenever the complaint was against 'authority' an attempt would be made to obtain the official attitude; but that if someone chose to refuse an invitation to appear, this would not be exploited to discredit the body concerned. The ITA recognised that there would be occasions when a company would wish to refer to the fact that it had extended an invitation. Whilst it was important that, by virtue of its refusal to state its case, the official body should not effectively veto discussion on the matter, it was desirable that every effort should be made to ensure that the absentee's point of view was explained as fairly and responsibly as possible.

So the STV programme had erred in two respects. Moreover, not only did it fail to make any effort to put the local authority's case but the interviewer even went on to tell viewers what three questions he would have put to them had they chosen to appear, leaving them of course unanswered. The impression created was therefore one of an elected local authority either unwilling or unable to justify its actions to its constituents. The company readily acknowledged that a serious breach had occurred.

In July 1964 there was an STV documentary called *Sink or Swim*. It dealt with the industrial situation in Britain and the crying need for greater cooperation between trade unions, employers and government if improve-ment was to be brought about. At first ITA staff showed disquiet that no Government spokesman was to be included and no mention of Government measures was even intended. But transmission was eventually approved on the understanding that the programme would clearly state that it was giving the views of only two of the three parties. Absence of a Government spokesman was condoned, provided the Industrial Training Act and the Contracts of Employment Act were both mentioned. This again seemed to imply that so long as the viewer was not misled, so long as he was left in no doubt that he was not getting all the divergent views on a situation, the law was being observed.

Yet when, in the first months of 1964, ATV had offered a three-part film series on China doubts were at once expressed. The film maker Felix Greene was known to be '*persona grata*' to the Chinese Communist authorities. No reassurance was found in the information that these authorities had given him 'unprecedented scope'.[3] Scripts were asked for. They confirmed suspicions that the series 'did not constitute an objective and impartial study of the subject'.[4] ATV were told that broadcast of a one-sided view of developments in China could not be justified even if it were made clear that it represented no more than the impressions 'for what they are worth' of one recent observer. Particular objection was taken to the scoop interview with Chou En Lai. It was described as an obvious propaganda piece, including imputations against United States policy that remained unchallenged.

The company were unwilling to accept this rebuff. They had, they believed, the most comprehensive, up-to-date film record of China available in the western world. Responsibly presented it could, they maintained, do much, whatever its shortcomings, to dissipate dangerous public ignorance about life in the largest country in the world. Exhaustive discussions followed. The outcome was an agreement to transmit the three programmes on certain conditions. Each of the three was to be introduced by a carefully worded statement which made clear Greene's strong sympathy with the Chinese people. Without going so far as to acknowledge bias, it pointed out that the Communist authorities had given him complete freedom to travel and film without supervision. The first two programmes were to be given postscripts in the form of a brief commentary by an independent expert. The third programme, that containing the Chou interview, was to be rounded off by a discussion in which an American and an English China watcher would take part. That was the form in which the programmes were shown after 10.30 p.m. on three successive Mondays in February and March 1964.

The behaviour of the ITA could well have seemed capricious. The statutory duty to ensure due impartiality related specifically to 'the news in whatever form' as well as to matters of political or industrial controversy, or current public policy. Programmes about conditions in China need not, one might plausibly argue, be included automatically in either of those categories. But any statement by eminent people on political, industrial or social issues could be seen as news, once it was promulgated in the mass media. In that sense, the accuracy and impartiality required of the news, *in whatever form*, might be held to embrace all factual public affairs programming of potential topical interest. The Authority was inclined to contend that the impartiality rule applied to all matters of public interest on which more than one responsible opinion was or could be held, irrespective of whether they could be defined as matters of political or industrial controversy or current public policy.

The issues raised by a programme in Rediffusion's *This Week* series shown on 3 August 1967 were more straightforward. It dealt with air safety and purported to show that passengers ran greater risks when flying with independent air lines than they did with the national corporations; that these risks were still greater on non-scheduled charter flights; and that this unsatisfactory state of affairs came about because of the way in which the independent companies were run in order to cut costs and maximise profits. There had been two serious air crashes, at Perpignan and Stockport, in one week and, six weeks earlier, a Government enquiry into British commercial air services had been set up. There was no doubt therefore that this was an important matter of current public policy. The programme made much of the allegedly excessive hours worked by some air crews; and referred in particular to the dangerous consequences of pilot fatigue.

The Independent Air Transport Association claimed that the programme breached the Television Act because it presented a distorted and unbalanced picture of the British Air Transport Industry, based on misrepresentation, selective use of evidence and suppression of material facts. They first approached Rediffusion and got no satisfaction. Repudiation of the Association's charges at producer level was backed at company boardroom level. It was then that they appealed to the ITA, presenting after some weeks' delay a carefully drafted document stating their case in detail. Rediffusion were asked for, and supplied, an equally detailed rebuttal. The ITA conclusion was that the programme took from the outset a clear editorial line on a matter of current public policy; and that by giving it backing at boardroom level the company had adopted that line as its own opinion. The evidence produced in support of the case that the safety levels of the independent air lines gave grounds for serious public concern was considered irrelevant; whatever the rights or wrongs, the Act was breached by the clear determination to make a case. Rediffusion were told their programme 'was in obvious breach of the Act',[5] under which it was not possible for a programme, having investigated a matter of public policy and come to the conclusion that one of a number of conflicting views was the right one, to adopt and promulgate that point of view and try to prove it right.

The company had no option but to accept this ruling. Whether they agreed with it is another matter. They might well have thought this was not a case of conflict between points of view; rather one between a not disinterested view and undeniable facts.

No single ITV series was the occasion of more discussion between Authority and company than Granada's *World in Action*. In connection with no other programme was the Authority's censorship more patently displayed nor more regularly challenged. The repeated and sometimes traumatic encounters between Granada management and Authority, and the discussions of principle (as well as programme detail) which these involved, brought into sharp focus the practical programme implications of the due impartiality law as the ITA interpreted it.

In 1963 *World in Action* had become one of ITV's regular weekday evening current affairs programmes and there was no disputing its high quality technically. By 8 March, the newspapers from the *Daily Mail* and *Daily Telegraph* to the *Daily Herald* and the *Daily Worker* were reporting the Authority's unprecedented action in refusing to transmit one *World in Action* programme because it lacked due impartiality. The declared intention of this programme, scheduled for transmission on 4 March, was to demonstrate scandalous waste of public money in much recent and current defence expenditure. A two-day Commons debate on Defence was still unfinished and the company sent a script on the day of transmission in order to find out, they said, whether, in the Authority's view, it infringed undertakings given at the time of the abolition of the old 'Fourteen Day Rule'. The staff ruled that it did so but went on to say that there was also a serious lack of impartiality in the programme which militated against its transmission even after the debate was over. Sir John Carmichael viewed the programme and agreed. Granada submitted amended versions which failed to satisfy. The programme was therefore withdrawn and both company and Authority made press statements. Both agreed that the facts of mis-spending reported in the programme were correct. The Authority added, however, that impartiality had not been preserved and because of the Act's requirements in this respect 'that must be the end of the matter'. Granada's statement said the company had no quarrel with the ITA 'who are bound by their interpretation of the Television Act',[6] the effect of which, they claimed, was 'to give programme companies less freedom than the BBC'. Support for this contention was forthcoming when a carefully chosen extract from the banned programme was shown in the BBC's *Panorama*. The Authority regarded the BBC's action as a rather shameful stunt.

Most commentators, including *World in Action*'s executive producer, Tim Hewat, professed difficulty in understanding why a programme should be suppressed for telling the truth. 'A factual, if over-dramatic presentation

was . . . suppressed because it implied criticism of the Government,' wrote
'Observer' in the *Financial Times*. Only the *Daily Mail* noted that the facts
had been selected to support a pre-formed judgement: 'Successes may have
been few and far between but it [the programme] mentioned none'. This
was to be the nub of most Authority rulings on impartiality over the coming
years. They rested on the simple, possibly naïve, belief that those accused in
public of misdeeds should be entitled to 'duly impartial' treatment, however
well-founded the accusations. That is to say whatever could also be said in
justification, explanation, mitigation or defence, should be given equal
public hearing. It was an attitude of mind that crusading journalists like
Hewat, his colleagues and successors found hard to accept.

It was not going to be easy to find a working compromise between these
two positions. When, after a summer break, *World in Action* returned in
September 1963, its first programme *The Guns* led to further Authority
action. The programme dealt with the deplorable living conditions of black
Africans in South Africa and neighbouring Portuguese Angola. In characteristically strident, melodramatic style it painted a picture of seething
incipient revolt in the first case and, in the other, bloody guerilla warfare
against cruel, oppressive, white colonial overlords. Hill received letters of
protest from the Portuguese Ambassador and the South Africa Foundation.
These listed alleged inaccuracies and complained, above all, of a tenden-
tious, patently biased, presentation. Not all charges of inaccuracy could in
fact be substantiated. There was certainly, however, some carelessly worded
scripting. Authority Members viewed the programme and found it not
impartial. They then went on to decide that henceforth all *World in Action*
and other current affairs programmes from Granada should be seen before
transmission by Authority staff.

Authority programme officers thus had the uneasy task of trying to turn
that ruling, with its negative and restrictive implications, to good account.
It could have been no more than a pre-emptive check on 'difficult' programmes but it was hoped that it could lead to more regular interchanges
between themselves and Granada current affairs producers, and that these,
in their turn, could perhaps contribute in time to greater mutual
understanding so that otherwise laudable journalistic zeal could be more
closely aligned with inescapable statutory responsibilities. But for the time
being at least that was not to be. For one thing, the Granada Board's high
sense of personal involvement and responsibility did not allow them to
countenance policy discussions and decisions about their programmes with
production executives rather than with themselves. Secondly, by the very
nature of television current affairs production, preview of transmission-

ready programmes, or even scrutiny of transmission scripts, could not be a very sensible or practical way of obviating lapses. It would seldom be possible to do either far ahead of scheduled transmission. Time to discuss and to make consequent desirable changes would therefore be limited. Banning or postponement of the programme could easily become the only available options. Such factors tended to make the ITA men appear to company production staff as busybody bureaucrats.

Nevertheless the first period of this pre-broadcast supervision passed with little or no overt friction. Minor changes in scripts were suggested and were made without too much difficulty. True the script of an 'enquiry' into Moral Rearmament had been found unacceptably biased; and was approved for transmission only after a couple of re-writes and finally a virtual remake. The many letters of critical protest that followed left the ITA unperturbed. The underlying tensions did not again emerge fully until the following June 1964. A programme on the allegedly inadequate training facilities available for British competitors in the Olympic Games was judged by Authority staff to be neither accurate nor impartial. It had probably been timed to coincide with a Commons debate on an Opposition motion cricising the Government's provision of funds for sport and other leisure activities.

Granada were not prepared to make all the changes requested, and so the programme was not transmitted. The company were told that, quite irrespective of the inaccuracies and careless use of figures they were in breach of the Act because the programme took a clear editorial line and presented only the one point of view on a matter of current public policy. The debate was itself evidence that an alternative point of view existed. Questions were asked in the House about the Authority's high-handed act of censorship.

The incident brought letters from Fraser to Peers and Bernstein painstakingly spelling out once more his interpretation of due impartiality. Whenever there are significant differences of opinion about the subject of a current affairs programme, he said,

then right at the start it must be the producer's aim so to shape the programme that these differences are fairly expressed or described . . . and the programme must not itself adopt one point of view rather than another . . . It should be impossible to tell from any programme on any subject within the field of current public policy or political or industrial controversy what are the opinions of the programme producers.

He accompanied these letters with a private note to Peers, expressing his regrets at having to write them: 'to me, as I am sure equally to you, these disputes and our failure to resolve them are becoming a very real anxiety. But we must not abandon the effort to reach a better understanding, and I will do all I can to play my part.'[7] Peers in due course replied. 'Your letters have not convinced me, but all at Granada are as anxious as you are to reach a better understanding and we will all do what we can to bring this about.'[8] So a meeting took place the following week, when Granada were told that, as a gesture of goodwill and in the interests of improved working relations, the company was to be relieved forthwith of the commitment to submit all scripts of *World in Action* for advance scrutiny. Fraser's recent letters should, it was said, have made clear to Granada what was expected of them, if they wished to avoid a reimposition of the commitment.

But good resolution was not enough. At the end of October *World in Action* presented a revised version of the Olympics programme to coincide with the return of the British competitors from Tokyo. Forman, who by now was acting as principal Granada go-between on such matters, had to be told that, although most of the questionable financial data in the earlier version had been removed, the programme still fell short of satisfying the requirements which the Authority considered necessary in order to comply with the provisions of the Act. Although relations remained friendly and as cooperative as an agreement to differ allowed, Granada were very obviously far from convinced that the ITA's understanding of due impartiality was the right one.

This would be well borne out in the months ahead. The following February a *World in Action* report on the Vietnam war concluded with a statement from Tom Driberg MP. It appeared to be a summing up and assessment of the mainly factual account given earlier, but in reality – as it seemed to the Authority – it was the expression of the views of one section of the Labour Party on a matter of current political controversy. But Granada saw no reason to be repentant.

Matters touched crisis point with the transmission on 3 August 1965 of a *World in Action* programme on the drugs industry. It accused the industry – with few exceptions – of gross overcharging for drugs supplied to the National Health Service and with giving false or misleading information in their advertising of patent medicines. The industry's much vaunted research activity (often adduced as the reason for high costs) was, the programme said, largely concerned with development of highly profitable alternatives, duplicating existing everyday remedies for the commonest minor ailments.

The drug industry reacted. A letter to Sidney Bernstein asked for a copy of the script. To Hill came a letter announcing the intention to make representations to the Authority that the programme did not comply with the provisions of Section 3(1)(e) of the Act. Authority staff agreed that the programme had not been impartial. Since the Government had recently set up a committee under Lord Sainsbury to investigate the drug industry's pricing policies, promotion, research and patents, they saw the subject matter of the programme as falling clearly within the area of current public policy. At the same time, with echoes of the Thalidomide story in mind, they agreed that the drug industry was not above criticism. Discussion with Granada produced an offer to the Association of the British Pharmaceutical Industry to appear in a second programme in which they would be able to give their side of the story to compensate for the very limited opportunity they had had in the first programme. The offer was refused.

The promised letter of representations from the ABPI turned out to enclose a voluminous document listing several items of alleged misleading or distorted statements in the programme. It asked for an agreed statement to be broadcast in which Granada would admit and apologise for their failure to preserve due impartiality.

But Granada was adamant that the ABPI was not owed an apology. They insisted that the programme was not a case for the prosecution to the virtual exclusion of any case for the defence: it was overwhelmingly a presentation of incontestable facts. Fraser vehemently disagreed and expressed his despair of ever getting Granada to understand that the Television Act and the terms of their contract prohibited them from doing what newspapers could do if they wished – take sides in a controversy. But Bernstein insisted in equally robust terms that the programme had presented nothing but facts. If the facts were unfavourable to the drug industry that was not due to editorial bias. It was not Granada which brought in the verdict. It was a case of the facts speaking for themselves. He suggested that there should be a meeting between Granada and Members of the Authority.

Hill agreed that this meeting should take place. It was not just desirable; it was necessary. For there were clearly fundamental differences of approach and understanding of the broadcasters' social and statutory responsibilities between the Authority and Granada. Some effort would have to be made to clear the air. The intervention of a General Election caused the proposed meeting to be delayed until 12 May 1966. The staff provided the Authority Members with a comprehensive written brief covering a whole range of other cases as well as the drug industry programme. One of them was a series on defence policy called *What Price Peace?* (February 1966). This had seemed to provide a very disturbing example of selective and misleading use of facts to support a pre-conceived editorial line. It concerned figures taken from a Gallup Poll relating to public attitudes towards nuclear arms.

The ITA staff brief was a painfully thorough job, but, unhappily for them, they failed to tell Granada that other programmes besides the drug industry one were intended to be discussed. Granada representatives therefore came unprepared. So discussion had to be confined mainly to this one programme, which had given rise to Bernstein's original request for a meeting. Sadly, little was apparently achieved apart from restatement of conflicting positions. No moves towards reconciliation of them were made. Hill stood firm: the Authority's job was to ensure the law was not contravened. It was against the law to put out programmes which did not give those criticised an adequate right of reply; and which, self-avowedly, conveyed a company viewpoint. Bernstein said that it was not a question of taking sides. There was undeniably a great deal wrong with the drug industry. That was fact, not opinion. He could not believe that it was the purpose of the Act to prevent public attention being drawn to those things that were wrong. In any case, Granada's legal advice had been that the drug industry was not covered by the section of the Act referring to due impartiality.

He was asked to provide a copy of this legal opinion, and what finally arrived at the beginning of September was a document from a QC, which stated that 'due' impartiality did not mean absolute impartiality (which was impossible), but a reasonable presentation of facts and arguments on both sides of a case. There could be cases, it said, where such a reasonable presentation of available facts produced more favouring one side at the expense of the other because that was the objective truth of the matter. There was no necessary obligation to try to give equal time (or lines of script) to both sides. Its second main argument was that, although the subject matter of the drugs programme was indeed a matter of public policy, it was not one which was 'current'. It did not therefore fall within the requirements of the Act.

The Authority's own opinion from Counsel dismissed these arguments. Given – inter alia – the appointment of the Sainsbury Committee there was no doubt that the programme had dealt with a matter of 'current' public policy. Moreover, whether or not a programme was duly impartial by virtue of its reasonable presentation of available facts and arguments was, under the terms of the Act (and programme contract), a matter for the Authority's opinion alone. And the Authority was under no obligation to give reasons for its opinion. Fraser was therefore instructed to write to Bernstein giving formal notice that a breach of contract had taken place.

There the matter rested. By this time the attention of the Authority Members was being claimed by preparations for a new round of contract awards. Questions on their interpretation of due impartiality could be raised with Granada spokesmen when they were interviewed on their application for a renewal of contract. There is no record of any serious disputes between the ITA and the company in this connection during 1967. Yet the basic cause of such disagreements – lack of any clear understanding between the Authority and the company about the governing principles of current affairs on television – had not evaporated. It would be well into 1969 before renewed efforts were made by both parties alike to reduce the incidence of sterile argument, to achieve more common understanding of the sometimes uncertain distinction between opinion and selected fact; and to define more defensibly and practically the nature of the due impartiality expected from what had long become – regardless of these troubles – one of the liveliest, most significant and successful current affairs departments in British television.

These were the ways in which some of the programmes of ITV in the years from 1963 to 1968 were affected by the legal requirement of due impartiality. About ten years later, in 1977, the Annan Report referred to the 'muddles that have grown up round due impartiality'[9], and attempted to define how it should be interpreted. It concluded that 'due impartiality should not be a shield behind which broadcasters shelter but a pass-key to open up public affairs'.[10] After this seemingly impeccable utterance, it went on to recommend that due impartiality 'should not preclude committed public affairs programmes from having a recognised place on the broadcasting outlets'.[11] The ITCA welcomed this recommendation, and in doing so they were voicing a view widely held amongst broadcasters. But the IBA's comment was that 'the recommendation glosses over the problems that occur in practice in fitting such committed programmes into a service that is duly impartial'.

33

THE NETWORKING TANGLE

In the light of the evidence from the Authority and from the companies, the Pilkington Committee had diagnosed the character of the network 'carve-up' that had come into being by the late fifties and early sixties and which was described in Chapter 33 Volume 1. The Report said:

> In summary, on the 'plural' form of organisation there has been superimposed a centralised control of programme planning. To say this is not to condemn the principle of networking. It is to recognise the reality of constitution behind the form. It is to recognise that between the commercial companies to which the franchises have been given there is little or no competition in the provision of programmes, so that the intentions of Parliament and the aim of the Authority have been frustrated: and that the companies, though independent of one another in the sense that no one company has a financial interest in any other, are not otherwise independent. The major companies are interdependent; the affiliates are dependent upon and, very largely, distributing agents for, the major companies. Finally, it is to recognise that the total franchise divided by the Authority into, and allocated to the companies by, areas has in effect been reassembled by the companies: and then divided by time.[1]

Soon after June 1962 pressure began to build. Here at least was an aspect of the Report with which the Government could go along in the certain knowledge that most MPs of whatever political persuasion would be in agreement. 'The present system,' said Bevins in the Commons debate on 31 July, ' . . . has a serious weakness. What it does is virtually to carve up the market between the four major companies and keep competition at bay.'[2] Even before the Report, the annual conference of the ACTT had passed a resolution calling upon their incoming General Council to examine the restrictions of the networking of television programmes originated by the smaller ITV companies 'by the virtual monopoly of network programmes by the major contractors'.[3]

As soon as it became clear in the first half of 1963 that the new Television Act would place the control of networking and of network prices in the hands of the ITA, the Standing Consultative Committee had work to do. The task it was set was so to adjust the existing network agreement as to remove the element in it which provided for a company to pay their network parent a proportion of their net advertising revenue unrelated to their actual 'take' of programmes.

The subject was potentially explosive. Fraser reported on 5 July that 'Captain Brownrigg favoured me this morning with his comments on our proposals for network programme prices, which he described as a bombshell sufficient to blow him to Wimbledon, where he was meaning to spend the afternoon'.[4] What sort of day Brownrigg had on the centre court is not recorded, but the fact is that within two weeks some new principles were agreed. Programmes prices paid by regional companies should be related to their net advertising revenue (i.e. to their capacity to pay): but collectively they should guarantee to take or pay for a fixed minimum number of hours of 'live' programmes per week, i.e. excluding fictional films, the purchase price of which would be shared by all companies on the basis of their population coverage. Certain expensive 'special event' programmes would also be outside the agreement, the costs being shared by all companies on a coverage basis. Fraser was able to tell the Authority on 25 July that negotiations had gone well and that an agreement might be ready for it to receive in September.

And so it was. It was the biggest concerted effort so far made by the companies and the ITA to secure a voluntary agreement on a matter involving the reconciliation of many conflicting interests. As a result of intensive negotiation amongst the Four and the Eleven separately, between each of the two groups, between each of them and the ITA and finally between all together, a consensus was found.

The SCC met on 21 August with Fraser, as usual, in the chair, and with remarkably few reserve members needing to attend. Adorian of A-R, Cecil Bernstein of Granada, Grade of ATV and Thomas of ABC were all present. By this time the British Regional Television Association (BRTA) had been formed, with Gill of Border TV as its first chairman and principal spokesman. The ITA had worked out a scale for assessing programme payments from the Eleven to the Four on the basis of their net advertising revenue after levy (NARAL). The Minutes read:

> . . . *Mr Cecil Bernstein* said that, as regards the supply of programmes from the Four to the Eleven, the Four were now prepared to accept the scale set

out in the ITA Paper coupled with a guarantee of 30 hours of live programmes a week being available for, and paid for by, the Eleven.

Mr Gill confirmed that the Eleven were prepared to accept the guarantee of 30 hours and a scale which provided the Four with an annual sum of £3 million for 30 hours a week . . . As regards the sale of programmes from the Eleven to the Four, it had been agreed that, if a regional company wished to offer a programme to the network, it would offer it to the Programme Planning Committee in the normal way and, if it was agreed that the subject was suitable and the slot available, the Programme Planning Committee would agree the budget . . . The agreed cost of the programmes would be shared by all companies in accordance with the official scale for live programmes . . .

The Chairman expressed his appreciation to the companies for the way they had reached agreement between themselves in settling the complex matter of network programme prices.[5]

Originally the Four had sought a payment of £3.5 million. As for the Eleven there had been much heart-searching: there were those who wished to be assured a guaranteed network provision and others who were fearful that a guaranteed offer coupled with a guaranteed 'take' might inhibit the exchange among regionals of their own programmes. What had become pretty clear, however, was that, in practice, the number of hours of live programmes available in the network would be substantially more than the guaranteed minimum. The current figure was running at around forty-four hours a week and nobody saw it falling in the future below thirty-eight. In other words there would be reasonable scope for the Eleven to exercise a choice between the network programmes on offer. The old 'affiliate' system was dead; the new agreement and the new Programme Planning Committee (subsequently called the Network Planning Committee) made it obsolete.

All this fell a long way short of 'free trade'. To what extent it would eliminate the worst features of the 'carve-up' remained to be seen. If, for the present, the monopoly remained, it had become a qualified monopoly, operating under the supervision of an Authority which now had complete power of control over the sale and purchase of programmes by the terms of Section 4 of the 1963 Act (which was to become Section 15 of the consolidated Act of 1964).

Over the five years between September 1963 and September 1968 no subject (with the possible exception of labour relations) occupied more collective management man-hours or imposed more stresses and strains on

ITV's plural system than the planning and pricing of the movement of programmes between what had now become the fourteen companies. This planning could be light, flexible and elastic, allowing for change and growth, or it could be rigid, tight and expressed in production quotas for each company that hardly ever changed. In the event, so much did the planning tend towards the second form that the Authority resolved that, in the contracts from 1968 on, there should be a lifting of many controls and a marked swing towards freedom and competition in the production and exchange of programmes. As the franchise trail wound its course through the first half of 1967, the talk was once again of free trade even though the ideal of a 'competitive optional network' that had been harboured by the founding fathers of 1954 had come to be seen as unattainable.

The arrangements prevailing by January 1967 came under five separate headings:

Movements from the Four to the Ten:
'Live' programmes were the most frequent. As we have seen, the ITA in 1963 decided that, as a matter of principle, payments for network programmes should be related to their value to the purchasing company and to that company's ability to pay. To give effect to this principle, a sliding scale related to the net advertising revenue after levy (NARAL) had been evolved. This was notified to applicants for the 1964 contracts so that they would be able, in preparing their applications, to know how much their basic supply of programmes would cost them. It was indicated that the Authority would not approve arrangements for the supply of programmes which led to a greater payment than the scale gave. It was weighted in favour of the company with a smaller advertising revenue and against the company with a larger one. An example of this was that in 1965/6 Border, with an advertising revenue of £575,000, paid £61,000 for its whole annual network programme supply, while Tyne Tees, with a revenue of £3,417,000 after levy, paid £601,000 for virtually the same amount of programmes.

However, instead of the scale running free so as to produce a collective payment from the Ten to the Four governed solely by their individual NARALS, the Ten agreed with the Four that they would each take (or pay for) not less than thirty hours a week of network programmes, in return for which the Four agreed to a ceiling of £3 million per annum for the first year (1964/5). As it happened, because NARALS increased more than was originally expected, this provided a good bargain for the Ten who, had the ceiling not been imposed, and had the scale applied to the actual income for that year, would have paid collectively that year not less than £3¾ million. For 1965/6, broadly similar arrangements continued, the collective payment of £3 million for thirty hours becoming £3.6 million and for the year 1966/7, the total payment had risen to £3.85 million. Even though the scale was not used to determine completely the actual payments by the Ten, it was used to allocate among them the agreed collective payment.

In practice, although the use of the scale meant that the value of the programmes (in terms of what they would earn for the purchaser) and the purchaser's ability to pay (which was governed by his advertising revenue) were adopted as the criteria of payment, the yield of the scale to the Four represented a broadly fair share of the average cost of a network programme.

For cinema films and American television films, the actual cost of acquiring the British rights was normally shared between the Four and the Ten on the basis of *unweighted* NARAL. For new British television film series, as with those produced by ATV production companies, e.g. *Danger Man* and *Thunderbirds*, the collective price to the regions was fixed by negotiation. The sale in these cases was to BRTA who divided up the liability for payment among the members according to unweighted NARAL. If the production of a successful programme like *The Avengers* was transferred from the television studio to the film studio, the cost to the Ten went up. As a live show, it would be available to the Ten for a cost of about £2400 per hour-long episode. As a film the cost to them per episode was likely to be about £5000 for two showings. This latter figure would be distributed also on the basis of unweighted NARAL, which meant that the smaller regions paid a higher proportion than they would if the scale had applied.

Distribution of Ten's payments among the Four

The collective payments made to the Four by the Ten were distributed in the proportions of: Rediffusion 25 per cent, Granada 25 per cent, ATV 30 per cent and ABC 20 per cent. This corresponded only very broadly with the required originations of the Four and bore no necessary relationship to the selection of programmes by the Ten. Any one of the Four which was less successful with its programmes than the others suffered no consequent financial loss so far as payment from the Ten was concerned.

Supply of programmes among the Four

There was a set of individual bilateral agreements. These agreements most often had the feature that the two parties agreed to make available to each other specified amounts (sometimes equal, sometimes unequal) of programme material, and each agreed to take a specified minimum amount (invariably less than the total on offer) with notional payments, usually unequal, being attached to the programmes. For example, the original Rediffusion/ATV agreement provided for an average minimum supply from ATV to Rediffusion of five hours of live programmes a week and of seven-and-a-half in the reverse direction. A schedule to the agreement gave a notional price for programmes ranging from £2000 for a one-and-a-half-hour drama, to £750 for a half-hour feature. Rediffusion paid 40 per cent of the scheduled price and ATV 20 per cent. This disparity reflected the value to Rediffusion, with its large London weekday audience, of an ATV programme, compared with the value to ATV, with its smaller Midland weekday audience, of a similar programme. As between ATV and Granada, the arrangement was that each company made available to the other the whole of its live output on the terms that for each hour taken Granada would pay ATV £700, while ATV paid Granada £420. The arrangement between ATV and ABC for weekends was quite different in that the payments made were much more realistic, and were negotiated for each show, or series of shows, taken by the other: the market-place bargaining between these two companies which we noted in Volume I continued to prevail.

Movements from the Ten to the Four
When a regionally produced programme was taken by one or more of the Four, the normal payment to the producing company represented a due proportion, on a NARAL basis, of the direct costs and of a standard figure (varying with the type of programme) for indirect costs.

Movement among the Ten
It was agreed that the selling company would receive from the purchasing company one half of what the latter would pay if the scale were strictly applied for a programme of that length from the Four.[6]

The guarantee on the part of the Ten to take a minimum weekly average for a minimum collective price had the disadvantage of discouraging regional programme production and the exchange of programmes between regionals. 'Why should we,' a company could ask themselves, 'produce more than we need of programmes of our own when we cannot fit them in easily without dropping a programme from the Four which we have to pay for anyway?' The reciprocal guarantee on the part of the Four to supply a minimum number of programmes was not in the event necessary as a safeguard to the Ten, for an adequate supply was secured by the need of the Four to fill their own programme schedules, quite apart from any origination requirements which the ITA imposed.

The Authority had come to believe that the distribution of the Ten's payments on a fixed percentage basis should cease. Companies selling to the Ten should be paid for what they sold. If they were successful they would earn more; if not, they would earn less. As things were, the main producing companies were shielded from competition in this respect. Moreover, the arrangements for the supply of programmes among the Four meant in effect that each was committed to taking, more or less blind, a fixed amount of programmes from others, regardless of quality. Here again it was believed that guarantees should go. Their abolition might also facilitate the entry of more regional programmes into the central areas.

In the Authority's view, the fixed production quotas and exchanges of the Four had become a hindrance to free growth and development and the selection of programmes on merit. By the time each had discharged their contractual obligation to produce their quota of programmes, they had produced between them more than enough programmes to meet all their own needs in their areas. Since none of them wished to be left with a programme they could not sell to the others, mutually beneficial arrangements were made by which each engaged to take a minimum quantity of programmes from the others. And since these arrangements helped them to spread the cost of producing their individual quotas, they had a severely limited interest in using programmes from the Ten. At the same time the division of the payments by the Ten in fixed proportions diminished the financial incentive to any of the Four to increase the supply of their programmes to the Ten by making them better and more attractive than those of the other three.

The ITA decided to do all it could to free the production and exchange of programmes from these rigidities. It envisaged that any network company would be able, over and above its own programmes, to select for its transmissions the programmes it preferred from all other companies, the regional companies no less than the other main companies. On the other side of the coin, they would no longer have a guaranteed sale of their programmes, however little these might deserve it, to other network companies. Thus the company, as a supplier, would do well or ill according to the merits of their product, and the size of their production would rise or fall over the years according to the demand for their programmes and so would their proportion of the annual payment. There would then be no 'take it or leave it' attitude to regional sales, but an incentive to produce programmes good enough to be preferred. A member of the Ten would be able to substitute for a network programme a programme of their own, or a programme from another of the Ten.

The consequence of these changes, so it was thought, would be that individual companies would be responsible singly for the combination of programmes which they proposed to transmit. That would accord with the theory on which the two Television Acts had been based. The central question was whether, against the economic forces within the system making for stability and regularity in programme production, it was a plan any less starry-eyed than the original dream of free trade under a 'competitive optional network'. Was it once again to prove to be a Utopian dream, a conception of the desirable which in the nature of things could not be achieved?

Whatever doubts or reservations there may have been – and if they did not exist already they were soon to be expressed by the surviving companies – the Authority proceeded to state in the contract details sent to applicants for post-1968 contracts that a number of changes affecting the networking of programmes would be introduced from the end of July 1968. In summary, these changes were fivefold. First, initially at least, the requirement on companies operating in the four central areas of London, Midlands, Lancashire and Yorkshire to produce a specified amount of programmes would be removed; secondly, the reciprocal guarantees of supply and purchase between the major and the regional companies would cease; thirdly, there would be freer choice in the selection of programmes by the major companies among themselves; fourthly, a change would be made in the method of payment for programmes exchanged among the major companies from that of payment on a notional basis to one related to programme costs; and fifthly, there would be a change in the scale of payments for network programmes.

After much discussion proposals were agreed between the companies in August 1967 covering the basis of payment for programmes up to the end of the contracts in July 1968. They were in no way revolutionary, and they received the ITA's agreement without argument but without enthusiasm. They elicited one wry comment from the Head of Finance, A. S. Curbishley: 'So we are apparently being asked to take not a single step in the direction of our declared 1968 wind-of-freedom objective'.[7]

If these words implied scepticism or even apprehension about the future course of events, such implications were to be amply fulfilled. The problems that were thrown up and which had to be teased out by all concerned, especially by the New Five and the ITA, could with little exaggeration be described as nightmarish. By the time the contracts took effect these complicated issues had not so much been resolved as buried beneath a welter of argument and counter-argument. Nevertheless, the new arrangements and procedures which haltingly took effect and became refined by means of trial and error proved in the next decade to be a basis for programme planning which was in the main free from the worst faults which existed under the old contracts. No record of this year-long struggle between the summers of 1967 and 1968 can be found in the annual reports, and nor even was its course charted in the proceedings of the Authority itself or of any of the regular committees like the PPC or the SCC. The discussions took place in those legendary smoke-filled rooms, and bulky but confused documentation in the files of the ITA and the companies are the only monument to the tribulations of chief executives and accountants.

The ITA wanted every company to be responsible singly for the combination of programmes they transmitted; it wanted all companies to be free to choose from the available supply those programmes which they thought best; it wanted a measure of competition between the network companies for the acceptance of their programmes by other companies; and it was opposed to any arrangement which compelled one company to accept in their schedules a minimum quantity of programmes from another. But it also yearned for a single standardised schedule in the main viewing hours; and it had become worried by the increasing diversity between the schedules of the three major weekday companies. The problem was how to secure such a standardisation, without which competition with the BBC was unlikely to be successful, but at the same time avoid the system of programme quotas which had nullified free competitive enterprise under the old dispensation. By January 1968 Forman was expressing in a forceful letter to Fraser the Granada view that competition between the majors to sell programmes both to each other and to the regionals was incompatible with cooperation in scheduling and planning. In their own case Granada needed a guaranteed outlet for their programmes in London, without which they could not hold or attract talent.

A fracture in the ITA's armour became manifest when Fraser agreed that there should, for an initial period, be a fixed division between the Five of the payments by the Ten. He did so in response to arguments that 'the attempt to reach agreement on the basis we had proposed was exercising a malign influence on the planning of the programmes. Instead of concentrating on the production of the best possible composite schedule of the Five, each company was jostling for a position in the composite schedule which would prove most financially rewarding to it.'[8] At the same time, he said that 'the

Five have been left in no doubt that "payment by results" remains our policy'.[9]

Some sort of solution began to emerge when the five companies ingeniously suggested a points system based on agreed prices for programmes. Each company would earn points for every programme taken by others, including the regionals. 'I do confirm' wrote Grade on behalf of the companies, 'that there will be no bulk deals to take programmes at anything other than the agreed scale of prices. In other words, all payments and receipts will simply be as per the agreed price list and based on actual usage.'[10] The system of tariff prices for different categories of programmes (as distinct from the actual costs which varied from one programme to another) proved to be the basis on which networking was to proceed under the new contracts. To reconcile this with its condition announced in the programme contract application forms, that the price basis for exchanges between the five central companies should reflect the full cost of the programmes concerned, the ITA made it a condition that companies should produce at agreed intervals actual direct cost figures for each programme, programme series or programme category for which a 'tariff cost' had been determined and details of their indirect costs during that period. The books would be made up, as it were, and any credits or debits adjusted between the accountants. That was on 12 June 1968 and at this point we must leave the continuing saga to be taken up in the next volume.

In parallel with the programme-pricing negotiations progress also had to be made in planning the supply of network programmes after July, not as hitherto by a mosaic of three weekday companies and two weekend ones but by three seven-day companies (ATV, Granada and Yorkshire), one 'long London' company (Thames), and one 'short London' company (LWT). Since rigid quotas were now taboo, some other basis had to be found for planning in quantitative terms the relative output of networkable programmes from each of the new Five. Without knowing the scale of potential usage of their wares by the network these central companies, especially the two new ones, would be in a hopeless situation. A nicely balanced exercise in 'indicative planning' was necessary, and this was based upon prospective NARAL – skilfully estimated by A. S. Curbishley – for the system as a whole and also the companies individually. Early in 1969, some six months after the new contracts came into force, a total of ninety-four programme hours was being sold by the Five to one another. Of this total ATV's share was rather more than a third, Thames' rather more than a quarter, Granada's and LWT's about a sixth each and Yorkshire's less than a tenth. The relatively high shares of ATV and to some extent of Thames were accounted for by the fact that the hourage included ITC and ABPC filmed series. It could not be said that a stable, mutually satisfactory system had yet been established, and nor could it be said with any certainty how much further the ITA's cherished plan for a genuinely competitive network would have to be compromised in order to lift ITV out of the state of recession and loss of confidence into which it had by that date sunk.

34

THE ADVERTISING SCENE

The net advertising revenue of the companies (before levy) in the year ending 29 July 1965 was £82,619,000; in the following year it fell to £82,017,000, but thereafter rose to £89,945,000 in 1967 and £95,930,000 in 1968, (say £375 million in 1981 terms). The fall in 1966 could largely be accounted for by the Government's decision to prohibit cigarette advertising on television which took effect on 1 August 1965.

National advertising was by far the largest provider of revenue, most of it coming from a relatively small number of large advertisers. Half of the income came from the advertising of food and drink; 20 per cent came from household equipment and stores; and pharmaceutical goods, toiletries and cosmetics accounted for a further 10 to 12 per cent. Local advertising on the separate stations accounted for no more than 2–3 per cent of total advertising revenue, but the percentage varied between one regional company and another.[1]

So the scene was seemingly set fair. ITV's principal source of income was rising by about 5 per cent a year. Despite rising costs, the levy and a deteriorating relationship with the trade unions, profits were high; between 1964 and 1968 the yearly profit averaged £18.3 million – a return of around 50 per cent on capital.[2]

ITV was able to take in its stride the changes in the system of advertising control which, following Pilkington, were called for in the new legislation. The Act gave statutory backing to control arrangements based broadly on a system developed by the ITA and the companies in the course of their cooperative control of advertising from the opening of the service in 1955. In the new Act, however, the position of the ITA was clarified and it was empowered to assume a more direct role in the setting of standards and in the day-to-day decisions relating to the acceptance of advertisements by reference to these standards.

The Authority had the duty and the power to exclude from television any advertisement that could reasonably be said to be misleading; and to define, in consultation with the PMG, the classes and descriptions of advertisements and methods of advertising that should not be accepted for broadcasting. In consultation with its Advertising Advisory Committee and with a panel of independent medical consultants, it drew up a comprehensive code of standards and practice which was published in July 1964, and with which manufacturers and traders and their advertising agencies must seek to comply if they proposed to use television for their advertising. Its specialist staff, together with the programme company specialists, examined the scripts and finished films of advertisements before they were accepted for television. The advice of members of the Medical Advisory Panel was taken about any advertisement for a proprietary medicine, treatment or appliance, any toothpaste, toilet product or food product for which a medical claim was made, any advertisement for veterinary goods, and many others. To supplement the daily discussion of individual advertisements between the specialist staffs of the ITA and the companies in relation to the rules, there was a formal link in a Joint Advertisement Control Committee under the chairmanship of the Authority's Head of Advertising Control.

Consultation with independent experts covered advertising well beyond the range of the medicines and treatments, medicated toilet products, toothpastes and veterinary goods specifically laid down in the Act. The advice of the appropriate member or members of the Medical Advisory Panel was sought for advertisements for foods, drinks, or sweets, for which any health or dietary advantage was claimed; for hairsprays, cosmetics and disinfectants; and for any other products on which the specialists' advice seemed to be desirable.

Of the 7500 scripts examined centrally in 1964/5, almost 1000 (13 per cent) for some 250 different products were in the medical and allied classes. 20 per cent required some amendment to ensure that the advertisements would be in line with the provision of the Code of Standards and Practice. On many points there could be differences of opinion. In some cases changes were required because long-standing beliefs were no longer accepted by medical practitioners – for example, as regards the connection, if any, between dandruff and other skin conditions. The results of research carried out abroad and accepted as the basis for advertising claims in their country of origin were not always accepted by the consultants of ITV and this had its effect on some advertisements. There had to be some changes in the wording or perhaps the inclusion of visual signs to make sure that 'presenters' would be taken by viewers to be commercial representatives of the advertisers and not understood to be doctors or other professionally qualified advisers. The latter could not be employed to present a proprietary medicine in a television advertisement. In a few cases it was necessary to object to one of the main propositions of an advertisement to such an extent that it had to be changed radically if it was to be accepted at all. They included several 'tonics', a product for the relief of rheumatic pain and a product for the treatment of dandruff.

Although the Television Act did not require it, the companies retained the services of independent consultants in analytical chemistry and engineering, whose advice was often sought on the technicalities of claims for paints, petrols, oils, adhesives, fertilisers, insecticides, polishes, domestic appliances, disinfectants and washing and cleaning products of all kinds. Discussion covered, amongst other things, the effects of lathering in washing products and washing-up liquids, the merits of additives in washing powders, the prevention of scaling on water-heaters in washing-machines, the germicidal properties of disinfectants and their effectiveness in floor cleaners, and the effects of grease-solvents.

So far as the hazards of cigarette smoking were concerned, the Government exercised its own power of direction. Since publication of the report on 'Smoking and Health' by the Royal College of Physicians in 1962, there had been no television advertising of cigarettes before about 9 p.m. and the advertisements had been governed by rules designed to exclude them from certain methods of presentation that were believed to have a special appeal for young people. Early in 1965 the Government came to the conclusion that the continuance of this advertising on television would be at variance with their general efforts to make cigarette smokers aware of the health hazards involved and to dissuade young people from starting the habit. A ban on the advertising of cigarettes on television was announced in Parliament by the PMG on 2 March 1965, effective five months later.

The established limitation in the amount of advertising to a maximum of six minutes an hour, averaged over the day's programmes, continued unchanged. Within that average there was a maximum of seven minutes in any one clock-hour subject to some flexibility, taking one hour with another, to fit in with the timing of programmes and the natural incidence of intervals in them. Rules designed to limit the number of advertising periods to an average of about three an hour were also maintained.[3]

In 1965 the Consumer Council – a newly established quango – made representations that thirty-six television advertisements for twenty-five products or services were typical of advertisements which, in the Council's opinion, were allowed in breach of the Authority's Code of Advertising Standards and Practice. Having checked some of the facts with ITA staff, the Council withdrew a number of these cases. There were left nineteen advertisements for seventeen products which the Council took to be in breach of the Code. All of them were for proprietary medicines and similar goods.

These representations were first considered in detail by the two main medical members of the AAC in consultation with the three general medical members of the Medical Advisory Panel. The AAC then considered them, taking account of the conclusions of these medical experts. The Committee checked the scripts and viewed the advertisement films in question in relation to those requirements of the Code of Advertising Standards and Practice which the Council believed to have been breached. It found no substance in the Council's claim that the Code was not being properly applied, and this conclusion was subsequently endorsed by the Authority.

Other advertising issues which came up for discussion and decision between 1964 and 1968 included such varied matters as the use of selective quotations from reviews in commercials for theatrical productions, the use of ITV programme personalities (such as news-readers) and/or actors identified with well-known TV fictional characters, advertising in the intervals between religious programmes; advertising by subsidiaries of ITV companies; the acceptability of commercials for sanitary towels and tampons; and the excessive repetition of the same advertisement in a sequence of advertising intervals. The subject of betting and football pool advertising lay dormant and did not come to a head until 1969.

Despite the stringency of all the controls, television, as the ITCA was to point out to the Annan Committee some years later, tended to draw the fire of those who were critical of advertising in all its forms.[4] This was a tribute to its effectiveness; and it can only be seen as remarkable that, after all the fuss about it in Parliament in 1954 and again in 1963, the volume of substantial public criticism was so small right through the sixties. 'Self-policing is self-protection.'[5]

Although, as we shall see in Chapter 37, it was not without critics, ITV's devotion to regionalism was as strong in the field of advertising as in programming. The relatively low percentage of regional as compared with national advertising on television should not obscure its value for the purposes of test-marketing; moreover, local preferences or limitations on distribution could be taken into account in the planning of the advertising agencies. In the main the companies maintained their individual sales departments, and joint selling by STV and Grampian, and Westward and Channel, were exceptions which the ITA accepted as justified by special circumstances. Here was an area where competition between the companies was genuine and sometimes intense, particularly in London. ITV in the sixties pioneered a trend towards regionalism and devolution which was increasingly followed in other media. 'A plurality of sales forces has a great deal to recommend it from the point of view of both the advertiser and the television company,' said the ITCA.[6]

Advertising charges were listed on the companies' rate cards in basic prices for 'spots' of seven, fifteen, thirty or sixty seconds' duration, varying according to the time of day. All rate cards made provision for discounts or surcharges. There were 'run of the week' spots sold at discount because day and time of transmissions were not specified, and there were 'pre-emptible' rates which allowed a spot to be sold at a cheaper rate than normal because it was subject to cancellation if another booking materialised at the full price. There were also volume discounts as well as specially reduced rates for local advertisers. On the other hand 'special positions' could be bought on payment of surcharges. The structuring of the rate cards was all-important, and a sales director could succeed or fail according to the skill and judgement which went into it. Only the 'form and manner' of the rate card was subject to ITA approval, because its statutory powers were limited to ensuring that there was no 'unreasonable discrimination' against or in favour of any particular advertiser. It had no jurisdiction over the prices charged.

Reporting to the Annan Committee the ITCA said:

Airtime salesmen throughout the television industry need to be . . . conversant with the marketing requirements of every one of their clients. They have to interpret complicated permutations of audience research data to media buyers in advertising agencies. They have, above all, to interpret sociological and marketing statistics about the area and product sales data, in a wide range of product fields, to marketing executives in industry whose decision it is whether to advertise in their market and how much to spend, whether to test-market a product or conduct some other kind of specialist marketing requiring television support. Sophisticated selling of this kind is essential if maximum revenue is to be obtained.[7]

Such was the advertising scene during the period covered by this volume. If, despite the forebodings of 1963, ITV remained a prosperous industry, whilst growing in stature as a public service broadcaster, much was due both to its collective self-discipline in the maintenance of advertising standards and to the professional skill of its sales executives. In each of these respects it gave a lead to other media, so that it was probably true to say that Britain provided not only the best broadcasting but also the best advertising in the world.

35

TECHNICAL BACKGROUND

The emphasis must be on the word 'background'. It is self-evident that the very existence of broadcasting and of its television component stems from the inventive genius of electrical and electronic engineers and that, furthermore, the institutions of broadcasting in Britain as in other countries were moulded by the technical characteristics of the creation and propagation of radio waves. Readers of Volume I will have seen the extent to which the very shape of Independent Television was conditioned by technical circumstances and its evolution over the years has been greatly influenced by progressive changes in these circumstances. The foreground history of ITV engineering remains to be written, and justice to it cannot be done, except inferentially, in a history with a predominantly political and institutional motif. This chapter is no more than a reminder of the existence of a world within which ITV, as viewers know it, grew to maturity and without which it could neither have existed nor thrived.

The first transmitting station at Croydon was based on a single laboratory prototype Marconi 10kW transmitter and an experimental omnidirectional aerial on a temporary 200ft tower with an effective radiated power of 60kW. If any fault developed there were no fall-back arrangements: yet in the first few months loss of vision was minimal. Meanwhile a second transmitter and new aerial tower were being built, together with the new stations at Lichfield near Birmingham, Winter Hill near Manchester and Emley Moor near Huddersfield.

The transmitter engineers recruited by P. A. T. Bevan, working in close collaboration with industry, concentrated on the task of making these early stations reach as many people as possible: aerials with complex directional power-radiation patterns: juxtaposition of vertical and horizontal polarisation: beam tilts, the use of frequency offsets. The early ITV programmes had to be accommodated within four Band III channels, all that the Government made available in the first years. To increase power the engineers pioneered, first at Lichfield and shortly afterwards at Croydon, the technique of using two high-power Band III transmitters delivering their outputs to a common aerial. It seems likely that Lichfield was the first occasion this idea had been put into practice in any country.

A major planning problem was to create an inter-city programme distribution network: for financial as well as engineering reasons this initially overshadowed in immediacy and importance almost every other aspect of engineering. The Post Office would provide, as it did for the BBC, the basic network of microwave and coaxial cable video links. But this still left open the problem of who would do the detailed network switching which, because of the regional shape being given to ITV, would require frequent switching between the various regional and local studio centres from which the advertisements as well as regional programmes would come. Such a network would involve a degree of switching vastly different from anything previously undertaken. The Authority asked the Post Office if they would be prepared to set up switching centres and run them. The Post Office, to put it mildly, were reluctant; their engineers had never previously been called upon to *control* the switching of television programme material.

The ITA recognised that this reluctance stemmed from a fear that engineers would have to monitor the programmes and to switch on cues that might well be delayed by over-running (for after all this was an era of 'live' television in the days before the videotape recorder revolutionised TV production). And so it provided a daily switching schedule indicating in hours, minutes and seconds exactly when the switching would be carried out. To preserve flexibility, arrangements were made to allow the schedule to be changed at short notice; otherwise the Post Office would simply switch away from any programme that over-ran by even a few seconds. 'Lines Booking' was a key unit at ITA, straddling the responsibilities of programme and engineering staff; its services to ITV as a whole deserve a meed of praise.

While transmitters and inter-city networks were ultimately the responsibility of the ITA, the studio centres were the creation of the programme companies. Soon a cluster of new studio complexes was being built. Television House in Kingsway; hurriedly converted film studios at Elstree and Wembley; underground at Foley Street in Central London; the Granville Theatre in Chelsea; Wood Green in North London; Alpha Studios in Birmingham; Quay Street and Didsbury in Manchester. These first studios were rushed. There was often no master time synchronisation, so that when switching to another studio the picture might shift an inch or two on every screen. But they worked. The basic design reflected a refreshingly new approach to television planning and design, based more on American than traditional British concepts.

As money flowed into the system greater sophistication became possible. The first 405-line videotape recorders arrived in 1958. In the wake of Granada in Manchester, ABC at Teddington established one of the most advanced purpose-built studio centres, introducing new ideas in control suites, new ideas for better communication between controllers and the studio floor. Gradually the equipment was taken out of the studios into technical areas where telecine machines or video tape machines or cameras could be assigned to any of the studios.

In a few years the system was transformed. Networking made technical cooperation and common standards between the companies essential. Even the engineering relationship with the BBC began to change about 1962 as more and more of the senior engineers found themselves sitting on the same national and international committees. However, ITV engineering still retained some of the feel and motivation of the early days – the desire to cut through establishment hierarchies; to believe that problems could be solved by small teams working closely with industry; not to fear borrowing ideas from across the Atlantic.

The availability of $4\frac{1}{2}$ inch image orthicon cameras fitted with the new wide range zoom lenses, the positive modulation characteristics of the original Blumlein 405-line waveform, all combined to provide brilliant black-and-white pictures of a definition and contrast of the highest quality.

Outside the studios ITV was also scaling new heights. The televising of the funeral (30 January 1965) of Sir Winston Churchill, using forty-five live cameras drawn from many companies and a commentary spoken by Sir Laurence Olivier, was a memorable occasion. Bevan said: 'The camera shots were often breathtaking, as indeed were the sound effects from many locations. I think most of us realised that we were seeing London as it had never been seen before and perhaps as we might never see it again. Tears were never far away.'[1] The programme beat the BBC's comparable offering to a first prize at an international competition in Cannes. Peter Morley, the producer, and his twelve directors from nine different companies would be the first to acknowledge the debt they owed to the engineers.

There was a notable outside broadcast achievement by Southern Television, and its coverage of the racing during Cowes Week was of unusual technical interest. This was originally accomplished from a 70ft 'Proud' class motor torpedo boat on which was erected a temporary studio. Southern then decided to buy the vessel and convert her into a first-ever marine outside broadcast unit. This unique vessel could transmit television programmes live from sea to shore, or tape-record programmes at sea. Marine events covered, in addition to Cowes Week, included the Fastnet race, the offshore power-boat race, water skiing and many other entertainment programmes, notably *A Tale of Two Rivers*, four delightful musical programmes recorded on the Thames and the Seine to contrast London with Paris. *Southerner* was equipped with three $4\frac{1}{2}$ inch image orthicon camera channels – two cameras at port and starboard on the forward deck and a third amidships on the deck cabin roof. The cabin became a vision and sound production control room, while below, internal bulkheads were removed to make an equipment room towards the bows into which, through a hatchway, the outside broadcast equipment (including a video tape-recording machine weighing 800lb) could be installed and removed by crane.

In engineering terms the sixties were a watershed for British television: the years of separation between the triumph of 405-line black-and-white VHF television and the coming of 625-line colour UHF television. The problems of choosing a colour system for the United Kingdom dominated the period 1962–7. NTSC, the original compatible colour system devised by the National Television System Committee of the USA and introduced there in 1954 had been dubbed 'Never Twice the Same Colour' – not from any basic fault of the system but because of the practical shortcomings of the total equipment. An attractive, if erratic, French contender was SECAM: and a marriage of some of the features of both systems produced PAL.

In the technical investigations of these systems, ABC at Teddington played a notable part, with a small team of dedicated engineers under the direction of ABC's young chief engineer, Howard Steele. While the BBC were largely in favour of adopting NTSC, a system they knew and had worked with, the ITV engineers were more willing to look at and see the advantages of the newer systems, SECAM and PAL. They also showed for the first time that it was possible to transcode signals from one system to another – and, for instance, that some of the considerable problems of working with SECAM in a studio could be overcome.

ITV in fact was the *only* organisation that put out experimental 405-line colour in all three systems. They showed that colour on 405 lines would have been attractive, though the start of BBC 2 in 1964 on 625 lines had virtually ruled out any possibility of avoiding a change of line standards.

In the outcome the UK – despite the often strong opposition of the BBC and some sections of industry – adopted PAL colour, a decision which there has never been any reason to regret. ITV, in an effort to get the system moving, agreed that colour should be radiated only on 625 lines and to facilitate this undertook, despite misgivings, to duplicate its programmes on UHF. The formal announcement to this effect was made by the PMG in January 1967.

Some months earlier Howard Steele succeeded Bevan as the ITA's Chief Engineer. By then it had built up a team of engineers with great expertise in the building and operation of transmitters and links; now they came under the direction of someone with expert knowledge also on the studio and colour side.

Colour posed for ITV, with its regional structure, some formidable problems if it was to match in technical quality the service of BBC 1 and BBC 2 which were essentially London-originated and distributed over a more or less fixed network of inter-city links. ITV network programmes, on the other hand, came from London, Birmingham and Manchester and sometimes other cities, with locally injected advertisements and a complex pattern of links. Could a jump from London to Aberdeen, Manchester to Plymouth, be made without perceivable changes of colour? Engineers, aware of the fickle nature of differential-phase and differential-gain, could readily appreciate the problem that ITV had set itself. Only engineers perhaps realised the full magnitude of the success that was achieved when ITV eventually went into colour in November 1969. The setting up – this time in close cooperation with the BBC – of a new network of transmitters, with the much higher powers, higher masts, and with the many more transmitters needed for UHF was begun in 1967. Pat Hawker has written:

The problems that faced ITV in 1967 were formidable: they have been recorded as a series of questions each of which required an engineering answer: 'Could the regional system cope with the challenge of colour based on a network of co-sited ITA/BBC UHF transmitters? How would it be possible to retain the necessary control over our own network of transmitting stations? How, with the much more complex networking involved in a regional system and the constant switching between the studios many miles apart, could we achieve a colour performance which would truly stand comparison with that of any monolithic broadcasting organisation anywhere in the world? Could our system, with its mixture of large and small companies, devise a viable duplicated colour system without any additional revenue from a new programme channel or any part of the colour licence revenue? Would it be possible to build the system at a rate which would allow colour to be networked right from the start and so help to share costs? Could the ITA provide all the new transmitters, ultimately at least 400–500, without a massive and un-economic build-up of the 300–400 operational staff required for the 40 VHF stations?[2]

Engineering solutions were found to all these problems, based on the concept of a network of *unattended* transmitters, no matter how high the power, or how crucial the station in the network. This meant the adoption of novel automatic and telemetry systems, much more reliance on semi-conductor techniques and the adoption for the highest-power stations of a new type of five-cavity klystron.

To maintain overall control of technical quality of the colour pro-grammes a new engineering section was created within the ITA to hammer out, in conjunction with the companies, comprehensive Codes of Practice, and to ensure that these were maintained in operational practice. Four main UHF transmitters in the largest regions were built in time for a simultaneous opening on 15 November 1969 so that ITV colour would, from the start, be available to almost half the population – and by 31 March 1970 a further four high-power transmitters would bring the new service within reach of almost 60 per cent of the population: an extremely rapid build-up by any standards. As an integral part of the new system, virtually identical colour control rooms were built in each ITV area: from these all the ITA transmitters, whether located at ITA or BBC sites, were supervised and the technical quality monitored and any faults reported to mobile maintenance teams.

The change to colour meant massive re-equipment and retraining by the programme companies. In practice it meant a good deal more, since the opportunity was taken to build several new studio centres: the Euston centre by Thames; an ATV centre in the heart of Birmingham; a start on the LWT centre on the South Bank; a new centre at Northam for Southern Television; the new ITN House with its special facilities for overseas broadcasters and regional companies; the new Leeds centre for Yorkshire Television, the first to be built for colour and 625 lines, although operating initially in monochrome. Existing studio centres for Granada at Manchester, for ATV at Elstree, for Thames at Teddington and for the regional companies were re-equipped for colour between 1968–71, so that by 1971 all companies (except Channel) were providing locally originated colour and handling network colour. By autumn 1970, Independent Television had in operation some 190 colour camera channels, 75 colour telecine machines and 60 colour-capable videotape machines, and from November 1969 was transmitting over 50 hours a week in colour. It was by far the most extensively equipped colour television operation in Europe, and it achieved probably the fastest initial build-up of colour ever attempted by a major broadcasting organisation.

Part V

END OF AN ERA

36

THE 'FRANCHISE TRAIL', 1967[1]

Since Bevins' statement in Parliament on 27 June 1963 (Chapter 24) a second competitive television service by at latest 1967 had seemed, if not a foregone conclusion, at least a genuine possibility. But in January 1966 Hill was telling colleagues that his recent conversations with the Labour PMG, Wedgwood Benn, had led him to conclude that an early policy statement on the future shape of broadcasting in Britain was very unlikely. Post Office civil servants were much more preoccupied with proposals arising from Prime Minister Wilson's scheme for a University of the Air (Chapter 31). In these circumstances the Authority saw no alternative but to offer existing companies a one-year extension of their contracts, i.e. until the end of July 1968. This extension was made subject to a reconsideration of the rentals.[2]

Rental policy was very much an ITA preoccupation at this time; discussions were due to take place in the near future with the Post Office and the Treasury. Rentals had been fixed at a level which made possible the accumulation of the substantial reserves that would be necessary to meet the extra capital expenditure that the creation of a second national service would demand.[3] Such expenditure would be additional to that required – White Paper or no White Paper – for more clearly foreseeable developments of colour and UHF duplication. But well-justified fears were entertained that with no ITV 2 in the offing the Treasury would be tempted to make another of its habitual raids on what it would see as an over-large ITA capital reserve. In the event the Treasury took £2.7 million in 1965/6 and £1.8 million in 1966/7, by which time the total of such appropriations since 1961 amounted to over £6.5 million.

By July 1966 there was still no sign of the awaited White Paper. The Authority therefore went ahead with its preparations for a new round of contract awards on the basis of a single ITV service. A Contracts Committee was set up with a remit to consider in the first instance three matters: the future pattern of franchise areas, future rental policy and the question of programme company diversification, in particular into other branches of the entertainment industry. This last was a relatively new development, born in part of ITV's continuing prosperity. Whereas earlier concern had been felt over the extent to which powerful outside interests occupied dominating positions in the control of some of the companies, now undesirable consequences were feared from the tendency of some ITV companies to acquire holdings in other profitable enterprises, some, but by no means all, of which related to broadcasting and public entertainment. There were worries too over the implications of ATV's widespread theatrical interests and Lew Grade's involvement in the Grade artists' agencies. For some outside critics, the exclusive contracts held by these agencies with so many leading performers, musicians and writers gave ATV a wholly disproportionate position of monopoly power within British broadcasting. But the Authority was not prepared at this stage to go further than a contractual obligation laid upon companies to keep it informed of any extensions of their own or of their major shareholders' interests outside the area of television broadcasting. The important need, it felt, was not necessarily a ban on such diversification but rather adequate information on which it could base a judgement whether the nature of the company had been materially changed or its performance as a programme provider significantly affected.

With a provisional timetable that envisaged the announcement of awards by June, it was important to decide what contracts were to be on offer. In other words, was there a case for change in the existing pattern of franchise areas? A hint that there might be room for a fifth 'major' had been dropped in 1964. Discussions on this question stimulated comment in the press. In November the *Daily Mirror* recorded both the likelihood of a London split between two independent contractors on a 4 day/3 day basis and the probability of a split in the Northern (Granada) area.[4] This report virtually coincided with various Authority decisions. The first was in favour of three seven-day companies, one in each of the Midlands, Lancashire and Yorkshire areas – with two companies operating respectively for $4\frac{1}{2}$ and $2\frac{1}{2}$ days in London. Secondly, it was thought that, with the possible exception of Wales, no changes need be made in the regional company pattern. Thirdly, contracts should be offered for a period of six years (the maximum possible under the 1964 Act), terminable on the introduction of a second service within that period. Fourthly, no decisions on rentals should be made until an announcement of the Government's much delayed decisions on colour and duplication of the 405 VHF and 625 UHF services.

On 15 December 1966 the Authority decided to make its intentions public. When two days later the *Guardian* reported the intention to split

Granadaland it was able also to record Sidney Bernstein's characteristic reaction: 'If the territory of Granada is interfered with in any way we shall go to the United Nations'.

Any uncertainty was removed when Hill made a full public statement on 21 December. It had been carefully timed to follow on the appearance the previous day of the long-awaited White Paper on Broadcasting. In this the key statement for ITV was the one saying 'no allocation of frequencies to a fourth television service will be authorised for the next three years at any rate'.[5] It said that a fourth television service would make large demands on resources. The three services already provided a large volume of programmes of various kinds and the Government did not consider that another television service could be afforded a high place in the order of national priorities.

This further set-back to the ITA's long-cherished hope for a second range of competitive commercial stations roused very little press reaction. The Bevins Levy had taken most of the steam out of the pressure for this way of cutting excessive profits. The programme companies had learned to live with the additional burden of discriminatory taxation and – despite their earlier cries of doom and despair – they had continued to prosper. Revenue, especially in the central areas, was still growing. But it was at best doubtful whether there would be enough to support both a second service and a levy charged on gross advertising income rather than on profits. So the Authority's desire to exploit ITV prosperity to the programme advantage of the viewer rather than that of the Treasury found some expression in the creation of a fifth major company; and it was on this decision that press attention was mainly focussed.

Most national newspapers quoted Hill as saying that income from advertising had now reached the point at which it could support five major companies. 'The people of Yorkshire deserve to have a company which is interested in Yorkshire,' he added. But for the *Huddersfield Daily Examiner*, viewers in West Yorkshire at least had not fared so badly under the *ancien régime*. 'Honesty must surely compel the hitherto subject peoples to acknowledge that the absolute authority wielded from Manchester has in the main been benevolently despotic.'[6] The *Guardian* saw other, incidental advantages. Companies, said its leader writer, should be 'strong and prosperous but they should not monopolise. The new pattern . . . should reduce the dominance of the four existing major contractors and increase the influence of the minor companies. The arrival of a fifth major company . . . could do a lot to improve the relationships between the big and the small.'[7]

It was obvious that the establishment of a fifth major contractor would affect the finances of the others. Overheads for ITV as a whole were likely to be increased; and these increases would be additional to those arising from the introduction of colour. To assist the BBC the December White Paper had conceded an additional £5 charge in the licences for viewers with colour receivers, but ITV would have to meet the cost of colour out of its advertising revenue. On the question of duplication during the period of changeover from 405-line VHF to 625-line UHF, the White Paper was non-committal; but the Authority could no longer defer determining rentals for its new contracts, taking account of both the deferment of ITV 2 and its wish to avoid further Treasury raids on accumulated reserves. By February 1967 agreement had been reached on this and most other outstanding issues. The total to be raised would be just over £7 million. (In 1964 the aim had been to get £8 million.) Individual rentals were set at levels ranging from £10,000 for the Channel Islands and £20,000 for the Borders to £750,000 for each of the two London, the Midlands and the Lancashire franchises, £800,000 for Central Scotland, £850,000 for the Southern Region and £600,000 for the new Yorkshire contract. Levels of average weekly production to be required from regional contractors were also fixed, ranging from three hours for the Channel Islands and four hours for the Borders to nine hours for Central Scotland and Southern England and twelve hours for Wales and the West. Measures of control over the methods and costs of programme exchanges between the majors and for the supply of programmes from them to the regionals were also proposed.

Advertisements inviting applications for contracts appeared on 28 February. Closing date was 15 April. In the event thirty-six applications were received and these were unevenly distributed over the fifteen regions. In six areas no competitor to the incumbent company came forward; but for the new Yorkshire seven-day franchise there were ten contenders, all of them newcomers to ITV. With applications from seventeen new groups in the field the Authority could feel it had good prospects of bringing fresh blood into the system.

The information that applicant groups were asked to give duplicated much that had been asked for in 1963. But that was to be supplemented by some of the matters mentioned in Lord Hill's press conference of January 1964, in which he had indicated the Authority's thinking as he put it 'on some aspects of company structure' (Chapter 27). Enquiries about proposed company financial structure, the spread and representative nature of shareholdings, as also about ultimate financial and policy control now included detailed questions about present intended diversification into pay television, large screen TV, sound radio and other entertainment-related activities. Applicant groups were also asked to state their intentions with regard to a programme magazine – whether they favoured a company-sponsored local publication or a national one with regional editions. On the technical side preparations (or plans) for studios had to cover the expected introduction of colour and UHF 625 lines.[8]

The thirty-six applications from thirty different groups, more than half of them newcomers, were the residue from the two to three hundred original requests for application particulars that had followed on the 28 February advertisement. Initial euphoria had clearly been tempered by realism. In more than one instance aspirant groups negotiated amalgamation with rival contenders for the same contract in order to pool resources. Even so, if there was any fact behind the *Sunday Times* story of City finance houses 'queuing'[9] to offer backing to promising contenders, this can only have been in respect of the two London contracts or, more likely perhaps, the new seven-day contract for Yorkshire. In the event, apart from Yorkshire, there were only three new applicants for the five central areas. Few people expected much change in the smaller regions. Still, when the applications were studied, there was seen to be in some of the new groups 'too much talent to be ignored'.[10] Much of this talent came from the BBC.

(i) YORKSHIRE

Prominent among the candidates for the Yorkshire franchise was a consortium called Yorkshire Independent Television which represented the fusion of two earlier would-be applicant groups, a Yorkshire-based one led by the Yorkshire Post Newspapers in association with the local picture theatre chain, Star Cinemas, and a London-based one made up principally of EMI, the *Daily Telegraph*, Penguin Books and British Lion Films, which Lord Goodman had brought together. Also very much in the running were Telefusion Ltd, a large and successful Blackpool-based TV rentals firm, with a big share of its business in Yorkshire; a group headed by Professor O. R. McGregor which had (as the Morris Finer group) made, and then withdrawn, an application for the Tyne Tees contract in 1963 (Chapter 27); the Yorkshire TV Producers' Group organised by Howard and Wyndham Theatres in association with Decca and Harraps, the educational publishers, and calling on the services of a number of award-winning ITV producers; and Trans York TV, of which local Yorkshire businessmen and steel magnates were leaders. The comedian Ken Dodd's 'Diddy TV' withdrew from the competition at an early stage.

The Authority soon concluded that the final choice would lie between the *Yorkshire Post* – Goodman group and Telefusion Yorkshire Ltd. If what was sought was new blood, with broadcasting and general communications professionalism, combined with representative personalities from the industrial, commercial life of the three Ridings, each of these two groups seemed to offer a veritable embarrassment of riches. If anything, the more glittering star cast belonged to the first of the two; 65 per cent of their £150,000 of voting shares and 62 per cent of total capital of £4 million were to be held by Yorkshire persons or companies. After the *Yorkshire Post*, EMI, under their energetic Chairman, Sir Joseph Lockwood, were to have been the second largest shareholder. But they had recently acquired control of the Grade Organisation's talent agency whose links with ATV, through Lew Grade, had already given the ITA concern, and consequently they withdrew. Eight newspapers were involved in the application of which five (*Yorkshire Post* and *Yorkshire Evening Post*, *Huddersfield Examiner*, *Halifax Courier* and *Scarborough Evening News*) were represented in the Board by the Managing Director of Yorkshire Post Newspapers Ltd.

The group's intended Managing Director was David Wilson of Southern Television, with a generous letter of agreement from John Davis, Southern's Chairman, in his possession. Their Director of Programmes was to be Granada's Tim Hewat, their Sales Director Peter Paine of Tyne Tees and ex-BBC Donald Baverstock was to be a principal programme adviser, making available the talents and experience of his associates Antony Jay, Elwyn Jones, Denis Norden and Sid Colin. The proposed Heads of Drama, of Features and Current Affairs and of Local News and Sport were recruits from the BBC.

Against this dazzling array, Telefusion Yorkshire Ltd could offer a Board presided over by Sir Richard Graham, a former High Sheriff of Yorkshire with Sir Geoffrey Cox of ITN as his Deputy Chairman. Gwyn Ward Thomas of Grampian would be Managing Director and the BBC's Aubrey Singer Director of Programmes. A bright young twenty-nine-year-old executive from the Telefusion parent company, E. Stuart Wilson, was to be Assistant Managing Director. Peter Willes, Rediffusion's Head of Drama, was also with them. There were to be twenty-two Directors in all, of which half were stated to be either resident or employed in the region. Of the proposed £5 million capital, the voting shares (£750,000) would be much more widely distributed than those of the Yorkshire Post group, being held by close on forty separate investors over half of whom were in Yorkshire. A list of small investors in non-voting stock included over 250 names, also mainly of

Yorkshire people. In all 67 per cent of the finance would come from companies or persons resident in the area. As with their rivals, 10 per cent of voting shares would be offered to Yorkshire universities. The parent Telefusion company which had about one million rental subscribers in the Lancashire–Yorkshire area, was to be the largest single shareholder with 29 per cent of voting and 20.8 per cent of total capital (including non-voting and loan stock). Nine newspaper groups (subsidiaries of the S. Pearson Group) representing no fewer than thirty-one local Yorkshire weekly papers were to be holders of non-voting stock (about 5 per cent). Alan Whicker who had undertaken to provide a regular supply of documentary programmes would have a 5 per cent total holding including less than 1 per cent of voting shares. The London scriptwriters' company (ALS TV LTD) would have a 6 per cent holding of voting shares. A further £175,000 worth of shares would be held in reserve for company staff. Well-known television names among the proposed senior staff included a Head of Light Entertainment and a Head of Sport, both from the BBC.

The group declared its firm intention to produce in its first year a weekly average of ten hours of which half would be local, with the expectation of more in later years. This programme commitment was virtually the same as that of the Yorkshire Post group. There was in fact very little to choose between the declared intentions of the two groups in this respect. Both proclaimed ambitions to make high quality contributions to network drama, light entertainment and documentaries. The Yorkshire Post group emphasised their aim to inject an element of originality and 'excitement' into ITV programmes. This was countered by the Telefusion spokesmen with the claim that ITV had ceased to be 'people's television', had become too much 'producers' television', intellectually inbred and London orientated. Telefusion also showed awareness of the ITA's recent preoccupation with the pattern and balance of the programme schedules, particularly at weekends. As a supplement to the detailed programme plans given in their application, they brought to their interviews a draft schedule containing suggestions for an improvement in the quality and balance of ITV's weekends. They declared an intention not to diversify the company's operations beyond programme making and allied fields.

The Authority seems to have been inclined to fear that the formidable array of talent assembled by Yorkshire Independent Television contained too many strong, independent personalities who might in the event find it difficult to work together as a team. But if the balance was finally tipped in Telefusion's favour this must also have owed much to the able way in which their written statement of programme philosophy and intentions was further developed and explained at their interview, notably by Sir Geoffrey Cox.

Thus at their meeting on 9 June the Authority resolved to offer the seven-day Yorkshire contract to Telefusion Yorkshire Limited. It was an offer with conditions which made it not far short of a shot-gun marriage with the Yorkshire elements in the rival group. Management control would stay with Telefusion, but the proposed holding by the parent Telefusion company would have to be reduced from the intended 29 per cent of voting capital to not more than 18 per cent and their total investment limited to some £900,000. An opportunity to invest to a total of £850,000 should then be offered to the *Yorkshire Post*, the Huddersfield, Halifax and Scarborough newspapers, Yorkshire Cooperative Societies and the Trade Unions associated with them in the application. The intention to invite a £75,000 investment by Yorkshire universities was to be implemented and the new company's name was to be changed to exclude the word 'Telefusion'.

By the beginning of July, Yorkshire Independent Television Ltd had decided on a voluntary winding-up and had stated their consent to the change of name of *Telefusion (Yorkshire) Limited* to *Yorkshire Television Limited*. In the event, Singer did not take up the post with the new company for which he had been designated: instead, Donald Baverstock offered his services to Ward Thomas and was appointed Yorkshire Television's Director of Programmes on 14 July.

On 30 November Lord Aylestone, the new ITA Chairman, went to Leeds to lay the foundation stone of Yorkshire Television's studios, the first in Europe to be built and designed from the outset with colour in mind. At the official luncheon which followed this ceremony, he spoke of the Authority's policy of regional diversity. Of the area to be served by this first major company to be appointed since 1955 he said: 'It would be difficult to find a more natural, homogeneous identifiable region in the Kingdom . . . Yorkshire Television will take a special place in Independent Television'. In the years ahead, it did.

(ii) LONDON

The proposed new division of the London week created the possibility of a weekend contractor with sufficient resources to rank as a major network company. Instead of the contract currently held by ATV, for a Monday to Friday operation in the Midlands supplemented by a Saturday and Sunday one in London, there would be a full seven-day contract for the Midlands and a separate London weekend one. The latter might include anything up to half the broadcast hours on Fridays. There were long debates at the ITA before deciding where the dividing line between the two ITV London operations should be drawn. Without some Friday hours the weekend company would not receive enough advertising income to enable it to play a full programme role as a major producing company. On the other hand if the weekday London contractor was expected to continue to provide programmes (including schools broadcasts) during less lucrative weekday morning and afternoon hours, it seemed reasonable to let them have some share in the more lucrative evening time on Fridays. There was moreover the belief that weekend audiences had a distinctive character and characteristically different programme expectations from those of typical weekday viewers. The question was therefore narrowed down to deciding at what time – 6 p.m. or 7 p.m. – the viewers' weekend mood took over. A decision was not finally reached in favour of 7 p.m. until all applications for the weekend contract had been received and all three of the applicant groups had been interviewed.

Applications came from TVR, a London based broadcast and recording facilities company that had also applied for the Yorkshire and the London weekday contracts; from a totally new consortium brought together by David Frost in partnership with ITN's first editor, Aidan Crawley, who was by now MP for West Derbyshire; and from ABC.

With the creation of seven-day franchises in the North and in the Midlands, ABC would be left out on a limb. It is true that they did put in applications for both the new seven-day contracts in Lancashire and the Midlands. But, like other existing contractors, they were invited to state an order of preference and they made it clear that their much preferred goal was the short London contract. They had acquired highly relevant experience and a deserved prestige from their weekend service in the Midlands and the North. Howard Thomas was confident that they would turn this experience to good account, and certainly do better than ATV, were they to be given the stronger position in the system that a London base would provide. Given that Hill and his colleagues were concerned to improve the image of ITV's weekend, the time when opinion formers and other people of public power and influence were thought most likely to be viewers, the company that had been a pioneer of adult education and televised religion, that had produced *Tempo, Armchair Theatre* and *The Avengers* seemed made for the job.

ABC's written application and the performance of Thomas and Tesler at the interview on 4 May revealed that their thinking about possible weekend schedule improvements chimed in closely with the Authority's own. ATV, after much heart searching, had eventually decided to make the Midlands their first preference, as it was likely to be the more financially rewarding of the two. With their production centre at Elstree, they would still be able to make substantial contributions to the network. There could be little doubt that, in the absence of more promising competition bringing in talented new blood, the London weekend contract would go to ABC, with ATV getting the seven days in the Midlands.

It was in this frame of mind that the Authority approached interviews on 5 May with Rediffusion and the Frost–Crawley group. At the first of these, the Authority was interested to note the presence of the General Manager (McMillan) and his deputy (Lord Windlesham), the Director of Programmes (Bennett) and the Director of Sales (Guy Paine) because at the company's previous interview in 1964 it had commented on the absence of any television professionals on Rediffusion's Board of Directors. But by May 1967 these and Arthur Groocock, Company Secretary, made up one half of the Rediffusion TV company's ten-man Board.

It was quite understandable that Wills should still feel, and also display, fully justifiable pride in having been one of the more courageous and farsighted of ITV's early pioneers. Yet to Hill and his colleagues Wills' own outspoken confidence in the ability of the Board and management of Rediffusion Television Ltd to cope with any present or foreseeable problems arising for the ITV system seemed to betray a degree of complacency. He broadly hinted that the Authority could best carry out its statutory public duties and responsibilities by appointing well-run, competently-staffed companies (like Rediffusion) and then letting them get on with the job without further interference. It was his view – and he did not conceal it – that the Authority should renew the Rediffusion contract forthwith, in much the same way as his BET air and bus services had been annually renewed almost automatically.

The impression thus received, justified or not, was unfortunate because the achievements of Rediffusion to the general benefit of ITV had been and continued to be substantial. And the contributions made to the interview by both McMillan and Bennett showed that their programme people were thinking seriously and constructively about future developments and desirable improvements in the ITV programme service.

At the immediately following interview – that with the Frost–Crawley consortium – Bennett reappeared as the intended Programme Controller of this new applicant group, as also did Guy Paine as Director of Sales. But the Crawley group had more to offer than two Rediffusion renegades. Perhaps the most significant feature of this application for the London weekend franchise was the further evidence it offered of the emergence (already well-illustrated by the Yorkshire applications) of professional broadcasters as a class of contenders for ITV contracts in their own right on the basis of their achieved public standing and prestige as successful programme makers and performers. The group stressed that while the stability and financial and business expertise of a potential programme company was obviously a paramount consideration, there was no reason why the people who knew about television, cared about television, and did television should not have an effective voice in the running of that company, through a substantial equity holding.

It was proposed to raise £15,000 in voting and £1½ million in non-voting shares, with up to £3,075,000 in unsecured loan stock. Some 30 per cent of the share capital (voting and non-voting) would be allocated to senior management, programme people and other 'artistic interests'. No one would have more than a 10 per cent interest. David Frost, described as 'co-creator' of the consortium, would hold £750 (5 per cent) of voting shares and £75,000 non-voting. He could not have a seat on the Board because it was envisaged that he would present one of his forty-five-minute programmes on each of the three nights and these would certainly include controversial matter. The prospective Deputy Chairman was John Freeman, at that time still High Commissioner in New Delhi but better known to the British public for his BBC *Face to Face* interviews. Managing Director would be Michael Peacock, who would resign from controllership of BBC 1 to take up the post. Proposed Deputy Managing Director was Dr Tom Margerison, Science Editor of the *Sunday Times*. Corporate business interests and management experience was present in the persons of Lord Campbell of Eskan, Chairman of Statesman and Nation Publishing Ltd, Sir Christopher Chancellor, Chairman of Bowaters, Sir Geoffrey Kitchen, Chairman of Pearl Assurance, Duncan McNab, Chief Executive Officer of the London Cooperative Society, the Hon. David Montagu of Samuel Montagu Ltd, the merchant bankers, Sir Donald Stokes of Leyland Motors and Arnold Weinstock of GEC. Virtually all the loan capital and 52 per cent of the equity would come from seven corporate shareholders, five of whom were represented on the fifteen-man Board. Other corporate shareholders, not represented on the Board, were Imperial Tobacco Co Pension Trust, Lombard Banking, the two publishing houses of William Collins and Weidenfeld & Nicolson, University College, London and Magdalen College, Oxford. All investors, it was stated, had accepted the principle that expenditure on high quality programming should take precedence over dividends.

Four programme units were planned. The Drama, Music and Arts unit would he headed by Humphrey Burton from the BBC. Head of the Entertainment Unit would be Frank Muir, and he would have the benefit of a service of programme ideas plus one certain programme series a year from scriptwriters Galton and Simpson. Head of Public Affairs Unit was to be Clive Irving, former Managing Editor of *The Sunday Times* and creator of that paper's 'Insight' feature. In charge of the Children's, Educational and Religious Unit would be Doreen Stephens, currently Head of the BBC Television's Family Programmes Department. Intended Chief Engineer was Bill Fletcher who as Chief Engineer, Operations, was masterminding the BBC conversion to colour.

Even if the Authority Members had not themselves thought that ITV had lost some of its early drive, had exhausted the appeal of novelty and was running out of ideas, they had had the thought presented to them repeatedly in contract applications both from existing companies like Granada or ABC and, of course, from several of the ten Yorkshire hopefuls. And they naturally agreed. Vigorous BBC competition had reinforced a company tendency to play safe with assured audience winners. This reluctance to take risks and the resulting sameness and predictability of schedules had been a principal ground, as we have seen, for the Authority's campaign to get a 'new look' in the pattern of programmes. Here lay precisely the chief attractions of the Crawley–Frost consortium. It included both at Board and senior staff levels people who could claim at least some credit for the BBC's revival as well as one or two of the livelier minds in ITV programme circles. The group members made much of this as an earnest of their credibility as a major ITV company. Perhaps a more coolly critical look at their relative lack of television *company management* (as distinct from programme) experience might have been in place. (It was after all a prominent feature of the two most promising Yorkshire applications.) However that may be, what the Authority saw itself being offered was an array of talent and a record of success as a most plausible justification for the ambition they shared to combine high standards of programme quality with the wide audience appeal on which company profitability would depend. The group asserted confidently – and they were believed – that they could give a new look, a unity and distinctive style to ITV's weekend schedules. They were also critical of the existing programme journals and suggested that improvement could be best achieved by one centrally produced ITV publication with regional editions but with a consistent editorial standard equal to the task of presenting the '*right image*' of Independent Television.

They would start with eight-and-a-half hours of own productions, increasing to ten hours as their planned newly-built studio complex came into operation. In addition to three Frost programmes acting as a kind of stylistic link over the three weekend evenings, a forty-minute news magazine on Sunday afternoons was promised, a regular arts programme (including serious music) later on that afternoon, thirty minutes of religious programmes additional to the Sunday church services, a regular drama series on Fridays and a major new play on Sunday evenings. They obviously felt that they possessed collectively sufficient flair and skill in programme presentation to meet any competition the BBC might throw against them. The enthusiasm and self-confidence displayed were impressive. When to these was added an apparently active involvement in the consortium's plans of so glittering a galaxy of leaders in the worlds of business, industry and commerce, the case became overwhelming. This was the group which had to be given the London weekend contract.

So the problem was, what to do about ABC? 'A possible decision,' wrote Fraser (encapsulating much preliminary discussion) 'is that ABC and Rediffusion be told that the Authority is prepared to offer the contract to a new company, formed by the two companies, in which majority control is exercised by ABC, but of which the profits as nearly as possible be divided equally between the two.'[11] This was the solution adopted by the Authority at its meeting on 9 June. 'With our principle of programme quality in mind,' said Lord Hill at his 12 June press conference, 'the combination of these two companies seemed to the Authority to offer the possibility of a programme company of real excellence.'[12] Despite the honeyed words, the decision seemed condescending and insulting to Wills, and a comparable interpretation was put upon it by numerous informed observers who had not forgotten the stoicism this company had displayed in supporting a loss in the early stages of ITV, amounting in 1981 terms to some £20 millions.

But personal feelings were one thing, sound business prospects were another. Negotiations for the merger went forward, even though Wills and his colleagues with their unshaken belief in the virtues of risk-taking private enterprise must have found abhorrent the degree of interventionism displayed by the Authority in the conditions it attached to the contract offer. In addition to ABC having a small majority of voting shares and providing Howard Thomas and Brian Tesler as, respectively, Managing Director and Director of Programmes, the Board of the new company was to have a majority of ABC nominees and a chairman who was preferably to be independent of both sides. There should be equal division of profits. All this – board composition, shareholding and general management arrangements, including even senior staff appointments and choice of studios – was to be presented for Authority approval by the end of July. When the

Authority met on 27 July, Hill could only tell Members that the merger
'appeared to be viable'. Good progress was being made, he said, in the
negotiations. Agreement had been reached that the main production centre
would be at ABC's Teddington studios. ABC would close its own London
office and its Manchester studios. Rediffusion's Television House in
Kingsway, the original home of the ITV companies, would be retained. The
future of their Wembley studios was still uncertain.

But final agreement on all aspects of the merger was only reached after
long and painful negotiation. The Authority had placed itself in a position
which did not enable it to stand aside and more than one three-cornered
meeting was necessary during the late summer and autumn. When by mid-
October definite information had still not been received about the terms of
the merger a clear and early statement was sought from both companies
whether or not a final agreement could be expected. The prolonged
uncertainty was having an inevitable effect on staff morale. In fact strike
threats and brief stoppages by ACTT, NATKE and the ETU had taken place
throughout September. ABC were off the air for an hour on 8 October. On
the following day, *World of Sport* was lost. Two days after Fraser's letter a
billed Frost interview with Edward Heath was blacked. 'We want to know,'
said George Elvin of the ACTT, 'whether our members are going to be re-
employed when the new companies take over.'[13]

A reply giving the terms of the ABC–Rediffusion agreement was
eventually received on 20 October and within a week these were approved.
The new joint company was now to be called 'Thames Television', and the
ABC Chairman, Sir Philip Warter, would take the chair. There would be five
further directors from ABC and four from Rediffusion. Among senior staff the
Heads of Drama (Lloyd Shirley) and Light Entertainment (Philip Jones)
came from ABC; Heads of Current Affairs (Jeremy Isaacs) and Religion and
Education (Guthrie Moir), and Outside Broadcasts (Grahame Turner)
came from Rediffusion. Remaining staff would be recruited in approximately equal proportions from the two sides.

But the future of Rediffusion's Wembley studios still remained undecided
and it was an issue of harassing complexity. With the modern Teddington
studios available and capable of extension, the controlling interest in the
new Thames Television felt it had no need for Wembley. Rediffusion would
have been glad to sell it as a going concern to the new weekend consortium,
but the latter aspired to build an entirely new studio centre on a central
London site and had in mind the site of the old Vauxhall gasworks on the
South Bank. It was within the powers the ITA had reserved to itself to require
the consortium to buy from Rediffusion, who urged it to do just that. But the

ITA could not bring itself to force the consortium into Wembley. This would have seemed a betrayal of the high ideals to which it had subscribed by appointing the consortium in the first place. Where would they have the best chance of producing the best of which they were capable? Not where it would suit Rediffusion/ABC for them to go, not where it would be cheapest for them to go, not even where the staff transition would be easiest. It was in the new and prestigious home of music and arts on the South Bank.

When it became apparent that the newcomers were prepared to go elsewhere (Pinewood) for temporary premises whilst the South Bank studios were under construction – and this with the ITA's tacit agreement – Rediffusion finally gave in and reluctantly agreed to a short-term rental of Wembley to the consortium, which had now become London Weekend Television. All this time – and understandably enough – ABC and Rediffusion staff were in a ferment. But at last the merger was a reality and the tensions were eased. It had been a mammoth task accomplished with skill and mutual forbearance by Paul Adorian of Rediffusion and Robert Clark of ABC, assisted by Thomas and Fraser. At certain crucial stages they had the advantage of having their negotiations 'moderated' by Baroness Sharp.

Another condition attached to the London weekend contract offer concerned shareholdings. London Weekend were asked to include as substantial shareholders the *Daily Telegraph*, a disappointed member of the unsuccessful Yorkshire Post group, *The Economist*, and the *Observer*. It was suggested that about £1 million of capital should be offered to the three in an approximate ratio of 4 : 4 : 2. Crawley lost no time. Two days after being offered the contract, he wrote to say that negotiations had already been concluded with the *Observer* and the *Telegraph* and that those with *The Economist* should be completed in another forty-eight hours. The London Weekend Board thus acquired three new directors, the Hon. David Astor representing the *Observer*, the Hon. Michael Berry representing the *Telegraph* and Sir Geoffrey Crowther representing *The Economist*.

(iii) CENTRAL SCOTLAND

Both *The Economist* and the *Observer* would have been large shareholders (the latter with 15 per cent of total capital) in a group competing with Roy Thomson's STV for the Central Scotland franchise. It was led by the Rt. Hon. Joseph Grimond, MP for Orkney and Shetland since 1950 and who had been until recently leader of the Liberal Party. Others in this consortium included Alasdair Milne, a member of the three-man consultancy partnership formed with two other former BBC executives, Baverstock and Jay; Tom Taylor, President of the Scottish CWS; Steven Watson, Principal and Vice Chancellor of St. Andrews University; and the Glasgow MP and history professor, Esmond Wright. This line-up was supported by an array of television talent and experience comparable to that in the London Weekend consortium. Much of it again was drawn from the BBC. They were all in Fraser's words very obviously 'new elements we would like to have'. A plan was therefore very seriously considered to arrange another merger, this time between the Grimond group and STV. The transfer of *The Economist* and the *Observer* interests was indeed part of that plan. These two, together with John Menzies Ltd, the wholesale newsagents, who withdrew before the interview on 19 May, would have supplied 30 per cent of the total proposed capital. So there was room for manoeuvre. Several possible schemes were discussed. All had a central aim to reduce further the Thomson holding in STV, and, simultaneously, to spread the ownership more widely among the Scottish public in particular. But none was in the end thought feasible. No such proposal was even put either to the Grimond group or to STV. Among other factors, the Authority seems to have felt that, notwithstanding their impeccable Scottish backgrounds, too high a proportion of those involved in the Grimond application had interests, main activities and residence outside the area served by the station. So the contract was offered once again to Scottish Television.[14]

In addition to Thomson and their Deputy Chairman, James Coltart, Managing Director William Brown and Programme Controller Francis Essex had aquitted themselves well at the Authority interview. They gave every sign of having been well briefed on the ITA's main preoccupations at that time. It was also a fact that the company whose output had for a time attracted well-justified criticisms, had over the previous couple of years achieved marked improvements which the Authority was keen to encourage. The contract offer did, however, have conditions attached. The Thomson Organisation's holding of voting shares was to be still further reduced from 55 per cent to 25 per cent. The surplus was to be disposed of to people and interests, as widely spread as possible, unconnected with the Thomson Organisation. Not less than three new directors were to be appointed to the Board and these were to be figures of some standing in Scottish life but also unconnected with the Organisation. All these conditions were accepted and in due course – it took a good year – meticulously carried out.

For Thomson personally the least onerous of these conditions was the further reduction in his shareholding. Lord Hill relates how Thomson asked him to make the formula 'not more than 25 per cent'.[15] If the ITA did him a good turn when it brought him into ITV in 1957, it certainly did him another by forcing him to unload when shares were at peak prices in 1967/8. He was not slow to express his gratitude when a slump came along in 1968/9!

(iv) THE MIDLANDS

Given the approach taken by the Authority to the London situation, award of the seven-day contract in the Midlands to ATV seemed virtually inevitable. But this did not protect their application from searching critical appraisal. On their programme record, discontent with the company's commitment to the Midlands region was still strongly felt at Brompton Road. And their application seemed to indicate no clear plan for a substantial shift of programme operations from Elstree to Birmingham. On the other hand, what emerged most strongly at the interview, as it was bound to do, was the impression of Lew Grade's personality – his evident total personal commitment, not to say identification, with Independent Television, his ebullient spirit of entrepreneurial showmanship and willingness to take risks in the cause of the system's success. Despite their reservations, Authority Members shared with the general public at that time an inability to picture an ITV without its Lew Grade. At the same time they might well have perceived a grain of truth in Dennis Potter's view that the Palladium show had 'by now reached the particularly ripe kind of decay where one actually looks forward to the sudden drama of cheerful suds swirling through the high zone wash or slobbery dogs gobbling up their tinned meat and liver'.[16]

If the main focus of ATV's interest could this time round be more fully and successfully concentrated on the Midlands, a changed Sunday evening might be easily achieved. This meant the introduction of unequivocal contractual obligations. The formal contract offer to ATV therefore re-iterated and reinforced the regional commitment conditions of the 1964 contract, which had not been fully met or even pressed for. But now with a seven-day franchise involved the imperative was stronger. Once again it was said that Robin Gill, Grade's deputy, should take up residence in the region, or failing that, a full-time member of the Board should be appointed, ranking immediately below the managing director, resident in the Midlands and responsible for the Midland operation. In addition it was required that a Midland programme controller of standing comparable to that of programme controllers in other major companies should be appointed. Not less than six weekly hours of programmes would have to be produced in the region and two to three hours of these should be other than purely local programmes. To that end, a full-scale Midland television centre would be required. Two additional directors were to be appointed, and these were to be local residents actively associated with the public life of the area. In filling any job vacancies arising from the new contractual commitments prior consideration should be given to those already working in ITV.

The company's letter of acceptance on the stated terms also gave information about consequent management appointments. Lew Grade would become ATV's Deputy Chairman, as well as being Joint Managing Director with Robin Gill. Bill Ward, who was already a Board member and in charge of production at Elstree, would be appointed an Executive Director, take up residence in the Midlands and, as Midlands Production Controller, have full responsibility for the company's Midland production output. Arrangements were, it was stated, already in hand for the creation of a new Midlands Television Centre. It was not, however, until a full year later, in June 1968, that the announcement was made of the appointment of two additional directors living in and associated with the life of the Midlands. They were Dame Isabel Graham-Bryce, a former ITA Member who, besides undertaking a variety of other public work, was a very active Chairman of the Oxford Regional Hospital Board; and Sir George Farmer, a Director of the Leyland Motor Corporation and Chancellor of Birmingham University since 1966.

(v) NORTH WEST ENGLAND

Granada was another central company from which the Authority had sought reassurances in the conditions attached to their contract renewal in 1964. Yet in their case, none of these related to the structure, control and ownership of the company. Among the directors and voting shareholders there was virtually no participatory representation of the regional public. This was still the situation in 1967, as it had been in 1963. But at the earlier date the Authority had been more concerned, in the case of this company especially, to have better channels of communication between its own staff and that of Granada. This was in recognition rather than in discouragement of Granada's proclivity for adventurous programming and the pursuit of difficult or contentious topics in documentary and current affairs. By 1967 things had much improved. Discussions involving at times a clear conflict of opinion on matters related to provisions of the Act still occurred. But these were now more likely to be on the substance of the case – rational debates involving professional legal advice rather than irritable disputes on whether advance information had been adequate or supplied in good time. It was in this spirit that the resulting 'creative tension' was treated during the Granada interview on 4 May 1967. Sidney Bernstein claimed that, while they never questioned the final decision, they had always wanted the right to argue the point.

But what had been overlooked in 1963 could not be neglected in 1967. This the more so because there was a competitor in the field; and this competitor based its appeal mainly on its almost exclusively regional origins and character. Granada, said this group, projected no more than an outdated folk image of the County Palatine and its surrounding region. They, by virtue of their membership and associations, could do fuller justice to the rich and varied industrial, agricultural and cultural life of the area. Heading the Palatine Television consortium was Charles Carter, Vice Chancellor of Lancaster University and Chairman of the North West Economic Planning Council. Other personalities associated with the group were George Wedell, former Secretary to the Authority and by now Professor of Adult Education at Manchester University, and a number of local authority worthies. They proposed planning their programmes with the help of advisory panels chaired by local people of distinction in their respective fields such as Lord Bowden of the University of Manchester College of Science and Technology; Percy Lord, Lancashire's County Chief Education Officer; the Bishop of Blackburn; and Liverpool City Councillor, Lady Simey. The Head of Programmes would be Michael Redington, currently a senior producer with ABC. A number of other Lancastrian personalities and experienced television professionals were also, it was claimed, interested in joining the group. But it was very clear to the Authority that this hurriedly assembled consortium was still in an embryonic state, with as yet no firm commitments from intended management or key programme staff. The Authority felt it would be taking too great a gamble in preferring them to the proven all-round competence of Granada.

Nevertheless the point had been well taken. The contract offer to Granada did not this time neglect the question of regional representation. A member of the company's Board with full-time executive responsibilities must in future be resident in the area. Further, at least two new directors, living in and recognisably associated with the public life of the area should be appointed. In choosing these, consideration should be given to one from one of the region's universities. For good measure, the contract offer added a requirement that any transfer of programme production from Manchester to London studios (to save increasingly onerous travel costs) could only take place with prior Authority approval. The contract was formally accepted in these terms, but it was not until a full year later, after personal correspondence between Fraser and Sidney Bernstein, that the names of two additional Granada directors were submitted to and approved by the Authority. They were F. C. Williams, Professor of Electrical Engineering at Manchester University; and J. P. Jacobs, a Liverpool businessman, managing director of a large textile firm.

(vi) SOUTH WEST ENGLAND

Only a matter of days before final application date did it become public knowledge that Peter Cadbury's company had opposition. Tor Television had as its chairman the Yeovil MP John Peyton. In addition to a number of West Country businessmen, the group included several television (mainly drama) professionals. The group's application laid special emphasis on their proposed contribution to children's programmes. They were strongly critical of Westward's performance in this field, as well as deploring what they held to be the generally poor professional quality of most current local output. However, the Authority did not find their statement of their own programme thinking particularly impressive. A staff note for the Authority gave a different view of Westward's programmes. It laid stress on the substantial progress made by the company in the past three years, once they had given up their initial mistaken programme and management policies. Now, having concentrated management and programme control in Plymouth under Bill Cheevers, they were doing all that could be asked of them. A new contract was duly offered to Westward and accepted.

(vii) SOUTHERN ENGLAND

Southern's opposition was somewhat stronger and the application by the Southern Cross consortium was certainly more thoroughly thought out. It will be recalled that in 1963 the Authority had felt obliged to press for greater regional participation in the boardroom control of Southern's affairs. Their new competitor, led by Lord De l'Isle, intended to have a board of nine members, four of whom were resident in the area. Two others had their main business interests in the area. Southern Cross proclaimed their firm intention to keep their company's financial roots in the region so that the profits of the company would be seen to be ploughed back into the area. Of their proposed voting capital of £1 million, 10 per cent each would be owned by two trusts, called respectively the Southern Trust and the Talent Trust. The first of these would have in its membership a wide range of individuals, representative of public and business life in the area, as well as such public institutions as the Chichester Festival Theatre, the Glyndebourne Trust, to say nothing of fifteen local newspapers. The Talent Trust would be designed to give talented professionals – all of them potential programme contributors – an indirect financial stake, through membership of the Trust, in the programme company. A new studio complex would be built in Brighton, which the group contended would be a better, more strategically placed, centre for coverage of the whole Southern region than Southampton. It would, for example, help to overcome the alleged feeling by viewers in the eastern extremities of the area that their interests had been neglected.

Although their rivals claimed that Southern Television had totally failed to establish themselves as a television programme company either in the minds of the national viewing public or in professional broadcasting circles, Southern's own application provided documented evidence to the contrary with a list of some dozen recent programmes and series they had produced which had been shown on all or part of the national network. These included a contribution to ITV children's programmes of which they could justifiably be proud.

When Southern's Chairman, John Davis, was once more taxed by the Authority with the company's lack of financial roots in the region, he remained unrepentant. He could not see any advantage which would accrue to the image of ITV from putting the shares in Southern Television on the market. It was his belief that the shares would be traded on the London stock market and would be unlikely to end up in the possession of local people. He went on to point out that the two major corporate investors in Southern – Associated Newspapers and Rank – already had some 75,000 shareholders, a high proportion of whom were Southern region residents.

This apparent self-contradiction may not have gone unnoticed. But what the Authority did fix on was the absence from the interview of any spokesmen for Southern's senior programme executives. If the Members were expected to regard the company's programme achievement and future potential as factors outweighing the disadvantage, as they saw it, of

Southern's financial structure, an opportunity to discuss programme matters with such people was, surely, essential. An invitation was formally extended to a second interview, at which this deficiency could be made good. It took place on 19 May and was attended by Berkeley Smith (Programme Controller), Jack Hargreaves (Executive Producer), A. F. Jackman (Head of Programme Planning) and Terry Johnston (Head of News and Current Affairs). These were in addition to David Wilson, G. R. Dowson and Professor Asa Briggs as representatives of the Board.

In preparation for this meeting Wilson sent the Authority a detailed list with explanatory notes of his company's programme output, both local and networked, since the start of their current contract. A staff note was also provided by Fraser which stated that Southern had produced Independent Television's best country programmes and that *How*, an informative programme of charm and originality, was the best new children's programme to arrive in the ITV schedules for many a year. The note went on to say that in Berkeley Smith, Jack Hargreaves, Stephen Wade and Terry Johnston, Southern had as strong a creative programme team as existed in the regions. The programme men did themselves and their company full justice. Some well-roasted chestnuts were pulled out of the fire. Southern were duly offered a contract with no special strings attached.

(viii) WALES AND THE WEST

Lord Derby had some difficulty in falling in with the ITA timetable of interviews, and he did not in correspondence find Hill helpful in making an adjustment. Nevertheless, following the submission of a reasonably workmanlike TWW contract application, he was prudent enough to inform the Authority that the 44 per cent of voting shares in TWW held by the *News of the World* and the *Liverpool Daily Post and Echo* would be, if it so wished, reduced to 38 per cent, and an opportunity was also taken to explain that projected changes in the representation of Welsh interests on TWW's Board had been held over because of the serious illness of Sir Grismond Philips, chairman of their Welsh Board. Apart from these two matters, on which they believed the Authority might need reassurance, there is no evidence that the Chairman and directors of TWW entertained any doubts that they would be considered in all other respects fully qualified to remain programme contractor for the ITV region in Wales and the West.

At the time of their application TWW had seventeen members of their main Board (not counting Sir Grismond Philips, who died on 8 May). Of the seventeen, ten did not live in the area and six were seventy years old or older. The management headquarters was in London where (apart from the Chief Engineer and the Managers of the Bristol and Cardiff studios) virtually all their management staff were based. This included the Programme Controller, Bryan Michie.

Michie had been a protégé of Jack Hylton who, as was seen in Volume 1, was one of the chief founders of the company. But Hylton's death in 1965 altered the balance of power, enhancing the influence of the *News of the World* interest, which had hitherto been balanced by Hylton's wide-ranging professional entertainment and arts interests. Not only Michie but other senior executives like Alfred Francis, the former Managing Director, and Frank Brown, the Publicity Director, now lacked a powerful patron, respected and trusted by Lord Derby. These three men had little to do with the contract application.

The company would have been wise if they had made better known, both to the Authority and more widely, what they considered to be the positive advantages of their London base. Some of the arguments were summarised in notes supplied to the author in 1979 by Frank Brown:

> The advantages of a London base were considered by the company to outweigh its disadvantages. They straddled two sensitive and disparate areas, brought a little closer together when the Severn bridge was eventually built. Working from London prevented a misinterpretation of decisions which could have followed its transfer to either Bristol or Cardiff where it was planned to have equally balanced programme production facilities and budgets.
>
> A London base allowed for an extremely efficient system for handling film programmes and commercials, many of which were 'bicycled' around the growing number of contracting companies. It allowed TWW to play a prominent part in the formation and servicing of the British Regional Television Association which clarified common industry policies by the smaller companies within the framework of the Independent Television Companies Association, dominated by the majors. TWW played a prominent part in establishing a separate and more competitive film purchasing policy for the regional companies.

These arguments were inconclusive but they were by no means ill-considered, and certainly the company might have done more to dispel the belief – which was widespread – that their management were 'remote' from the areas they were serving.

TWW's competitors were a new consortium led by Lord Harlech, former British Ambassador in Washington and current President of the British Board of Film Censors. It was born of the fusion of two groups, one from the Bristol area and one from Wales and had as a consequence an unusually large Board of some two dozen directors, divided equally between the two sides of the Bristol Channel. The West Country contingent included several prominent Bristol businessmen, some of whom also had interests in the arts, like William Poeton, managing director of a group of engineering companies, founder and Chairman of the Bristol Arts Centre. The Chairman and Managing Director of the *Bristol Evening Post*, Walter Hawkins, was also of their number. They were shortly to be joined by Harold Sylvester, Bristol's Chief Education Officer who was about to retire. On the Welsh side there were some well-known names, such as BBC broadcasters John Morgan and Wynford Vaughan Thomas, the latter their proposed Programme Controller; and stars of film and theatre, Richard Burton and Stanley Baker, and Geraint Evans, the opera singer. Welsh cultural activities were well represented by the poet Alun Llewelyn-Williams, Director of Extra Mural Studies at Bangor, a former member of the ITA's Welsh Committee and himself a frequent broadcaster; and QC Alun Talfan Davies, who beside being on the governing bodies of the Aberystwyth and Swansea University Colleges was very active in the promotion of contemporary Welsh literature. Also on the Board were Gerald Bright – better known to the general public as Geraldo of dance band fame; and Eric Thomas (of Woodall's Newspapers) who had, it may be remembered, played as managing director a very creditable role in the salvage operation that filled the last days of the ill-fated WWN company.

There were to be £50,000 'A' voting shares of which the directors at any one time would between them always hold half. The other half would be held between nine named corporate bodies, all connected with the area, such as Imperial Tobacco and Harveys of Bristol pension funds, the *Newport Argus* newspaper and the *Bristol Evening Post*, the General Piped TV Co. of Neath and the Bath & Portland Stone Company. There would be as well £400,000 'B' non-voting shares and £2 million of 7½ per cent unsecured loan stock which it was hoped to repay within four years of air date: 60 per cent of these two pieces of capital had already been applied for. The remainder was being held for possible future public issue.

In their written application this group made statements very reminiscent of those in that of the London weekend consortium, e.g. 'that although the station must be run on sound business principles and on a profitable basis, this should not be the sole consideration but that emphasis should be placed

on the development and encouragement of artistic, cultural and educational activities in the area'. Head Office and administrative centre would
be in Cardiff. Board meetings would be six to eight times a year, alternating
between Bristol and Cardiff. There would be an executive committee of the
full Board, meeting much more often. They did not name an intended
Managing Director.[17]

The programme parts of the Harlech application held great appeal for
the Authority, and contained no traces of the speed at which they had been
composed. They were extremely well-written and displayed a particularly
thoughtful approach to regional television. They propounded a thesis that
the world-wide spread of mass communication media had – paradoxically –
stimulated in the public a resurgence of regionalism, a heightened sense of
regional identity calling for fuller expression through the arts and patterns
of life. 'In this light,' they said, 'the West of England and Wales have
potentially a remarkable contribution to make . . . a source of programmes
on all aspects of life.' The region, they claimed, had produced more people
of talent in the crafts of communication, actors, singers, writers, than any
area of comparable size in the world. Especially in the case of those of Welsh
origin, such individuals had retained strong emotional ties with their
homeland. For Richard Burton, Stanley Baker and Geraint Evans, a Welsh
TV station seemed to offer a welcome means for the expression of their
cultural patriotism. All three, together with Harry Secombe, had made firm
programme commitments to the Harlech group, because 'they believe, and
the group shares their belief, that the television station should make a
contribution both financial and in talent to the development of live theatre,
opera and the cinema in the area'. Such declarations were bound to appeal
to the ITA with its persistent public commitment to regionalism as the main
distinguishing characteristic of the television system for which it had
responsibility.

TWW for their part were content to 'stand on their record'.[18] It is true that
record was not a bad one, even though latterly there had been from time to
time expressions at staff level of ITA discontent and pressures for improvement in schedule balance. But, as must surely be the case in ITV contract
awards where there is competition, the decision had to depend on a
balanced judgement of the future potential of each of the competing
applicants. On the one side supporting evidence for that potential could of
course be found in a record of past programme achievement. On the other,
similar evidence could be sought only in the impression made by the
statements and personalities of the applicants, supported in some degree by
a record of past achievement in other, related, activities. In neither case,

however, could past successes offer a one hundred per cent guarantee of future achievement. Other factors must, and on this occasion did, intervene.

At their interview by the ITA the Harlech delegation, notably in the persons of Poeton, Morgan and Harlech himself, were more impressively convincing than the TWW spokesmen. Leaving aside their presumed and necessary merits as businessmen and managers, they showed themselves to be able professional communicators, skilled in the art of adapting their discourse to the character and known expectations of their audience. In particular, the concluding statement by Lord Harlech was the finest piece of spoken prose heard at any of the thirty-six ITA interviews. It was a polished, clearly well prepared performance, drawing together, as he put it, the main strands of their case, re-emphasising both dedication to regionalism and commitment to that spirit of public responsibility that would dictate a conservative dividend policy.

By contrast, TWW spokesmen seemed ill-prepared and confused, at times even self-contradictory. They appeared not to have foreseen the possibly decisive importance of the interview, nor to have anticipated the likely course of the interrogation. It is odd that at this crucial juncture in the affairs of his company Chapman-Walker's flair (to which, as we saw in Volume 1, ITV owed much) should have seemingly deserted him.

So, inevitably as it now seems, on 10 June, letters were presented to both groups informing them that Lord Harlech's group was being offered the contract. The offer was conditional on purchase from TWW – if TWW were willing to sell – of the latter's studio installations in Bristol and Cardiff; and on the offer to TWW of a 40 per cent interest in the non-voting stock of the new company. Harlech were also told that (apart from that 40 per cent and any other holdings outside the area the Authority might permit) the remainder of their total share and loan capital should be allocated equally between Welsh and West Country interests.

Lord Derby's reaction to the 'bombshell'[19] decision by the Authority was immediate. He was outraged and said so. Telegrams and letters went to Hill expressing 'bewilderment and astonishment' and conveying the 'vehement feelings' of his Board that they were entitled to a further hearing before the decision was made final. In these and in other communications, some of which were released to the press, the recurrent theme was a sense of grievous injustice, revealing feelings of deeply wounded pride. At no time in the past ten years, it was claimed, had TWW's management been told of serious inadequacies in their performance. Any complaints had always been promptly acted upon. They even believed, they said, that they had answered the 'routine questions' put at their interview, to the Authority

Members' entire satisfaction. If there were indeed genuinely grave short-comings in the public service they had over ten years so conscientiously striven to render, then elementary justice to directors, management staff and over 8000 shareholders demanded that they should have been told of them in advance. Since that had not been done they should in all fairness be given now an opportunity of hearing what these criticisms were, in order that they might give their answers.

Hill remained unmoved. In a letter to Derby which he also released to the Press, he reminded TWW's Chairman that all ITV contracts were for a fixed, pre-stated period with no presumption of automatic renewal, and that Derby himself had said as much to his shareholders after the 1963 decisions.[20] If fairness demanded anything it must surely be that all applicants for a contract, old and new, should be given an equal chance. Admittedly newcomers could offer only promises in lieu of performance. 'But if promise is never to be preferred to performance, then every television company will go on for ever.'[21] Both contenders had been equally free to present their case. The Authority chose the applicant they had unanimously judged to be the better. It was its duty to do so. He rejected the suggestion that Authority freedom of choice should be inhibited by the knowledge that a company's shares were publicly quoted. That too could imply permanent tenure for incumbent contractors. Investors buying such shares were *ipso facto* speculators operating in the knowledge that company contracts had a limited assured life. As for the original founder shareholders, any who had retained an original £1000 purchase had a holding worth at latest prices £10,000 and would have also received over the past ten years a further £10,000 in dividends, after tax. It was no pleasure to the Authority to be parting from a company with which it had worked for ten years. It would be easier to leave things alone. But that was not what the Television Act said it should do. However adequate its programmes, a company always lived with the risk that it would encounter a better competitor. In the nature of things, it might not happen often. This time it did. That remained the Authority's position.

The Authority made no official, public rebuttal of the complaint that they had given no warnings of dissatisfaction with the company's programme performance. Since its case was that the decision arose from a judgement of potential, not of past performance, it could not logically do so. There had been occasions when headquarters staff had had to act in support of regular complaints from their colleague, the Welsh officer, over the unsatisfactory balance of TWW's local programming. Details of these were put together, but they do not appear to have had any bearing on the decision that was taken to reject Lord Derby's request to be allowed to make further representations.

The dismissal of TWW was treated by the press as the outstanding sensation of the 1967 contract decisions. 'The main surprise of ITA's new deal,'[22] said *The Times*. There was some criticism of the arbitrary nature of the proceedings. 'Perhaps it should have been expected,' said the *Telegraph*, 'that Lord Hill would reach the conclusion that contracts awarded perforce somewhat arbitrarily in the beginning could be as arbitrarily reallocated now, especially where they had reaped a rich harvest in the interim.'[23] The lessons to be drawn were probably most neatly summed up by a *Guardian* leader of 21 June. It said:

> TWW has obviously been sadly upset to discover that the Television Act of 1964, as interpreted by the ITA, means what it says. Television franchises do not last for ever . . . Television Wales and the West, like all other independent television companies, is a public utility contractor, and TWW must not complain if the duly authorised public licensing authority decides to change to a contractor which it regards as better qualified.

However, still clearly deeply resentful, the directors of TWW turned their attention to the future interests of their shareholders. By late November 1967 negotiations had been concluded for the sale to Harlech of the Bristol and Cardiff studios and facilities. (This was extended to include stocks of programme material and unused film rights.) The agreed price was £1.6 million. In this welcome decision the Authority found the reassurance it had sought from the beginning that the future employment of TWW staff, as well as pension and other rights, would be in large measure safeguarded. At the same time a second decision was made by TWW not to take up the 40 per cent investment in Harlech. From the outset of the negotiations they had disclaimed any interest in this possibility and eventually, with their agreement, the Authority absolved Harlech from making any formal offer. In due course shareholders were offered instead a cash hand-out from their company's liquid balance of some £2¾ million plus a proportionate issue of new shares in TWW (Enterprises) Ltd, the company formed to manage their diversified interests in such enterprises as opticians Dollond and Aitchison and the Donmar Theatrical Companies. Once this operation was completed, the television company went into voluntary liquidation at the end of July 1968.

Further trauma symptoms may perhaps be read into the comparative readiness with which TWW even entered into an agreement to cede (for half a million) the last few months of their television contract to Harlech. As a result the new company went on the air, with Authority agreement, not as originally intended on 30 July, the date on which all the other new contracts came into force, but on 4 March 1968.

For their final week, TWW, or their programme staff at least, had sufficiently recovered their equilibrium to be able to bid their viewers 'Goodbye' with a flourish. On Saturday 2 March they screened a special star-studded edition of their popular success *Discs a Gogo*; and on the Sunday evening at 10.35 p.m. a big name spectacular was shown. It was compered by Bernard Braden and included Morecambe and Wise, Tessie O'Shea, Ivor Emmanuel, Manfred Mann, Stan Stennett, Clifford Evans and many other popular entertainers who had appeared for TWW during the previous ten years. Unkind critics could say it was a bill that fairly represented where TWW's main programme interests lay. The show was called *All Good Things* . . . It was immediately followed – after the commercial break – by *Come to an End*, a brief valedictory spoken by John Betjeman.

(ix) GENERAL

None of the remaining franchise decisions presented problems. In six areas, the existing contractors were the only applicants; and Anglia, Border, Channel, Grampian, Tyne Tees and Ulster Television were all offered new contracts without any special conditions attached other than those applying to all companies, new and old. Only in the case of Border did the Authority reserve to itself the right to require the managing director and programme controller to take up residence in the area; and this condition was not in the event included in the terms of the contract.

There were three general conditions all companies were asked to accept. The first of these referred to the age of company directors. Some applications from incumbent contractors revealed not only that some of their Board members had been there a long time but also that they included a higher proportion of the elderly than, in the ITA's view, seemed appropriate for a young medium. It was prescribed that in future retirement age for ITV company directors should be seventy years. Only on express approval from the Authority could a director stay on after that age; in no case would an extension beyond seventy-five be permitted.

Secondly, there was the question of the programme weeklies, on which opinions had been sought from all contract applicants. Hitherto the seven different publications used to advertise ITV programmes had been regarded as an exclusively company concern, not subject to Authority control or supervision. The most widely distributed was *TV Times*, of which seven regional editions appeared. Hill and his colleagues found that, whatever the advantages of regional diversity in programme terms, it did not in these publications lead to a consistently high standard likely to do credit to the public image of ITV. They therefore proposed that a central publishing company should be set up, on the model of ITN, to produce a single nationwide programme paper for the whole of ITV, but with regional editions.

An able inter-company working party was set up with the task of elaborating a workable plan. It was brilliantly successful and by late June a plan was adopted and given Authority approval. There would be a new company called Independent Television Publications (ITP). It would have on its Board representatives of all the ITV companies with the exception of Channel, which, with the agreement of the ITA, would continue to be able to supplement its income by production and sale of *Channel Viewer*. The new national programme magazine would take over its title from *TV Times*. The Director General would attend all *TV Times* Board meetings, in the same way as he attended those of ITN.

The third general condition attached to every new contract offer referred to the establishment of a common ITV fund to support the arts and sciences. It was Marshall McLuhan who had observed that new media of public communication nearly always take over as their subject matter the previously existing older media. Television was seen by many people as voraciously parasitic on the live arts, especially those of theatre and music. The companies had generally come to acknowledge their obligation to help in the public support for the nurture and development of those arts and sciences on which their activities so largely depended. Patronage had been exercised by most of them over the past ten years, usually and under-standably in their own service areas. The total sums disbursed in this way amounted to well over £1¼ million by 1967. Such expenditure was of course over and above the greatly increased opportunities for gainful employment created by the coming of ITV for a wide range of artists, writers, craftsmen and performers. However, the ITA concluded that still more might – and ought to be – done through a central ITV fund to which all companies should contribute. It was made a contractual condition. All companies accepted it in principle.

(x) AN APPRAISAL

The events and decisions recorded in this chapter were the most surprising and dramatic in the history of ITV thus far. Moreover, for some fifteen years the feeling that a grave injustice was done to Rediffusion has remained strong, and not only amongst those who were adversely affected by it. For TWW the situation was different. There, a straight choice was made between one application and another. If at this time TWW were out of form there was, of course, no reason why they could not have recovered it in a reasonable time. But they were drawn against a lively challenger and they lost the fight on points. On their behalf it might be argued that, unlike James Coltart of STV, Lord Derby did not receive any timely personal warning from Lord Hill that his contract might be in jeopardy.[24]

It would have seemed to Wills and some of his colleagues that the position in 1967 had improved since 1964 when the contracts were previously under review. The old A-R had been restructured on lines commendable to the ITA, and Wills, rather against his better judgement – had obligingly modified his own concept of the correct organisation for running an efficient programme company in order to meet the views held at Brompton Road. Now the ten-man Board of Rediffusion Television included no less than five full-time professional television executives. The success he had so stoutly claimed for his company in 1964 had by common consent continued unabated in the intervening three years and consequently, as he saw it, the renewal of their contract for a further term should have been a fixed point in any new mosaic the ITA might wish to devise. No reason that he could see existed for changing the franchise of the most important of all companies: he saw no need to look beyond the fact that his company, to which all Independent Television owed so much, remained in excellent shape, and were providing an all-round public service which brought credit to the system and a good financial return to the shareholders. The fact that changes were to be made in the structure of ITV in the North and the Midlands, and indeed in London also (as a result of transferring Friday evenings to the weekend contractor) seemed irrelevant to Rediffusion's just claim. Consequently, he felt able to lead from strength at the interview, and he did so.

So far as personal relationships were concerned he was conscious of a certain lack of rapport between Hill and himself and he believed that Hill did not like him. But he saw this as a business matter in which personal likes and dislikes were surely not important. Within his own company, he had been informed by McMillan at an earlier stage of the latter's wish to join in a bid for the Yorkshire contract: he had raised no objection to it and had so informed his Board. He did not know that two other professional members of his Board, Bennett and Paine, were prominent among the consortium seeking the London weekend franchise. Regrettably – one might even say deplorably – they had elected not to tell him. Had he known, Wills would doubtless have thought it well to inform the Authority that he did not wish to stand in the way of his staff seeking to better themselves financially. To him, as a businessman, they would have been clear cases of ambitious young men scenting the prospect of financial gain through shares in the equity of the new company. The possibility that their behaviour might be seen by Members of the ITA as evidence of desertions from an unhappy ship would not have occurred to him. Understandably, when he subsequently heard of their secret defection, he considered it to have been little short of treachery.

Unquestionably the reputation of Rediffusion Television at Brompton Road stood high. If Authority Members were not directly aware of the company's high standing from their own observation the reports from their staff could not have left them with room for doubt. Perhaps the rather overbearing manner of Wills and his deputy, Lord Tangley, at the interview would have been a surprise, not to say a shock, to some of the newer Members. But the older hands, including Hill, who had experienced it all before in 1964, were undisturbed. Hill told the author as recently as 1981 that he had never felt anything but respect for Wills.

To an informed observer the scenario would have seemed fairly easily predictable. A new major company would be appointed to take over the seven days in Yorkshire and, without question, Granada would be offered seven days in Lancashire and would accept. ATV's tenure of the London weekend was probably going to be terminated, but, since their immense resources and potential were virtually indispensable, they would be invited to take seven days in the Midlands. If, against expectations, ATV were offered an enlarged weekend franchise in London, then ABC would undoubtedly get the Midlands; but it was more likely that ABC would be invited to take over in London at the weekends, working from their new studios in Teddington. Rediffusion would have its 'long London' contract renewed, subject to the loss of Friday evenings.

What changed the whole picture was the emergence of the London weekend consortium and their brilliant success in selling themselves to the ITA. Persuaded that this consortium offered an opportunity which just could not be missed, the ITA had then to face the consequences. 'It had to have its chance whatever the repercussions,'[25] wrote Hill. Lose Rediffusion? Unthinkable. Throw ABC to the wolves? Indefensible. Put them together and you would have acquired for London ITV such an array of talent as had not previously been dreamed of. A merger of two such dissimilar companies to manage what was still the most important of all the franchises might, thought the ITA, be a tricky business, but it was extremely unlikely that either company would pull out and leave such a rich plum to the other. As

Chapter 27 has shown, this was not the first time that the Authority had considered involving A-R in a marriage of convenience. Since on that occasion Wills had peremptorily rebuffed an attempt to coax him into matrimony, Hill had no inclination to resort to that approach again. This time it had to be 'take it or leave it'.

But, if a marriage was arranged, were the partners to be equal in all respects with alternating chairmen and joint managing directors? This would be an equivocal arrangement – a recipe for disaster. The nettle had to be grasped. The decision was that Howard Thomas with his able and experienced lieutenants, Brian Tesler, Programme Controller and George Cooper, Director of Sales, should be top dogs. John McMillan had no comparable lieutenants (for they were going to the successful weekend applicant) and his principal remaining aide – the thirty-five-year-old Lord Windlesham (formerly David Hennessey) was still rather an unknown quantity. It was a painful decision, and, so far as McMillan personally was concerned, a brutal one. Not only to Wills and his colleagues but to many detached observers, it seemed to add insult to injury.

'I have never been given a reason for the treatment accorded to Rediffusion Television Limited,' wrote Wills to the author on 15 July 1981. One supposes it might have been thought that an attempt to explain the overall background would inflame rather than defuse the situation. What has been written in the preceding paragraphs offers not so much 'a reason' as a credible explanation. There is a striking contrast between the clarity and conviction with which the dismissal of TWW was defended in public and the failure to provide justification for the forced marriage of ABC and Rediffusion, with the former as the dominant partner, saving in terms of its being a 'repercussion' of the decision about the London weekend.

It would be pointless to ask in conclusion whether, if the London weekend consortium and Harlech had not been thrust into the arena, Independent Television would have been worse, or better, or about the same. Suffice to say that its best years of achievement lay ahead. Thames rapidly became a dominant force in ITV affairs and London Weekend, after agonising upheavals, eventually came good. Harlech, too, after a shaky start, became a sound and workmanlike company, providing an enterprising programme service, which was none the worse for bearing no very marked resemblance to the one so elegantly described in their application.

Despite any appearances to the contrary, the decisions were not Lord Hill's alone. The Authority Members acted collectively in dispensing their justice, rough though it undoubtedly was. Two years later one of them publicly expressed his doubts whether the decisions had been right.[26] There was, of course, no provision for any appeal. Clearly, they fell somewhat short of observing Lord Chief Justice Hewart's dictum 'Justice should not only be done, but manifestly and undoubtedly be seen to be done'. But they were not a court of law and they discharged their unpleasant task with a proper regard for the duty imposed upon them by Parliament.

37

OUTLOOK UNSETTLED

Television had long been a continuing source of copy for the press, but there had probably never been a more massive accumulation of column inches than that evoked by the events of 1967. Comment was varied and diffuse. Certain themes, however, tended to dominate. The arbitrary and secret nature of the selection process and the apparent concentration of power in a body not itself directly answerable to the electorate naturally came in for comment. The fairness or otherwise of particular decisions, though not overlooked, gained less attention than the reminders these provided that ITV contracts generally were of limited life, with all the financial consequences for investors of that fact. A few commentators chose to consider what the changes might mean for the future not only of ITV but of British television generally, including the BBC. At his Press Conference announcing the new contracts Hill had stated the two principles which had guided the Authority's decisions. First was the quality of the programmes. Second was the refusal to accept that companies once appointed should be 'there for all time' irrespective of the quality of new applicant groups.

On 28 June an adjournment debate[1] in Parliament was initiated by the Liberals. It was opened by Dr Michael Winstanley, himself a frequent broadcaster for Granada. While agreeing that the ITA had done no more than discharge the duty laid on it by Parliament, he drew attention to some aspects of the system which were the subject of public disquiet. He wondered, for example, whether machinery could not be devised for making the contract award procedure more open to public scrutiny and for allowing the possibility of appeal by a rejected applicant. He also touched on the problem of company diversification into non-TV interests and seemed not too happy over the extent of press participation, in some cases actively encouraged by the Authority. If the press were to be in effect subsidised by television earnings would it not be thereby inhibited in exercising its traditional watchdog role? From the Labour benches, Christopher Rowland praised the Authority's conduct. It had, he said, asserted its rights and shown its prime interest to be programme quality, not profit levels. It had been right, he felt, to reach its decisions in secrecy; but he considered that 'once the decisions have been reached, the applications of successful applicants and a résumé of the evidence they put to the ITA should be published'.

Paul Bryan, who had resigned as a director of Granada on becoming Conservative Party broadcasting spokesman, was equally complimentary, while admitting that the changes had shocked the industry. Some of the Authority Members were themselves, he suspected, 'secretly aghast at how bold they had been'. On balance, he believed that the shake-up, and especially the resulting general post of talent, could well have a reinvigorating effect. He agreed that disquiet existed over the secrecy of the proceedings and would be prepared himself to support a system of public hearings, if it could be shown to be workable – which he doubted. All in all, he thought the ITA had an unanswerable case for what it had done. There could therefore be every reason for allowing both the Authority's contract prospectus and the written applications of the successful companies to be published. He concluded by urging a relaxation in the controls on hours of television broadcasting. Now that the BBC had two channels, it was absurd to limit ITV companies to the hours that BBC 1 was on the air.

The PMG, Edward Short, who intervened at this stage, did not accept the idea of public hearings, that the Authority should give reasons for its decisions or that there should be a right of appeal against them. 'My conception of a public corporation in this country is that we should either back it up or sack it, but not muck it about.' He fully backed the TWW decision, repeating in substance the public statements already made by Hill. On press participation, he thought the Authority was taking the right line: some 'ownership of shares by representative newspapers [was] extremely valuable, but not to the extent of control by a single newspaper or press interest'. On excessive profits, he recalled that their control was the purpose of the levy introduced by the 1963 Act. He reminded members that levy plus corporation tax already took three quarters of company profits and he assured the House that he would not hesitate to exercise his power to reduce or increase the levy by Order if that were thought necessary. He offered small hope of a second commercial channel, standing by the arguments previously put in Wedgwood Benn's White Paper, and concluded by pointing out that 'nine years from now, an opportunity will arise for a fundamental review' of the whole broadcasting system because BBC and ITA licences would be terminating on that date. 'I cannot see the present kind of organisation lasting for very much more than the decade we have ahead of us.'

Robert Cooke, an old campaigner for a competitive broadcasting system, regretted the Minister's statement about the fourth channel for that very reason. He even suggested that ITA engineers should not be so active in trying to prevent overlap between transmitters serving adjacent company areas. Overlaps meant more competition and were therefore desirable. If no second commercial service was planned, deliberate overlaps creating more competition were the next best thing. Hugh Jenkins of Actors' Equity spoke for the workers in television, emphasising the uncertainty about continuity of employment and career prospects introduced by the reminder the Authority had given that ITV company contracts had limited lives. If the only permanent organisation in ITV is the Authority, he said, it should be the Authority's responsibility for maintaining the continuity of employment that the companies could not offer. Without reasonable career prospects for those who actually make the programmes, the Authority's assumption of a dominant role could have damaging rather than beneficial consequences for the programme service. It would also do much to obviate such difficulties if the levy were imposed on company earnings net of programme expenditure. This, he thought, would encourage companies to apply more resources to their programmes and less to investment in enterprises outside the industry.

The Liberal leader Jeremy Thorpe, in replying to the debate, touched on themes already discussed, the great power conferred on those given even temporary control of the television medium, and the consequent need for Parliament to keep a watchful eye. He disapproved of the PMG's dismissal of the proposals that the ITA should give reasons for its contract decisions and that there should be possibility of an appeal against them. 'Some sort of appellate body would be useful. There is real disquiet and I do not think that the Postmaster-General has recognised it in the way he should.' Thorpe had himself in the past worked for the Current Affairs Department of Rediffusion. He certainly still had old friends and colleagues on the staff of that company, many of whom were at the end of June 1967 in a state of anxiety over their professional future.

These variations on already well-worn themes were the dominant characteristic of a rather perfunctory Parliamentary occasion. Neither then nor in the welter of press comment was there any real hint of the shape of things to come during the years immediately following the start of the new contracts at the end of July 1968. The startling and disconcerting developments in 1969 and 1970, when ITV encountered its biggest set-back since 1956, are outside the scope of this volume, but it is necessary in this concluding chapter to refer to some of the plain facts about economic trends in the industry which received little public attention until the National

Board for Prices and Incomes reported on ITV in October 1970.[2] It is also necessary to look at the developments that had been taking place in ITV's industrial relations over the years since 1964. We shall then see that the issues which dominated 1967 – important as they undoubtedly were – obscured other issues of no less importance which, even if they were perceived at all, were not held to be relevant to the award of the new contracts.

As we saw in Chapter 34, the average annual increase in revenue from 1965 to 1969 was about 5 per cent. This was reasonably well ahead of the average rate of inflation but it was modest compared with former years. The companies could no longer rely on a growing audience, because population coverage of the service was nearing its maximum and an improved BBC 1, supplemented by BBC 2, was making inroads in ITV's share of the total audience. On the other hand, over the same period, total costs were rising more steeply – from approximately £44 million in 1965 to nearly £65 million in 1969. It was the companies' belief that inflation had a much more direct impact on costs than on revenues. Moreover, as the Prices and Incomes Board pointed out, an exceptionally big increase in 1968 was largely attributable to an increase of nearly 25 per cent in administration expenses. These included significant terminal and redundancy payments by ABC, Rediffusion and TWW, following the 1967 contract awards. 'But for these payments total costs would have increased in 1968 by no more than 7 per cent.'[3] Of course, by the time this report came to be published in October 1970 a more serious and permanent further increase had become evident, namely that created by the establishment of an additional franchise area in Yorkshire: ' . . . we estimate that at least a third of the total increase in costs in 1969 over 1968 can be attributed to the introduction of the Yorkshire company'.[4]

The progressively deteriorating trend since 1965 in the relationship between revenue and costs was obscured by the continuing high rate of return on capital employed. A return of around 50 per cent on capital (see Chapter 34) compared with a rate of return in the manufacturing industry generally over roughly the same period of some 13 per cent.

The graph taken from the NBPI report and reproduced on the page opposite displays at a glance the economic history of ITV in the second half of the sixties. It was only after the new contracts came into operation at the end of July 1968 that, as will be seen in the next volume, the alarm bells rang out loud and clear, but it will be seen from the graph and from the preceding paragraphs that coming events did cast their shadows before.

This was so particularly if manpower costs and the course of industrial

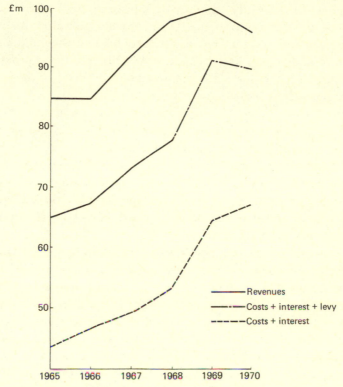

Revenues, levy, interest and total costs excluding taxation 1964–9 (actual) 1970 (estimated)

The centre line does not take account of the increased scale of levy announced in the 1969 Budget and effective from July of that year.

Source: NBPI Enquiry

relations are taken into account. During the course of the 1964 contracts some 40 per cent of total company costs went in wages and salaries of staff and fees to actors, writers and other freelance workers. The percentage increase in the wage and salary bill over the period we have been examining was 36 per cent – a figure appreciably higher than the comparable national one.[5]

What were the developments in industrial relations which had given rise to these startling figures? Back in 1964 an increase in the scale of the levy in the April Budget coincided with the expiry of the pay agreement with the ACTT, and by July – aided by a well-timed strike and a personal intervention by the new Labour Prime Minister, Harold Wilson – the union had secured rises of $17\frac{1}{2}$ per cent spread over a three-year period, together with increased holidays and improved working conditions. The view has been expressed by

Peter Seglow in his study of trade unionism in television that if the companies had not given in so quietly in 1964, the troubles which arose in 1966–8 would not have assumed the proportions they did.[6] But the settlement brought two-and-a-half years of virtual industrial peace, even if it meant pay increases for ACTT technicians well ahead of those in other industries generally.

From late 1966 onwards individual companies began to experience further industrial troubles, culminating in March 1967 in a dispute at ATV, with ACTT members demanding premium payments for recording programmes in colour for export to the United States. Despite concern in the industry that conceding the demand would constitute a precedent for new pay rates when ITV itself went over to colour, Lew Grade settled. He was reported to have said that failure to do so would lose his company orders worth more than £$\frac{1}{2}$ million.[7]

Then came the contract changes announced on 11 June, and within a few days staff reactions began to manifest themselves; and especially so on the part of the technicians, for, just as they had stood most to gain from ITV prosperity, so they stood most to lose from the big upheaval. Beginning with an overtime ban on ABC in the Alpha studios at Birmingham early in July through to a stoppage of work – also at Alpha – towards the end of January 1968, there were at least a dozen strikes, overtime bans or brief programme blackouts, mostly by the technicians, affecting ABC, ATV, ITN, Rediffusion and STV – all resulting directly from the outcome of the contract decisions. It would be wrong to say that trouble over the dislocation of staff was unforeseen, but the extent of the repercussions was altogether beyond expectations. In the end, after countless protracted meetings between managements and unions, with the ACTT making the main running, *The Times* was able to write in March: 'the union (ACTT) had achieved its declared aim of eliminating the word "redundancy" '.[8]

Seglow describes the outcome as follows:

Technicians employed by the old TWW company were taken on the books of the new contractor – Harlech – without loss of seniority. Displaced technicians at Alpha were taken on by ATV, those at Associated Rediffusion went to the two new London companies – Thames and London Weekend. The same arrangement was made for the London-based employees of ABC Television. ABC's employees at Didsbury, on the outskirts of Manchester, were taken on by the new Yorkshire station operating out of Leeds to which they and their families would now have to move. Technicians displaced at ABC, Associated Rediffusion, and Alpha received severance payments because, it was argued, they had lost accumulated seniority as their employment had been terminated. These payments were rather in excess of their entitlements under the Redundancy Payments Act. Bearing in mind that there was no interruption in their employment these terms may seem generous, but from the point of view of the affected technicians, they should be seen within the context of the large fortunes that had been amassed by the companies between 1955–6 and 1967. Moreover, the terms had only been achieved by a determined struggle by the unions in general, and the ACTT in particular, which had held some 130 negotiating meetings with the companies.[9]

Looking back on these events when they gave collective evidence to the Annan Committee in March 1975 the ITV companies said:

> The industry's labour relations machinery was severely strained by the re-allocation of franchises in 1967. Some 3000 employees were displaced: roughly one-third of the total employed in the industry. The companies gave an undertaking to all the unions that there would be no re-dundancies. Discussions took place over many months, and in the event all displaced staff were re-deployed, but only after a period of anxiety to them and their families. The freedom of the new companies to recruit staff of their own choice was undesirably limited.[10]

Insecurity was the enemy against which the ACTT fought with such conspicuous success. It was a condition which permeated ITV as it prepared to enter a new contract period. The time was one of national economic recession – devaluation in November 1967 and severe pay restraints in April 1968 – and it was apparent that the franchise trail had after all been no gold rush. Advertisers were holding back and the only certainty was that costs would continue to rise. The advance into colour had to be paid for. The consequences of ITA policy were cost inflationary. The balance of power had swung perceptibly towards the unions. The rival from which so many key men had sought to transfer a year or so earlier was a strong force to be reckoned with. These factors, together with the inevitable reaction from the 1967 upheaval, were daunting, and it almost seemed as if ITV had reached the edge of a precipice.

And yet the new contracts on which ITV was about to embark, and which were destined to last for more than a dozen years, marked a period when the programme output attained the highest level of quality and achieved widely-acclaimed success.

NOTES AND REFERENCES

PREFACE

1. *Report of the Committee on Broadcasting 1960* (HMSO) (Cmnd. 1753). The membership of the Pilkington Committee was: Sir Harry Pilkington (industrialist), Mr H. Collison (trade union leader) (later Lord Collison), Mr Elwyn Davies (Secretary of the University of Wales), Miss Joyce Grenfell (actress), Mr Richard Hoggart (university teacher), Mr E. P. Hudson (Scottish company director), Professor F. H. Newark (Law Faculty, Belfast), Mr J. S. Shields (grammar school headmaster), Mr R. L. Smith-Rose (technical expert), Mrs Elizabeth Whitley (housewife), Mr W. A. Wright (footballer), Mr Peter Hall (theatrical producer), Sir Jock Campbell (industrialist) (later Lord Campbell of Eskan). Peter Hall and Sir Jock Campbell, however, resigned early in 1961. Additionally a key figure was D. G. C. Lawrence, the Committee's secretary and Post Office civil servant, of whom on page 4 the Report records 'his responsibilities have been extensive throughout and in recent months have included the translation of our earlier discussions, hearings and decisions into a complete first draft of our Report, amounting to about 150,000 words'.
2. Lord Hill of Luton, *Behind the Screen* (Sidgwick & Jackson, 1974).
3. R. Bevins, *The Greasy Pole* (Hodder & Stoughton, 1965).

CHAPTER 1: TYNE TEES

1. Application Form Part III ITA File 15.
2. ITA Paper 145(57).
3. Report of a meeting between Fraser, C. C. Darling and G. Black on 14 January 1958, ITA File 7009/1.
4. Ibid. Memorandum by Pragnell dated 14 March 1958.
5. Letter to C. C. Darling dated 24 September 1958 ITA File 7009/2.
6. ITA Minutes 97(58).
7. Correspondence about shareholdings ITA File 7009/1.
8. *The Times*, 22 September 1960.
9. *News Chronicle*, 21 January 1959.
10. *Guardian*, 8 June 1960.
11. *Darlington Northern Echo*, 14 January 1961.
12. *Northern Despatch*, 17 January 1961.
13. *Guardian*, 14 June 1962.
14. ITA File 3095/4/5.
15. *Evening News*, 2 May 1963.
16. ITA Minutes 173(63).
17. *Darlington Northern Echo*, 28 January 1963.

CHAPTER 2: ANGLIA

1. Letter from Fraser dated 20 June 1958, ITA File 7010/1.
2. 4 July 1958.
3. *Report of the Committee on Broadcasting 1960*, Vol II, Appendix E (HMSO) (Cmnd. 1819–1) p. 1193.
4. *Eastern Evening News*, 16 July 1958.
5. ITA File 7010/1.
6. Ibid. Memorandum Fraser to P. A. T. Bevan (ITA Chief Engineer) dated 16 September 1958.
7. Ibid. Fraser to Lord Townshend dated 14 October 1958.
8. ITA Minutes 97(58).
9. ITA Minutes 98(58) and 99(58).
10. ITA Minutes 101(58).
11. ITA Paper 35(59).
12. ITA Minutes 106(59).
13. Letter to Townshend dated 5 June 1959, ITA File 7010/1.
14. *Ipswich Evening Star*, 28 October 1959.
15. *Eastern Daily Press*, 28 October 1959.
16. *Daily Telegraph*, 28 October 1959.
17. *Eastern Daily News*, 27 October 1960.
18. Letter to Townshend dated 14 December 1959, ITA File 7010/1.
19. Quoted by Martin Jackson in the *Daily Express*, 24 January 1963.
20. *The Sunday Times*, 24 September 1961.
21. *Daily Telegraph*, 23 January 1962.

CHAPTER 3: ULSTER

1. ITA Minutes 91(58).
2. ITA Minutes 97(58).
3. *Belfast Evening Telegraph*, 9 September 1958 (Ulsterman's Diary).
4. ITA Minutes 99(58).
5. Letter to Fraser dated 11 February 1959, ITA File 7011/1.
6. Ibid. Letter from Fraser to W. MacQuitty dated 24 April 1959.
7. Ibid. Letter dated 23 February 1959.
8. Ibid. Letter to Lord Antrim dated 25 February 1959.
9. Ibid. Memorandum to N. Stevenson dated 12 June 1959.
10. Ibid. Letter to Stevenson.
11. Ibid. Letter dated 25 June 1959.
12. Quoted in the *Guardian* 10 March 1959.
13. Memorandum dated 25 August 1959, ITA File 5089.
14. Quoted by L. Marsland Gander in the *Daily Telegraph*, 2 November 1959.
15. *Northern Whig*, 2 November 1959.
16. *Daily Telegraph*, 2 November 1959.
17. Ibid.
18. Handwritten note on memo by Stevenson dated 23 November 1959, ITA File 5089.
19. *Belfast Newsletter*, 30 January 1960.
20. Robert Ray in *Belfast Telegraph*, 25 April 1960.
21. *Belfast Telegraph*, 27 September 1960.
22. *Guardian*, 26 October 1960.

23. Ulster Television evidence to Pilkington. Pilkington Report, Vol. II, Appendix E, p. 726.
24. Ibid.

CHAPTER 4: WESTWARD

1. James Thomas in the *Daily Express*, 17 December 1959.
2. ITA Paper 92(58).
3. ITA Minutes 117(59).
4. Letter to Fraser dated 14 June 1960 ITA File 7012/1.
5. ITA Paper 140(60).
6. ITA Paper 146(60) and ITA Minutes 130(60).
7. *Financial Times*, 7 February 1961.
8. *Western Morning News*, 18 December 1959.
9. *Western Evening Herald*, 11 February 1961.
10. *Exeter Express and Echo*, 18 October 1960.
11. Letters Pragnell to G. Bailes dated 1 October 1959 and 11 April 1960, ITA File 7012/1/1.
12. Statement to Douglas Marlborough of the *Daily Mail* on 12 March 1961.
13. *Western Morning News*, 2 May 1961.
14. *Plymouth Independent*, 3 September 1961.
15. Martin Jackson in the *Daily Express*, 26 January 1963.
16. ITA Paper 234(62).
17. *New Daily*, 4 March 1963.
18. *The Sunday Times*, 17 February 1963.
19. ITA Minutes 176(63).
20. Reported in the *Daily Express* 2 August 1963.

CHAPTER 5: CHANNEL

1. ITA Paper 103(59).
2. ITA Paper 8(60) and ITA Minutes 118(60).
3. Contract application by Channel Islands Communications (Television) Ltd, ITA File 18/1.
4. ITA Paper 5(61) and ITA Minutes 135(61).
5. ITA File 7013/1.
6. Ibid. Letter Krichefski to Pragnell dated 14 July 1961.
7. *Guernsey Evening Press*, 5 August 1961.
8. Letter to Pragnell, ITA File 7013/1.
9. Ibid. Memorandum to Sendall dated 19 February 1962.
10. Ibid. Letter Pragnell to Killip dated 22 January 1962.
11. Letter dated 25 October 1965, ITA File 5094.
12. *Daily Telegraph*, 17 June 1963.

CHAPTER 6: BORDER

1. ITA Paper 8(60) and ITA Minutes 118(60).
2. ITA Minutes 119(60).
3. ITA Paper 23(60).
4. ITA Minutes 120(60).

5. Application Form Part 1, ITA File 17.
6. Letter Pragnell to Burgess dated 4 May 1960, ITA File 7014/1.
7. ITA Paper 105(60) and ITA Minutes 128(60).
8. Letters Pragnell to Gill dated 22 August 1961 and Gill to Pragnell dated 24 August 1961, ITA File 7014/1.
9. *Cumberland Evening News*, 24 August 1960.
10. *Isle of Man Weekly Times*, 28 July 1961.
11. *Television Mail*, 1 September 1961.
12. Ibid.
13. Border Television Annual Report and Accounts 1961/2 p. 6, ITA File 7014/1.
14. *Daily Telegraph*, 30 July 1962.

CHAPTER 7: GRAMPIAN

1. ITA Paper 63(60).
2. ITA Minutes 124(60).
3. ITA Paper 123(60).
4. Report of meeting held on 27 January 1961, ITA File 7015/1.
5. Ibid. Letter W. H. Wilson to Pragnell dated 30 March 1961.
6. Ibid. Memo Stevenson to Sendall dated 2 June 1961.
7. Ibid. Letter I. Tennant to Mrs Dunlop dated 30 May 1961.
8. Ibid. Letter O'Donnell to Fraser dated 14 July 1961.
9. Ibid. Letter Pragnell to J. Lindsay dated 21 July 1961.
10. *The Times*, 5 July 1961, quoting Tom Johnston.
11. Letter dated 12 December 1961, ITA File 7015/1.
12. ITA Paper 7(62) and ITA Minutes 152(62).
13. Letter to Fraser dated 16 January 1962, ITA File 7015/1.
14. ITA Paper 19(62).
15. ITA Minutes 154(62).

CHAPTER 8: WWN

1. ITA Minutes 129(60).
2. Letter dated 30 September 1960, ITA File 3072.
3. ITA Paper 172(60).
4. ITA Minutes 131(60).
5. ITA File 23.
6. Letter Pragnell to J. Alban Davies dated 26 May 1961, ITA File 3072.
7. ITA Papers 136(61) and 138(61), ITA Minutes 142(61), also 'Independent Television in Wales', paper presented to the Pilkington Committee *Report of the Committee on Broadcasting 1960* Vol. 1, Appendix E (HMSO) (Cmnd. 1819) pp. 538–41.
8. ITA Minutes 142(61).
9. Letter Pragnell to Haydn Williams dated 2 June 1961, ITA File 7016/1.
10. ITA Minutes 143(61).
11. *The Times*, 26 July 1961 and *Daily Express*, 25 July 1961.
12. Memo Fraser to Sendall dated 28 June 1961, ITA File 7016/1.
13. *South Wales Evening Post*, 8 September 1961.
14. ITA Minutes 158(62) and correspondence May and June 1962, ITA File 7016/1.
15. Ibid. Letter Lyn Evans to Sendall dated 26 March 1962.

16. Ibid. Letter to Pragnell dated 11 April 1962.
17. *Western Mail*, 28 November 1961.
18. Letter to F. H. Copplestone dated 23 August 1962, ITA File 7016/1.
19. ITA Paper 240(62) and ITA Minutes 169(62).
20. ITA Minutes 173(63).
21. ITA Paper 62(63).
22. ITA Minutes 176(63).
23. Letter to Emrys Roberts dated 20 May 1963, ITA File 7016/1.
24. ITA Minutes 177(63).
25. Letter to Fraser dated 28 May 1963, ITA File 7016/1.
26. Ibid. Memo dated 28 August 1963.
27. Ibid. Letter dated 29 January 1964.
28. Ibid. Letter dated 18 May 1963.

CHAPTER 9: 'DISQUIET' AND 'DISSATISFACTION'

1. Pilkington Report, p. 2.
2. H of L 3 June 1959 Col. 574.
3. Conversation between Richard Hoggart and Joseph Weltman on 31 July 1979.
4. Hoggart had, however, read a paper on 'The Quality of Cultural Life in Mass Society' at a Congress for Cultural Freedom in Berlin in July 1960. Some of the ideas expressed in that paper reappeared in the Pilkington Report.
5. Pilkington Report Vol. II, Appendix E, Paper No. 179.
6. Ibid. Paper No. 174.
7. Ibid. Paper No. 258.
8. Ibid. Paper No. 252. They had been disappointed by the failure of their application for the East of England contract.
9. Pilkington Report Vol. I, Appendix E, Papers Nos. 75 and 76.
10. The eleven cities were: Aberdeen, Belfast, Bristol, Cardiff, Carlisle, Dover, Glasgow, Newcastle, Norwich, Southampton and Plymouth.
11. The ACTT said to Pilkington that they believed too much of the profit was going to shareholders: not enough to programmes; and the actors union, Equity, suggested that companies should be contractually bound to spend a stated proportion of their income on programmes. This, they suggested, could lead to a larger amount of better quality home productions and would be especially desirable in the national regions such as Scotland.
12. Pilkington Report p. 66.

CHAPTER 10: PROGRAMME BALANCE

1. Pilkington Report para. 326.
2. ITA Annual Report and Accounts 1958/9, p. 16.
3. Pilkington Report para. 187.
4. Pilkington Report Vol. II, Appendix E, Paper No. 133.
5. Ibid. Paper No. 156.
6. Ibid. Paper No. 149.
7. Pilkington Report para. 187.
8. In its Annual Report for 1959/60.
9. Pilkington Report para. 190.
10. Pilkington Report Vol. II, Appendix E, Paper No. 232.

11. Ibid. Paper No. 238.
12. This unfortunate situation was made even more uncomfortable for the Authority when a third person, still in membership, namely Dame Frances Farrer, actually wrote to the Committee, in her personal capacity, recommending that on no account should a third channel go to commercial television because that would spread further 'the dead level of popular approach'. But Dame Frances had already shown herself as temperamentally averse to the disciplines of board discussions leading to agreed decisions involving collective responsibility. Moreover, her attendance at meetings had been spasmodic. She was a former General Secretary of the National Federation of Women's Institutes. This Federation informed the Committee that opinion generally amongst its membership favoured a third service for the BBC if there was to be one at all. Pilkington Report Vol. II, Appendix E, Paper No. 261.
13. Pilkington Report para. 191.
14. Ibid. paras. 194–5.

CHAPTER 11: TELEVISION VIOLENCE AND THE YOUNG

1. Pilkington Report paras. 118 and 167.
2. Ibid. paras. 120–1.
3. SCC Minutes 53(60). Pilkington Report paras. 168 and 172.
4. One company's (ATV's) policy was described in their written evidence as follows: 'Of paramount importance is the avoidance of themes or scenes likely to prove distressing to children. Extreme suffering, whether of human beings or animals; violence and brutality (particularly when shown in close-up); and incidents which may be regarded as over-stimulating to young viewers, are avoided. Where points of doubt arise it is the policy of the Company in respect of programming intended for children, to re-write, amend or totally delete the incident'. Pilkington Report Vol. II, Appendix E, Paper No. 109.
5. Pilkington Report para. 168.
6. *Children and Television Programmes* (BBC and ITA, 1960) p. 17.

CHAPTER 12: THE IMPACT OF TELEVISION ON SOCIETY

1. Pilkington Report para. 156.
2. Regrettably the *procès-verbaux* of committees of enquiry are, unlike those of Parliamentary committes, rarely published; but this is what Tomlinson said and he confirmed it to the author in November 1979. He added in a letter that the Committee seemed to be trying to say that the ITA ought to be a kind of moral watchdog. He himself was much opposed to this point of view, believing that what is appropriate in the pulpit is out of place in a public body. Attempts to *impose* morality (as distinct from *proclaiming* it) were usually disastrous.
3. The Director-General of the BBC, Mr (later Sir Hugh) Carlton Greene had expressed the opposite view. Yet in 1968 the Chairman of the BBC (Lord Hill) was able to say that Greene 'had achieved a transition to a service that seeks to mirror life as it is – warts and all' (*The Sunday Times*, 1 September 1968).
4. Pilkington Report para. 169.
5. Ibid. para. 171.
6. Proceedings of Conference on Crime Prevention 29 November 1961, ITA File 3088.
7. '*Television as the Archetype of Mass Communications*' (International Encyclopaedia of the Social Sciences, 1968). Also reprinted in *Speaking to Each Other*, Vol. I (Chatto & Windus, 1970) p. 165. Republished in Penguin Books, 1973.

8. ITA Paper 108(62).
9. The programmes were: ITV Westerns – *Bonanza, Outlaws, Gunsmoke*; ITV Crime – *77 Sunset Strip, No Hiding Place, Top Secret*; BBC Westerns – *Laramie, Wagon Train, Bronco, Frontier Circus*; BBC Crime – *The Big Pull, Perry Mason, Z Cars, The Defender, The Franchise Affair, The Andromeda Breakthrough*.
10. Pilkington Report para. 174.
11. Ibid. para. 175.
12. SCC Paper 58(57). He also added: 'I think we all now take the view that circumstances are now very favourable for a further advance towards what the Act calls proper balance . . .'.
13. SCC Paper 33(62).
14. Pilkington Report para. 184.
15. Ibid.
16. Graham Greene's *Complaisant Lover*, which ATV were intending to produce with Sir Ralph Richardson in the lead, had to be dropped because of the author's objections to cuts which the company had agreed with the Authority should be made. The play was later broadcast by the BBC, without cuts.
17. Pilkington Report para. 185.

CHAPTER 13: ADVERTISING

1. Associated-Rediffusion's memorandum to Pilkington dated December 1960 contains the following: '. . . Independent Television was intended by the Television Act to be, and very largely is, a responsible service designed to give an alternative to the BBC. It depends upon advertising for its finance but is not to be controlled or unduly influenced by advertising interests.' Pilkington Report Vol. II, Appendix E, Paper No. 108.
2. Pilkington Report para. 651.
3. Pilkington Report Vol. II, Appendix E, Paper No. 252.
4. Pilkington Report para. 243.
5. Ibid. paras. 249–50.
6. Ibid. para. 233.
7. Ibid. para. 52.
8. Ibid. para. 246.
9. Ibid. para. 247.
10. Ibid. para. 254.
11. Ibid. para. 255.
12. Pilkington Report Vol. I, Appendix E, Paper No. 69.
13. Granada found the task so daunting (or unrewarding) that they ceased to show advertising magazines for most of 1958.
14. *Inter alia* in the ITA Annual Reports for 1956/7 and 1957/8. The 1958/9 Annual Report also claimed that they had 'a substantial following amongst viewers'.
15. SCC Minutes 67(61), SCC Paper 51(61), ITA Paper 289(61).
16. ITA Paper 288(61).
17. Pilkington Report para. 260.

CHAPTER 14: MORE CHANNELS AND LONGER HOURS?

1. *The Times*, 17 July 1962.
2. 'In a free society control of the means of communication should be diversified not centralised.' Pilkington Report Vol. I, Appendix E, Paper No. 81.

3. Ibid.
4. Pilkington Report Vol. 1, Appendix E, Paper 31.
5. Ibid. Paper No. 30.
6. By this time it had already become established practice that on Christmas Day, Boxing Day and on other national holidays the control over hours was substantially relaxed to allow virtually day-long television.
7. ITA Minutes 134(60).
8. Pilkington Report Vol. 1, Appendix E, Paper No. 81.
9. Pilkington Report Vol. 11, Appendix E, Paper No. 110.
10. Pilkington Report para. 935.
11. Ibid. para. 932.
12. Ibid. para. 935.
13. Ibid. para. 934.
14. Pilkington Report Vol. 11, Appendix E, Paper No. 112.
15. Ibid. Paper No. 255.
16. Ibid. Paper No. 133.
17. Ibid. Paper No. 251.
18. Pilkington Report para. 904. This paragraph recording hostile criticism from one past Chairman, one past Member and one Member who had been still serving was a devastating blow to the ITA. Years later, in a letter to the author, Lord Clark was to comment: 'I had no idea that they (his comments to Pilkington) had been so destructive and I am sorry to think that they may have made things more difficult for the ITA' (letter of 17 April 1979).
19. Ibid. paras. 858–914.
20. Ibid. para. 1053.
21. Ibid. para. 884.
22. Ibid. para. 663.

CHAPTER 15: 'ORGANIC CHANGE'

1. Pilkington Report para. 554.
2. Ibid. para. 563.

CHAPTER 16: NEWSPAPER INTERESTS

1. Pilkington Report Vol. 1, Appendix E, Paper No. 91.
2. ITA Annual Report and Accounts 1954/5 p. 6.
3. Pilkington Report Vol. 1, Appendix E, Paper No. 91.
4. Pilkington Report para. 631.
5. Ibid. para. 633.

CHAPTER 17: MISCELLANEOUS PILKINGTONIANA

1. Pilkington Report para. 641.
2. Ibid. para. 642.
3. Ibid. para. 644.
4. Ibid. para. 453.
5. Ibid. para. 280.
6. Ibid. para. 284.

7. Ibid. para. 290.
8. Ibid. para. 292.
9. Ibid. para. 647.
10. Ibid.
11. Ibid. para. 652.
12. Ibid. para. 303.
13. Ibid. para. 437.
14. Ibid. para. 660.
15. Ibid. para. 662.

CHAPTER 18: A SUITABLE CASE FOR TREATMENT?

1. H of L 1 March 1961 Col. 95.
2. Ibid. Col. 219.
3. Bevins, *The Greasy Pole* p. 85.
4. *Broadcasting* (HMSO, July 1962) (Cmnd. 1770) para. 80.

CHAPTER 19: FIRST REACTIONS

1. All quotations in this chapter are from newspapers dated 28 June 1962 unless otherwise stated.
2. *The Economist*, 30 June 1962.
3. *The Times* and the *Daily Telegraph*, 29 June 1962.
4. Jubilee address at Columbia Teachers College, New York, May 1963, reproduced in *Speaking to Each Other*, Vol. 1, pp. 185–200.
5. Pilkington Report Vol. II, Appendix E, Paper No. 269.

CHAPTER 20: MORE MATURE REFLECTIONS

1. ITA File 3055/3.
2. *Broadcasting*, July 1962.
3. *The Times*, 4 July 1962.
4. *Broadcasting*, July 1962 paras. 77–8.
5. Ibid. para. 81.
6. SCC Minutes 75(62).
7. *Daily Mail*, 11 July 1962.
8. In his letter of 2 July to the Home Secretary Kirkpatrick had pointed out that the Exchequer was drawing some £24 million from ITV; £15 million in tax from the companies, £8 million in Advertising Duty and £1.3 million in tax from the ITA.

CHAPTER 21: LORDS AND COMMONS HAVE THEIR SAY

1. H of L 18 July 1962 Cols. 605–736; H of L 19 July 1962 Cols. 737–66 and 770–849.
2. *Evening Standard*, 19 July 1962.
3. ITA Paper 136(62).
4. H of C 31 July 1962 Cols. 421–541.
5. Now (1982) Baroness Pike of Melton, a past Chairman of the Authority's General Advisory Council and, since June 1981, Chairman of the Broadcasting Complaints Commission.

CHAPTER 22: TENSION AT ST. MARTIN'S-LE-GRAND

1. ITA Minutes 164(62).
2. SCC Minutes 77(62).
3. ITA Minutes 165(62).
4. Formerly of the Sudan Government Civil Service (between 1939 and 1959) where he had held senior positions in the Ministry of Finance.
5. Interestingly both he and Carmichael had been together in Sudan Government service in the early forties, German as Assistant Director of Posts.
6. Letter dated 12 October 1962, ITA File 3055/6.
7. ITA Paper 115(62).
8. Letter to Fraser dated 2 November 1962, ITA File 3055/6.
9. Director of the London School of Economics and Member of the Authority since August 1960.
10. ITA Minutes 168(62).
11. Bevins, *The Greasy Pole*.
12. 'This is Mr Bevins' opportunity to have his paragraph in British social history as one of those Postmasters General to whom a big chance was given and who had the courage to make the right decision against enormous pressures.' Richard Hoggart in the *Observer*, 7 October 1962.
13. *Reynolds News*, 26 August 1962.
14. *Daily Express*, 23 August 1962.

CHAPTER 23: THE WHITE PAPER AND BILL: DECEMBER 1962

1. *Broadcasting* (HMSO, December 1962) (Cmnd. 1893).
2. Ibid. para. 14.
3. Ibid. para. 11.
4. Ibid. para. 28.
5. Ibid. para. 24.
6. Ibid.
7. Ibid. para. 27.
8. *Financial Times*, 19 December 1962.
9. Ibid.
10. *Yorkshire Post*, 19 December 1962.
11. *The Times*, 20 December 1962.
12. Television Bill (HMSO, 20 December 1962) Clause 2(1)(a).
13. Ibid. Clause 2(1)(c).
14. Ibid. Clause 2(2)(a).
15. Ibid. Schedule 1 Clause 1(4).
16. Ibid. Clause 7(4).
17. Ibid. Clause 10(1)(c).
18. Ibid. Clause 10(2)(a).
19. Ibid. Clause 13. This clause in the Bill was shortened during the Committee stage because it was thought to be unduly detailed. The reference to 'different companies' was lost but the provision about planning survived and in later years became the statutory basis for the policy of 'complementarity'.
20. Ibid. Clause 15(1).
21. *Financial Times*, 21 December 1962.

22. *Sunday Telegraph*, 23 December 1962.
23. *Observer*, 23 December 1962.
24. *Financial Times*, 21 December 1962.
25. Undated document handed to the author by Norman Collins. See also Chairman's statement in Associated Television Ltd. Annual Report dated 1 August 1963.
26. Letter Carmichael to Bevins dated 16 January 1963, ITA File 3052.
27. *Daily Mirror*, 31 January 1963.
28. *Sunday Telegraph*, 17 February 1963.
29. *The Times*, 22 February 1963.

CHAPTER 24: PASSAGE OF THE SECOND TELEVISION BILL: 1963

1. H of C 25 February 1963 Cols. 907–1031.
2. Bevins, *The Greasy Pole*, p. 90.
3. ITA Minutes 173(63).
4. H of C Standing Committee B, 12 March 1963, Col. 58.
5. Ibid. Col. 90.
6. H of L 9 July 1963 Col. 1320.
7. H of L Standing Committee B, 14 March 1963, Col. 141.
8. H of L 18 July 1963 Cols. 355–74.
9. H of C 24 June 1963 Cols. 1017–32.
10. In fact at its 7 July meeting the Authority decided to inform the Minister of its decision in principle to appoint a General Advisory Council.
11. Pilkington Report para. 426.
12. H of C Standing Committee B, 19 March 1963, Col. 174.
13. H of C Standing Committee B, 14 March 1963, Cols. 132 and 129.
14. H of C Standing Committee B, Col. 114.
15. H of C 24 June 1963 Col. 1073.
16. H of L 18 July 1963 Col. 348.
17. H of L 22 July 1963 Col. 586.
18. H of C 24 June 1963 Col. 1065.
19. Ibid. Cols. 996–1002.
20. Ibid. Cols. 1003–14.
21. Ibid. Col. 1011.
22. Ibid. Cols. 1014–17.
23. H of C Standing Committee B, 9 May 1963, Col. 1024.
24. H of L 29 July 1963 Col. 1010.
25. H of C Standing Committee B, 7 May 1963, Col. 971.
26. 'This would involve the Authority in continuous management questions . . . Since with the Authority's guidance ITN has become world-famous and a credit . . . to British broadcasting, cannot we be spared the imposition on us of management duties of this kind?' Letter Carmichael to Bevins 6 March 1963, ITA File 3052.
27. H of C Standing Committee B, 25 April 1963, Col. 671 and H of C 27 June 1963 Col. 1756.
28. H of C Standing Committee B, 2 May 1963, Col. 834.
29. H of C 27 June 1963 Col. 1782.
30. Ibid. Cols. 1796–7.
31. Ibid. Cols. 1808–15.
32. *Financial Times*, 29 June 1963.

CHAPTER 25: THE LEVY

1. SCC Minutes 83(63).
2. *Sunday Telegraph*, 17 February 1963.
3. Bevins, *The Greasy Pole*, p. 88.
4. Ibid. p. 90.
5. Ibid. p. 96.
6. ITA Paper 86(63).
7. *Investors' Chronicle*, 19 April 1963.
8. Letter to Carmichael dated 14 March 1963, ITA File 29.
9. ITA Paper 67(63).
10. ITA Paper 82(63).
11. Record of conversation between Pragnell and the PMG, ITA File 29.
12. Ibid. Letter to Carmichael.
13. ITA Paper 101(63).
14. ITA Paper 98(63).
15. H of C Standing Committee B, 25 April and 30 April 1963, Cols. 703–17.
16. H of C Standing Committee B, 30 April 1963, Cols. 742–5.
17. Bevins, *The Greasy Pole*, p. 101.
18. Ibid. p. 104.
19. Ibid. p. 105.
20. H of C Standing Committee B, 2 May 1963, Cols. 845–6.
21. Ibid. Col. 848.
22. Ibid. Col. 864.
23. H of C Standing Committee B, 30 April 1963, Cols. 796–7.
24. *Daily Telegraph*, 8 May 1963.
25. Bevins, *The Greasy Pole*, p. 108.
26. Ibid.
27. Ibid. p. 109.
28. H of C 27 June 1963 Col. 1773.
29. Ibid. Col. 1777.
30. ITA Minutes 177(63).
31. ITA Minutes 179(63).
32. H of L 22 July 1963 Col. 482.

CHAPTER 26: ENTER LORD HILL

1. Lord Hill of Luton, *Behind the Screen*, p. 16.
2. Ibid. pp. 17–18.
3. ITA Paper 163(63).
4. SCC Paper 44(63).
5. Lord Hill of Luton, *Behind the Screen*, pp. 20–1.
6. ITA Minutes 180(63).
7. *Broadcasting*, December 1962, para. 11.
8. Over a full fifteen years thereafter the Deputy Director General concerned (the author) failed to accomplish this task. Under his successor, Colin Shaw (Director of Television), the omission was rectified with the publication by the IBA in March 1978 of *Television Programme Guidelines*.
9. ITA Paper 138(63) and SCC Paper 45(63).
10. ITA Paper 169(63).

CHAPTER 27: NEW INSTITUTIONS: NEW CONTRACTS

1. Conversation with the author and Weltman in April 1980.
2. Lord Hill of Luton, *Behind the Screen*, pp. 20–1.
3. Pilkington Report para. 563.
4. H of C 25 February 1963 Col. 919.
5. ITA press notice dated 16 September 1963.
6. Lord Hill of Luton, *Behind the Screen*, p. 19.
7. *Observer*, 5 December 1963.
8. ITA Paper 244(63).
9. *Financial Times*, 10 January 1964.
10. The Sydney Box bid for British Lion did not succeed and before the end of the year the ailing film company had been taken over wholly by the National Film Finance Corporation.
11. Letter Wedell to Orr dated 3 January 1964, ITA File 41/Cl.
12. Letter Howard Thomas to the author dated 5 August 1981.
13. Transcript of Authority interview with Granada on 2 January 1964, ITA File 41/D1.
14. ITA press notice dated 16 September 1963.
15. ITA press notice dated 8 January 1964.
16. *Daily Telegraph*, 9 January 1964.
17. *Guardian*, 9 January 1964.
18. *Daily Express*, 9 January 1964.

CHAPTER 28: COLLECTIVE PROGRAMME POLICIES

1. E. G. Wedell, *Broadcasting and Public Policy* (Michael Joseph, 1968) p. 177.
2. PSC Minutes 1(64).
3. ITA Paper 88(65).
4. Letters Bernstein to Sendall dated 14 February 1966 and 20 October 1966, ITA File 3043/3A.
5. Lord Hill of Luton, *Behind the Screen*, pp. 33–6.
6. PPC Paper 12(66).
7. PSC Paper 1(67).
8. Cox to the author, November 1981.
9. *Ten Years of Independent Television* (Television Mail, September 1965) p. 86.
10. Cox to the author, April 1981.
11. PSC Paper 3(66).
12. There is no record of this meeting, but the late Cecil Bernstein's recollection was that Fraser and I conveyed that the introduction of a longer news at 10 p.m. should be taken as a requirement amounting to a direction. Probably more exact is McMillan's recollection that he and Bernstein were themselves convinced of the need urgently to demonstrate the companies' capacity for collective innovation without receiving directives from the Authority. (Conversation September 1981).
13. Letter to R. B. Henderson dated 1 March 1967 ITA File 5005.
14. PPC Paper 6(67).
15. *Crossroads* was to remain at four episodes a week for the next thirteen years until 1980 when, against the backcloth of new franchise awards, and for similar reasons, it was decided to settle for three episodes a week. This was the number originally proposed to Grade in 1967.
16. PPC Minutes 13(67).

17. psc Paper 16(67).
18. ita Annual Report and Accounts 1968/9, p. 13.
19. Report to the Network Planning Committee by the Sports Working Party dated 11 June 1964, ita File 5010.
20. Network Planning Committee Minutes 10 August 1964.
21. Report to the Chairman of the Network Planning Committee dated 13 April 1966, ita File 5010.
22. ppc Paper 11(66).
23. Letter Cecil Bernstein to Sendall dated 19 October 1966, ita File 5010/3.
24. ita Minutes 221(66).
25. ppc Minutes 12(67).
26. Lord Hill of Luton, *Behind the Screen*, p. 39.
27. Letter to Sendall dated 27 December 1967, ita File 5010/3.
28. See Volume 1, Chapter 33.
29. ita Paper 109(65).
30. ppc Minutes 9(66).
31. *The Times*, see in particular issues dated 8 February, 9 February, 11 February, 16 February, 17 February and 18 February 1966.
32. See Volume 1, Chapter 35 (iii).
33. H of C 23 February 1966 Cols. 398–400.
34. Letter Sendall to McMillan dated 8 February 1966, ita File 3049/7.
35. ita press notice dated 17 February 1966.
36. ppc Paper 6(66).
37. ita Paper 121(66).
38. Letter Cox to Sendall dated 26 October 1966, ita File 5005/12/1.
39. *Daily Mirror*, 24 October 1966.
40. *The Times*, 1 November 1966.
41. scc Paper 12(68).
42. scc Minutes 121(68).

CHAPTER 29: PROGRAMMES AND PUBLIC ATTITUDES

1. *25 Years on ITV 1955–1980* (Independent Television Books and Michael Joseph, 1980).
2. Lord Hill of Luton, *Behind the Screen*, pp. 34–5.
3. N. Swallow, *Factual Television* (The Focal Press, 1966) p. 208.
4. ita Paper 70(66).
5. Pilkington Report Vol. ii, Appendix E, p. 1262.
6. M. Whitehouse, *Cleaning Up TV: From Protest to Participation* (Blandford Press, 1967).
7. Now (1982) Sir Roy Shaw, Secretary General of the Arts Council.
8. Greene in *The Listener*, 17 June 1965.
9. Whitehouse, *Cleaning Up TV*, p. 143 footnote.
10. ita File 3057c.
11. Whitehouse, *Cleaning Up TV*, p. 236.
12. Letter Mrs Whitehouse to Lord Hill dated 19 April 1967, ita File 3057c.
13. Ibid.
14. M. Tracey and D. Morrison, *Whitehouse* (Macmillan, 1979).
15. gac Minutes 3(64).
16. Letter to Sendall dated 4 September 1962, ita File 580/2/1.
17. Ibid. Memo dated 27 December 1963.

18. 'Too Much Reviewing' by Peter Black in *Contrast*, Summer 1963 (British Film Institute).
19. A. Wilson, *Tempo: The Impact of Television on the Arts* (Headway Publications, 1964).
20. Ibid. p. 8.
21. Letter Sendall to Forman 13 June 1966, ITA File 583/2/44.
22. Perhaps the principal new work published in Britain was William Belsen's *The Impact of Television* (Crosby Lockwood, 1967).
23. One such exception was a study of the production of a seven-programme documentary series, *The Nature of Prejudice*, made in the autumn of 1967 by ATV and transmitted over most of the network in the spring of 1968. See *The Making of a Television Series* by Philip Elliott (Constable, 1972).
24. P. Black, *Mirror in the Corner: People's Television* (Hutchinson, 1972) p. 226.

CHAPTER 30: POLITICAL TELEVISION

1. PPC Minutes 3(64).
2. Directive dated 20 August 1964, ITA File 5012/1.
3. SCC Paper 4(66).
4. SCC Paper 15(64).
5. SCC Paper 25(65).
6. SCC Paper 3(65).
7. SCC Paper 16(66).

CHAPTER 31: SPECIAL CLASSES IN THE SIXTIES

1. Letter Fraser to Sidney Bernstein dated 13 October 1960, ITA File 3006/4.
2. SCC Paper 1(62).
3. SCC Paper 12(62).
4. *Broadcasting*, July 1962 para. 37.
5. Letter Sendall to Wolstencroft dated 14 August 1962, ITA File 3006/4.
6. ITA Minutes 168(62) and SCC Paper 79(62).
7. ITA Minutes 169(62).
8. Letter Wolstencroft to Sendall dated 4 October 1962, ITA File 3006/4.
9. Ibid. Letter Sendall to Wolstencroft dated 15 October 1962.
10. Ibid. Letter Wolstencroft to Sendall dated 5 November 1962.
11. Ibid. See exchange letters Weltman and Johnson of January 1965.
12. AEAC Paper 1(63).
13. Paper presented by Joe Weltman at a Conference on Educational Television organised by the BBC and Sussex University, May 1966.
14. H. Wiltshire and F. Bayliss, *Teaching Through Television* (National Institute of Adult Education, 1965).
15. AEC Paper 11(69).
16. AEC Papers 12(70), 35(70) and 4(72).
17. *Religion in Television* (Independent Television Authority, 1964).
18. In a recorded interview with Kenneth Harris.
19. Report of the ITA Consultation on Religion in Television 20/24 September 1965, ITA File 5008/1/27E.
20. Report of the 4th ITA Consultation on Religious Television 1/5 April 1968, ITA File 5008/1/44F.

CHAPTER 32: DUE IMPARTIALITY

1. Pilkington Report Vol. II, Appendix E, Paper 113.
2. Transcript of *On the Braden Beat* of 12 February 1966, ITA File 5081/2/11A.
3. Letter R. J. Heller to Sendall dated 20 January 1964, ITA File 5081/2/21.
4. ITA Paper 45(64).
5. Note of a meeting held on 5 December 1967, ITA File 3049/8.
6. ITA Paper 57(63).
7. Letters dated 7 August 1964 ITA File 5083/2/13.
8. Ibid. Letter dated 19 August 1964.
9. *Report of the Committee on the Future of Broadcasting* (HMSO, 1977) (Cmnd. 6753) para. 17.8.
10. Ibid. para. 17.10.
11. Ibid. Recommendation No. 1173 p. 485.

CHAPTER 33: THE NETWORKING TANGLE

1. Pilkington Report para. 550.
2. H of C 31 July 1962 Col. 431.
3. Letter G. H. Elvin to Fraser dated 1 April 1960, ITA File 7066.
4. Ibid. Memo to Pragnell dated 5 July 1963.
5. SCC Minutes 89(63).
6. This summary is based on a paper submitted to the ITA's Contracts Committee in January 1967 by A. W. Pragnell.
7. Note dated 4 September 1967, ITA File 7066.
8. Ibid. Memo Fraser to staff dated 19 February 1968.
9. Ibid. Memo to Chairman dated 26 February 1968.
10. Ibid. Letter to Fraser dated 25 March 1968.

CHAPTER 34: THE ADVERTISING SCENE

1. Report 156 from the National Board for Prices and Incomes: Costs and Revenues of Independent Television Companies (HMSO, October 1970) (Cmnd. 4524) pp. 10–11.
2. Ibid. para. 83.
3. Much of this information was first recorded in Chapter 7 of the ITA Annual Report and Accounts 1964/5.
4. ITV Evidence to the Annan Committee (Independent Television Companies Association, March 1975) p. 121.
5. Ibid. p. 122.
6. Ibid. p. 126.
7. Ibid.

CHAPTER 35: TECHNICAL BACKGROUND

1. Chairman's Address: Electronics Division of the Institution of Electrical Engineers, October 1966.
2. *Independent Broadcasting* (Independent Broadcasting Authority, September 1976) 'Times Remembered: 21 Years of TV Engineering' by Pat Hawker, to whom the author is much indebted for permission to make extensive use of this article.

CHAPTER 36: THE 'FRANCHISE TRAIL', 1967

1. *The Franchise Trail* was the title of a play by Nemone Lethbridge which was transmitted by London Weekend Television late in 1968.
2. ITA Minutes 211(66).
3. ITA Annual Report and Accounts 1965/6, pp. 66–7.
4. *Daily Mirror*, 21 November 1966.
5. *Broadcasting* (HMSO, December 1966) (Cmnd. 3169) para. 19.
6. *Huddersfield Daily Examiner*, leader 22 December 1966.
7. *Guardian*, 22 December 1966.
8. Conspectus as issued to all applicants.
9. *The Sunday Times*, 'Insight' column 12 February 1967.
10. *Guardian*, 17 April 1967.
11. ITA Paper 62(67).
12. ITA press release dated 12 June 1967.
13. Quoted in the *Daily Express* 15 October 1967.
14. In *Behind the Screen* Lord Hill made plain that his personal inclination was to award the contract to the Grimond Group: 'They put up an excellent show with Alasdair Milne and Alastair Burnet outstanding'. He stated that Fraser strongly advised reappointment of STV (p. 52).
15. Ibid. p. 54.
16. *New Statesman*, 28 April 1967.
17. After the contract award it was made known that the occupant of the post was to be Tony Gorard, who had been successively Chief Accountant and Company Secretary with Anglia.
18. Lord Derby at TWW Annual General Meeting 18 May 1967 as quoted in *Western Mail*, 19 May 1967.
19. *Daily Telegraph*, 13 June 1967.
20. 'The new Licence which was granted to us on the 30th July 1964 extends our franchise for all practical purposes for three years. Moreover, this Licence provides for an extension at the discretion of the ITA for a further period of three years.' Extract from TWW Limited Chairman's Statement and Directors' Report & Accounts, 31 December 1964.
21. Black, *The Mirror in the Corner*, p. 189.
22. *The Times*, 12 June 1967.
23. *Daily Telegraph*, 13 June 1967.
24. In his memoirs Hill states that he had told Coltart that unless there was a speedy and substantial improvement in programme quality the chances of gaining another contract seemed to him remote. Lord Hill of Luton, *Behind the Screen*, p. 51.
25. Ibid. p. 45.
26. Sir Sydney Caine, *Statement on TV Policy* A Supplement to Hobart Paper 43 (The Institute of Economic Affairs, July 1968).

CHAPTER 37: OUTLOOK UNSETTLED

1. H of C 28 June 1967 Cols. 422–69.
2. Report No. 156 Costs and Revenues of Independent Television Companies.
3. Ibid. para. 57.
4. Ibid. para. 58.
5. Ibid. para. 112.

6. P. Seglow, *Trade Unionism in Television* (Saxon House, 1978) p. 133.
7. *Daily Mirror*, 29 March 1967.
8. *The Times*, 23 March 1967.
9. Seglow, *Trade Unionism in Television*, pp. 146–7.
10. ITV Evidence to the Annan Committee, p. 114.

INDEX

'A' rentals, 212
A' the Airts, 68
ABC Television,
    company, xiv, 2, 4, 53, 113, 114, 115, 213,
        218, 345–6, 364–5; affiliation
        with: Channel Television, 46–7;
        Grampian Television, 62; Ulster
        Television, 26, 27; Westward Tele-
        vision, 35; application for the
        London ITV contract, 1968– , 341,
        345; application for the North East
        England ITV contract, 4; merger with
        Rediffusion Television to form
        Thames Television, 345–6, 364–5;
        Pilkington Committee, evidence to,
        113, 114, 115; submission to the ITA
        for franchise extension to cover the
        Borders ITV area, 53
    contract, ITV, Midlands and the North
        weekend service, 1956– , 2, 53; exten-
        sion to cover Borders ITV area pro-
        posal, 53
    contract, ITV, Midlands and the North
        weekend service, 1964– , 211; appli-
        cation, 213, 218; conditional ap-
        pointment, 218
    engineering, 27–8, 62, 327
    finance: network payments, 312–3; share-
        holdings, 213, 218
    programmes, 2, 48, 88, 144, 238, 242, 250,
        262, 263, 275–6, 277, 278, 279, 281,
        285, 288; adult education, 144, 275–
        6, 277, 278, 279, 285; arts, 9, 48, 263;
        current affairs, 250; drama, 262, 341;
        first transmission date, 2; local, 88;
        networking arrangements, 313;
        popular music, 65; religious, 288,
        290; schools, 281; sports, 238, 242
    staff, xiv, 46–7; redundancy payments,
        370, 372–3; seconded to Channel
        Television, 46–7; strike by ACTT

        members, 346, 372; taken on by ATV
        and Yorkshire Television, 372
    studios, 325, 326, 346, 364, 372; Alpha
        Studios, 325, 372; Teddington, 326,
        346, 364
    transmitting stations, 2, 72, 325; overlap
        with Wales, West and North area,
        72; population coverage, 2
    see also Volume 1 for origins and develop-
        ment of the company
ACTT see Association of Cinematograph,
    Television and Allied Technicians
ALS TV Ltd, 339
ATV see Associated Television
ATV Network see Associated Television
Abbreviations, xvi–xvii
Abercorn, Duke of, 23, 24
Aberfan disaster, television coverage, 252–3,
    265
About Anglia, 18–19, 21, 295
Adams, Mary, 258
Additional payments see Exchequer Levy
Adorian, Paul, as Managing Director,
    Associated-Rediffusion, xiv, 309, 347
Adult Education (Advisory) Committee
    (ITA), 146, 211, 276, 277, 278, 279, 284,
    285
Adult education programmes, 27, 31, 114,
    142, 144, 146, 165, 184, 274–84, 285
Advertising, television, 103–9, 164–5, 167–
    8, 319–23
    controls, 103–9, 164–5, 167–8, 181, 204,
        319–23; Advertising Advisory
        Committee, 103, 104, 128, 153, 157,
        164, 165, 181, 204, 320, 322; amount
        and length of advertisements, 106,
        107, 143, 167, 321; Code of Advertising
        Standards and Practice, 107, 167, 168,
        174, 181, 204, 319, 320, 321–2; Copy
        Committee, 103, 105, 153, 157, 204;
        distinction between advertisements